Schools Council
Research Studies

Children
and their Books

The final report of the Schools Council research
project on Children's Reading Habits, 10–15,
University of Sheffield Institute of Education

Schools Council
Research Studies

Children
and their Books

Frank Whitehead
A.C. Capey
Wendy Maddren
Alan Wellings

Macmillan Education

First published 1977

ISBN 0 333 22322 5

Published by
MACMILLAN EDUCATION LTD
Houndmills Basingstoke Hampshire RG21 2XS
and London

Associated companies in New York Dublin
Melbourne Johannesburg and Delhi

Text set in 10/12 pt IBM Press Roman,
printed by photolithography, and bound
in Great Britain at The Pitman Press, Bath

Contents

Tables   viii
Acknowledgements   xiii
Members of the research team   xiv
Foreword   xv

1 Previous research   1
United States surveys 1920–40   1
Jenkinson's 1938 survey in Great Britain   7
Scott's 1942 survey in New Zealand   11
Some related research studies 1941–58   12
Surveys in Great Britain since 1955   14

2 The research design and procedures   20
Introduction   20
Sampling – general principles   21
The sample design   24
The primary sample   26
The secondary sample   27
Collecting the data   28
The children's questionnaire   29
The questionnaire administration instructions   33
The pupil assessment sheet   34
The school questionnaires   34
The follow-up interviews   35
Handling the data   37
Coding and associated procedures   38
The computer analysis   40

3 The questionnaire survey   41
A – THE SAMPLE   41

B – THE QUANTITATIVE FINDINGS   51
Amount of book reading   51
Amount of periodical reading   54
Amount of television viewing   55
Relationship between book reading, periodical reading and
    television viewing   56
Social class and book reading   61
Ability and attainment and book reading   62
Social class and periodical reading   66
Ability and attainment and periodical reading   68
Social class and television viewing   70
Ability and attainment and television viewing   71
Interim summary of the main quantitative findings   71
Some other relevant variables   73
The influence of the family   77
The influence of school type   78
Single-sex and mixed secondary schools   84
School organization and methods   85
Streaming, mixed ability, vertical grouping and setting   87
Structured versus integrated timetables in the primary schools   91
The provision of class libraries in secondary schools   92
Type of book provision in English lessons   95
Difficulties associated with the investigation of school variables   98
The relative importance of the different variables (two
    computer programmes)   100

C – THE QUALITATIVE FINDINGS   108
Diversity of book reading   108
Classification of books into seven categories   110
Amount of book reading by categories   112
Classification of children into five types of book reader   119
Amount of book reading and reading of quality books   120
Quality and narrative book reading (boys only)   122
Social class and type of book   122
The 246 widely read books   125
The most widely read books in each age group   129
The influence of book availability in school on 10+ book reading   133
Sources of books read   137
Social class and book source   140
Liking scores and book source   141
Liking scores and book type   143
Books left unfinished   145
Books re-read   146

School stories, detective stories, historical stories, pony
   stories and science-fiction   148
The non-narrative books   150
Favourite writers   151
Classification of periodicals into six categories   153
Amount of periodical reading by category   154
Classification of children into five types of periodical reader   156
Percentage reading named periodicals in each age group   158

4 The follow-up interviews   162
Sub-sample, procedure and purposes   162
The 10+ interviews   165
The 11+ interviews   175
The 13+ interviews   178
The 15+ interviews   190
Postscript (and interview summary sheets)   196

5 The books children prefer   206
Some theoretical considerations   206
Some widely read books examined   227

6 The comics children choose   255
Then and now   255
The favourite four   260

7 Conclusions and recommendations   271

Appendices   293

I   Sampling details   294
II   Children's questionnaire   299
III   Instructions for the administration of the children's
   questionnaire   309
IV   Assessment sheet   311
V   School questionnaires   313
VI   Authors of quality narrative books   330
VII   Supplementary primary school questionnaire   334

Tables

1	Response of schools	41
2	Response of children	42
3	Children in different types of secondary schools — our sample compared with population of England and Wales 1970–71 (percentages)	43
4	Social class of sample (percentages)	44
5	Class composition: comparison of our sample with 1966 sample census (percentages)	44
6	Percentages in social class groups NM and M	46
7	Distribution of children, by sex and age, allocated to the different grades for ability and attainment (in percentages)	47
8	Social class and ability	48
9	Relationship between ability and attitude to the school — all age groups together	49
10	Family size by sex and social class	49
11	Family size by ability, sex and social class	50
12	Average number of books read during one month	51
13	Type of book reader as percentage of each age group	52
14	Average number of periodicals read regularly (by sex and age)	54
15	Distribution of children regularly reading periodicals by sex and age (in percentages)	54
16	Average number of hours spent watching television	55
17	Types of television viewer as percentage of sex and age grouping	56
18	Relationship between book and periodical reading	57
19	Relationship between book reading and television viewing	59
20	Relationship between periodical reading and television viewing	60
21	Type of book reader as percentage of each age group, subdivided by social class	61
22	Type of book reader by ability and attainment	63
23	Type of book reader by ability and attainment (percentages based on four categories of book readers)	65

24   Type of periodical reader as percentage of each age group,
      subdivided by social class   67
25   Type of periodical reader by ability and attainment   69
26   Type of television viewer by social class   70
27   Type of television viewer by ability and attainment   72
28   Distribution of children visiting the public library regularly
      by sex and age (in percentages)   74
29   Type of book reader as percentage of 10+ age group, by type
      of school   78
30   Type of book reader as percentage of 12+ age group, by type
      of school   80
31   Type of book reader as percentage of 12+ age group, by
      comprehensive sector against selective sector   81
32   Average number of books read in a month, according to
      school type   81
33   Type of book reader as percentage of 14+ age group by type
      of school   82
34   Type of book reader as percentage of 14+ age group, by
      comprehensive sector against selective sector   83
35   Average number of books read in a month at 14+, according
      to school type   84
36   Types of book reader as percentage of 12+ age group in single-
      sex and mixed schools   .   84
37   Types of book reader as percentage of 14+ age group in
      single-sex and mixed schools   85
38   Type of book reader at 10+ as percentage of each type of class
      organization   87
39   Type of book reader at 12+ by different type of class
      organization   89
40   Type of book reader at 14+ by different type of class
      organization   90
41   Type of book reader as percentage of 10+ children subjected
      to different types of timetabling   91
42   Type of book reader as percentage of 12+ age group, by two
      types of library provision   92
43   Type of book reader as percentage of 14+ age group, by two
      types of library provision   93
44   Type of book reader as percentage of 12+ age group, by two
      types of book provision for English lessons   96
45   Type of book reader as percentage of 14+ age group, by two
      types of book provision for English lessons   97
46   Diagrammatic representation of AID analysis for 10+ age group   102

47   Diagrammatic representation of AID analysis for 12+ age
      group   104
48   Diagrammatic representation of AID analysis for 14+ age
      group   105
49   Independent variables specified by General Linear Hypothesis
      programme as giving, in combination, the best prediction of
      amount of reading for the 10+ age group   106
50   Independent variables specified by General Linear Hypothesis
      programme as giving, in combination, the best prediction of
      amount of reading for the 12+ age group   107
51   Independent variables specified by General Linear Hypothesis
      programme as giving, in combination, the best prediction of
      amount of reading for the 14+ age group   107
52   Categories of book as percentage of all book titles listed   113
53   Categories of book as percentage of all book reading (age
      groups combined)   113
54   Categories of book reading as a percentage of all book reading
      for each age-and-sex grouping   115
55   Narrative and non-narrative book reading as percentage of all
      book reading   116
56   Quality and non-quality book reading as percentage of all book
      reading   116
57   Average number of books of each type read by children in
      different sex and age groups   118
58   Distribution of children in different narrative/non-narrative
      book-reading categories, by age and sex (in percentages)   118
59   Distribution of children in different quality/non-quality
      categories by age and sex (in percentages)   121
60   Quality of book reading by amount of book reading   121
61   Distribution of boy readers according to their choice of
      books (in percentages)   123
62   Type of book reader (quality/non-quality) by social class   123
63   Non-narrative books as a percentage of total book mentions
      for social classes M and NM, by sex and age   124
64   Most widely read books in the 10+ age group   130
65   Most widely read books in the 12+ age group   131
66   Most widely read books in the 14+ age group   132
67   65 quality narrative books judged suitable for 10+ children,
      their availability in schools (spring term 1972), and number
      of times read by 10+ children in March 1971   135
68   (a) Number of books from each source per 1000 boys   138
      (b) Number of books from each source per 1000 girls   138

69 Book source as a percentage of total number of book
   mentions for each age-and-sex grouping, by social class   140
70 Liking scores of children in different age-and-sex groupings
   (as percentage of total book mentions)   141
71 Book source by liking score ('my own' omitted)   142
72 Mean liking scores for all books for each age-and-sex grouping 143
73 Mean liking scores for different book types   144
74 Percentage of narrative books left unfinished   145
75 Proportion of narrative books from different sources left
   unfinished (percentages)   145
76 Book mentions which were re-readings, as a percentage of all
   book mentions   146
77 Average number of book mentions which were re-readings, for
   each age-and-sex grouping   147
78 Percentage of book mentions which were re-readings in each
   book category, for each age-and-sex grouping   147
79 Number of readings of five types of fiction, as percentage of
   total book readings for each age group   149
80 Named favourite writers as a percentage of all children in each
   age-and-sex grouping   152
81 Number of times authors were named as favourite writer,
   compared with the number of their books read during the
   month   153
82 Types of periodical, as percentage of total number of
   periodicals read   154
83 Average number of periodicals in each category per head   155
84 Average number of periodicals per head in each category, for
   each age-and-sex grouping   156
85 Types of periodical reader as a percentage of all children for
   each age-and-sex grouping   157
86 Percentage of children regularly reading named periodicals
   (a) 10+ age group   158
   (b) 12+ age group   159
   (c) 14+ age group   160

Acknowledgements

Our first debt of gratitude is to the heads, staff and pupils of the 381 schools who completed the written questionnaire, and to the many local authorities who gave their cooperation so readily; the second, to the Statistics Division of the Department of Education and Science who gave such unstinted help in the drawing of the sample; and the third, to the staff at the Science Research Council's Atlas computer who skilfully piloted the research team through many unforeseen problems, particularly during the earlier stages of our work.

We would also like to thank Professor A. M. Walker, Dr D. J. Scott, and Dr C. W. Anderson, all of the Department of Probability and Statistics at Sheffield University, for their advice over our statistical analyses; Mr N. H. Baines, Mr P. Froggat, Mr R. K. Richards and others of the Sheffield University Computing Services Department for their help in transferring the data to the ICL 1907 computer at Sheffield; and Professor D. W. Harding for reading and commenting on part of the draft report.

'A study of reading habits' is reprinted by permission of Faber and Faber Ltd from *The Whitsun Weddings* by Philip Larkin.

Note

This report is the outcome of incessant collaborative discussion between the four co-authors and also, at an earlier stage in the research programme, with Fred Inglis who was a member of the research team from 1969 to 1971. At the final stage of writing, however, the responsibility for particular chapters was distributed as follows:

1   Frank Whitehead
2   Alan Wellings
3   Wendy Maddren and Frank Whitehead
4   Frank Whitehead
5   Frank Whitehead and A. C. Capey
6   A. C. Capey
7   Frank Whitehead

MEMBERS OF THE RESEARCH TEAM

Frank Whitehead (*Director*)
Fred Inglis (September 1969–December 1971)
Alan Wellings (September 1969–December 1971)
Pamela Trivett (October 1971–June 1972)
A. C. Capey (from January 1972)
Wendy Maddren (from October 1972)
Mrs Jean Wilde (*Secretary*)

Foreword

This is the final report from the Schools Council research project, Children's Reading Habits, based at the University of Sheffield Institute of Education from 1969 to 1974 under the direction of Frank Whitehead. The inquiry sought to discover the extent and kind of children's voluntary reading, what satisfactions they seek from books, and what environmental factors influence their choice.

In 1971 a national questionnaire survey was conducted with some 8000 children of 10, 12 and 14 years old in 193 primary and 188 secondary schools. To supplement the written questionnaries follow-up interviews were held with 576 children in 34 different schools throughout the country.

This report provides all the information which could not be contained in the project's interim report, Schools Council Working Paper 52, *Children's Reading Interests.* It outlines major studies of children's reading, describes the project's research design, and concludes with recommendations to teachers and parents which have special significance in the light of the Bullock Report.

This is the first survey of children's voluntary reading using a stratified random sample so selected that its findings can justifiably be generalized to the total relevant populations of children in England and Wales.

A Study of Reading Habits

When getting my nose in a book
Cured most things short of school,
It was worth ruining my eyes
To know I could still keep cool,
And deal out the old right hook
To dirty dogs twice my size.

Later, with inch-thick specs,
Evil was just my lark;
Me and my cloak and fangs
Had ripping times in the dark.
The women I clubbed with sex!
I broke them up like meringues.

Don't read much now: the dude
Who lets the girl down before
The hero arrives, the chap
Who's yellow and keeps the store,
Seem far too familiar. Get stewed:
Books are a load of crap.

Philip Larkin

The day I read a book
I can't remember when
But one of these days
I'm gonna do it again.

Jimmy 'Schnozzle' Durante

1 Previous research

In the English-speaking world in the past eighty or ninety years numerous studies have been undertaken of children's leisure-time reading interests, the earliest such study in Great Britain having been published in 1888, while in the United States of America the earliest studies appeared in 1897. During the 1920s and 1930s there was an intensification of effort in this field, particularly in the United States and, by 1940 — according to one writer — the number of studies reported totalled as many as two hundred. A full survey of this research would be a valuable contribution to educational history; but with such a vast amount of work to draw upon, this chapter cannot do more than pick out a few of the more important studies and comment briefly on the issues they raise.

UNITED STATES SURVEYS 1920—40

A natural starting point is offered by the three large scale surveys which were reported in the United States in the 1920s — namely Jordan (1921, revised and augmented 1926), Terman and Lima (1925), and Washburne and Vogel (1926). In each of these studies the main inquiry was pursued by using the children themselves as informants and by asking quite a large number of them to provide information about their reading and about how much they had enjoyed it. Thus in 1917—18 Jordan gave 3598 pupils a questionnaire asking for the names, in order of preference, of the five books and five magazines that they liked best of all the books and magazines they had ever read; the same procedure was repeated in 1925 with 1559 pupils in two different cities. Similarly, in their principal inquiry, Terman and Lima asked 1827 children in Grades 1 to 8 to list the four or five books they had most enjoyed reading during the previous year. Washburne and Vogel's inquiry was on a more ambitious scale, and took in 34 cities in varied parts of the United States. As many as 36 750 children in 34 schools filled in a 'ballot' on every book they read during the school year 1924—25, and in all 9300 books were reported on.

One serious weakness of all three studies is that very little information is

1

given about the population from which the child-subjects were drawn or
about the methods used in sampling this population. It seems to have been
assumed (quite erroneously) that, so long as a considerable number of
children were involved, it would be legitimate to generalize from their
reading habits and preferences to those of 'children at large'; and this absence
of rigour in sampling methodology has continued to characterize almost all
research into children's reading not only in the 1920s but in later decades as
well. In reality, of course, if any generalization of findings is to be made,
great care needs to be taken to define the population under consideration, to
ensure a representative sample from it, and to avoid possible sources of
bias — a set of related problems which will be discussed at some length in
relation to the present investigation.

Even so, each of these pioneering studies does raise certain issues which
are of continuing interest and relevance. Jordan, for instance, seems to have
been well aware of the difficulty of obtaining trustworthy information from
children's own statements and responses, and he supplemented his questionnaire survey by extended visits to eight public libraries during which he
compiled 'popularity scores' for individual books based partly on observation
of withdrawals and partly on the librarians' assessments of popularity. From
this section of his data he concluded that the reading interests of boys and
girls are very dissimilar, particularly between the ages of $10\frac{1}{2}$ and $13\frac{1}{2}$, and
that at these ages boys are inclined principally towards fiction concerned
with war, scouting, school, sports, and strenuous adventure, while girls are
attracted above all to fiction which portrays home or school life, or a
combination of both. Furthermore, in an observation which anticipates a
finding of our own survey half a century later, he reported that, in regard to
non-fiction, the boys' interests centred round what-and-how-to-do books,
whereas the girls — except for 'a few books on cooking, crocheting, dramatics
and poetry' — failed to show interest in non-fiction.

However, the major part of Jordan's study consisted of his questionnaire
survey, and he makes explicit mention of two major sources of error which
may contaminate data collected by this means. In the first place, he writes:
'Children are likely to write down what is expected of them and not what
they really like, and may write down nothing when some real preference
exists which they prefer not to reveal.' In his questionnaire administration he
tried to meet this difficulty by emphasizing that the school authorities
would not see the answers of individual students, and by asking the pupils
to write their first names only, 'as an aid in helping [them] lose their
identity'. And in the second place he notes that: 'The choices are too
greatly influenced by what the children read in school . . . The fact that a
book is used in school ensures its being read by comparatively large numbers;
and even if only a small proportion of users like it, its position of popularity
will be relatively too high.' Jordan's questionnaire, it will be remembered,

asked children to write down the five books and magazines they liked best of all those they had ever read, a procedure which concentrates wholly upon preference, leaves ambiguous the recency of the reading, and provides no information about amount of reading. From the answers, however, Jordan compiled lists of the most popular books for boys and girls separately in four age groups (7–11, 12–13, 14–16, and 17–18). He also classified the books under the headings: novels, stories, adventure, biography, history, poetry, science, travel, information and humour. The ill-defined and arbitrary nature of some of these categories is too self-evident to need underlining, though it should perhaps be added that in this respect they are no different from the categories used in most subsequent studies. When the questionnaire survey was repeated in 1925, it was found that the same types of books in almost the same proportions were chosen as in 1917, although there was a certain amount of change in the individual titles and authors mentioned, so that in the lists of most popular books between one-third and one-half were common to both dates.

Terman and Lima's book *Children's Reading* reports findings from several disparate studies, including one which was linked with Terman's extended programme of research into the abilities of gifted children. As a preliminary to this more specialized study, however, the authors report on reading records that were kept for two months by a control group of 808 unselected children aged between 6 and 16 in three small Californian cities. The tables compiled from these records show that at ages 10–11 these children were reading an average of 2·0 books per month, at ages 12–13 an average of 3·0 books per month, and at ages 14–15 an average of 2·5 books per month. The authors comment that these figures were probably higher than they would have been at that time for the United States as a whole, since other studies had shown much variation according to region, with children in urban communities reading more than children in rural communities. They also mention that in their own control group 13% of the children over 8 years of age read no books at all during the two-month period, whereas other studies had shown that in some localities as many as 30% or 40% of children read nothing at all except school texts. When the reading records of this control group were compared with similar records kept by a group (number unspecified) of gifted children with IQ 135 or higher, it was found that the gifted children were reading much more than the unselected children (between two and three times as much, in fact), and that the quality of their reading was also much higher. One minor point which seems worth mentioning relates to a sex difference in regard to re-reading; Terman and Lima report that in the reading records of 2000 children (the composition of this group is not made clear) 30% of the books read by girls were re-readings, whereas the corresponding figure in the case of the boys was only 18%.

Terman and Lima also gave a questionnaire to 1827 schoolchildren in grades 1 to 8 (In this group the unselected and gifted children were combined.), asking each child to list the four or five books he or she had most enjoyed reading during the last year. From the replies the authors compiled two lists of the books most liked by boys and girls respectively. At the top of the boys' list came (in descending order of popularity) *Treasure Island* , *The Call of the Wild*, *Tom Sawyer*, *Robinson Crusoe*, and *The Three Musketeers*; while at the top of the girls' list came *Little Women*, *Anne of Green Gables*, *Ivanhoe*, *Little Men*, and *Treasure Island*. It is noticeable that all the most-liked books are fiction (though this was partly due to the very wide range of non-fiction titles mentioned), and that only five titles appear in both the boys' list and the girls' list. Since these five titles are *Treasure Island*, *The Call of the Wild*, *The Three Musketeers*, *Ivanhoe*, and *A Tale of Two Cities* we may agree with the authors that such overlap as exists is wholly due to girls reading boys' books. The authors also comment that the differences between the two lists confirm that boys prefer stories of adventure and mystery whereas girls prefer stories of school and home life.

Washburne and Vogel's study first appeared in 1926 as *The Winnetka Graded Book List*, but was later re-published under the title *What Children Like to Read*. Their survey had involved the cooperation of some 800 teachers in various parts of the United States and, in choosing schools, the research team 'tried to get as wide as possible a variety of types, in cities of various kinds and sizes, well distributed among different sections of the country'. In the event 36 750 children in 34 schools (20 public schools, 9 private schools, and 5 university and normal training schools) filled out what was described as a 'ballot' on every book they read during the school year 1924—25; in effect, this means that in reporting on a book each child ticked one of the following statements:

> One of the best books I ever read.
> A good book, I like it.
> Not so very interesting.
> I don't like it.

Over 100 000 ballots were received in respect of some 9300 separate books. From these the researchers first took the 800 books on which twenty-five or more children's judgements had been received, and submitted this list to thirteen children's librarians with the request that they mark them as either: (1) of unquestionable literary merit, (2) of sufficient value to include in the list though not of high literary merit, (3) not recommended because of low literary merit, or (4) not recommended because of subject matter unsuitable for children. 110 books were excluded because three-quarters of the children's librarians considered them either 'too trashy' or 'unsuitable in subject matter', and this left the 686 titles which were included in the book list. The children's reading ability had been measured by the Stanford Silent Reading Test, and each book on the list was next graded according to the median reading grade of those children who had both read and liked it. Within the list itself books were listed in order according to a 'popularity index' which consisted of the product of the number of cities in which the book was read multiplied by the number of children who read and liked it. It should perhaps be mentioned that, within the resulting list, there was a marked orientation towards nineteenth century classics (perhaps an inevitable outcome of the selection procedure used), and that it seems likely that, in a number of cases (e.g. *The Merchant of Venice*, *A Midsummer Night's Dream*, and *Silas Marner* at age 13), the book had been read because it was prescribed as classroom reading rather than because it was voluntarily chosen.

Apart from the unprecedentedly large number of children involved in it, the Winnetka study has particular interest because it prompted a few years later an unusually searching re-analysis of the data by Shuttleworth. In his monograph *A Critical Study of Two Lists of Best Books for Children* (1932) Shuttleworth compared the Winnetka list (allegedly derived almost entirely from children's own choices and likings) with lists constructed by the Institute of Character Research at the State University of Iowa according to principles based entirely on 'competent adult opinion'. In the Iowa studies (the results of which were published in *A Guide to Literature for Character Training* by Starbuck et al., Vol. I, 1928, Vol. II, 1930) each book was carefully read by at least three of the staff of the Institute and thereafter graded into five (recommended) levels of merit or four (non-recommended) levels of demerit; the most suitable grade for each book was also determined by the judgement of these adult readers. The first issue examined by Shuttleworth was the extent to which the two lists agreed in regard to grade-placement; his conclusion was that they agreed well with each other in regard to *relative* grade-placement (in other words the books which were common to the two lists occurred in closely similar order) and also that they could be shown to agree well in regard to *absolute* grade-placement if certain corrections were made to compensate for the Winnetka survey's failure to obtain an adequate sampling of ballots from the earlier and later grades. Shuttleworth next turned his attention to the question of how far adult opinion was agreed as to the merit of children's books. Though critical of the nature of the scale that the Winnetka survey's thirteen librarians had been required to use, he was able nevertheless to argue (by re-analysis of the data) that the librarians were highly reliable in their judgements and that they agreed quite well ($r = 0.63$) with the expert readers of the Institute of Character Research, who had also agreed well among themselves.

More significant for our own purpose is the section in which Shuttleworth addressed himself to the question of how far selection of best books by competent adult opinion gives the same result as selection of best books on the basis of children's choices. He pointed out that the Winnetka survey recorded five possible indices of children's choices. These were:

1   The number of children reading and reporting on a book
2   The number of cities in which a book was read (ranging between one and thirty-four)
3   A so-called 'popularity index' obtained by multiplying the number of children reading and liking a book by the number of cities in which it was read
4   'Percentage liking' — i.e. the percentage of children ticking the first two statements on a 'liking scale'
5   'Interest value' — a measure obtained by assigning numerical values of 100, 67, 33, and 0 to the four statements on the 'liking scale' and averaging the resulting scores.

Shuttleworth pursued his inquiry by presenting a table showing the inter-correlations of these five indices for 156 books placed in grade V and 156 books placed in grade VI and on which at least eight librarians' judgements were available. This table shows clearly that measures 1, 2 and 3 correlate highly, and that measures 4 and 5 correlate highly, but that the cross-correlations are very low. 'Obviously', Shuttleworth commented, 'both sets of figures do not measure the same thing.' He went on to argue convincingly that the most probable interpretation is that measures 1, 2 and 3 are primarily measures of availability, and that measures 4 and 5 should be accepted as more valid measures of the true appeal of books to children. Shuttleworth's final step was to examine the correlations between competent adult opinion and the various measures of child appeal.

He found that adult opinion correlated positively with measures 1, 2 and 3, but showed either zero or negative correlations with measures 4 and 5. His comments on this finding are worth quoting: 'That competent opinion gives slightly positive correlations with number of ballots, number of cities, and "popularity index" may be due to the dependency of availability upon the recommendations of librarians and others who prepare lists of books for purchase by school and city libraries. The negative correlations between competent opinion and percentage-liking and interest-value were a complete surprise. There is no way of interpreting these data so as to yield the conclusion that there is any substantial correlation between what children like and what adults approve.' Two important issues have therefore been brought into prominence by Shuttleworth's re-analysis of the Winnetka survey. The first is the extent to which 'availability' (adult-controlled in a variety of ways) may underlie and determine lists and popularity-ratings which seem on the face of things to be an undiluted expression of children's

reading preferences. The second is the existence of a serious discrepancy
(to be noted again in a number of later studies) between what children
choose to read of their own volition, and what adults judge good for them.

In the next study which calls for mention, Lazar's *Reading Interests,
Activities and Opportunities of Bright, Average and Dull Children* (1937), a
questionnaire was administered to 4300 children aged 10, 11 and 12 in
eleven elementary and two junior high schools in New York. On the basis
of their IQ scores the pupils were classified into three groups, bright, average
and dull; and an inventory record was also compiled for each pupil to give
information about socio-economic background. Among the main findings
reported were that girls were reading more books per month than boys, that
bright pupils read considerably more than dull or average pupils, and that
the dull group contained the largest percentage reporting 'no books read'.
Analysis of the data showed that intelligence was more closely related to the
number of books read than was socio-economic status. On the other hand,
while the number of books in the home showed a substantial correlation with
the intelligence of the children, it was found that there was an even closer
association between the number of books in the home and socio-economic
status. One intriguing minor point is connected with the finding that,
whereas many of the girls in the sample were interested in boys' books, the
boys were not much interested in girls' books; Lazar further reported that
the girls who read boys' books were chiefly bright girls, while the boys who
read girls' books were chiefly dull boys. A further characteristic of Lazar's
sample that deserves mention is the fact that more than 60% of the parents
were foreign-born and that in about 44% of the homes a foreign language
was spoken; while these rather high percentages were probably not untypical
of the population of New York City at that period, they may suggest a need
for caution in extrapolating Lazar's findings to other communities.

JENKINSON'S 1938 SURVEY IN GREAT BRITAIN

We move next to the first survey of any considerable size to be carried out in
Great Britain, Jenkinson's *What do Boys and Girls Read?* This was published
in 1940, but the questionnaires had been administered in 1938 to 1570 boys
and 1330 girls between the ages of 12 and 15 in Hull, North Lincolnshire
and the East Riding of Yorkshire. It is no disparagement of the very real
achievement of this pioneering study to say that in certain respects
Jenkinson's methodology betrayed defects which weaken our confidence in
his findings and make it difficult to compare his results with those of our
own survey. In the first place the sampling was such as to introduce an
unmistakable over-representation of the more able children, though the
extent of this bias cannot now be ascertained. The questionnaire was
administered in seventeen senior elementary schools (all urban) and

eleven secondary schools (all urban, except for three which were in a small country town, and at that time selective and/or fee paying). This distribution between types of school means already that selected pupils had more chance than unselected pupils of being included in the survey; this imbalance does not really matter, however, since all Jenkinson's tables are given separately for each type of school. What is more bothering is the fact that in any school with more than one stream the questionnaire was given only to the A stream. It is true that we are told that, of the nine boys' senior elementary schools from which answers came, only three had A forms, the other six being single-stream schools; consequently we can deduce that for the boys' senior schools the under-representation of the less able pupils, though serious, would not be such as completely to invalidate any conclusions drawn from the resulting tables. We are not given any information about the girls' senior schools, but can perhaps guess that the situation here would be roughly similar.

It seems likely however that many (if not all) of the Secondary Schools were two-stream schools, so that we are bound to suspect that the findings of this part of the survey may apply only to the more able half of the secondary school population. Certainly it seems possible that these characteristics of the sample may go some way towards explaining the unusually high figures Jenkinson obtained for 'number of books read out of school'. In the secondary schools these ranged between 5·0 books per month and 6·0 books per month for the boys, and between 5·9 books per month and 6·5 books per month for the girls. And, even in the senior schools, the comparable figures − though lower − were still very high by comparison with those obtained in a number of subsequent studies; thus Jenkinson's senior school boys read between 3·9 and 4·3 books per month according to age, while his senior school girls read between 5·1 and 5·3 books per month. Even more striking is the very small percentage of children in Jenkinson's sample who claimed to have read no book during the previous month. In the case of the girls this percentage was at all ages so tiny as to be negligible; in the case of the boys it amounted to 4% among the secondary school boys at age 14+, and to 5·9% among the senior school boys at the same age. It certainly seems hard to accept these figures at their face value; though it must be admitted that, by making allowances for the flaws in sampling methodology already mentioned, we cannot accomplish more than a partial explaining-away of them. The conclusion which Jenkinson drew from his questionnaire data was that: 'The overwhelming majority of boys of these ages (and even more so of girls) are, in modern conditions, likely to acquire "the reading habit" without any encouragement from the schools.' Unfortunately one cannot at this distance in time be entirely certain as to whether or not this conclusion was, in 1940, an over-optimistic one.

The second area in which Jenkinson's conclusions need to be treated with caution relates to his handling of the book titles listed by his children as having been read during the previous month. Jenkinson seems to have been unaware of Shuttleworth's study, and he nowhere indicates any appreciation of the extent to which 'availability' may have determined the books which the children chose to read out of school time. It is consequently a weakness of his survey that no information was sought about the source from which books had been obtained, and that lists of 'most popular books' and 'most popular authors' were based solely on the number of times books had been read, without any attempt having been made to find out (by a 'ballot' or 'liking scale') how much children had enjoyed the reading of them. In addition the books were classified into twelve rather unsatisfactory and by no means unambiguous categories: school story, detective story, story of home life, adventure story, love story, historical story, collection of stories (e.g. an annual), humour, sport, travel, biography and technical. Admittedly the children themselves had been asked to assign their books to one of the first seven of these categories (the last five were added later), but Jenkinson comments that in this respect the children's own statements 'were useful, but were not felt to be binding'.

Jenkinson does indeed seem to have been aware of the overlapping nature of some of his categories, and of the difficulty of assigning a book with any certainty to a category without having read it oneself. Nevertheless, despite these reservations, Jenkinson's lists of books and authors and his comments on them have a good deal of interest. He reports that his 1570 boys had read during the month 7371 books; whereas the 1330 girls read 7651 books. He does not state how many separate and individual titles were mentioned, but to judge from the quite extensive lists of adult fiction titles given for each age group it would seem probable that the total number of distinct titles must have been very considerable, and that the diversity of book reading which was a striking feature of the response to our own questionnaire in 1971 may well have been in evidence in 1938 also. The criterion for Jenkinson's lists of 'most popular adult books' was a 'standard of popularity' aimed at ensuring that any book included would have been read during a year by two pupils out of five; this extrapolation from the records for a single month produced lists too long to be reproduced here. If we confine ourselves to the most widely read titles (those read during a single month by ten or more boys or girls in each age and school type), we can cite the following in descending order of 'wide reading':

Secondary school boys:
- 12+ *Treasure Island, Robinson Crusoe, David Copperfield, Tom Brown's Schooldays*
- 13+ *Treasure Island, Tom Brown's Schooldays, Westward Ho, The Invisible Man*

Secondary school girls:
  12+   *David Copperfield, Lorna Doone, Alice in Wonderland, Treasure Island, A Christmas Carol*
  13+   *The Thirty-nine Steps, Lorna Doone*
  14+   *The Thirty-nine Steps, David Copperfield, Jane Eyre, Lorna Doone*

Senior school boys:
  12+   *Treasure Island, Robinson Crusoe, Tom Brown's Schooldays, Oliver Twist*
  13+   *Treasure Island, Robinson Crusoe, Tom Brown's Schooldays, A Christmas Carol, David Copperfield*

Senior school girls:
  12+   *Oliver Twist, Alice in Wonderland, The Water Babies, David Copperfield*
  13+   *Oliver Twist, The Old Curiosity Shop, Gulliver's Travels, A Christmas Carol, A Tale of Two Cities, David Copperfield, Uncle Tom's Cabin, The Water Babies, Treasure Island.*

If these examples from the upper end of Jenkinson's much longer lists seem notably conservative (and even nineteenth century) in character, it must be stressed that they do not misrepresent the lists themselves, which contain very few recent books and hardly any that are without some considerable literary merit. The explanation of this emerges when we discover that Jenkinson (somewhat idiosyncratically) interpreted the term 'adult fiction' as meaning 'books which would be and are read with pleasure and interest by moderately sensitive and refined adults'. Thus he omitted from his lists authors such as Edgar Rice Burroughs, 'Sapper' and Edgar Wallace (though rather inconsistently he did include Ethel M. Dell, Zane Grey and Gene Stratton Porter). Jenkinson's lists of 'most popular adult authors' and 'most popular adult books' were in fact therefore confined to those books and authors he himself approved of, and they are placed in their correct perspective when we note that 'adult fiction' (as defined by Jenkinson) amounted to less than one-fifth of the total book-reading by his sample. (If we take the sub-groups separately, we find that only for the senior school boys aged 14+ (23·6%) and for the secondary school girls aged 14+ (31·4%) and 15+ (35·8%) did it account for more than one fifth of the total).

If we read Jenkinson's book with the care it deserves, the emphasis will fall above all upon his quite explicit statement that the private reading of children between the ages of 12 and 15 is 'largely chosen from inferior books, magazines, and newspapers'. It was indeed in highlighting the vast and seemingly unbridgeable gulf between what children chose to read in their own leisure time (ephemeral stories of adventure, school or home life, crime, war or detection — mainly trash by adult standards) and what they

were given to read in English lessons that Jenkinson's book was so
influential. The schools had supplied their English syllabuses, and the book
includes dispiriting lists of the texts studied in class at the different age levels.
The secondary school lists are dominated by eighteenth and nineteenth
century classics, with essays by Addison, Goldsmith and Lamb looming
large, and the more modern writers represented by *Eothen*, *An Inland
Voyage* and *The Mirror of the Sea*; the senior school boys' lists are the only
ones to make any very noticeable concession to juvenile tastes, by including
fiction by Wells, Buchan and Conan Doyle. On the whole the evidence
assembled in these lists provides firm support for Jenkinson's assertion that,
at these ages: 'Adult tastes are imposed on children, and this is a mistake.'
Fortunately Jenkinson's book was widely read, and its message was evidently
heeded. In the post-war period the literature prescribed in school English
syllabuses came to include more fiction, more books written during the
twentieth century, and more books written specially for children. (The
changed climate can be traced in publishers' lists of the period; a good
example of the new trend was the appearance in 1950 of Heinemann's *New
Windmill Series*.) Slowly, moreover, in line with Jenkinson's recommendations,
opinion among English teachers began to move away from 'much teaching
of few books' towards the provision of a wider and more varied supply of
books (e.g. through the classroom library) and an increasing concentration
upon developing the pupils' own reading tastes and interests.

SCOTT'S 1942 SURVEY IN NEW ZEALAND

A few years later Jenkinson's questionnaire was used in New Zealand by
W. J. Scott with only slight modifications and a few additions. Although
Scott's book, *Reading, Film and Radio Tastes of High School Boys and
Girls*, was not published until 1947, the survey it records had been carried
out in 1942 with a sample of 3972 pupils between the ages of 13 and 18.
The scope of the present survey does not permit a detailed review of Scott's
findings (which were in many respects closely comparable with Jenkinson's),
particularly since the age range studied was rather older than the one we are
concerned with; but three points deserve brief mention. First, in regard to
amount of leisure-time reading, Scott's figures for 'number of books read
per month' (5·0 for boys and 5·9 for girls) were only slightly lower than
those reported by Jenkinson. Second, the percentage of pupils who had read
no books during the month was also low — approximately 4% of Scott's total
sample. Since Scott's sample seems to have been quite a good cross-section
of the school population, these facts should perhaps induce us to moderate
our scepticism about Jenkinson's data and incline us to the view that
Jenkinson's high figures for book reading were indeed a genuine reflection
(only a little distorted by sampling flaws) of a certain phase in our cultural

history. The third point to be made is that Scott's 3972 pupils entered nearly five thousand separate books on the questionnaires — a clear indication that great diversity of reading was already present among adolescents at that time.

SOME RELATED RESEARCH STUDIES 1941–58

At this point we must turn aside from reading surveys proper to mention three studies of a slightly different kind which have nevertheless a certain relevance. The first is Robert L. Thorndike's monograph *A Comparative Study of Children's Reading Interests* (1941). Thorndike's aim was to explore the topics which interested children at different ages between 8 and 16, and for this purpose he constructed a questionnaire in which 88 fictitious book titles were listed, each with a brief descriptive note. The following examples will indicate the nature of the questionnaire:

> 1   *Lonesome Laddie Finds a Friend*
>   How a stray dog found a new master and showed his true love.
> 27   *The Revenge of Pahonkas*
>   An Indian chief gets his revenge against the white man who had wronged him. A story of life on the frontier.
> 53   *Murder in the Green House*
>   Who killed Jeb Wilson? Whose were the giant footprints in the hall? Dr Van Tine puts his wits to work.

For each title the pupil was asked to answer the question 'Would you like to read this book?' by placing a circle round one of three answers ('Yes', 'No', 'Uncertain'); and the questionnaire was administered to 2891 children in schools in New York City and New York State. The respondents were then divided into sub-groups by sex, age, and three ability groupings (bright, average and slow) based on IQ scores. Interest scores were computed for each sub-group, and the correlations between sub-groups were studied. Thorndike's main conclusions were that at these ages there is a consistent pattern of boy-interests and, to a lesser extent, of girl-interests cutting across all age and intelligence differences, that sex is a conspicuously more important than age or intelligence as a determiner of reported interest patterns, and that in expressed reading interests bright children (median IQ 123) are most like a group of mentally slower children (median IQ about 92) who are two or three years older than they are. The study is noteworthy for its ingenious method of isolating for study one set of factors which motivate children's reading preferences; it does not, of course, take into account other factors (such as reading difficulty) which come into play when real books as opposed to invented titles are in question.

The second study which falls on the fringe of our area of concern is George W. Norvell's *The Reading Interests of Young People* (1950). This dealt not with voluntary or leisure-time reading, but with pupil-reports on books or selections studied in class. Data had been collected over a twelve-year period from 50 000 children between the ages of 12 and 18 by 625 teachers in schools in New York State, the pupils being required to tick each title either 'very interesting', 'fairly interesting' or 'uninteresting'. From these data, interest scores were computed for any title for which a minimum of 300 pupil-reports was available, according to the formula: 'To the number of pupils reporting "very interesting" add half the number reporting "fairly interesting", then divide by the total of all pupils reporting, to give a percentage score'. Although the scoring procedure seems a little arbitrary, Norvell claimed to have grounds for believing that 'selections with an interest score of 70·0 have proved generally acceptable for class study'.

The striking fact which can be extracted from this study by Norvell is that at that time two-thirds of the selections most widely used in high school literature classes failed to meet even this criterion of acceptability to pupils — surely a remarkable manifestation of the discrepancy (first brought to light by Shuttleworth) between adult assessments of what is suitable for children and the opinions of the children themselves. Norvell's positive recommendations were similar to those advanced ten years earlier by Jenkinson, namely, that 'part of the class programme in literature consist of the reading or study in common . . . of a list of selections *known to be well liked by both boys and girls*, but that a second part of the programme consist of wide reading of individually chosen selections carried out under the guidance of the teacher.' There seems to be little room for doubt that in the past quarter of a century this approach, with its increased emphasis on individualized reading schemes, has steadily gained ground in both British and United States schools. In an appendix to *The Reading Interests of Young People* Norvell presented some experimental evidence to show that, at high school level, a classroom procedure built around wide reading produced better results than one confined to class study of a small number of texts.

It is worthy of note, however, that in 1958 Norvell published a companion volume, *What Boys and Girls Like to Read*, which took as its province the reading of younger children and presented interest score data about books read in class by 24 000 pupils in grades 3 to 6. In this volume he was also able to add for some grades comparisons between books studied in class and books read independently, and these showed that on average, in grades 4 to 6, a book studied in class was better liked than the same book read independently. The implications of this finding are not wholly clear, but it might be taken to suggest that the balance of advantage between class reading and individualized reading varies somewhat according to age level. It seems possible that these younger children still lacked the fluent mastery of reading skills that would enable them to take as much enjoyment from a book in an independent reading as in a class reading accompanied by discussion.

The third, rather differently oriented study which needs to be mentioned, is an investigation carried out by D. V. Connor in Australia and reported in an article entitled 'The relationship between reading achievement and voluntary reading of children' in *Educational Review*, Vol. 6, pp. 221–27 (1954). His subjects were 214 12-year-olds drawn from three schools in a metropolitan residential-industrial area, and their reading attainment was assessed by Parts 1, 2 and 4 of the Australian Council for Educational Research Reading Tests. In addition two instruments, consisting in each case of a questionnaire-cum-rating scale, were constructed for assessment of voluntary reading habits and interests in respect of (1) quality of reading material and (2) quantity of reading material. For the whole group the degree of relationship between reading habits and reading attainment was found to be 0·58 (0·45 when intelligence was held constant). The group of 214 pupils was then divided into three sub-groups according to whether they were 'being subjected to the "treatments" of good, medium or poor reading habits'. It was considered that the groups were already equated on age, grade, and socio-economic status, and the method of 'paired comparisons' was used to equate the groups on intelligence and sex. During this matching process the number of subjects was reduced to 150. The 'effect' of good, medium and poor reading habits was then examined by subjecting the reading attainment scores of each group to analysis of variance. Significant differences were shown to exist between each group, and Connor's conclusion was that 'the good readers (in terms of reading attainment) are the ones who also read more and better quality reading material, and poor readers read less and poorer quality material'. Connor added, however, 'it is not known whether this is a causal relationship . . . it may well be that good reading achievement tends to cause children to select or have at their disposal "good" reading material and to engage in good reading habits, rather than vice versa'. This study is remarkable for the rigour of its experimental method and the sophistication of its statistical treatment, and it must be regarded as providing unusually firm evidence of an association between voluntary reading and reading attainment which other investigators have often tended to assume rather than to demonstrate.

SURVEYS IN GREAT BRITAIN SINCE 1955

If we return now to the type of survey which has been the main focus of our interest in this chapter, we shall find that, although there have been a number of further studies of this kind in the post-war period in Great Britain, these have invariably been subject to certain limitations either in their scale or in the objectives they set themselves. One type of self-imposed limitation is exemplified by J. D. Carsley's study 'The Interests of Children (aged 10—11) in Books' published in *The British Journal of Educational Psychology* Vol: 27, 13—23 (1957), for — although the number of children answering questionnaires was quite large (2040 pupils in 30 schools in the Merseyside area) — they were deliberately confined to a single age group. Moreover, although the design of the questionnaire was such as to elicit a good deal of interesting information about such matters as the source of books read at home, children's preferences for favourite books in their private reading, or the amount of time spent by children in reading and in watching television respectively, no figures are given for amount of leisure-time book reading, and in general the data which had been accumulated is not presented in a way which makes it easy to compare it with that put forward in other studies.

Television and the Child (1958) by Hilde T. Himmelweit, A. N. Oppenheim and Pamela Vince provides an example of a study with a field of inquiry limited in a distinctly different way. This lavishly funded survey was focused primarily on the television viewing of the young, and reading enters into it only as one of those aspects of children's lives where television may be expected to exert an influence. The main survey was carried out among 10—11 year-olds and 13—14 year-olds in London, where about two-thirds of the children had television at home, and also in Bristol, Portsmouth and Sunderland, these areas having been chosen as ones in which about one-third of the children had television at home. The design of the sample made it possible to assemble two groups of children, viewers on the one hand, non-viewers (or controls) on the other hand, which made up a total of 1854 children in all and which had been carefully matched on age, sex, intelligence and social background. In the course of a comparison between the reading of these two groups the authors argued that under the influence of television children initially read less, with books suffering more than comics; but that, after a few years of viewing, book reading returns to its original level, whereas the diminution of comic reading remains.

We shall re-examine these arguments in a later chapter, at the same time raising the doubt, in the light of our own findings, as to whether generalizations made at a period when television viewing was a minority activity can safely be extrapolated (as they often have been) to a phase of culture in which almost every home contains a television set. For the moment, however, we will confine ourselves to the amount of book reading reported by this 1955 sample. Among the 10—11 year-olds, viewers were found to have read an average of 2·5 books per month, while non-viewers had read 2·7 books per month. Among 13—14 year-olds, viewers had read 2·2 books per month while non-viewers had read 2·5 books per month. It is clear that these figures are markedly less than the ones reported by Jenkinson in 1940. Of interest

also are the figures for non-book-readers. Among the 10–11 year-olds 19%
of both viewers and non-viewers reported that they had read either no book
or only part of a book during the month. Among the 13–14 year-olds this
percentage stayed roughly the same (21%) for non-viewers, but had climbed
to 28% in the case of viewers. It should perhaps be added that the percentage
of non-book-readers was greatest (36%) among the 13–14 year-old boys who
were viewers, though it was also high (35%) among 13–14 year-old viewers
who were of average ability (IQ between 100 and 114).

As a contrast to the two surveys just mentioned (each of which covered
quite a large number of children) we may mention next *Books Girls Read*
(1967) by M. J. Lane and K. A. Furness-Lane, which deliberately confined
itself to the pupils at a single girls' comprehensive school in London.
Unfortunately this limitation of scale was not compensated for by an
accompanying rigour in methodology, and indeed the authors seem to have
been completely unaware of any of the earlier inquiries which had been
carried out into children's reading. Nevertheless, it may be of interest to
mention the mean number of books read out of class during the previous
month by their rather small sample (220 girls selected at random from a
total school population of about 1600); their figure was 3·35 books per
month, which is considerably lower than the figures presented by Jenkinson
and Scott, but rather higher than those presented by Himmelweit. However,
the Lanes' discussion of their data is almost wholly confined to an interesting
but highly speculative suggestion that their girls could be divided with very
few exceptions into three groups – firstly, a group dominated by the values
of their peers, and predominantly concerned either with juvenile culture or,
at an older age range, with the 'pop' adolescent sub-culture; secondly, a
smaller group oriented towards 'a typical adult female life style, centred
round a romantic conception of marriage, the home, children and the
nuclear family'; and thirdly, a still smaller group who were 'centrally
involved . . . with intellectual or at least educational pursuits'.

Our next example, *Children in the Library* (1968) by I. J. Leng, could
well serve as a model for a really thorough and meticulous study of a
limited field. Leng confined himself to a study over the period of one year of
the books borrowed from a public library by the 1055 children between the
ages of 6 and 13 who lived within a one-mile radius. Of these 1055 children,
555 (53%) actually used the library during the year, and the greater part of
the book consists of a careful and sensitive analysis of their borrowing, an
account which can be recommended without reservation but certainly cannot
be summarized in a brief space. It is important to remember, however, that
Leng's observations apply only to those children who use a public library,
and that in many areas this group would form a smaller percentage of the
total age group than they did in the small Welsh town he was studying. Leng
does in fact demonstrate that in the case of his own sample library users

differed from non-users in several respects. The most important differentiating factor was that of sex, since 'the bulk of children who join are girls, and the majority of those who abstain are boys'. In addition, children who were library members were chiefly characterized by their relatively high level of attainment in school work, by the high proportion gaining grammar school places, and by their tendency to be of higher intelligence and to come from families of not more than three children.

The last survey which we shall mention here, that carried out by J. J. Taylor, was also restricted in that the inquiry was limited to the pupils in four secondary schools in a single geographical area, namely, the North Midlands. Taylor's study originally constituted a thesis submitted in 1970 for the M.Phil. degree of the University of Nottingham, but his conclusions have been summarized in two articles in *The Use of English*, Vol. 24, No. 1 (1972) and Vol. 25, No. 1 (1973) and also in an article in *Reading*, Vol. 7, No. 3 (1974). The schools concerned were two grammar schools and two secondary modern schools each with a mixed four-form entry, and the questionnaires were completed in respect of a four-week period in February 1967 by all the pupils in the first four years, a total of 1926 children.

Taylor found that, in their reading of comics, the children maintained an average of more than 3 comics per week in the first and second years of all four schools, and that, although the amount of comic reading dropped somewhat among fourth-year grammar school pupils, there was a marked tendency for boys and girls to remain quite heavily addicted to comic reading throughout the age range studied. As far as book reading was concerned Taylor was able to show that, throughout all four years, secondary modern boys read significantly less than secondary modern girls, grammar school boys or grammar school girls. He also showed that among secondary modern pupils the number of books read fell significantly, as between the first and second years on the one hand, and the third and fourth years on the other hand, but that over the same age range the amount of reading of grammar school pupils did not change significantly. In computing the average numbers of books read during the month Taylor omitted those children who had read no books, so that his averages are not really comparable with those of other investigators. Even though they have been artificially inflated by this omission, Taylor's figures remain quite low. Thus, for secondary modern boys the number of books per month ranges between 1·6 and 2·2, while for secondary modern girls it ranges between 2·3 and 2·7. For grammar school boys the figure remains steady throughout the age range at 2·6, whereas for grammar school girls it ranges only between 2·6 and 2·9.

Taylor pointed out that while in the fourth year all but a small fraction of the grammar school pupils were maintaining the rate of book reading achieved in the first year, in the secondary modern schools in the fourth year the practice of book reading had been abandoned by one in five of the girls and by one in four of the boys. Taylor himself claimed that, even allowing for the bias in Jenkinson's sampling, his own figures suggested a marked decline in book reading as compared with 1940. We have of course no means of knowing to what extent these four schools were representative of schools throughout the country. Nevertheless, given its limited and local character, this study was a thorough and valuable one, many of the findings of which tally quite well with the findings of our own national survey which was carried out four years later. We shall refer to some detailed points of comparison, showing both resemblances and differences, in later chapters.

We will conclude this necessarily foreshortened review of previous research by indicating some of the points which emerged from it to act as guidelines for our own research team when we started upon our task. First it seems clear that, if applied to children of 10 or more years of age, a written questionnaire can elicit valuable information about children's reading habits and tastes, particularly perhaps if it is focused primarily on obtaining a factual report of what they have read during a specified and not too lengthy period of time. However, since availability has been shown to be so very influential in determining what children read, it is important to supplement this factual record with opportunity for children to express their degree of liking for what they have read, and to complete the picture by obtaining as many data as possible about the sources from which books have been obtained. Secondly, since all the British surveys have been local in scope and limited in scale, there was a clear need in the 1970s for a national survey using a sample large enough and representative enough to justify generalizing the resultant findings to the country's children at large. Moreover, it seemed important that such a survey should attempt to set reading in its context in the social and cultural life of the children concerned by assembling relevant information about such matters as television viewing, the influence of family circumstances, and of the school milieu. It was with these considerations in mind that we set to work in the autumn of 1969 to fashion our research instruments and to draw our sample of children.

BIBLIOGRAPHY

Carsley, J. D. (1957). 'The interest of children (10—11 years) in books', *British Journal of Educational Psychology*, **XXVII**, 13—23.
Connor, D. V. (1954). 'The relationship between reading achievement and voluntary reading of children', *Educational Review*, 6, 221—7.
Himmelweit, H. T., Oppenheim A. N. and Vince P. (1958). *Television and the Child.* Oxford University Press.
Jenkinson, A. J. (1940). *What do Boys and Girls Read?* Methuen.

Jordan, A. M. (1921, revised 1926). *Children's Interests in Reading*. University of North Carolina Press.

Lane, M. J. and Furness-Lane, K. A. (1967). *Books Girls Read*. Society of Young Publishers.

Lazar, M. (1937). *Reading Interests, Activities and Opportunities of Bright, Average and Dull Children*. New York: Teachers College Contributions to Education, No. 707.

Leng, I. J. (1968). *Children in the Library: A Study of Children's Leisure Reading Tastes and Habits*. Cardiff: University of Wales Press.

Norvell, G. W. (1950). *The Reading Interests of Young People*. New York: Heath.

Norvell, G. W. (1958). *What Boys and Girls Like to Read*. Morristown, New Jersey: Silver Burdett Company.

Scott, W. J. (1947). *Reading, Film and Radio Tastes of High School Boys and Girls*. New Zealand Council for Educational Research.

Shuttleworth, F. E. (1932). 'A critical study of two lists of best books for children', *Genetic Psychology Monographs*, **XI**, 4.

Taylor, J. J. (1972). 'The reading of comics by secondary school pupils', *The Use of English*, **24**, 11–15.

Taylor, J. J. (1973). 'The voluntary book reading habits of secondary school pupils', *The Use of English*, **25**, 5–16.

Taylor, J. J. (1974). 'The voluntary reading habits of secondary school pupils', *Reading*, **7**, 11–19.

Terman, L. M. and Lima, M. (1925). *Children's Reading*. New York: Appleton.

Thorndike, R. L. (1941). *Children's Reading Interests. A Study Based on a Fictitious Annotated Titles Questionnaire*. New York: Teachers College

Washburne, C. and Vogel, M. (1926). *Winnetka Graded Book List*. Chicago: American Library Association.

2 The research design and procedures

INTRODUCTION

Although educational research is usually justified by an expectation that its results will be useful, researchers must not only present their results, they must also show how they produced them. What were the methods used and were they appropriate to the nature of the inquiry? How much weight of interpretation can the research findings bear? These and similar questions need to be examined explicitly.

The boundaries of our research are to some extent arbitrary; we had to exclude much that would be useful and relevant. This was inevitable since an integral part of the original concept was that most of the study should be statistical and produce results generalizable to the whole of the populations of children sampled. In research of this kind the investigators have to decide beforehand which variables of the multitude which suggest themselves are to be assessed and how this can best be done. Clearly, in the present case, the success of our research depends to a large extent on the adequacy of the ideas we developed about the contextual structure of children's reading habits and on our success in defining and assessing the relevant variables. However, we have tried to illuminate the research other than by statistics; we hope that on our broad statistical sketch we have been able to map out some of the more important regions in finer detail on the basis of interviews with children, discussions with teachers and a close examination of a large amount of children's reading material.

The first stage of our research was to plan and carry out a survey of children's reading; we had to decide what data we should try to collect, what methods we could best use to collect it, from whom it should be collected and to what analysis it should then be subjected. All of these four factors were interdependent; decisions about a scheme for one of them became constraints within which decisions about the others had to be taken. To follow on from our survey, we had to plan a schedule of interviews with children and other smaller scale investigations to fill out the survey data and follow up some of the hypotheses suggested by it.

In the remainder of this chapter, there will be discussion of the principles and practice according to which we conducted our sampling, constructed and used our questionnaires, handled the survey data we collected and conducted our follow-up investigations. The reader should bear in mind that it is for convenience of discussion that these topics are treated separately, and that in practice considerations relating to each of them were interlocking and mutually constraining.

SAMPLING – GENERAL PRINCIPLES

We wanted our research to produce data from which we could generalize to as large a part as possible of the population of children in England and Wales aged 8 to 16. The key to the validity of such generalization, in any kind of scientific research, is sampling.

A sample is a number of things drawn from the whole population of those things – a sub-set of a set. The number of samples or sub-sets which can be drawn from any particular population or set clearly depends on the number in the population or set; there are as many possible samples containing a given number as there are possible combinations of that number which can be drawn from the total number in the population.

Clearly, we are all familiar with the idea of sampling to this extent. It is a practical convenience for everybody, not just the scientist, to use an examination of a small part of something as a guide to the quality of the whole – as a farmer will look at a handful of grain when he is buying a sack. On the basis of this kind of examination we draw conclusions about the whole of an article, consignment, or other kind of thing we are examining. For these everyday purposes we rely on our past experience of the goods we are examining, and their particular source as a guide to how much we should examine and what kind of examination we should make. We will have learned that some goods are of highly consistent quality for example, and that if a small part is satisfactory then the rest is likely to be; other goods we will have experienced as highly variable and needing more thorough inspection.

When a scientist draws a sample the principles are basically the same. The practice is different in that precise quantification is required of all the information he derives from it, including a precise statement about the likelihood of the measured characteristics of the sample being a reflection of those same characteristics in the population from which it was drawn.

Instead of just using his personal past experience as a guide to how large a sample to take, the scientist, of course, uses the collective past experience that is embodied in sampling theory. The theory essentially describes how large a sample should be, and how it should be selected, for a given level of likelihood of its characteristics being a reflection of those of the population.

The theory says, in effect:

1   that if a sample is randomly selected, then a quantitative statement
    can be made about the probability or likelihood of it being similar
    to the population (a statement which might take the form: there is
    a 95% probability that 10-year-old children in the population
    sampled read between 2·5 and 3·5 books in November 1968);
2   that the larger a sample is, as a proportion of the population, the
    more precisely can this probability figure be given.

This last consideration is obvious enough to require no further general
discussion, but the notion of randomness is less clear. In everyday speech the
term 'random' tends to be used loosely and as a near synonym of 'arbitrary'.
In sampling contexts a sample is drawn randomly when every member in that
sample has been selected in such a way that every member of the population
from which it was drawn had an equal chance with every other member of
being selected.

Consider a hypothetical sampling situation and suppose we wish to draw
a sample of 50 from a school with a population of 1000 children. Some of
the ways in which we could select our sample are:

1   Get all the children assembled in the school hall and just wander
    around picking out 50;
2   Still in the hall, we could pick the 50 children nearest to us, or
    furthest from us;
3   We could arrange all the children's names alphabetically and pick
    the first 50 (or the last, or 50 starting from any initial letter).
4   We could take 50 random numbers* between 1 and 1000 and count
    off the children as they walk past us, selecting the children
    representing our random numbers.

Clearly there are other methods of selection too, but the four above
illustrate some considerations in sampling. Thus:

1   will not produce a random sample; it is a technique which suffers
    from the near certainty that our own psychological dispositions
    will lead us to select according to some criterion such as dress,
    sex, friendliness, etc.
2   suffers from the fact that children are likely to cluster together on
    the basis of similarity or friendship and such clusters will not be
    random.

*There are several published sets of tables of random numbers, e.g. those of
Fisher, R. A. and Yates, F. (1963).

3   will meet the criterion of randomness since there is no relationship
     between the initial letters of names and other individual
     characteristics.
4   by definition will produce a random sample.

Techniques 3 and 4 will produce what is called a 'simple random sample' –
'simple' because (a) there is only one stage to the process of drawing the
sample and (b) the members of the population are not sampled with a vew to
selecting into the sample the same proportions of each sex, age group, etc., as
are in the total population; 'random' because each child had an equal chance
of being selected, just as if his name had been drawn from a perfectly mixed
up set of names in a hat.

Any information we now collect about the characteristics of our random
sample – average age, sex proportions, average IQ and so on – also describes
the population of 1000 children with a degree of probability we can
calculate. Obviously, though, if before sampling we divide the children into
groups defined by the characteristics we are most interested in then we shall
get a sample which reflects the population even more accurately. This is
called stratification.

As an illustration, suppose we divided the population by age and sex, and
then took the sample. We should start by constructing a matrix and entering
the children into the cells in this fashion:

	Male	Female	Total
12 years and over	200(10)	100(5)	300
11 years and under	300(15)	400(20)	700
Totals	500	500	1000

Suppose the children were divided into the different categories in the
frequencies, f, shown. We can now sample from each cell in this matrix in
the proportion $\frac{50}{1000} \times f$ so that the sample from each cell is in the same
proportion to the population in the cell as the whole sample is to the whole
population. The figures in brackets in the cells are the numbers we shall
select (randomly of course) from each cell.

Stratified random sampling enables us to attach a higher probability to
statements made about the population on evidence from the sample than is
possible with simple random sampling.

One further possible elaboration of sampling procedure needs to be
described. Suppose that we want members of our sample to be clustered
together in groups (e.g. in a school, or a parliamentary constituency –
grouping making it possible to get at a whole group in one go), either for

convenience in collecting information about them, or because we also wish to find out things about the place or institution to which the group belongs. In this event we should first sample the places or institutions and then sample the appropriate number of individuals in these places or institutions, at each stage using simple or stratified sampling. This procedure is called two-stage sampling, and, in principle, any number of stages can be used in drawing a sample.

Just one further term needs explanation; this is 'sampling frame': before drawing a sample from a population we need some kind of listing of that population from which to work. In sampling people the sampling frame might be the register of voters, the register of disabled, a list of society members, official returns of numbers in educational establishments, etc. In any sampling exercise the first step is to find the most suitable sampling frame — suitable in terms of representing the target population and of being as far as possible up to date.

THE SAMPLE DESIGN

The basic sampling design was chosen with regard to a number of constraints, some outside our control, like the availability of a suitable sampling frame, others, like the choice of population to be sampled, largely determined by the original research brief, and others still, like our decision to sample at three age points, being the choice of the research team.

The only suitable sampling frame for children of school age is that provided by the annual returns of schools to the Department of Education and Science (DES) of the numbers on roll in December and showing the ages of all children as at the preceding 1st September (except for direct grant schools where age was recorded as at 31st December). Our target date for carrying out the survey was February 1971 and so we were able to use the 1969 DES return, judging that the number of deaths and removals between the date of the return and our survey would have no significant effect. The DES were able, and very willing, to programme their computer to provide us with information from the return in suitable forms.

We wanted to sample from children in maintained schools (excepting special schools and all-age schools) and direct grant schools in England and Wales. We decided to exclude schools in authorities with a middle school form of organization, considering that such schools were too recently established to form a distinct category as far as reading patterns were concerned and thus their inclusion would unjustifiably complicate the administration of our sampling.

We decided to sample children in three year-groups — those aged 10 at the beginning of the school year, those aged 12, and those aged 14. We concluded that the largest sample the research team's resources could handle would be about 10 000, that is 3000 or so in each age group. By the date of the administration of the questionnaire (in the event, March 1971) about half the children had reached their next birthday, but we have continued to refer to the age groups as 10+, 12+ and 14+ children.

Given all of these considerations, the choice of a basic sample design followed fairly naturally. It would have to be a two-stage sample, selecting first the schools, and then the children within the schools. We were interested in comparing reading patterns between regions of the country and between different types of school and so adopted these two factors for stratifying the schools before sampling them.

Since we had decided to exclude middle schools we agreed that a useful simplification of the sampling would be achieved by drawing 12+ and 14+ children from the same secondary schools. We also decided that it would be administratively very convenient if we took the same size group of children from each school and, with this in mind, we chose to sample schools by probability proportional to size, a procedure which will be explained here.

Sampling with probability proportionate to size is a convenient way of selecting a sample from unequal size units (schools, in our case) so that the final sample consists of groups of convenient and equal size. The following hypothetical example demonstrates how the criterion of randomness is achieved. Suppose we are sampling in two stages a group of 10 children from a cell in which there are two schools, one with 400 pupils, the other with 600. First the school from which the pupils are to be sampled is chosen by selecting a random number between 1 and 1000. Clearly this gives the first school 4 chances in 10 of being chosen, the second 6 chances in 10. If the first school is chosen each pupil in it will have 10 chances in 400, if the second school 10 chances in 600. Overall each pupil will have had the same number of chances, i.e.

$$\frac{400}{1000} \times \frac{10}{400} = \frac{1}{100}$$

$$\frac{600}{1000} \times \frac{10}{600} = \frac{1}{100}$$

The initial print-out of primary school statistics we received from the DES computer (see Appendix I (a)) consisted of a table of ten columns and six rows (ten regions of the country and six types of primary school — Junior with infants (boys); Junior with infants (girls); Junior with infants (mixed); Junior (boys); Junior (girls); and Junior (mixed)). In each cell of this table was printed the number of schools it contained and the number of children in these schools who were aged 9 on 1st September, 1969. We noted that the single-sex primary schools contained only 2·25% of this population and so decided only to sample the mixed schools (a population of 589 055 pupils in 14 959 schools) as a further way of simplifying the administration of our sampling.

We wanted about 3000 primary school children in our sample from a target population of nearly 600 000 — a ratio of about 1:200 — and so from each cell in the DES table we needed to end up with $\frac{1}{200}$ of the number of children it contained. In practice this 'sampling interval' of 1:200 had to be adjusted, (a) because we were in this first stage selecting schools by probability proportionate to size with a view subsequently to selecting 16 children from each school, and (b) because we had decided to draw a double size sample of schools, using schools 1, 3, 5, etc., as our basic sample with, in effect, another sample comprising schools 2, 4, 6, etc., as a second sample from which we could replace any schools which, for whatever reason, turned out to be unable to take part in the project. Thus, the basic sampling interval for each cell was $\frac{200 \times 16}{2}$ (i.e. 1600). For some cells this interval needed slight further adjustment so that the population of children in the cells, divided by 1600, produced as nearly as possible a whole number of schools. This last step, of course, produced small differences in sampling intervals between cells and it was our intention to correct for these in analysis. In practice, the effect of such corrections proved so marginal that we decided against using them.

The schools were selected by asking the DES computer to choose a random number between one and the number representing the calculated sampling interval for each cell and then 'count through' the children in each cell using the random number interval and print out for us the schools where it 'selected' a child in the cell population.

In the second stage of the sampling procedure, discussed more fully below, simple random sampling was used, with no stratification. The children were selected from lists supplied by the schools by using tables of random numbers. We could, of course, have stratified in this second stage using such factors as sex, ability, social class, and so on. In practice, all except the first of these would have been difficult to define for our purposes, and this kind of stratification would in any case have added considerably to the complexity of our sampling administration. In the event, the balance of sexes in our achieved sample was reasonably satisfactory (see Table 2, Chapter 3).

THE PRIMARY SAMPLE

Having chosen not to sample from single-sex primary schools, as described above, we decided to aim for a sample of 200 from the total of 14 959 mixed primary schools, a ratio of about 1:75. In practice our procedure

produced a list of 197 primary schools, distributed among the twelve cells
of our primary school tabulation as shown in Appendix I (b). At the same
time we had drawn a second list of 197 schools (see above), distributed in
the same way, as 'second choice' schools.

When the local education authorities administering the schools in our list
were approached we discovered that one large authority had adopted middle
school organization in September 1970, converting its junior schools into
middle schools for 8–12 year-olds. This affected three schools in our sample
but we decided to retain the 10+ children in these schools. When we
approached the schools in our list ten were unable to take part in the survey
and were replaced by schools from the same regions and of the same types
from our 'second-choice' list.

The schools were asked to send us a complete list of all their pupils who
were aged 10 on 1st September, 1970. These lists were numbered and with
the aid of random number tables 16 pupils were chosen in each school. In
one rural school there was only one 10-year-old child and so the second
choice school was substituted. In twelve other schools there were fewer than
sixteen 10 year-olds and so the whole age group in these schools was included
in the sample. Two schools proved to have changed their 'type', or had been
misclassified, and were dropped from the sample, and two other schools
belatedly decided not to participate, so there were 193 schools in the final
primary sample.

THE SECONDARY SAMPLE

The secondary school sample was drawn according to the principles and
procedures described in the two preceding sections using a table (Appendix
I (c)) provided by the DES showing the numbers of schools and the combined
totals of pupils aged 11 and 13 as at 1st September, 1969 (31st December in
the case of direct grant schools).

We decided not to include the two direct grant, mixed schools in our
sample and also decided that the other direct grant schools – the single-sex
comprehensive schools and the single-sex comprehensives and single-sex
too few for it to be worth sampling them across all ten regions. These schools
were sampled separately, as described later.

The remaining eighty cells of our secondary table, containing in all 4353
schools, were sampled using the same procedure as for the primary sample
to produce a list of 180 schools, a ratio of about 1:25. Just as with the
primary sample, a 'second choice' sample was also drawn.

For the direct grant schools, the single-sex comprehensives and single-sex
'secondary (other)' schools the sampling interval was calculated for the
complete row of the table – across all ten regions – for each type of school.
These rows were then treated as single cells and sampled to produce 2 Direct

grant (boys) schools, 2 Direct grant (girls), 5 Comprehensive (boys), 5 Comprehensive (girls), 3 Other (boys), and 2 Other (girls), a further 19 schools bringing the total secondary sample up to 201 schools (see Appendix I (d)).

Local authorities asked us to avoid using three schools, one because of its small size, and the two others because of their recent involvement in research studies. Substitute schools of the same type and region were used from the 'second choice' list. Altogether 33 of our sample of 201 schools were replaced from our second choice list — those just mentioned, schools wrongly designated in the DES print-out, and others which were unable or unwilling to take part.

From the sample of 201 schools, we 'lost' 13: 8 which we found to have been wrongly designated only when it was too late to use replacements; 2 which failed to return the questionnaires; 2 which returned only partial sets of questionnaires; and 1, most of whose questionnaires disappeared in the post. These losses reduced the final sample to 188.

The pupils within the secondary schools were sampled in the same way as were the primary children. When schools sent us their lists of pupils 6 schools proved to be Junior High schools, containing no 14+ children. These schools were retained in the sample.

COLLECTING THE DATA

Our research objectives were both descriptive and analytic. We wanted to map out children's reading to show how much they read of different kinds and qualities of material and then to explore the relationships between their reading behaviour and those other aspects of their total experience we thought might be associated with it.

From the children in our sample we wanted to collect information about their reading, about their choices among other activities and about their individual family situations. From teachers we wanted to know about each child's ability, attainment and attitude to school and also about the schools themselves — organization, curricula, English syllabuses, book use, and teaching emphases.

Our basic tools were two questionnaires, one for the children (with slightly different versions for primary and secondary pupils) and one for the schools (again in two versions, with the primary questionnaire to be completed by the head teacher, the secondary by the head of English). For teachers' assessment of individual pupils we designed a multiple-choice assessment sheet. For teachers administering questionnaires to children we composed a sheet of instructions and also, of course, we devised a variety of *pro-forma* letters and other forms to meet various administrative contingencies.

THE CHILDREN'S QUESTIONNAIRE

This questionnaire is reproduced as Appendix II. In the process of developing and refining this questionnaire we used schools in the Sheffield area to test different versions and used the penultimate version in our pilot study for which we drew a sample of about 400 children from West Riding and Sheffield schools. (Both West Riding and Sheffield are 'middle school' areas and so were not included in the main sample).

There is a common basic logic to the construction of any kind of questionnaire, test, schedule, or scale intended to collect information from or about individuals. It applies whether the information is required about facts of experience, about attitudes, about motivations or about knowledge. Firstly, the tasks of the instrument need precise definitions and these have then to be tried out in operational forms until an appropriate level of confidence is reached about the validity and reliability of the instrument. Reliability, in principle, lies in the extent to which a respondent will give the same answers over repeated applications of an instrument. Validity is the measure of how far an instrument is finding out what it is intended to find out.

Although the logic can be spelled out, construction of questionnaires and similar devices is an art rather than a science. For a full discussion of the logic and design of questionnaires of the kind we used the reader is referred to Moser (1967) and Oppenheim (1966). Only the particular considerations affecting the form of our Children's Questionnaire will be discussed here.

We chose, at a very early stage in the project, to rely for the main body of data on the once-only completion by the children in our sample of a questionnaire mailed to their schools and administered by teachers. There were other courses open to us and some of them were considered very seriously. While still collecting the data in 'one shot', there is a range of possible techniques ranging from (a) individual interviews conducted by a trained interviewer to (b) group administration of questionnaires by 'remote control'. The nearer the chosen technique is to (a) the greater the control that can be exercised over the method of collection (e.g. interviewers can be trained and their performances checked), and the fuller and more complex the questions can be (follow-up questions can be asked, accuracy of understanding checked, and so on). Also, the use of interviewers can produce a higher response rate; individuals can be sought out by the interviewers.

The problems with interviewing as a technique are those of expense and administrative complexity. For us to use it would have meant a much smaller sample. We chose (b), the 'remote control' technique, and to compensate to some extent for its shortcomings provided a full, carefully constructed set of questionnaire administration instructions for the schools, and strove to make the questionnaire as simple and unambiguous as possible.

We judged, correctly as it turned out, that schools were sufficiently accustomed to giving pupils forms to fill in, and to making returns, to guarantee us a high response rate (see Table 2, Chapter 3 — response rates between 84·8% and 91·4%).

Data collection at one point in time is discussed above. Our main research variable is in the nature of a habit; reading is a recurrent pattern of behaviour. Ideally, to collect information about someone's reading behaviour, it should be observed over a representative period of time. In principle, this is what Leng (1968) did, except that his 'observation' was confined to the use of public library books. For one year he recorded the books borrowed by children from the children's section of a public library, arranging that each borrower completed a single questionnaire when he returned a book to establish whether he had read it. This technique is only workable with books from a predetermined and supervised source, but 'self-recording' — perhaps some kind of diary — would be a way of incorporating the time dimension into the data-collecting process.

The diary technique is widely used; it is common within schools for children to be encouraged to record aspects of their activities in this way and it has been used as a research tool (see, for instance, Smalley). However, it was clear that we had to rely on the schools to supervise our data collecting, and to ask them to organize a diary-keeping programme for a month, for example, would have been unreasonable. It would also have invited a much lower response rate. In the event, we asked children to recall which books they had read during the month preceding their completion of the question-naire. The contingent memory problem will be discussed later.

Our definitions of the objectives of the Children's Questionnaire were that it should:

1   Provide measures of children's reading behaviour in terms of (a) the amount of reading done, particularly of books but also of more ephemeral forms of reading matter, and (b) preferences among different kinds of reading.
2   Show what sources children used for books they read.
3   Provide information about children's use of non-literary media.
4   Provide an indication of children's attitudes to their schools.
5   Uncover those family and social differences which we supposed might relate to different levels of engagement with reading.

In turning these objectives into operational forms and combining them into a questionnaire we had to observe a number of constraints.

We had opted for remote control collection of data, and the contingent opportunity to use a large sample which, in turn, would produce data in such quantities that it would have to be coded for the computer by a team of coders for whom we should have to specify as simple a set of procedures as possible. The form of the questions and the format of the questionnaire were designed with this in mind. Wherever possible we used multiple choice questions, accompanying these with symbols for use in the coding stage, and where such questions were not possible — lists of books, TV programmes and periodicals, for example — we anticipated the answer classifications we should later use in the coding procedure. (The coding procedures are described in a later section of this chapter.)

We decided that we would use the same basic questionnaire for all three age groups in the sample, for reasons of economy. The wording and format, therefore, represent our judgement of what would be comprehensible to most 10+ children, while not seeming unacceptable to 14+ children. (We did insert two extra questions for secondary pupils — one about intended age of leaving school and one about attitude to English lessons. The latter we thought inappropriate for primary pupils, many of whom would be following an integrated curriculum.)

It is an obvious requirement for any questionnaire that it should be easily understood but this requirement was strengthened for us by our wish that teachers should not be involved in explaining questions and so introduce additional variability into the administration conditions. Evidence from the completed questionnaires suggests that our intention that it should be comprehensible to most 10 year-olds was achieved in that a number of teachers commented that, while they had expected the questionnaire to be difficult for 10 year-olds, they found to their surprise that with few exceptions they had coped with it perfectly well.

Our pre-pilot questionnaires incorporated the whole range of questions which we thought could usefully be asked in relation to our research objectives. They demonstrated two general points: (1) that we were asking too many questions for most children to complete the questionnaire within the average timetabled period of 30–40 minutes — an objective we thought desirable for schools' convenience; (2) that a number of questions, e.g. about cinema-going, radio listening, gramophone listening, conditions under which reading was done, and so on, did not discriminate sufficiently between children to justify our retaining them. These two factors led to a progressive reduction in the size of the Children's Questionnaire — the version we used in the pilot study was about two-thirds the length of the first versions, the final version just over half the length.

The core of the Children's Questionnaire was a fold-out sheet asking children to record their book reading in the preceding month, to indicate whether they had re-read a particular book or failed to finish it, where they had obtained each book and how much they liked it. It must be acknowledged that this is a deceptively simple and straightforward form of questioning and that we have to justify asking children to recall their book reading over the one-month period.

It was implicit in our adoption of a 'one-shot' data collection policy that a question demanding recall over a specified period time would be necessary as a base for statements about the amount of children's book reading. Reflectively, of course, our assessment that this sort of question was acceptable removed one of the obstacles to 'one-shot' data collection. Clearly, however, it is the case that the question 'What books have you read over the past month?' is likely to produce response errors on a different scale from those produced by a question like 'What book are you currently reading?' The members of the research team asked themselves the recall question and acknowledged that they were not very confident in their answers. On the other hand, when we tried out the question and discussed it with schoolchildren they showed a level of confidence which, when we first encountered it at least, we found surprisingly high, and it was this that led us to our conceptualization of the problem and to our accepting the use of the recall question.

Psychologists have long since demonstrated that remembering and recalling are not the same thing. We all have the experience of not being able to recall something like a name to order, only to have it come into our consciousness shortly after, or to be able to select it from a list of names. We have not forgotten the name, we have simply been unable to recall it at a given moment. Further, our ability to recall something is not randomly determined, it depends both on the immediate and on the more long-term situations in which we find ourselves, and on the extent to which these provide, respectively, cues and structures relating to what we are wishing to recall.

In view of this sort of analysis, we felt that our recall question was justifiable, given:

(a)   that children would be set by the questionnaire and the administration situation to think about their book reading, being cued to varying degrees by the preamble to the questionnaire: by our invented examples of titles and authors; by progressive remembering after entering the first title, and by being in a classroom where reading was a regular activity.

(b)   that school life provides a structure of which book reading is an intrinsic part and which offers temporal reference points (beginning and end of term, half-term, special events, and so on) which we could ask teachers to refer to as a way of 'marking-off' the period of a month.

We did carry out some explicit investigation of the validity of the Children's Questionnaire and the results of this reassured us further about the recall question, as well as enabling us to check the other questions. The only practical validity criterion available to us was the correspondence between children's answers to questionnaires and the information derived from probing interviews of the children who had completed them. A proportion of the children who completed each version of the trial questionnaire (after a period ranging from an hour to a week or so) were interviewed after completing it. They were asked the same questions as in the questionnaire and encouraged also to talk about how they had construed the questions, how they had 'marked off' the period of a month for their book list, and how far their answers about periodicals, television, library use, and so on, represented their typical behaviour. The correspondences between questionnaire answers and interview data were high and indicated that the final questionnaire discriminated between children, and represented their individual behaviours sufficiently to justify the weight we should subsequently place on the data it produced.

Our follow-up interviews after the main survey also provided some validation evidence for the questionnaire, albeit *post facto*. In no case did we feel it appropriate to reclassify a child on the basis of interview evidence compared with his original answers to the questionnaire.

Evidence about the validity of the questionnaire also, of course, provided some indication of its reliability, although we did also carry out a test/re-test procedure with one version of the questionnaire, spacing administrations one week apart. There was very little variation in children's answers between the two administrations.

To sum up, we are convinced that, as an example of a postal survey questionnaire, the Children's Questionnaire did very adequately the job it was designed for. It was not intended as a basis for finely scaling the differences in children's reading and related behaviours but we are confident in making the distinctions we have based on it.

THE QUESTIONNAIRE ADMINISTRATION INSTRUCTIONS

These are reproduced as Appendix III and their rationale will for the most part be clear. Their objectives were to bring about as much uniformity as possible in the administrations of the Children's Questionnaire and to try and make the pupils feel as unconstrained as possible by supervising teachers through urging on these an invigilating rather than a helping role.

The proviso in instruction 1 was intended to serve the functions of:

(a) locating the answers of the whole sample in the same period and, to some extent, in the same stage of the school term (although term dates vary between authorities);

(b)   making sure that children's reports of their TV viewing referred to a weekday evening.

Instruction 2 was related to the identification of each child in the sample by a code number, which enables us to link individual questionnaires with the teachers' assessments of children and to link children with their questionnaires when we came to the follow-up interviews of a proportion of the sample.

We had no reliable way of checking that all schools followed our instructions in all details but casual inquiries at schools subsequently visited generally produced a willing and encouraging account of how far they were met. Basically, we relied on the procedures being a familiar part of school life.

THE PUPIL ASSESSMENT SHEET

This is reproduced as Appendix IV and needs little elaboration. We typed the code number identifying each child in the first column, the child's name in the second.

THE SCHOOL QUESTIONNAIRES

There were two versions of this, one for primary schools, addressed to the head teacher, the other for secondary schools addressed to the head of English. These questionnaires are reproduced as Appendix V(a) and Appendix V(b).

Defining the aims of these questionnaires was more difficult than for the Children's Questionnaire. In general, we were looking for ways of characterizing those differences between schools which we thought might relate to differences in the quantity and quality of the book reading of their pupils. We decided to focus the questionnaires most strongly on English teaching in the schools and on the opportunities they provided for access to literature. In addition, we asked whether schools were streaming or setting their pupils, both generally and in relation to English; whether, in the case of primary schools, an integrated curriculum was followed; whether the school was on a single or divided site; and what sort of area schools drew most of their pupils from. We also collected information about sex and type of the schools as a cross check on the information we had from the DES which we had found in some instances to be outdated.

The main part of the questionnaires relates to our supposition that schools probably have a crucial influence as to the extent that they are able to model for some children a positive attitude to the use of books and the enjoyment of literature and that different levels of success in this respect would partly be reflected in their English teaching — its organization, emphases and objectives — and in the size, composition and accessibility of their stocks of literature. We think the data our questionnaires produced about book stocks can be taken as fairly accurate, but two difficulties faced our questions about English teaching. First, that of devising questions adequate to catch the variety of approaches to English in the schools and, second, that we were not necessarily doing more than collecting the possibly unrepresentative opinion of the one person who completed the questionnaire (and in whose school there could anyway be a variety of approaches to English).

Our data did enable us to produce a variety of school typologies but we were to some extent trying to catch shrimps with a herring net.

The constraints on the design of the School Questionnaires were fewer than with the Children's Questionnaire. There would be only about 400 of them, compared with nearly 8000 from the children, so that the data coding could be more easily handled. Also, of course, we could adopt more normal standards for the comprehensibility of questions and ask for information which might actively have to be sought out by the respondents.

THE FOLLOW-UP INTERVIEWS

In about 10% of the schools in the main sample children were interviewed by a member of the research team, mostly in the first two terms of the 1971—72 school year. Our hope had originally been that by October/November 1971 the analysis of the survey data would have progressed far enough to show us fairly clearly what the objectives of the follow-up should be. In fact, difficulties in card punching delayed the start of analysis and we went ahead with our interviews rather than leave more than a year between the survey and the follow-up.

To structure our interviews with children, and to ensure that each interviewer covered more or less the same ground, we composed an interview schedule. The practice when we met one of the children was to ask the child first to complete a copy of the Children's Questionnaire and then, referring where appropriate to his answers about periodicals, books, TV, newspapers, and so on, to follow the sequence of inquiries incorporated in the schedule.

The main object in the encounter with the child was to get him or her talking freely and to explore the finer contextual details of the experiences and activities touched on in the questionnaire.

This is a summary of what we asked:

1   *About comics and magazines* —
     Do you buy them, if not, who does?
     Which is your favourite, and why?

Which comics and magazines did you read about a year ago?
Which parts do you read?
Do you read a newspaper, which parts?

2   *About non-narrative books* —
Why did you choose (title)?
Are there any books you like looking things up in?

3   *About narrative books* —
How did you come to choose (title)?
What parts did you specially like/dislike?
Why is (name) your favourite writer?
Do you have any specially favourite books?
What did you specially like about a year ago?

4   *About reading generally* —
Where do you do most of your reading?
Do your parents like to see you reading?

5   *About family and leisure* —
What do your parents like you to do when you're not at school?
How do you usually spend your spare time?
What do you like doing best?
What do you usually do when you get home from school?
In which parts of the evening do you usually watch TV?
Do you usually watch for more or less time than you watched
  last evening?
Does the family have the TV on so that you can watch when you
  feel like it?
Do your parents ever stop you watching TV because they think it's
  too late or because you might be frightened?
Do you watch TV on Saturday and Sunday afternoons?
What else do you do at weekends?
What time do you usually go to bed on schooldays/at weekends?

6   *About aspirations* —
What do you want to be when you leave school?

These questions were, of course, no more than a guide for the interviewer
and were adapted and supplemented as seemed appropriate. A fuller discussion
of the follow-up interviews is contained in Chapter 4.

Miscellaneous

One of the more memorable contingencies we had to meet arose from the
condition imposed by one large authority that we must not ask children
about their father's occupation; about whether they lived with their parents;
whether or not their mothers worked; and how many siblings they had. We

circumvented this prohibition by constructing a form similar to the Assessment Sheet and asking the schools to provide us with the information, as far as they were able. In most cases, they did so.

HANDLING THE DATA

Our research was of the kind that is only possible if a computer is available for analysis of the immense quantities of data that are produced. The raw data, however, have to be converted into a form that can be fed into the computer — a process known as coding. Our questionnaires were designed with this in mind, and the coding procedures were largely worked out as the questionnaires were constructed, some of the coding procedures being incorporated in the format of the Children's Questionnaire.

Basically, a digital computer can only work with information in binary form, i.e. everything fed into it has to be a statement that something exists, or does not. Coding the raw data meant, in effect, constructing for each case (child) in our sample a table with a large number of rows and columns such that there was a cell, or combination of cells in this table for all answers we wanted to retain from the completed questionnaires.

In practice, the table comprises computer punch cards with 12 rows and 80 columns. The computer can be instructed by its programme to read any combination of the 960 cells on a card to determine which cells are punched and which are not. In this way the computer recalls the information recorded for each child and can subsequently be instructed to perform statistical operations on this information. For each case in our survey there was a set of three punch cards, i.e. nearly 24 000 in all, over 200 000 items of information.

In the case of questionnaires containing only multiple-choice questions it is possible to pre-code all of the possible answers to that a card-punch operator can transfer information directly from questionnaires to punch-cards. This pre-coding involves printing on the questionnaire an indication of which row and which column of a card is to be punched for any particular answer. We did pre-code all the multiple choice questions on our Children's Questionnaire and the codings could be seen in the left hand columns of all pages except 2 and 3.

Questions which ask the respondent for lists (e.g. books, periodicals) or to which the possible answers are too many for a complete listing of alternatives in the questionnaire (e.g. newspapers) are of the kind which can only be coded after the set of questionnaires has been completed.

The research team was helped by a team of coders, mostly university students, in the early part of the 1971 summer vacation. It was a complex and in some ways nerve-racking operation since it had to be planned in minute detail before the team started work and any mistakes in procedures might be too costly in time and labour to remedy subsequently.

CODING AND ASSOCIATED PROCEDURES

On the set of three cards for each child in our sample we wanted to include his answers to the Children's Questionnaire, information provided about him by the school, and information about his school from the School Questionnaire. For punching onto cards this data had to be entered in coded form on a coding sheet, a specially printed representation of three punch cards with cells large enough to have written in them a symbol indicating which row(s) of each column should subsequently be punched on the cards by the punch operator.

Three different kinds of procedure were involved in the coding:

1   The simple transfer from the Children's Questionnaire to the coding sheet of the appropriate pre-coded symbols for the multiple-choice questions.
2   Entering symbols on the coding sheet for the non-pre-coded answers to the Children's Questionnaire, Assessment Sheet and School Questionnaire by reference to a set of keys incorporated in a basic manual drawn up for the coding team.
3   Analysing the information from the complex parts of the Children's Questionnaire — about books, periodicals, TV programmes, and occupations, particularly — and deciding in what forms to classify it before incorporating these classifications in further keys as a basis for coding.

Instructions for the first two kinds of procedure mentioned were incorporated in a basic manual and these operations were carried out by the coding team. The third procedure was more complex and involved a lot of preparation before data could be entered on coding sheets. This preparation and coding was done by members of the research team.

Pages 2 and 3 of the Children's Questionnaire contained the data which were most difficult to handle. We had first to decide how much of the information on these pages should be coded. The coding team had simply coded the number of titles entered; we had to decide how to deal with the individual titles and how to classify books into categories before coding the information about whether the books had been re-read or unfinished, the sources of books and how much they were liked.

We carried out an extensive preliminary analysis of book titles, going systematically through every questionnaire and constructing an alphabetical card index so that the title of every book mentioned was recorded, together with the number of times it occurred. In all, there were 7557 titles. We decided to index for the computer every title that was mentioned ten times or more. There were 246 of these and each was allocated a code so that, where one or more of these titles appeared in a child's questionnaire, the computer record for that child would contain the fact.

To retain some information about books mentioned fewer than ten times we decided to classify every book mentioned by its category and code this information for every book mentioned by children. The categories we adopted are discussed in Chapter 3.

For the format of the book coding we treated each book as a 'sub-case', allocating 12 sets of 6 columns on card 2 of each child's set of three cards for the maximum of 12 books which we had allowed space for in the Children's Questionnaire. The coding for each of the books mentioned by a child took up all or part of one of the sets of 6 columns.

For the 'favourite author' question we made a preliminary list of all the names mentioned by children and decided to reference by a code each author occurring ten times or more. There were 55 of these.

We did not code the individual titles of periodicals mentioned by children, but we did develop a two-way classification system in terms of which each title mentioned by a child was coded. The classification was into: (a) 'literate' or 'non-literate' ('literate' representing periodicals which consisted wholly or mainly of continuous prose while 'non-literate' represented those consisting wholly or mainly of picture-strips), and (b) juvenile; boys' pre-adolescent; girls' pre-adolescent; pop/teen; romantic; domestic/romantic; information general; information specific; sport; and unclassifiable. This classification was essentially an attempt to summarize what we felt to be the most salient distinctions in the tremendous variety and number of periodicals mentioned by children. In the course of our later analysis we found that the system had been too complex, in that some of the sub-categories shaded into one another in a way that made valid discrimination between them impossible. We therefore conflated sub-categories, in the computer, into the six categories which are shown in our analysis of types of periodical in Chapter 3, Section C.

We classified fathers' occupations on the basis of the Registrar General's *Classification of Occupations* (HMSO 1970) and used the categories professional; intermediate; skilled non-manual; skilled manual; partly skilled; unskilled; unclassifiable; unemployed, disabled or deceased with no classifiable indication of former occupation.

Information recorded by children about mothers' occupations was, predictably perhaps, much less clear than that for fathers' and we decided not to attempt to classify it.

The coding organization

The logistic details of the organization of the coding are too numerous to present fully but a few aspects of it need to be mentioned.

Our main concern was to minimize coding errors, i.e. errors in identifying the correct codes and in transcribing them onto the coding sheets. We approached this objective in two ways. First, we tried to combine coding tasks so that every member of the coding team had a routine varied enough to hold his interest while not being so complex that the complexity would be a source of error. Second, each coder's work was continuously sampled for accuracy so that if he did enter an 'error condition' only a limited batch of his work needed to be re-coded and he could, if it was thought necessary, be transferred to a different job.

The coding operation for the main survey benefited greatly from our coding experience in the pilot study. We were able to select as the core of the main survey coding team those coders who had proved particularly effective in the earlier exercise.

THE COMPUTER ANALYSIS

The early stages of the data analysis were carried out on the Science Research Council's Atlas computer at Chilton using a programme system called the *Multiple Variate Counter* (MVC). It later became necessary to transfer our data from Chilton to the Sheffield University Computer Service, and this necessitated converting the data format on the cards to enable us to use the *Statistical Package for the Social Sciences* (SPSS), which has, in fact, proved to be a powerful and flexible programme system for our purposes.

BIBLIOGRAPHY

Fisher, R. A. and Yates, F. (1963). *Statistical Tables for Biological, Agricultural and Medical Research*. Oliver & Boyd.

Leng, I. J. (1968). *Children in the Library*. University of Wales Press.

Moser, C. A. (1967). *Survey Techniques in Social Investigation*. Heinemann Educational.

Oppenheim, A. N. (1966). *Questionnaire Design and Attitude Measurement*. Basic Books.

Smalley, L. M. (1958). 'A practicable diary technique for time sampling the everyday life of children', *Educational Review*, **10**, 233–47.

Stuart, A. (1962). *Basic Ideas of Scientific Sampling*. Griffin.

Yates, F. (1960). *Sampling Methods for Censuses and Surveys*. Griffin.

3 The questionnaire survey

A – THE SAMPLE

It will be recalled that our sample was drawn using information provided by the Statistics Division of the Department of Education and Science. In the first instance we sought the cooperation of a stratified random sample of 398 schools spread throughout England and Wales. The schools which agreed to participate were then asked to administer our questionnaire to children whose names had been randomly selected from lists supplied by each school. (For a full account of our sampling procedure see pp. 24–28). Clearly the

Table 1   Response of schools
(a) All schools

School type	Design sample	Achieved sample	Achieved sample as % of design sample
Primary	197	193	98·0
Secondary	201	188	93·5
All	398	381	95·7

(b) Secondary schools

School type	Design sample		Achieved sample (12+)		Achieved sample (14+)	
	Number	%	Number	%	Number	%
Direct grant	4	2·0	4	2·1	4	2·2
Grammar	36	17·9	35	18·6	35	19·1
Sec. mod.	89	44·3	85	45·2	84	45·9
Comp.	55	27·4	54	28·7	50	27·3
Other	17	8·5	10	5·3	10	5·5
TOTALS	201	100·1	188	99·9	183	100·0

randomness of our sample was dependent both upon a high response rate from the schools and upon a high response rate from the selected children within the schools. In the event the schools responded remarkably well, and our achieved sample of 381 schools fell short of our design sample by only 17 schools in all (see Table 1(a)). The distribution of the secondary schools between different types in both the design sample and the achieved sample is shown in Table 1(b).

It can be seen that in general the correspondence between the design sample and the achieved sample is quite close, though there is in the achieved sample for each age group a shortfall in the number of schools in the category 'other', and as a result there is a slightly higher proportion of grammar, secondary modern and comprehensive schools than there should be. It will be noted that five of our secondary schools were either junior high or junior comprehensive schools with no 14+ children, and this fact reduced a little further our achieved sample for the 14+ age group.

As far as the response of the children themselves was concerned, the most important cause of loss was absenteeism, though we also lost a few children who had left their school before the questionnaire was administered and a few whose questionnaires were lost in the post. In addition there was the inevitable failure of a few individual children who were at school on the day the questionnaire was administered to return a satisfactorily completed questionnaire booklet; some of these were very backward children, some were recent immigrants still unable to cope with written English, and some remained unaccounted for. Table 2 sets out the relevant information about the children's response for each of the three age groups.

Table 2   Response of children

Age group	Number approached	Left school	Absent	Not answered	Achieved sample All		Boys	Girls
		%	%	%	n	%		
10+	3004	0·6	6·3	1·6	2747	(91·4)	1402	1345
12+	3001	0·5	10·4	2·1	2612	(87·0)	1353	1259
14+	2923	0·7	12·6	1·9	2480	(84·8)	1307	1173

The rate of absence among the older children may seem rather high. It is perhaps worth noting, however, that our figures for absence are not very different from those revealed in a survey carried out in 1974 by the Association of Education Committees on behalf of the DES, which found that 9·9% of all pupils in middle and secondary schools were absent on the day selected, January 17th 1974 (*Times Educational Supplement*, 2nd August 1974).

In the meantime it is useful to compare our sample with the national population in respect of the percentage of children in each of the different types of secondary school.

Table 3 Children in different types of secondary schools —
our sample compared with population of England and Wales
1970—1 (percentages)

School type	12+ Sample	Population	14+ Sample	Population
Direct grant	2·2	1·9	2·5	2·9
Grammar	19·1	15·2	20·5	15·8
Sec. mod.	45·6	46·2	45·3	45·6
Comp.	27·5	29·4	26·1	28·7
Other	5·5	7·3	5·7	7·0
	99·9	100·0	100·1	100·0
Number of children	2587	570 886	2475	544 580

From Table 3 we can see that by comparison with the national population for the age groups in question, our sample is slightly overweighted with grammar school pupils and has correspondingly too few pupils in comprehensive and 'other' schools. This disproportion is due mainly to the shortfall in 'other' schools in our achieved sample already mentioned, but comparison with Table 1(b) suggests that it has also been intensified by the fact that the response rate from grammar schools and direct grant schools was slightly higher than that from other types of secondary school.

It has been shown (Hall and Jones, 1950) that the father's occupation is the most effective single indicator of the social level of the home; and we therefore obtained a measure of the social class of the children by classifying their father's occupation in terms of the Registrar General's classification. Clearly one difficulty about this procedure is that it is inevitably dependent on the child's accurate perception and description of his father's job. As it turned out a little over 10% of the 10+ age group failed to give a description of their father's occupation which was adequate for our purposes, whereas for the 12+ and 14+ age groups this proportion had dropped to 7% and 5·6% respectively. Table 4 shows the distribution of our sample, at each age, among the Registrar General's six social classes. (These are I — professional, II — managerial and technical, III — skilled non-manual and skilled manual, IV — semi-skilled and V — unskilled.)

Table 4   Social class of sample (percentages)

Age group	Class I	Class II	Class III N	Class III M	Class IV	Class V	Father died/ retired	Inade- quate reply	No answer
10+	2·8	13·0	10·8	38·7	15·8	4·1	4·1	9·0	1·6
12+	3·9	17·0	11·1	39·7	13·8	3·6	3·8	5·6	1·4
14+	4·0	16·9	9·4	39·9	14·8	4·2	5·3	4·4	1·2

We now have another indication as to how far our sample is representative of the population as a whole. The best check we have is the sample census data of 1966, for unfortunately comparable tables were not yet available from the 1971 census. The census figures for social class are for males aged fifteen or over, whether economically active or retired. This is not exactly comparable with our sample, as our class composition is of males aged about 27 or over with at least one child aged 10+, 12+ or 14+; it will serve well enough, nevertheless, as a rough guide. In Table 5 we have excluded the three 'class unknown' categories, and have merged class IIIN (skilled non-manual) with class IIIM (skilled manual) to make our figures comparable with the census figures.

Table 5   Class composition: comparison of our sample with 1966 sample census (percentages)

Sample	Class I	Class II	Class III	Class IV	Class V	TOTAL
Ours	4·1	17·7	56·8	16·9	4·6	100·1
Census	4·5	15·7	50·3	20·6	8·8	99·9

The differences between our sample and the census figures are very much what we would expect. We must remember that the exclusion of private and public schools from the sample can be expected to reduce class I and class II, particularly the former, but this is counterbalanced by the relatively high numbers of direct grant and grammar school children.

It is not unreasonable to suppose that the resultant of these two con-flicting trends will be a slightly smaller class I and a rather larger class II. Table 5 also shows, however, that as compared with the 1966 census, our sample contained a distinctly lower proportion of class IV and class V. This may be the consequence of a lower-than-average response rate from children in these social classes, either because of greater absenteeism or lower standards of literacy. It must be remembered also that special schools were excluded from our sample, and this may have had some influence on the sample's class-composition, since some (though not all) of the conditions catered for in special schools are probably class-biased. There is also the possibility that some children tended, either deliberately or unconsciously, to upgrade their father's occupation when completing their questionnaire.

When we came to analyse the data, we found that the nine-category classification used in Table 4 was rather unwieldy; and we decided therefore to conflate these nine categories into a smaller number of new ones, if this could be done meaningfully. The first and most obvious step was to merge the three last categories ('Father deceased or retired', 'Inadequate information', 'Questionnaire not answered') into a single new category, namely 'Class not known'. We then examined the other six categories in relation to book reading and periodical reading. We found that, for all except the 14+ boys, the book reading for class IIIM (skilled manual) and class IV (semi-skilled manual) was very similar indeed; and there was clearly a strong case for merging these two categories into a single category which would then comprise about 55% of the children in each age/sex group. The book reading pattern for class V (unskilled manual) showed certain points of dissimilarity, but since class V made up only about 4% of the sample it did not seem to merit a separate category; and it was therefore merged with the other two manual categories. The three non-manual categories (classes I, II and III) showed no very marked affinity with each other; but they were even more dissimilar from the non-manual categories, and we decided therefore to merge them all into a single non-manual category, particularly since the resulting new category constituted only some 30% of the sample. The most appropriate classification for our purposes was therefore a straightforward manual/non-manual dichotomy. (The only group not really suited by it was the 14+ boys for whom a three-way split of classes I + II, class III, and classes IV + V would have been more appropriate.) The pattern in regard to periodical reading was very similar, and here again the dichotomous manual/non-manual division suited all but the 14+ boys. There was rather more variation, in this case, between skilled and semi-skilled manual groups, but the manual/non-manual split was the obvious choice.

Table 6 shows the percentage of children in the manual and non-manual categories for each of the sex and age groupings. If we compare the class composition of the different sub-groups we find that there are no significant differences between boys and girls, and that for girls the differences between the age groups are not significant. Among the boys however there is a smaller percentage from non-manual homes at 10+ than at either 12+ or 14+, and this difference is significant at the 5% level of probability. It is not easy to find a convincing explanation for this difference. In subsequent pages we shall refer to the two social class groups as social class NM and social class M respectively.

We consider next the ability and attainment of our sample. It will be recalled that we asked the schools to assess their children according to five

Table 6   Percentages in social class groups NM and M

Social class	10+ Boys	Girls	12+ Boys	Girls	14+ Boys	Girls
Non-manual	25·5	27·9	32·3	31·8	30·1	30·6
Manual	59·8	57·4	57·3	57·0	58·8	59·0
Not known	14·6	14·7	10·4	11·2	11·2	10·4
TOTALS	99·9	100·0	100·0	100·0	100·1	100·0
n	1402	1345	1353	1259	1307	1173

grades, which had been defined on the assumption that 20% of the total age group *in all schools* would fall into each grade. To help them in their assessment we suggested the following criteria: grade A would comprise those children capable of passing in four or more subjects at GCE O-level; grade B those capable of passing in four or five CSE subjects; grade C those of average ability (some of whom would be capable of passing one or two CSE subjects, while others would not attempt CSE at all); grade D those of below average ability but without serious reading disabilities; and grade E, backward children — those needing remedial teaching. Clearly, assessment along these lines is no easy matter, particularly in secondary schools where the teachers may have a very incomplete range of abilities within their charge, and are often, moreover, distinctly uncertain as to what range they do have, in comparison with other secondary schools. In the event, as Table 7 reveals, the primary schools achieved a fairly even distribution of the 10+ children between the five grades. If we take the sexes together, there are rather too many 10+ children in the middle grade (grade C) and correspondingly too few in the lowest grade (grade E); but part of this imbalance may be justified in that the special schools which were left out of our sampling will have drawn off some of the least able children and that the response rate can be assumed to have been lower for grade E pupils than for other ability grades. Table 7 shows, however, that in the case of the 12+ and 14+ children, the secondary schools tended to allocate rather a high proportion of the sample to grades A, B and C and were evidently reluctant to classify more than a handful of their pupils as belonging to grade E. There are two factors which may account, in part, for this skewed distribution. In the first place, as Table 3 showed, our sample for these age ranges was overweighted with pupils from grammar schools and direct grant schools. In the second place, the rate of absence was rather high for these ages, and there may have been a tendency for the absentees to include a disproportionately high number of the less able children. Nevertheless, even with these qualifications, it seems clear that the uneven allocation of older children to the five grades must be attributed

Table 7 Distribution of children, by sex and age, allocated to the different grades for ability and attainment (in percentages)

Grade	10+ Boys	Girls	All	12+ Boys	Girls	All	14+ Boys	Girls	All
A	20·2	21·3	20·7	27·7	31·2	29·5	25·8	30·1	27·9
B	17·9	24·2	21·0	23·4	24·7	24·1	30·6	30·3	30·5
C	27·0	29·7	28·3	26·6	25·0	25·8	23·6	23·7	23·6
D	21·7	18·7	20·2	16·5	14·7	15·6	15·8	13·7	14·8
E	13·2	6·1	9·7	5·8	4·4	5·1	4·2	2·2	3·2
TOTALS	100·0	100·0	99·9	100·0	100·0	100·1	100·0	100·0	100·0
n	1369	1311	2680	1269	1213	2482	1243	1144	2387

largely to the difficulty which secondary school teachers have in forming a just estimate of their pupils' position relative to the total spectrum of ability and attainment.

It is natural to ask how far ratings for ability and attainment are associated with the social class of the child. Table 8 sets out for each age and sex grouping the percentages allocated to the five ability and attainment grades, and inspection of this table makes it clear that very much higher percentages of children are allocated to the high ability grades in social class NM than in social class M. It is worth noting, too, that when social class is held constant, there is still a tendency to place more children in the higher ability grades at 12+ and 14+ than was the case at 10+, and that at these older ages there is an evident reluctance (regardless of social class) to assign pupils to the lowest grade.

A further point which emerges from Table 7 is that, for every age group, there is a consistent tendency to rate girls higher for ability and attainment than boys. Table 8 makes it clear that this tendency persists even when social class is held constant. The reasons for this are not immediately apparent, but some further light on the phenomenon may be deduced from Table 9. In addition to asking schools to assess children for ability and attainment, we also asked them to rate each child on a three-point scale according to his general attitude to the school, and high ratings on this scale turned out to be closely associated with ability and attainment.

Since the same trends are present in each age group, we have in Table 9 considered all ages together for the sake of conciseness in presentation. We can see from this table that, even when ability is held constant, girls have higher 'attitude' ratings than the boys, and that in general the pattern of relationship between the two variables is quite similar for each of the two social classes. Certainly Table 9 suggests that there is a strong association between ability and attainment and (favourable) attitude to school. How this association should be interpreted remains uncertain, however. It may be that the girls in the sample are in fact better achievers than the boys in terms of school attainment, and that this higher attainment is believed by the teachers to be the outcome of a positive attitude towards school; it may be that the girls are more cooperative than the boys, and that as a result they are more successful in terms of school attainment; or it may be that the girls are simply quieter and more docile than the boys, and that this docility leads to their being given an erroneously high rating for ability and attainment.

Table 8   Social class and ability

(a) Social class NM

Ability	10+ Boys	Girls	12+ Boys	Girls	14+ Boys	Girls
A	36·9	36·3	48·8	52·8	44·2	53·7
B	23·1	30·4	24·2	24·4	33·3	25·4
C	23·6	22·3	18·2	16·7	16·4	15·0
D	11·5	9·1	6·5	4·1	4·8	5·1
E	4·9	1·9	2·4	2·1	1·3	0·8
TOTALS	100·0	100·0	100·1	100·1	100·0	100·0
n	347	372	418	390	378	354

(b) Social class M

Ability	10+ Boys	Girls	12+ Boys	Girls	14+ Boys	Girls
A	15·4	17·2	17·7	22·5	18·7	19·5
B	16·6	22·1	23·9	25·5	30·5	33·4
C	29·3	33·8	31·0	29·3	25·7	28·4
D	25·3	20·8	21·4	17·9	20·6	16·5
E	13·4	6·0	6·0	4·8	4·5	2·2
TOTALS	100·0	99·9	100·0	100·0	100·0	100·0
n	819	745	735	689	734	673

We have already touched on the matter of home background with our description of the sample in terms of social class. We can now fill out the picture a little with our information on family size, whether or not the parents have a television, and whether or not the mother goes out to work.

One would not expect to find much variation in the figures for family size within different sex/age groups, and there is in fact very little. What does become relevant here is social class, as we can see from Table 10.

Table 9   Relationship between ability and attitude to the school — all age groups together

(a) Social class NM

Ability	Boys					Girls				
	A	B	C	D	E	A	B	C	D	E
Attitude										
High	73·1	30·8	21·0	8·4	6·5	80·3	51·7	22·1	16·4	29·4
Medium	26·1	62·9	68·9	53·0	45·2	18·4	46·3	71·9	65·7	35·3
Low	0·8	6·4	10·0	38·6	48·4	1·3	2·0	6·0	17·9	35·3
TOTALS	100·0	100·1	99·9	100·0	100·1	100·0	100·0	100·0	100·0	100·0
n	498	299	219	83	31	527	294	199	67	17

(b) Social class M

Ability	Boys					Girls				
Attitude										
High	73·1	38·9	17·4	8·1	8·6	74·0	54·0	21·9	12·9	6·6
Medium	25·1	57·3	74·3	60·0	45·2	22·8	44·0	68·4	61·8	51·6
Low	1·8	3·8	8·3	32·0	46·2	3·2	2·0	9·7	25·3	41·8
TOTALS	100·0	100·0	100·0	100·1	100·0	100·0	100·0	100·0	100·0	100·0
n	390	529	649	507	186	412	563	640	380	91

Table 10   Family size by sex and social class (percentages)

No. of siblings	Boys Class NM	Class M	Girls Class NM	Class M
0	9·5	8·2	9·7	7·3
1	32·7	26·4	35·0	26·9
2	31·6	24·4	27·0	22·8
3	15·1	16·4	16·0	17·0
4	6·6	9·6	6·1	12·1
5	2·0	6·7	3·1	6·1
6	1·7	3·4	1·7	4·0
7	0·5	2·1	0·7	1·9
8+	0·4	2·7	0·7	2·0
TOTALS	100·1	99·9	100·0	100·1
n	1188	2382	1134	2182
Mean no. of siblings	1·95	2·53	1·97	2·32
Mean family size	2·95	3·53	2·97	3·32

We note that for both sexes, the proportion of families with fewer than four children is higher amongst social class NM, whilst the proportion of families with more than four children is higher in social class M.

If we wish to see how ability and attainment is associated with family size, the picture is clearer if we consider small families (0—2 siblings, i.e. 1—3 children) as opposed to large families (3 or more siblings, i.e. 4 or more children).

Table 11   Family size by ability, sex and social class

Ability	Boys Social Class NM Siblings			Social Class M Siblings			Girls Social Class NM Siblings			Social Class M Siblings		
	0—2	3+	n	0—2	3+	n	0—2	3+	n	0—2	3+	n
	%	%		%	%		%	%		%	%	
A	78·2	21·8	499	72·5	27·5	393	79·1	20·9	531	72·9	27·1	414
B	73·6	26·4	307	63·8	36·2	536	68·1	31·9	298	63·6	36·4	566
C	67·3	32·7	220	56·8	43·2	657	66·2	33·8	201	49·9	50·1	645
D	67·1	32·9	85	48·7	51·3	515	54·4	45·6	68	44·5	55·5	389
E	53·1	46·9	32	54·6	45·5	187	50·0	50·0	18	40·9	59·1	93

Table 11 shows that even within the same ability groups, children in social class NM come from smaller families than those in social class M — except in the case of grade E children where the numbers are too small to be meaningful. For grades A to D, the chi^2 test gives a significant result (at 1% level) only when boys and girls are considered together. This table also shows that within each social class group, there is a consistent relationship between family size and ability, small families being regularly associated with high ability.

When we turn to our data on working mothers, we must remember that this does not enable us to distinguish between those children whose mothers are at work only for a few hours whilst they are at school, and those who regularly come home to an empty house — or indeed are unable even to gain entry until their mother returns from work. Our interviews suggested that there were a number of children who were conscious of 'hanging around', indoors or out, until their mothers came home. Be that as it may, our data show that rather more than half our sample had working mothers, and that in general there is a higher proportion for girls than for boys, and a higher proportion in social class M than in social class NM.

Finally, we look briefly at television ownership. This is consistent through-out all the sex/age groups, varying only from 98·2% (10+ girls) to 98·7% (12+ boys). If we now look at social class within the sex/age groups, we find that only for 12+ girls do social class NM have a higher television ownership than social class M. If we take all sex/age groups together, the percentages having a television set at home are 98·1 and 98·8 for social class NM and social class M respectively. Although this difference seems very small, the numbers involved when we take the whole sample are so large that a chi-square test does show a significant difference at the 5% level.

There is no difference in the television ownership of the different ability groups in social class NM, but in social class M, ability group E has a lower rate of television ownership than the others (96·6% as compared to 99·0%), and this difference is significant at the 5% level.

B – THE QUANTITATIVE FINDINGS

We come now to a description of the reading and television viewing of the sample. First we consider the amount of book and periodical reading, and the amount of television viewing; then we examine the relationships between these three, and the influence upon them of various home and school factors. Finally, in Section C we look at the more qualitative aspects of our data.

Amount of book reading

In the first place we were interested to know how much voluntary reading children do today, and the simplest way of presenting this is to show the average number of books read by the children in the sample during the month under study. It should be remembered that the month in question covered the last week in February and the greater part of March, a time of the year when one can perhaps reasonably expect that the amount of children's reading would be neither at its highest peak nor at its lowest ebb.

Table 12   Average number of books read during one month

Age group	Boys	Girls	Both sexes
10+	2·68	3·28	2·95
12+	1·99	2·48	2·21
14+	1·78	2·15	1·95
All age groups	2·16	2·66	2·39

From Table 12 it seems clear that English children in 1971 were not by any means such confirmed book readers as the children Jenkinson reported on in 1940. Indeed, if one accepted Jenkinson's figures (which fell within the range of 3·9 to 6·5 books a month), one could truthfully say that children in 1971 did not read half as much as children did in 1940. However, our figures are more nearly in line with those of Professor Hilde Himmelweit in

Television and the Child (Oxford University Press, 1958). In her survey of children in London, Bristol, Portsmouth and Sunderland in 1955 it was reported that children aged 10+ were reading 2·7 books a month, and children aged 13+ were reading 2·5 books in a month. For children who were television viewers these figures dropped to 2·5 books a month at age 10+, and to 2·2 books a month at age 13+. It can be seen from Table 13 that our 10+ children were reading rather more books than the Himmelweit survey children of the same age. On the other hand, the Himmelweit survey children aged 13+ were reading rather more than our 12+ children and distinctly more than our 14+ children.

However, any direct comparison with Himmelweit's data is unsatisfactory because of the differences in sampling procedure. Whereas we drew a random sample from the whole population, the Himmelweit survey used a factorial design with the following three factors for each age group: sex, social class (middle class and working class), ability (IQ lower than 100, IQ between 100 and 114, and IQ higher than 114). (Presumably 'middle' and 'working class' referred to the non-manual and manual occupations of the fathers, though this was not made entirely clear.) The effect of this factorial design would be to include in the sample a higher proportion of middle class children than in the population as a whole, and a lower proportion of less able children. Our figures in Table 12, however, agree with both Jenkinson and Himmelweit in showing that at all ages girls consistently read more books than boys.

It will be realized, of course, that Table 12, which is concerned solely with the average number of books read, tells us nothing about the dispersion of reading within the sample. The usual statistical measure here, the standard deviation, is not easy for most people to conceptualize, and we have preferred therefore to present our information in terms of the percentage of children in four different reading categories (Table 13).

Table 13   Type of book reader as percentage of each age group

Type of book reader	10+		12+		14+	
	Boys	Girls	Boys	Girls	Boys	Girls
Non-reader	15·8	9·4	33·2	23·3	40·0	32·4
Light (1–2 a month)	39·9	35·9	33·9	33·4	29·4	32·9
Moderate (3–4 a month)	28·0	30·6	21·5	29·1	21·1	21·1
Heavy (5+ a month)	16·3	24·1	11·4	14·3	9·5	13·6
TOTALS	100·0	100·0	100·0	100·1	100·0	100·0
n	1402	1345	1353	1259	1307	1173

In Table 13 we can see spread out in more detail the fact that there is a consistent tendency for children to read fewer books as they grow older. Not only is there a reduction at 12+ and 14+ in the average number of books read, but there is also, at these ages, a steep increase in the percentage of non-book-readers. The wording of our questionnaire permitted children to include books they had started but had not finished, so that if the changes were due not to an outright loss of the reading habit but rather to a slower turnover of books (either because of the greater length or complexity of the older children's books, or because the books were read more slowly owing to increased pressure of other activities on leisure time), we would expect the category of light book readers to increase at the expense of the moderate or heavy book-reading categories. In fact, however, there has been a steady shift at 12+ and 14+ not only towards the lower book-reading categories but also into the non-book-reading category; and we are forced to conclude, from the table as a whole, that a substantial number of children abandon the book-reading habit as they grow older. Thus among the girls, while there were only 9·4% in the 10+ age group who had read no book at all during the sample month, this percentage has risen to 23·3% at 12+ and to 32·4% at 14+. At all ages, however, there are fewer non-book-readers among the girls than among the boys; and the corresponding figures for boys are indeed even more disturbing. The percentage of non-book-readers among the 10+ boys is itself by no means negligible at 15·8%, but by age 12+ the corresponding figure has already climbed to 33·2% and at age 14+ it actually reaches a staggering 40%. One certainly cannot feel happy about the situation thus revealed.

It should be made clear, however, that although the non-book-readers include some pupils who are weak or backward at reading, most of them have the ability to read books if they choose to do so. Indeed in the two older age groups, as we shall see later, more than two-thirds of the non-book-readers have been assessed by their teacher as average or above average in ability and attainment, so that for these pupils, certainly, their condition is one of 'won't read' rather than 'can't read'. Nevertheless if we try to look on the bright side, we can extract from Table 13 the fact that there are still quite a number of children who read quite a few books. Thus to read three or more books a month seems a creditable achievement in face of the massive competition from television and other modern distractions. Yet at 10+ more than half of the girls (54·7%) and more than two-fifths of the boys (44·3%) accomplish this much reading. Admittedly this group of dedicated book readers has dwindled considerably by age 12+, so that among the girls the percentage has fallen to 43·4% and among the boys to 32·9%; and at age 14+ the proportion dwindles still further. Nevertheless even among the 14+ boys (the group in our sample that reads fewest books) there are still as many as 30·6% who have read three or more books during the month; and it seems clear that at this age, if we take both sexes together, there is a firm core of nearly a third of the age group who are genuinely committed to book reading.

Amount of periodical reading

The children were also asked to list all the comics and magazines which they read regularly. Unsurprisingly the answers revealed extensive reading of comics and magazines by the majority of children throughout the age range. The average number of periodicals read regularly by boys and girls at the three age levels is shown in Table 14. It can be seen from this table that at all ages girls read more periodicals than boys, and also that there is some decline in periodical reading in the higher age groups, though this is not as marked as in the case of book reading. Thus as we move from the 10+ age group to the 12+ age group we find that the average number of books read is reduced by about a quarter both for boys and for girls, whereas in the case of periodicals the corresponding figures are about one-tenth for girls and one-fifteenth for boys. Again for boys between age 12+ and age 14+ the average number of books read per month and the average number of periodicals read regularly declines by about the same proportion (approximately one-tenth); for girls, however, the average number of books

Table 14   Average number of periodicals read regularly (by sex and age)

Age group	Boys	Girls	Both sexes
10+	3·13	3·52	3·29
12+	2·93	3·25	3·07
14+	2·68	3·18	2·91
All age groups	2·92	3·33	3·10

Table 15   Distribution of children regularly reading periodicals by sex and age (in percentages)

No. of comics and magazines	10+ Boys	Girls	12+ Boys	Girls	14+ Boys	Girls
0	17·0	12·1	18·8	12·6	20·8	12·3
1—3	45·3	44·9	47·5	47·9	49·0	50·0
4—6	28·4	30·3	25·8	31·1	24·3	29·6
7—12	9·3	12·7	7·9	8·3	5·8	8·2
TOTALS	100·0	100·0	100·0	99·9	99·9	100·1
n	1402	1345	1353	1259	1307	1173

diminishes more than the average number of periodicals between these two ages.

Once more, however, it is perhaps more revealing to present the information in the form of a table (Table 15) which shows the percentage of children at each age in different reading categories. In this table we can see spread out in more detail the heavier periodical reading of girls as compared with boys, and the small but consistent decline in the amount of periodical reading with increasing age, particularly in the case of the boys.

Amount of television viewing

Our information about television viewing was obtained by asking each child to indicate the number of hours he had spent watching television on the previous evening. Information obtained in this way should be fairly accurate, given the limited demand upon memory span. To ensure compatibility in the answering of this question, the questionnaires were administered only on a Tuesday, Wednesday, Thursday or Friday, so that in every case the figures obtained related to a weekday evening. (Our personal interviews later with a proportion of the children showed that weekend viewing was highly variable according to the individual and the family, but often quite extensive.) The average number of hours spent watching television on weekday evenings during term time is shown in Table 16.

Table 16   Average number of hours spent watching television

Age group	Boys	Girls	Both sexes
10+	2·76	2·70	2·73
12+	2·51	2·52	2·52
14+	2·28	2·13	2·21
All age groups	2·52	2·46	2·49

This table confirms the well known fact that children of these ages spend a considerable part of their evening watching television. In general boys watch rather more than girls, but this difference is significant ($p = 1 \cdot 0\%$) only at 14+. For both sexes the average amount of time spent viewing decreases as age increases but not at all dramatically.

Table 17 shows the spread of television viewing among different age and sex groupings.

It will be seen that there is some diminution in the percentage of very heavy viewers (4 hours or more) at 12+ as compared with 10+, and that this diminution becomes even more pronounced at 14+. Only at 14+, however, is there a noteworthy increase in the percentage of non-viewers or of very

Table 17   Types of television viewer as percentage of sex and age grouping

Television viewing	10+ Boys	Girls	12+ Boys	Girls	14+ Boys	Girls
Hours 0	5·1	4·9	5·6	5·2	8·0	10·9
0−1	9·1	10·0	9·4	11·2	14·4	15·6
1−2	19·0	17·7	23·9	21·1	21·3	22·6
2−3	19·2	22·2	23·3	23·9	23·1	21·6
3−4	19·3	20·8	18·2	18·2	18·2	14·9
4+	28·3	24·4	19·6	20·3	15·0	14·4
TOTALS	100·0	100·0	100·0	99·9	100·0	100·0
n	1377	1336	1336	1241	1291	1162

light viewers (0−1 hours). At 14+, it would seem, there is a significant reduction in the television viewing of some children; and it seems a fair guess that this is due to two influences working (either singly or in combination) − increased homework, and increased social activities with the peer group.

Relationship between book reading, periodical reading and television viewing

In any attempt to examine the relationship between book reading, periodical reading, and television viewing we have some difficulty in deciding on the number of categories which will most helpfully reveal underlying trends. In Table 18, which sets forth the relationship between book reading and periodical reading, we have adopted a three-way split for each of our cross-tabulations, largely because this enables us to keep in view the non-readers who form, in each case, a minority in which we are particularly interested.

In Table 18, then, those whom we separated out in Table 13 as 'light book-readers' and 'moderate book-readers' are combined together in a single large category which we may call 'medium book-readers' − i.e. those who read between 1 and 4 books per month. Similarly, in Table 18, we have combined together in a single category − which we may call 'medium periodical readers' − all those who regularly read between 1 and 6 periodicals. Thus Table 18 shows, for each age and sex grouping, the percentage of non-book-readers, medium book readers, and heavy book readers who are also non-periodical-readers, medium periodical readers and heavy periodical readers. It is evident from this table that the relationships we are concerned with are complex and not easily summarized. Nevertheless, if we interest ourselves first in the non-book-readers, we can see (from inspection of the first column for each age-and-sex grouping) that although the overwhelming majority of these children (75% or more) are either medium or heavy

Table 18 Relationship between book and periodical reading

(a) Boys

Age groups	10+			12+			14+		
Books	0	1—4	5+	0	1—4	5+	0	1—4	5+
Periodicals	%	%	%	%	%	%	%	%	%
0	21	16	15	21	18	18	25	19	15
1—6	69	76	67	71	75	73	68	77	80
7+	10	7	17	8	7	10	7	5	6
TOTALS	100	99	99	100	100	101	100	101	101
n	221	952	229	449	750	154	523	660	124
n as % of total	16	68	16	33	55	11	40	50	9

(b) Girls

Age groups	10+			12+			14+		
Books	0	1—4	5+	0	1—4	5+	0	1—4	5+
Periodicals	%	%	%	%	%	%	%	%	%
0	20	12	10	17	11	12	11	12	17
1—6	74	77	72	74	81	77	81	80	77
7+	6	12	18	9	8	11	8	9	6
TOTALS	100	101	100	100	100	100	100	101	100
n	127	894	324	293	786	180	380	634	159
n as % of total	9	66	24	23	62	14	32	54	14

readers of periodicals, this proportion is even higher for medium book readers and heavy book readers in the same age-and-sex groupings, with the exception of the 14+ girls where the trend is reversed. There are, in fact, signs of an association between non-book-reading and non-periodical-reading which holds good for all except the 14+ girls. We gain further confirmation of this association if we compile 2 x 2 tables of non-book-readers/1+ book readers by non-periodical-readers/1+ periodical readers. Chi-square tests on these tables for all boys taken together and for 10+ and 12+ girls taken together show significant association at least at 1·0% level of probability.

If we next turn our attention to the heavy book readers, we notice that there is a tendency for heavy periodical readers to form a higher percentage of this category, at both 10+ and 12+, than of the medium book readers or the non-book-readers. For boys and girls at both these ages therefore there is a tendency for heavy book reading to go hand-in-hand with heavy periodical reading; this tendency is significant at the 0·1% probability level at 10+, but it is not significant at 12+ where the number of children who are both heavy book readers and heavy periodical readers is rather small. The number of children in this category at 14+ is even smaller, and here the trend is no longer discernible.

In Table 19, which shows the relationship between book reading and television viewing, we have again adopted a three-way split for our cross-tabulations, with the intention of keeping in view the crucial group of non-book-readers. It is certainly of interest to note that for each age-and-sex grouping heavy viewers (i.e. more than 3 hours viewing per weekday evening) form a higher percentage of the non-book-readers than of the medium book readers or of the heavy book readers. This table leads us to expect an inverse relationship between amount of book reading and amount of television viewing, and this expectation is confirmed if we divide the sample into light readers (0–2 books per month) and heavy readers (3 or more books per month) and again into light television viewers (less than 3 hours per weekday evening) and heavy viewers (more than 3 hours per weekday evening). Chi-square tests on these 2 x 2 tables show an inverse relation not only for the sample as a whole (at 0·1% level of probability), but also for boys and girls separately and for each age-group considered separately. Thus, for all sub-groups except 10+ children, the association is significant at 0·1% level of probability; for 10+ boys and for 10+ girls the probability level is 5·0%.

Although we have found within the 10+ and 12+ age-groups a direct relationship between amount of book-reading and amount of periodical-reading, and an inverse relationship between amount of book-reading and amount of television-viewing, it must be remembered that this does not necessarily imply an inverse relationship between periodical reading and television viewing.

Indeed from Table 20, which shows the relationship between periodical-reading and television-viewing, using once again a three-way split for each cross-tabulation, it would be more plausible to suppose a direct association between amount of periodical-reading and amount of television-viewing. Thus if we turn our attention to the non-periodical-readers we find that for both sexes at 10+ and 12+ and for the girls at 14+ there is a higher percentage of very light viewers among this group than among the medium or heavy periodical readers. At the same time heavy viewers form a higher percentage of the heavy periodical readers than of the medium periodical readers or the non-periodical-readers.

Table 20 therefore leads us to expect a direct relationship between amount of periodical reading and amount of television viewing, and this expectation is confirmed if we divide the sample into light periodical readers (0–3 periodicals) and heavy periodical readers (4+ periodicals) and again into light television viewers (less than 3 hours per weekday evening) and heavy viewers (3 or more hours per weekday evening). Chi-square tests on these 2 x 2

Table 19 Relationship between book reading and television viewing

(a) Boys

Age groups Books	10+			12+			14+		
	0	1–4	5+	0	1–4	5+	0	1–4	5+
	%	%	%	%	%	%	%	%	%
0–1 hrs TV	13	14	15	13	17	18	22	23	27
1–3 hrs TV	31	39	42	45	46	53	38	47	51
3+ hrs TV	56	47	43	41	37	29	40	29	22
TOTALS	100	100	100	99	100	100	100	99	100
n	209	942	226	449	750	154	523	660	124

(b) Girls

Age groups Books	10+			12+			14+		
	0	1–4	5+	0	1–4	5+	0	1–4	5+
	%	%	%	%	%	%	%	%	%
0–1 hrs TV	15	16	15	17	18	18	24	28	31
1–3 hrs TV	39	39	42	34	46	55	40	45	49
3+ hrs TV	46	45	43	48	37	27	36	27	19
TOTALS	100	100	100	99	101	100	100	100	99
n	127	894	324	293	786	180	380	634	159

Table 20 Relationship between periodical reading and television viewing

(a) Boys

Age groups	10+			12+			14+		
Periodicals	0	1–4	5+	0	1–4	5+	0	1–4	5+
	%	%	%	%	%	%	%	%	%
0–1 hrs TV	18	15	12	20	16	9	22	22	23
1–3 hrs TV	37	41	36	49	47	38	47	46	40
3+ hrs TV	44	45	52	32	37	53	32	32	37
TOTALS	99	101	100	101	100	100	101	100	100
n	225	630	522	245	637	454	260	638	393

(b) Girls

Age groups	10+			12+			14+		
Periodicals	0	1–4	5+	0	1–4	5+	0	1–4	5+
0–1 hrs TV	24	15	12	28	15	15	29	28	24
1–3 hrs TV	36	43	37	37	48	44	45	46	42
3+ hrs TV	40	42	51	36	37	42	26	27	34
TOTALS	100	100	100	101	100	101	100	101	100
n	162	598	576	152	597	492	141	584	437

tables show an association which is significant for each separate age-and-sex grouping. (The probability levels are as follows: 5·0% for 10+, 12+ and 14+ boys; 0·5% for 10+ girls; 10·0% for 12+ girls and 1·0% for 14+ girls.) For the sample as a whole the association is significant at the probability level of 0·1%.

Social class and book reading

Now that we have examined the interrelationship between book reading, periodical reading and television viewing, we must consider the other factors which may be influencing these activities. The most obvious matter to consider first is social class.

Table 21   Type of book reader as percentage of each age group, subdivided by social class

(a) Boys

Age groups Social class	10+ NM	M	12+ NM	M	14+ NM	M
Non-book-readers	8·9	17·8	24·7	36·9	28·2	45·2
Light book readers (1–2 books a month)	37·7	39·1	32·0	34·3	31·8	28·4
Moderate book readers (3–4 books a month)	30·4	27·9	26·8	19·5	26·0	19·3
Heavy book readers (5+ books a month)	22·9	15·3	16·5	9·3	14·0	7·2
TOTALS	99·9	100·1	100·0	100·0	100·0	100·1
n	358	839	437	775	393	768

(b) Girls

Non-book-readers	5·3	10·0	11·8	27·0	21·4	37·4
Light book readers (1–2 books a month)	24·3	40·3	30·5	34·4	30·1	34·0
Moderate book readers (3–4 books a month)	36·5	29·1	34·8	27·6	26·2	19·7
Heavy book readers (5+ books a month)	33·9	20·6	23·0	11·0	22·3	9·0
TOTALS	100·0	100·0	100·1	100·0	100·0	100·1
n	375	772	400	718	359	692

Table 21 shows us the breakdown by social class of the four different types of book reader. For each sex and at every age we note that there is a much higher percentage of non-book-readers or light book readers among children of social class M than among children of social class NM; and conversely that there is a much higher percentage of moderate and heavy book readers among children of social class NM than among children of social class M. This table would indeed lead us to expect a positive association between amount of book reading and social class, and if we construct 2 x 2 tables for non-book-readers and light book readers on the one hand and moderate and heavy book readers on the other, we find that chi-square tests indicate that for each age-and-sex grouping and also for the sample as a whole children whose fathers are in a non-manual occupation are inclined to read more books than children whose fathers are in a manual occupation. For the 10+ boys this difference is significant at the 0·5% level of probability; for every other age-and-sex grouping it is significant at the 0·1% level. If we take the sample as a whole the difference is significant beyond the 0·1% level.

The strength of this general trend should not conceal from us, however, the existence of groups who run counter to it. Thus it is important to keep in mind the rather high proportion of 12+ and 14+ boys from non-manual families who are either non-book-readers or at best light book readers; indeed Table 21 shows that at 14+ nearly a third (28·2%) of boys from non-manual families are non-book-readers. And even among the 14+ girls from non-manual families (as Table 21 similarly reveals) there are more than a fifth (21·4%) who are non-book-readers.

We can look at the information given in Table 21 in a slightly different way by considering the percentage of children in the two social classes M and NM within each of the four categories of book reader. When we do this (table not reproduced here) we find that, as far as the boys are concerned, the increase in non-book-readers between 10+ and 12+ is accompanied by an increase in the percentage of social class NM boys in this category. However, between 12+ and 14+ the class composition of the four book-reading categories does not change very much. For the girls, on the other hand, it is social class M girls who appear to be giving up book reading between 10+ and 12+; whereas there is again comparatively little change in the class composition of the book-reading categories between 12+ and 14+.

Ability and attainment and book reading

We must next examine the relationships between amount of book reading and 'ability and attainment'. In Table 22 we have conflated ability groups A and B, and ability groups C, D and E, to make the data more manageable.

From Table 22 it is clear that there is a much higher percentage of non-book-readers and light book readers among the pupils graded average or

Table 22 Type of book reader by ability and attainment

(a) Boys

Age groups Ability groups	10+		12+		14+	
	A and B	C, D and E	A and B	C, D and E	A and B	C, D and E
Non-book-readers	8.4	20.0	24.5	41.0	29.2	54.4
Light book readers (1–2/month)	34.3	43.6	30.5	37.9	29.1	28.0
Moderate book readers (3–4/month)	34.7	23.8	27.1	16.0	27.4	13.5
Heavy book readers (5+/month)	22.6	12.6	17.9	5.2	14.3	4.1
TOTALS	100.0	100.0	100.0	100.1	100.0	100.0
n	522	847	649	620	701	542

(b) Girls

Age groups Ability groups	10+		12+		14+	
	A and B	C, D and E	A and B	C, D and E	A and B	C, D and E
Non-book-readers	6.0	12.7	15.5	32.0	22.1	47.5
Light book readers (1–2/month)	25.3	43.6	29.3	39.7	33.9	31.8
Moderate book readers (3–4/month)	34.6	27.6	34.0	22.8	25.6	14.6
Heavy book readers (5+/month)	34.1	16.1	21.1	5.4	18.4	6.2
TOTALS	100.0	100.0	99.9	99.9	100.0	100.1
n	596	715	679	534	691	453

below average for ability and attainment, and conversely there is a much higher percentage of moderate or heavy book readers among those graded above average for ability and attainment. Moreover this generalization is true for every age-and-sex grouping. Table 22 would thus lead us to expect a positive association between ability and attainment and amount of book reading, and in fact if we construct 2 x 2 tables for non-book-readers and light book readers on the one hand and moderate book readers and heavy book readers on the other, we find that for each age-and-sex grouping children graded above average for ability and attainment tend to read more than children graded average or below for ability and attainment. This association holds good at a probability of less than 0·1% for each sex-and-age grouping. Again, however, the consistency of this trend should not conceal from us the existence of minority groupings which run counter to it. Thus in Table 22 the feature which is most likely to catch our eye is the high proportion of non-book-readers among the low ability children at 12+ and 14+. Particularly striking (and disturbing) is the fact that at 14+ more than half the boys and nearly half the girls graded average or below for ability and attainment are non-book-readers. At the same time we need to notice also that at this age the percentage of non-book-readers among the above average children is also much too high for comfort. Thus among the above average 14+ boys nearly a third (29·2%) are non-book-readers, while among the above average 14+ girls more than a fifth (22·1%) are non-book-readers. If we compare the 10+ with the 12+ figures, moreover, it becomes clear that a number of above average pupils (boys particularly) are becoming alienated from the reading habit at a very early stage in their career in the secondary school. Thus among the above average 10+ boys only 8·4% are non-book-readers; among the above average 12+ boys the corresponding figure has already climbed to 24·5%.

Again we can look at the information presented in Table 22 in a slightly different way by considering the percentage of children of different ability and attainment gradings within each of the four categories of book reader. The data are presented in this form in Table 23.

Table 23 does not reveal any trends which we could not discern from Table 22, but it does tell us slightly more about them. Thus we can see that at 14+, for both boys and girls, about 40% of the non-book-readers are children of ability and attainment grades A or B; and that less than 30% are of ability and attainment grades D or E. If we combine together ability and attainment groups A, B and C, and consider children who have been graded average or above by their teachers, the results are even more striking. Thus, at 12+, 68·0% of the boys who are non-book-readers fall into this category, and 65·9% of the girls. And at 14+ we find that 70·8% of the boys who are non-book-readers have been graded as average or above, while as many as 73·0% of the girls who are non-book-readers have been so graded. Even

Table 23 Type of book reader by ability and attainment (percentages based on the four categories of book reader)

(a) Boys

Age groups	10+				12+				14+			
Books read per month	0	1–2	3–4	5+	0	1–2	3–4	5+	0	1–2	3–4	5+
Ability group A	10·3	15·3	25·6	32·4	16·5	23·8	38·5	50·7	14·4	22·8	38·9	53·3
B	10·3	17·3	21·7	20·0	22·0	21·9	25·5	27·7	26·6	34·6	33·6	28·7
C	27·7	28·5	25·1	25·8	29·5	31·6	21·8	12·8	29·8	25·6	15·8	9·0
D	27·2	24·6	17·5	16·4	22·8	16·9	11·3	7·4	22·0	14·6	10·2	6·6
E	24·4	14·2	10·2	5·3	9·2	5·8	2·9	1·4	7·2	2·5	1·5	2·5
TOTALS	99·9	99·9	100·1	99·9	100·0	100·0	100·0	100·0	100·0	100·1	100·0	100·1
n	213	548	383	225	413	433	275	148	500	356	265	122

(b) Girls

Age groups	10+				12+				14+			
Books read per month	0	1–2	3–4	5+	0	1–2	3–4	5+	0	1–2	3–4	5+
Ability group A	9·4	14·0	23·3	34·0	15·2	21·4	42·4	57·6	13·0	28·3	42·0	56·1
B	18·9	18·6	27·8	29·9	22·8	27·0	23·2	25·6	28·5	33·6	30·9	25·8
C	33·9	36·3	27·3	21·7	27·9	28·0	26·0	11·0	31·5	21·4	21·8	13·5
D	26·0	23·3	16·4	11·9	25·0	18·5	7·1	4·7	22·6	14·8	5·3	3·2
E	11·8	7·8	5·2	2·5	9·1	5·1	1·4	1·2	4·3	1·9	0·0	1·3
TOTALS	100·0	100·0	100·0	100·0	100·0	100·0	100·1	100·1	99·9	100·0	100·0	99·9
n	127	463	403	318	276	411	354	172	368	378	243	155

allowing for the uneven allocation of children at this age to the five ability
and attainment grades (see Table 7) the clear inference must be that the
swing away from book reading at 12+ and at 14+ is not due *mainly* to
deficiency in the skills of reading.

One other issue raised by Table 22 deserves mention. As we noted earlier,
in our discussion of Table 7, there is a consistent tendency for girls to be
rated higher than boys for ability and attainment. How far does this higher
ability and attainment among the girls (however one explains it) account for
the fact that girls are inclined to read more than boys? Inspection of the
comparable columns in Table 22 would suggest that this can be only a partial
explanation; and in fact our analysis of the full table from which Table 22
has been condensed shows that although the higher ability and attainment
rating of the girls accounts to a certain extent for the larger amount of
reading they do, this is by no means the whole story. Even when we hold
ability and attainment constant, girls of a given ability group tend to read
more than boys of the same group, so that there is clearly some factor other
than ability involved.

One further problem must be mentioned here. It will be recalled that
Table 8 showed that there is a strong association between social class and
ability and attainment. Is it perhaps the case then that, in reality, Table 22
does no more than duplicate Table 20?

To explore this, we constructed a table (not reproduced here) in which
for each age group and for each social class (M or NM) we broke down the
percentage of children in each reading category as between above average
(A and B) pupils and average and below (C, D and E) pupils. From this it
became clear that there is a distinct tendency (within the same social class
groupings) for children graded average or below to read fewer books and for
children graded above average to read more books. If we take the sample as
a whole and construct 2 x 2 tables for children in ability and attainment
grouping A together with B and C, D and E together against children reading
less than 3 books and children reading 3 or more books the differences are
significant at 0·1% level of probability for both M children and NM children.
It would seem probable therefore that the social class difference cannot be
held to account fully for differences in amount of book reading, and that
differences in ability and attainment (however we account for these) must
also be brought in as one of the explanatory factors. This issue will be
returned to later in our argument.

Social class and periodical reading

We may move on now to examine the influence of social class on the amount
of periodical reading. The basic information is presented in Table 24, and

Table 24   Type of periodical reader as percentage of age group subdivided by social class

(a) Boys

Age groups Social class	10+ NM	M	12+ NM	M	14+ NM	M
Periodicals read 0	18·2	15·9	19·2	17·0	17·3	20·8
1—3	52·0	42·8	55·1	44·9	53·4	48·4
4—6	22·6	30·9	21·1	29·2	24·2	24·6
7+	7·3	10·5	4·6	8·9	5·1	6·1
TOTALS	100·1	100·1	100·0	100·0	100·0	99·9
n	358	839	437	775	393	768

(b) Girls

	10+ NM	M	12+ NM	M	14+ NM	M
Periodicals read 0	12·8	11·1	13·8	11·1	13·4	11·1
1—3	52·3	41·6	54·0	45·4	56·0	47·7
4—6	25·1	32·8	26·5	34·4	24·8	31·9
7+	9·9	14·5	5·8	9·1	5·8	9·2
TOTALS	100·1	100·0	100·1	100·0	100·0	99·9
n	375	772	400	718	359	692

Note: Equally, if we hold ability and attainment constant and construct 2 x 2 tables for M children and NM children against children reading less than 3 books and children reading 3 or more books, the differences are significant at 0·1% level of probability for children graded A or B, and at 0·5% level of probability for children graded C, D and E.

from this table we can see very rapidly that the relationship between social class and periodical reading is very different from that between social class and book reading.

Thus if we look in the first place at those children who read no periodicals regularly, we note that almost invariably these non-periodical-readers form a higher percentage of the NM children than they do of the M children: the only exception here is in the case of the 14+ boys where the general tendency is reversed and the non-periodical-readers form an exceptionally high percentage (20·8%) of the boys from M families. If we extend the scope of our observation to include the light periodical readers (i.e. 1—3 periodicals) we find that for every age-and-sex grouping the non-periodical-readers and the light periodical readers taken together form a higher percentage of the NM children than they do of the M children. Conversely, moreover, the moderate and heavy periodical readers taken together consistently form a

higher percentage of M children than of NM children. This table leads us
then to expect an *inverse* relationship between social class and amount of
periodical reading; and if we construct 2 x 2 tables for non-periodical-readers
and light periodical readers on the one hand and moderate and heavy
periodical readers on the other hand we find that for all age and sex groups
except the 14+ boys those children whose fathers are in a manual occupation
are inclined to read more periodicals than children whose fathers are in a
non-manual occupation. This association holds at 0·1% level of probability
for each age-and-sex grouping, except for the 14+ boys in whose case the
difference is not significant.

Ability and attainment and periodical reading

The next logical step is to examine the relationship between ability and
attainment and amount of periodical reading, and the basic information is
set out in Table 25 where, as in Table 22, we have conflated ability
groups A and B, and ability groups, C, D and E to make the data more
manageable.

It can be seen from Table 25 that the relationship between ability and
attainment and amount of periodical reading is more complicated and much
less easy to disentangle. It is evident, of course, that whatever the ability
group concerned, the vast majority of children are either light periodical
readers or moderate periodical readers. If, however, we look at the non-
periodical-readers we find that in all cases these form a higher percentage of
the average or below average pupils than of the above average pupils (though
admittedly the difference is not always a very great one). On the other hand,
if we look at the other extreme – the heavy periodical readers who regularly
read seven or more periodicals – we find that for five out of the six age-and-
sex groupings these form a higher percentage of the average or below average
pupils than they do of the above average pupils. (The exceptional case is that
of the 10+ girls where there is an unusually high percentage of heavy
periodical readers among both types of pupil.) What this may suggest, therefore, is that among the average and below average pupils there are two groups
who differ from the norm in the amount of their periodical reading – on the
one hand the non-periodical-readers and on the other hand the heavy
periodical readers, both of which groups form a higher percentage of their
ability group than their equivalents among the above average pupils. It is
worth mentioning before we leave Table 25 that at every age the percentage
of non-periodical-readers among the boys is markedly higher than among
the girls.

When we try to examine the separate effects of ability and attainment
and social class on amount of periodical reading, the picture which emerges

Table 25 Type of periodical reader by ability and attainment

(a) Boys

Age groups Ability groups	10+ A & B	C, D & E	12+ A & B	C, D & E	14+ A & B	C, D & E
	%	%	%	%	%	%
Periodicals read 0	12·1	20·2	18·3	19·2	19·0	22·7
1–3	47·5	43·3	51·0	44·2	52·4	44·6
4–6	31·6	26·7	24·7	27·3	24·5	24·7
7+	8·8	9·8	6·0	9·4	4·1	7·9
TOTALS	100·0	100·0	100·0	100·1	100·0	99·9
n	522	847	649	620	701	542

(b) Girls

Age groups Ability groups	10+ A & B	C, D & E	12+ A & B	C, D & E	14+ A & B	C, D & E
	%	%	%	%	%	%
Periodicals read 0	9·6	14·5	10·8	13·7	11·6	12·8
1–3	48·8	41·1	54·2	40·8	54·4	43·9
4–6	28·0	31·9	28·3	35·2	26·9	34·0
7+	13·6	12·4	6·8	10·3	7·1	9·3
TOTALS	100·0	99·9	100·1	100·0	100·0	100·0
n	596	715	679	534	691	453

is not easy to interpret at all confidently, and we are therefore not including the table which we constructed for this purpose.

Social class and television viewing

In our examination of the influence of social class and of ability and attainment, we come finally to amount of television viewing. Table 26 shows for each age-and-sex sub-group the percentage of M and NM children who fall into each of our six television-viewing categories.

Table 26   Type of television viewer by social class (in hours per weekday evening)

(a) Boys

Age groups	10+		12+		14+	
Social class	NM	M	NM	M	NM	M
	%	%	%	%	%	%
Hours 0	5·1	4·4	6·7	5·2	8·7	7·2
0−1	11·6	8·4	11·1	8·5	17·9	13·6
1−2	22·9	17·3	29·1	21·3	23·8	19·9
2−3	20·9	20·0	27·5	21·5	20·5	24·9
3−4	20·3	19·0	13·9	20·4	17·4	17·7
4+	19·2	31·0	11·8	23·1	11·8	16·6
TOTALS	100·0	100·1	100·1	100·0	100·1	99·9
n	354	823	433	766	391	763

(b) Girls

Hours 0	4·8	5·0	7·1	4·0	16·2	8·9
0−1	12·0	9·0	15·9	8·9	15·9	16·2
1−2	20·9	16·2	24·5	19·4	25·1	21·4
2−3	24·9	22·1	26·0	23·9	22·6	21·4
H 3−4	20·6	21·3	15·4	20·8	11·5	15·7
4+	16·8	26·5	11·1	23·1	8·7	16·4
TOTALS	100·0	100·1	100·0	100·1	100·0	100·0
n	374	766	396	707	358	687

Table 26 makes it clear that there is a very consistent pattern of heavier viewing among social class M children as compared with social class NM children. Thus, if we divide our sample into light television viewers (less than three hours per weekday evening) and heavy television viewers (three or more hours per weekday evening), we find that for each age-and-sex sub-group there are significantly more heavy viewers among the M children than among the NM children, and vice versa. The most marked difference between M and

NM children seems to occur in the heaviest viewing category (i.e. those who watch four or more hours television on a weekday evening); indeed at 12+, for both boys and girls, the percentage who fall into this category is twice as high for M children as for NM children. It is noticeable that among all the sub-groups in this table the percentage of children who watch no television at all is very small; the only exception to this is the NM girls at 14+, where the percentage who do no viewing amounts to almost one-sixth (16·2%).

Ability and attainment and television viewing

In Table 27 we have again conflated ability and attainment groups A and B and groups C, D and E to make the data more manageable.

Table 27 makes it clear that there is a consistent pattern of heavier viewing among children graded low for ability and attainment as compared with children graded high for ability and attainment. Thus, if we again divide our sample into light television viewers (less than three hours per weekday evening) and heavy television viewers (three or more hours per weekday evening) we find that for each age-and-sex sub-group there are significantly more heavy viewers among the C, D and E children than among the A and B children, and vice versa.

Interim summary of main quantitative findings

To take stock of our findings before proceeding to the next stage, we have established first that girls read more books and periodicals than boys, but that the amount of television watched is much the same for both sexes. Furthermore the amount of both book reading and periodical reading diminishes with age, with book reading declining faster than periodical reading. This change is accompanied by a considerable increase in the percentage of non-book-readers. Television viewing also decreases with increasing age, but only by quite modest amounts.

When we examined the relationship between book reading and periodical reading and television viewing, we found that for all age-and-sex groups except for 14+ girls there was a positive relationship between amount of book reading and amount of periodical reading. We also found an inverse relationship between amount of book reading and amount of television viewing, and a positive relationship between amount of periodical reading and amount of television viewing, both of these trends being present for all age-and-sex groupings.

The next stage of our inquiry was an investigation of the influence first of social class and then ability and attainment. As far as social class is concerned we found that:

Table 27 Type of television viewer by ability and attainment (in hours per weekday evening)

(a) Boys

Age groups Ability groups	10+ A & B	10+ C, D & E	12+ A & B	12+ C, D & E	14+ A & B	14+ C, D & E
	%	%	%	%	%	%
Hours 0	3·7	5·9	6·5	4·8	7·3	8·7
0–1	9·8	8·7	9·9	8·9	16·2	12·3
1–2	22·4	17·0	26·8	20·2	22·9	18·0
2–3	22·4	17·1	25·3	20·2	23·9	22·9
3–4	20·4	18·8	16·9	20·5	17·5	19·5
4+	21·4	32·5	14·6	25·4	12·3	18·6
TOTALS	100·1	100·0	100·0	100·0	100·1	100·0
n	519	825	645	610	699	528

(b) Girls

Age groups Ability groups	10+ A & B	10+ C, D & E	12+ A & B	12+ C, D & E	14+ A & B	14+ C, D & E
Hours 0	4·0	5·8	4·8	5·5	10·8	10·8
0–1	9·9	10·3	12·6	9·2	16·9	13·7
1–2	21·0	15·2	23·6	18·1	24·9	19·3
2–3	23·5	21·4	26·3	21·6	23·4	20·2
3–4	20·5	21·0	17·8	18·9	15·0	14·6
4+	21·1	26·3	14·9	26·7	9·2	21·3
TOTALS	100·0	100·0	100·0	100·0	100·2	99·9
n	596	706	673	524	688	445

(a)   throughout the sample there was a tendency for children with fathers in social class NM to read more books than children with fathers in social class M.

(b)   for all age-and-sex groupings except the 14+ boys, children with fathers in social class M are inclined to read more periodicals than children with fathers in social class NM.

(c)   throughout the sample there is a tendency for children with fathers in social class M to watch more television than children with fathers in social class NM.

As far as ability and attainment is concerned we found that:

(a)   for all age-and-sex groupings children graded above average tended to read more books than children graded average and below.

(b)   in the case of periodical reading the picture was a more complex one, but that over all there was a tendency for children graded above average to read fewer periodicals than children graded average or below.

(c)   throughout the sample there was a consistent pattern of heavier viewing among children graded low for ability and attainment than among children graded high.

We noted, however, that it is difficult to interpret these findings with confidence since we have already shown an association between ability and attainment and social class (see Table 8) such that very much higher percentages of children in social class NM than in social class M were allocated by schools to the higher ability grades. However, as far as amount of book reading was concerned, we were able to show that, even when social class was held constant, there was a distinct tendency for children graded average or below to read fewer books and for children graded above average to read more books.

Some other relevant variables

We will now mention briefly the relevance of certain other factors. There are eight further variables which were found to be positively associated with amount of book reading. These are:

(i)   *Smallness of family size*
If we take smaller families to be those in which the child has fewer than three siblings, we find that there are fewer smaller families among non-book-readers and light book readers than among medium and heavy book readers. It must be remembered however that family size is also correlated with both social

class and with ability and attainment. Nevertheless, chi-square tests on 2 x 2 tables of family size (less than 3 siblings by 3 or more siblings) by book reading (less than 3 books by 3 or more books per month) show a significant relationship between small family size and high book reading for children in ability groups A and B, in both social class M and social class NM.

(ii)   *Number of books owned by the child*
The full table (not reproduced here) of number of books owned by children in the sample shows that girls claim to own more books than boys (difference significant at 1·0% level for social class NM and at 5·0% level for social class M); and that, a little surprisingly perhaps, younger children claim to own more books than older children (difference significant at 5·0% level between 10+ and 12+ and at 1·0% level between 12+ and 14+). However children of higher ability claim to own more books than those of lower ability, while children in social class NM claim to own more than those in social class M; so that when we consider the relationship with book reading, we need once again to look at the social class and ability and attainment sub-groups separately. When we have done this however, we can assert with confidence that even when social class and ability and attainment are held constant, there is a positive association between amount of book reading and the ownership of a significant number of books (more than 10).

(iii)   *The child's regularity of visits to a public library*
We judged it reasonable to regard all children who visit the public library once a fortnight or more often as 'regularly visiting', and Table 28 shows the percentage of children in this category by sex and age.

Table 28   Distribution of children visiting the public library regularly by sex and age (in percentages)

10+ Boys	Girls	12+ Boys	Girls	14+ Boys	Girls
32·8	41·3	29·5	34·7	22·4	25·9

As can be seen, the percentage of children visiting regularly is higher for girls than for boys, and higher for younger children than for older ones. The difference between the sexes is significant beyond the 0·1% level; so also is the difference between the 10+ and 12+ age groups, and between the 12+ and the 14+ age groups. It is a cause for some concern that the proportion of children regularly visiting the public library is so low, particularly for the oldest age group. We note that the decrease between 12+ and 14+ is more pronounced than that between 10+ and 12+, and it seems possible that this may reflect a failure on the part of a number of children to make the transition from the junior section to the adult section of the library.

A further table (not reproduced here) makes clear the higher rate of public library visiting first by comparing children of high ability and attainment with those of low ability and attainment, and then by comparing children of social class NM with those of social class M; so that when we consider the relationship with amount of book reading, we need once again to look at the social class and ability and attainment sub-groups separately. When we do this we find that there continues to be a relationship between regular library visiting and amount of book reading for each of the four sub-groups; however, there is very little difference between the two social class groups, particularly for children of ability A or B; whereas, regardless of social class, the percentages visiting the library regularly are decidedly higher among the more able than among the less able, so that ability and attainment seems to be the more important factor here.

(iv)   *Parents' reading of library books*
It was found that a higher proportion of children's parents read library books in social class NM as compared with social class M, and that among children in ability and attainment groups A or B there is a higher proportion whose parents read library books than among children in ability and attainment groups C, D and E. Again therefore we need to take social class and ability and attainment into account when considering this variable. Nevertheless a table (not reproduced here) shows that, even when social class and ability and attainment are held constant, there is a positive relationship between amount of children's book reading and their parents' reading of library books. Chi-square tests comparing on the one hand those whose parents read library books against those who do not and on the other hand those who read 0—2 books per month against those who read 3 or more books per month show a relationship which is significant at 0·1% level of probability for ability and attainment groups A and B in both social class M and social class NM. For ability and attainment groups C, D and E in Social Class M the association is significant at the 0·5% level of probability; for the same ability and attainment groups in social class NM the association is not statistically significant, but in this case the numbers were small.

(v)   *The presence of quality newspapers among those taken by the family*
We found that there was no relationship between the number of newspapers and amount of book reading, but that there was a significant association between amount of book reading and the presence of quality newspapers among those taken by the family. (We had classified each of the national newspapers listed as either quality or non-quality: the quality papers were

Daily Telegraph, *Financial Times*, *Guardian*, *Journal*, *Observer*, *Scotsman*, *Sunday Telegraph*, *Sunday Times*, *Western Mail*, *Yorkshire Post*, while the non-quality papers were *Daily Express*, *Daily Mail*, *Daily Mirror*, *News of the World*, *People*, *Sun*, *Sunday Express*, *Sunday Mercury*, *Sunday Mirror*. (All local papers were placed in a third category.) A table (not reproduced here) showed that in each age-and-sex sub-group NM families were more likely to take quality papers than M families, and also that as we move down the ability and attainment scale there is a decline in the percentage of children reporting the presence of quality papers in the home. Clearly, therefore, both social class and ability and attainment are relevant factors here. Even when they had been taken into account, there was clearly a positive relationship between amount of book reading and the presence of quality newspapers in the home. Thus, if we construct 2 x 2 tables for amount of book reading (less than 2 books per month against 3 or more books per month) by type of newspaper (families taking quality newspapers against those who do not), we find that chi-square tests are significant at the following levels of probability: significant beyond the 0·1% level for children of ability and attainment A or B in social class NM; significant at 0·5% level for children of ability and attainment A or B in social class M; significant at 0·5% level for children of ability and attainment C, D & E in social class M.

(vi)   *Favourable attitude to school*
As far as the child's expressed liking for school was concerned, we found an association between ability and attainment and favourable attitude to school (as one would no doubt expect); but as far as social class differences are concerned the various sub-groups do not show a consistent pattern, and none of the differences is statistically significant. As far as this factor is concerned, therefore, ability and attainment is the linked variable which needs to be taken into account; a table (not reproduced here) shows that the association between amount of book reading and degree of expressed liking for school still holds when this has been held constant. In fact, if we construct 2 x 2 tables of book readers (non- or light readers against medium or heavy readers) by school liking ('very much' or 'quite a lot' against 'don't mind it', 'rather dislike it', or 'don't like it at all') we find that chi-square tests give significant differences beyond 0·1% level of probability for both ability and attainment groupings A and B, and for groupings C, D & E.

(vii)   *Favourable attitude to English lessons*
This variable relates only to the 12+ and 14+ children, since a question about liking for English lessons was judged to be inappropriate to primary school children who may not have had experience of clearly defined and identifiable English lessons. In the case of this variable there was no consistent relationship with ability and attainment, and any differences between

the two social class groupings were not statistically significant. A table (not reproduced here) showing the percentage of children in different reading categories for whom English lessons are 'favourite' or 'liked better than most' makes it clear that amount of book reading is positively associated with liking for English lessons, though the nature and extent of this association appears to vary somewhat as between the different age-and-sex sub-groups.

(viii)   *Age at which the child expects to leave school*
This variable too relates only to the 12+ and 14+ children, since it was thought unlikely that 10+ children would have sufficiently clear expectations or intentions for their responses to be worth recording and analysing. In the answers to this question there was very little difference between the sexes, an indication presumably that for the children themselves it is no longer the case that continued education is regarded as more important for boys than for girls. It became clear however that the expectation of staying on at school beyond age 16 was positively associated with both social class and with ability and attainment, so that we need to allow for both these factors when examining the relationship between expected school leaving and amount of book reading. However, a table (not reproduced here) makes it clear that even when social class and ability and attainment are held constant, there is still an association between amount of book reading and the expectation of staying on at school beyond age 16. In fact chi-square tests on 2 x 2 tables of amount of book reading (non-readers and light book readers against medium and heavy book readers) by expected age of leaving school (15 or 16 against 17 or 18) show differences which are significant beyond the 0·1% level, except for children of ability C, D or E in social class NM; in this sub-group the numbers are very small.

The influence of the family

If we attempt to sum up the main line of thought so far, we may perhaps say the following. Although there is no firm base-line in earlier research studies with which we can compare our own findings, there do seem to be some indications that children in 1971 were reading fewer books than children of comparable ages two or three decades earlier. It seems likely that this trend is associated with the tendency for books to count less in the modern world than they used to do. It might be suggested, however, that this shift in valuation will influence the individual child differentially through the social institutions in which he participates. The most important of these social institutions is almost certainly the family, and we have undoubtedly found some grounds for believing that, in our sample, family circumstances exert an important influence on the child's amount of reading. Thus a child with a father in a non-manual occupation is likely to possess more books and to see more quality newspapers in the home, and is more likely to visit a public library regularly and to have parents who read library books. We can fairly say that this child's home is oriented towards the use of books, and that this orientation is partly responsible for the fact that he is likely to have read more books than a child whose father is in a manual occupation. (Conversely the child whose father is in a non-manual occupation is likely to see regularly fewer periodicals — perhaps in part because on average he has fewer siblings — and to spend less time watching television.) Whether or not there is any causal connection between the two sets of phenomena, we can say also that the child with a father in a non-manual occupation is more likely to be assessed high by his school for ability and attainment, to express a favourable attitude towards school, and to record an expectation of staying on at school beyond the age of 16.

The influence of school type

The other social institution with powerful potential influence on the child is, of course, the school. We consider first the relationship between school type and amount of book reading. There is little differentiation in school type at the primary school stage, and it was therefore a little surprising that children in junior schools seemed to read less than children in junior-with-infant schools. The relevant figures for the 10+ children are shown in Table 29.

Table 29   Type of book reader as percentage of 10+ age group by type of school

Type of book reader	Boys Junior	Junior with infants	Girls Junior	Junior with infants
Non-	17·8	12·3	10·1	8·8
Light (1−2/month)	38·0	42·1	38·4	32·1
Moderate (3−4/month)	28·9	28·1	30·8	30·1
Heavy (5+/month)	15·2	17·5	20·7	29·0
n	757	604	711	579

Note: The three junior schools which had become middle schools at the beginning of the school year in which the questionnaire was administered were excluded from this table.

If we construct 2 x 2 tables comparing non-book-readers and light book readers against moderate and heavy book readers, chi-square tests show that there are significantly more non-readers and light readers amongst the girls in junior schools than amongst the girls in junior-with-infant schools, and this difference is significant at the 1·0% level of probability. The same difference is present among the boys, but is not statistically significant. If we take both sexes together the difference is significant at the 5·0% level. No unmistakable reason suggests itself to account for this difference. The junior-with-infant schools in our sample were somewhat smaller in their overall size (average number on roll approximately 300) than the junior schools (average number on roll approximately 370); and this does of course mean that there were, on average, decidedly fewer 10+ children in each junior-with-infants school, so that there may have been more individual attention available for each of them from the staff and head-teacher. It seems possible also that schools which have been concerned with the learning of reading from its very earliest stages tend to have a more reading-oriented ethos and that this has some influence on the amount of energy and enthusiasm devoted to the fostering of book reading at 10+. Nor should we neglect to mention the possibility that the children themselves have benefited from the absence of a break in continuity in the development of their reading progress, since it has sometimes been claimed that this break in continuity at the time of the change from infant to junior school has an adverse effect upon the reading development of some children.

Among the 12+ and 14+ pupils we found that school type was highly important in influencing the amount of book reading. In general terms the tendency was for direct grant school pupils to read more than grammar school pupils, for grammar school pupils to read more than comprehensive school pupils, and for comprehensive school pupils to read more than secondary modern school pupils. It is not of course surprising that the differences should be in this direction, in view of the positive association we have already demonstrated between ability and attainment and amount of reading. Owing to the differing levels of significance for the various sub-groups, however, it is necessary to treat the two age groups separately.

We start with 12+ pupils and present the figures for them in Table 30. If we construct 2 x 2 tables comparing non-book-readers and light book readers against moderate and heavy book readers, we find that the differences between direct grant schools and grammar schools are not statistically significant. There are however significantly more moderate and heavy book readers among the grammar school pupils than among the comprehensive school pupils, and this difference is significant at the 0·1% level both for boys and for girls and for the two sexes combined. Again there are significant differences of a similar kind between the comprehensive school pupils and the secondary modern school pupils, and in this case the signifi-

Table 30 Type of book reader as percentage of 12+ age group by type of school

(a) Boys

Type of book reader	Direct Grant	Grammar	Comp.	Sec. mod.
Non-	13·8	19·6	34·9	39·1
Light (1–2/month)	31·0	27·2	33·2	36·8
Moderate (3–4/month)	27·6	30·4	19·8	18·3
Heavy (5+/month)	27·6	22·8	12·1	5·8
n	29	250	364	606

(b) Girls

	Direct Grant	Grammar	Comp.	Sec. mod.
Non-	0·0	8·2	25·3	29·1
Light (1–2/month)	31·0	22·9	31·3	38·9
Moderate (3–4/month)	37·9	40·0	29·9	24·6
Heavy (5+/month)	31·0	29·0	13·5	7·3
n	29	245	348	573

cance levels are 1·0% for boys, 0·1% for girls, and 0·1% for both sexes combined.

However, the most meaningful comparison arises when we combine the secondary modern and grammar school pupils in our sample and compare them with the pupils in the comprehensive sector. The relevant figures (taking both sexes together) are shown in Table 31. In this case if we construct 2 x 2 tables comparing non-book-readers and light book readers against moderate and heavy book readers we find that the difference between the comprehensive sector and the selective sector is not statistically significant.

Another way of looking at the same data is in terms of the average number of books read per head during the month studied, and these figures are given in Table 32.

Table 31 Type of book reader as percentage of 12+ age group by comprehensive sector against selective sector

Type of book reader	Comp.	Grammar & Sec. mod. combined
Non-	31·2	28·7
Light (1−2/month)	32·1	33·9
Moderate (3−4/month)	24·1	25·2
Heavy (5+/month)	12·6	12·1
n	733	1705

Table 32 Average number of books read in a month according to school type

School type	Books per head	Standard deviation
Grammar	3·42	1·13
Sec. mod.	1·69	0·74
Gramm. with Sec. mod.	2·19	1·17
Comp.	2·13	0·93

If we now compare the comprehensive figure with the figure for grammar and secondary modern schools combined, we find that the variance of

$$\text{difference in means} = \frac{(1·17)^2}{119} + \frac{(0·93)^2}{55} = 0·027$$

$$\text{then SD} = \sqrt{0·027} = 0·16$$

Thus the difference in means (0·06) is about one-third of a standard deviation, and is not statistically significant.

We are therefore entitled to say that, in the case of the 12+ children, the amount of book reading of the comprehensive children is not significantly · different from that of the grammar school and secondary modern school children combined. This seems on the face of it to indicate that, in the amount of book reading this age group achieves, the more recently established comprehensive schools are doing at least as well as the former selective system. In fact, however, the 56 comprehensive schools in our sample included a number whose intake for the 12+ age group had been creamed off to a significant extent by selective schools. Thus, out of the 50 which answered our inquiry on this point, there were only 20 which said that creaming off had not taken place, whereas 5 said that their intake had been creamed off by less than 10%, 19 said that their intake had been creamed off by 10% or more, and 6 gave answers that could not be clearly interpreted. Since we have shown that there is a relationship between ability and attainment and amount of reading, it can therefore be argued that, at 12+, the comprehensive schools in our sample were actually achieving a higher level in regard to amount of book reading, allowing for the ability composition of their pupils.

We now turn to the 14+ age group for which Table 33 shows figures comparable to Table 30.

Table 33 Type of book reader as percentage of 14+ age group by type of school

(a) Boys

Type of book reader	Direct grant	Grammar	Comp.	Sec. mod.
Non-	3·1	26·9	42·0	45·7
Light (1−2/month)	28·1	20·7	33·0	30·9
Moderate (3−4/month)	37·5	31·4	17·7	17·4
Heavy (5+/month)	31·3	21·1	7·2	6·0
n	32	242	333	602

(b) Girls

Non-	0·0	16·9	36·5	38·9
Light (1−2/month)	17·2	30·8	33·0	34·5
Moderate (3−4/month)	31·0	31·2	18·6	17·2
Heavy (5+/month)	51·7	21·1	11·9	9·4
n	29	266	312	519

The differences revealed by this table are in the same direction as for the 12+ age group, but chi-square tests reveal a more variable pattern of significance levels. Thus if we take both sexes together the direct grant schools and the grammar schools show a difference significant at the 5·0% probability level. The difference between grammar schools and comprehensive schools is again significant at the 0·1% level for boys, for girls and for both sexes taken together. For this age group however the difference between comprehensive schools and secondary modern schools is not significant. It seems plausible to suppose that the closer similarity between comprehensive and secondary modern here is due to the nature of the comprehensive intake for this age group — a group more likely to have been creamed off by selective schools because the change to the comprehensive system was less advanced at the date of their transfer to secondary education; this is a point we shall return to in a moment.

For the 14+ group also we have compiled a table which shows type of reader by the comprehensive sector and the selective sector (grammar and secondary modern combined).

Table 34 Type of book reader as percentage of 14+ age group by comprehensive against selective sector

Type of book reader	Comp.	Grammar & sec. mod. combined
Non-	39·6	36·5
Light (1−2/month)	32·9	30·3
Moderate (3−4/month)	18·0	21·5
Heavy (5+/month)	9·6	11·7
n	657	1661

In this case, if we construct 2 x 2 tables for non-book-readers and light book readers against moderate and heavy book readers, we find that there are more moderate and heavy book readers in the selective sector, the significance level being 1·0%.

Once again we may try looking at these data in terms of average number of books per head read during the month. Table 35 shows the relevant figures. It is clear that in this case the advantage lies with the selective sector, though not to a very marked degree. However in this case our answers from the 50 out of the 56 comprehensive schools revealed that a much larger number of schools had been subject to a considerable amount of creaming off of their intake by selective schools at this age range. Indeed if we leave out of account comprehensive schools whose intake for this age group had been creamed off by 10% or more we are left with only 20 schools which could be regarded as genuinely comprehensive at 14+. For these 20 schools

Table 35   Average number of books read in a month at 14+ according to school type

School type	Books per head
Grammar	2·90
Sec. mod.	1·55
Grammar & Sec. Mod. combined	1·94
Comp.	1·74

the mean book average per head is 1·93, which is clearly not significantly different from the 1·94 for the selective sector shown in Table 35. It would seem reasonable to argue again therefore that for this age range too the comprehensive schools show a creditable achievement in regard to amount of book reading, if the ability composition of their pupils is taken into account.

Single-sex and mixed secondary schools

Another matter related to school type is that of the difference between single sex and mixed schools. This issue does not arise in relation to our 10+ children, since for that age group all the schools in our sample were mixed ones. The relevant figures for the 12+ children, however, are shown in Table 36.

Table 36   Types of book reader as percentage of 12+ age group in single-sex and mixed schools

Type of book reader	Boys Single-sex schools	Mixed schools	Girls Single-sex schools	Mixed schools
Non-	29·0	36·0	19·0	26·0
Light (1−2/month)	32·8	34·4	35·1	32·4
Moderate (3−4/month)	24·4	19·8	29·9	28·8
Heavy (5+/month)	13·7	9·8	16·0	12·8
n	524	817	501	747

Here if we contrast non-book-readers against book readers (all types combined, we find that for each sex there are significantly more non-book-readers in the mixed schools than in the single-sex schools, and the difference is significant at the 1·0% level of probability for boys, at 0·5% for girls, and at 0·1% if we take both sexes together. A similar finding emerges from the figures for the 14+ children, which are shown in Table 37.

Table 37   Types of book reader as percentage of 14+ age group in single-sex and in mixed schools

Type of book reader	Boys Single-sex schools	Mixed schools	Girls Single-sex schools	Mixed schools
Non	36·6	42·4	28·5	35·1
Light (1−2/month)	26·7	31·4	34·6	31·7
Moderate (3−4/month)	23·8	18·9	21·5	20·9
Heavy (5+/month)	12·9	7·2	15·5	12·3
n	525	776	480	690

Here again we find that there are, for each sex, significantly more non-readers in the mixed schools than in the single-sex schools, the significance levels this time being 5·0% for boys, 2·5% for girls and 0·5% if both sexes are taken together. This finding is not one that we had expected, and it is not at all easy to interpret. Perhaps the most plausible explanation is that the quality of book provision is more appropriate to the children's needs in single-sex schools, in that women teachers are more likely to be knowledge-able about books suitable for reluctant girl readers and men teachers more likely to be knowledgeable about books suitable for reluctant boy readers. It is no doubt true that, in a sense, the task of the English teacher in a mixed school is more demanding than that of a teacher in a single-sex school, since the latter has a smaller target area at which to aim, so to speak, and there are fewer books that he or she needs to have sampled or become acquainted with. However, it is quite possible that other factors have played a part which our analysis has failed to uncover. Possibly all we can say with certainty is that mixed schools need to be aware that, for whatever reason, certain of their pupils run a higher-than-average risk of becoming non-book-readers, and that there is a need for specially energetic measures to combat this danger.

School organization and methods

It will be recalled that, in addition to the information already available to us about school type, we sought to gain further information about school

organization and methods by sending out to each school a School Questionnaire which was completed in the case of primary schools by the head
teacher and in the case of secondary schools by the head of the English
department. A copy of each school questionnaire is reproduced as Appendix
V(a) and Appendix V(b) respectively. The schools were most helpful and
conscientious in filling in and returning these questionnaires, and it is with
great regret therefore that we have to report that this part of our investigation proved in the main to be disappointingly inconclusive.

We hoped in the first instance to identify the various characteristics which
differentiated 'high reading' from 'low reading' schools; and we therefore
picked out for each age group the 50 schools which had the highest average
book reading scores and the 50 schools which had the lowest average book
reading scores. We then set out to compare these two groups of schools in
the light of the information the schools themselves had supplied about their
own methods and organization. Regrettably this approach failed to produce
clear indications as to the characteristics which differentiated the two sets of
schools, and we therefore turned to the expedient of taking each school
variable separately and considering its relevance to book reading by means
of cross-tabulations with amount of reading similar to those used earlier in
this chapter for each of the home variables. Here again the results were, for
the most part, disappointingly inconclusive. Repeatedly we found that a
school variable which we had expected to show an association with amount
of reading did not in fact do so. Thus we thought it likely that, at 10+, the
amount of time 'spent on average each week listening to the teacher reading
stories to them' (question 3 in Appendix V(a)) would show a positive
association with the amount of reading undertaken by the children; this
hypothesis was not substantiated.

Again, we thought it likely that the amount of book reading would be
higher in primary schools where children were allowed to take books from
the school library home than in schools where children were not allowed to
borrow books to take home (question 6(c) in Appendix V(a)); this hypothesis
too we were unable to confirm. (Conceivably the explanation here is that
schools which do not allow books to be taken home take more positive steps
to make time available for reading during school hours; we had obtained no
information on this point, however.) We also thought it possible that in both
primary and secondary schools the ratio between the total book stock
(school libraries and class libraries combined) and the total number of
pupils would be associated with amount of book reading; in this case too we
found that our hypothesis was not substantiated, and we found it impossible
to conclude that the number of books available per pupil was a significant
school variable for our purposes. (Perhaps it is quality rather than mere
quantity of book provision that counts, but we were unable to obtain
information about this by means of a written questionnaire.)

In the end then we were left with only a small and rather miscellaneous group of school variables which seemed to be associated, either positively or negatively, with amount of reading. We shall therefore report next our findings in regard to this group of variables, and conclude the section with a brief discussion as to why this part of our investigation has yielded less illumination than we originally hoped it would.

Streaming, mixed ability, vertical grouping and setting

Of the school variables to be reported on, much the most interesting is that relating to the organization of classes. We start with the 10+ group where there were three possibilities: classes streamed by ability, mixed ability classes or the relatively infrequent situation in which the 10+ group was organized with other years in 'family' or vertical groupings. The data for the three types of organization are presented in Table 38.

Table 38   Type of book reader at 10+ as percentage of each type of class organization

(a) Boys

Type of book reader	Streamed classes	Mixed ability classes	Vertical grouping
Non-	20·3	15·6	5·0
Light (1−2/month)	39·4	38·7	48·8
Moderate (3−4/month)	24·2	28·7	33·1
Heavy (5+/month)	16·1	17·0	13·2
n	335	930	121

(b) Girls

Type of book reader	Streamed classes	Mixed ability classes	Vertical grouping
Non-	10·7	9·5	7·2
Light (1−2/month)	38·4	35·7	32·9
Moderate (3−4/month)	28·4	29·9	38·2
Heavy (5+/month)	22·5	25·0	21·7
n	271	910	152

In the first place we find from this table that the vertical grouping category contains a lower proportion of non-readers than the other two types of organization; and this difference is significant at the 0·1% level of probability when both sexes are taken together. Secondly, if we take vertical grouping and mixed ability together, and construct 2 x 2 tables for non-book-readers and light book readers against moderate and heavy book readers, chi-square tests show that there are significantly more non- and light readers in the streamed classes than in the other two types of organization, and this difference is significant at the 2·5% level of probability for both sexes taken together. This finding that children in streamed classes read less than children in mixed ability classes or in vertical grouping situations should perhaps send us back to reconsider our earlier finding (see Table 29) that 10+ children in junior-with-infant schools read more than children in junior schools. In our sample the schools with streamed classes at 10+ were predominantly in junior schools (31 junior schools with streamed classes as against 8 junior-with-infant schools), while the verticle grouping organization occurred with greater frequency in the junior-with-infant schools (18 junior-with-infant schools used vertical grouping as against 4 junior schools). The straight mixed ability 10+ class organization was more evenly divided between the two types of school, being used by 66 junior schools as against 60 junior-with-infant schools. This clearly raises the possibility that a contributory factor to the relatively poorer performance of the junior schools in regard to amount of reading was their greater tendency to organize their pupils in streamed classes; presumably in such a situation any benefit gained by the pupils who are assigned to a high stream is more than cancelled out by the adverse effect on the morale of those children who are relegated to a low stream.

It is important to note that streaming also appeared to have an adverse effect upon amount of reading at the secondary school level, though here of course the situation is more complex and the findings need to be interpreted with a certain amount of caution. (In grammar and secondary modern schools something akin to streaming has already taken place at the point of entrance to secondary education, so that to be in a mixed ability class in either of these types of school has a distinctly different connotation to being in a mixed ability class in a primary school or in a genuinely comprehensive school.) The relevant figures for the 12+ age group are shown in Table 39. The possible forms of organization are more numerous in this case, since we have to include not only streamed classes and mixed ability classes but also a system in which the age group is in sets for various subjects but not for English and a system in which the age group is in sets for various subjects including English. In analysing this table it seems appropriate to combine streamed classes with those groups which are in sets for various subjects including English and to contrast them with unstreamed classes taken together with those which are in sets for various subjects but not for English. If we construct 2 x 2 tables of non-book-readers and light book readers against

Table 39   Type of book reader at 12+ by different type of class
organization

(a) Boys

Type of book reader	Streamed classes	In sets except English	In sets including English	Unstreamed
	%	%	%	%
Non-	34·7	21·3	38·5	30·3
Light (1−2/month)	35·9	26·6	32·1	33·1
Moderate (3−4/month)	18·3	35·1	21·7	23·9
Heavy (5+/month)	11·1	17·0	7·7	12·7
n	596	94	221	393

(b) Girls

Non-	28·5	7·6	21·5	21·6
Light (1−2/month)	33·4	22·7	36·4	34·6
Moderate (3−4/month)	27·9	37·9	31·1	28·2
Heavy (5+/month)	10·2	31·8	11·0	15·6
n	548	132	228	301

moderate and heavy book readers we find that there are significantly more
non- and light readers among those who are either streamed or in sets for
English; and this difference is significant at 0·1% level of probability for
boys, for girls and for both sexes taken together.

We can also construct a similar table (see Table 40) for the 14+ children,
though it should perhaps be remembered that at this age, with GCE or CSE
exams beginning to loom ahead on the horizon, there is more pressure on
schools to either stream or set pupils according to ability, a fact which
perhaps accounts for the smaller *n*'s for unstreamed children in Table 40 as
compared with Table 39.

The interesting and indeed intriguing feature of Table 40 is that here the
difference is between those who were 'in sets but not for English' and the
other types of class organization, with those 'in sets but not for English'
reading more books. If we construct 2 x 2 tables by non-book-readers, we

Table 40   Type of book reader at 14+ by different type of class
organization

(a) Boys

Type of book reader	Streamed classes	In sets except English	In sets including English	Unstreamed
	%	%	%	%
Non-	41·6	31·6	39·5	40·3
Light (1−2/month)	26·6	26·9	32·4	32·3
Moderate (3−4/month)	22·4	26·3	17·7	22·6
Heavy (5+/month)	9·4	15·2	10·3	4·8
n	469	171	435	186

(b) Girls

	Streamed classes	In sets except English	In sets including English	Unstreamed
Non-	32·9	23·8	30·1	40·2
Light (1−2/month)	33·4	29·3	33·8	32·2
Moderate (3−4/month)	21·0	24·5	21·5	19·6
Heavy (5+/month)	12·7	22·4	14·6	8·0
n	386	147	405	199

find that there are significantly fewer non- and light book readers among the
'in sets but not for English' group as compared with the other three groups,
and this difference is significant at 0·5% level of probability for boys and for
girls taken separately, and at 0·1% level if both sexes are combined. Interpretation of this finding is somewhat hazardous, but we can perhaps
speculate that the retention of mixed ability teaching for English in a
situation where there is setting for other subjects may imply a particularly
strong commitment to this form of organization on the part of the English
teaching staff. It is evident however that at this age unstreamed classes as
such do not come particularly well out of any comparisons that one makes.
Taking the 12+ and the 14+ tables together we should perhaps say that they
provide some indication of an association in the secondary school between
amount of book reading and mixed ability teaching for English, but that the
evidence on this point cannot be regarded as conclusive.

Structured versus integrated timetables in the primary schools

Another school variable which proved to be significant related to the structuring of the timetable at 10+. In the school questionnaire (see Appendix V(a)) primary schools were asked to say, in question 1, whether the timetable for their 10+ pupils was 'structured according to the usual subject divisions', 'fully integrated' or 'partly integrated and partly structured according to the usual subject divisions'. The relevant figures for book reading are shown in Table 41.

Table 41   Type of book reader as percentage of 10+ children subjected to different types of timetabling

(a) Boys

Type of book reader	Structured	Integrated	Partly structured, partly integrated
Non-Light	13·3	8·0	16·7
(1—2/month) Moderate	39·3	48·3	39·3
(3—4/month) Heavy	27·2	35·6	27·6
(5+/month)	20·2	8·0	16·4
n	173	87	1142

(b) Girls

Type of book reader	Structured	Integrated	Partly structured, partly integrated
Non-Light	8·4	7·7	9·7
(1—2/month) Moderate	40·3	37·4	35·2
(3—4/month) Heavy	30·5	41·8	29·6
(5+/month)	20·8	13·2	25·5
n	154	91	1100

As can be seen from this table only a few of the schools followed a fully integrated timetable; nevertheless in these schools there were fewer non-book-readers, and this difference, though not significant for girls, was significant for boys at the 5·0% level of probability, and for both sexes taken together at the 2·5% level. The interest of this finding is that it tends to refute the claim sometimes made that more informal methods of teaching in the primary school are associated with lower levels of literacy and reduced emphasis on the role of books.

The provision of class libraries in secondary schools

There are two further school variables which deserve mention, both relevant to the secondary schools only. Among our primary schools the overwhelming majority provided class libraries for the 10+ age group, and whether or not they had a separate school library as well did not prove to be a significant differentiator in regard to amount of book reading. Among the 188 secondary schools all but four had a school library available for use by the 12+ age group, and all but three had a school library available for use by the 14+ age group. The groups which it is worthwhile to compare in regard to amount of book reading are therefore those schools which relied on the school library alone, and those which in addition provided class libraries for some or all of their 12+ and/or 14+ pupils. The two age groups need to be treated separately since the provision of class libraries was sometimes for the 12+ group only, sometimes for the 14+ group only, and sometimes for both. It should be added that the situation was complicated by the fact that in some schools a

Table 42   Type of book reader as percentage of 12+ age group by two types of library provision

(a) Boys

Type of book reader	School library only	School & class libraries
Non-	28·7	38·2
Light (1−2/month)	34·5	32·5
Moderate (3−4/month)	23·8	20·0
Heavy (5+/month)	12·9	9·3
n	634	636

(b) Girls

Non-	24·0	21·7
Light (1−2/month)	28·8	37·8
Moderate (3−4/month)	30·4	28·8
Heavy (5+/month)	16·8	11·7
n	621	590

class library was provided only for some classes in the age group in question and not for all classes. The relevant figures for amount of book reading are shown in Table 42 for the 12+ age group. In this case if we compare non-book-readers and light book readers on the one hand against moderate and heavy book readers on the other, we find that there are significantly fewer non- and light book readers in the 'school library only' category, the difference being significant at the 0·5% level for boys, at the 2·5% level for girls and at the 0·1% level if both sexes are taken together.

Similar figures for the 14+ age group are shown in Table 43.

Table 43   Type of book reader as percentage of 14+ age group by two types of library provision

(a) Boys

Type of book reader	School library only	School & class libraries
Non-	38·2	41·3
Light (1−2/month)	28·9	29·7
Moderate (3−4/month)	21·7	20·8
Heavy (5+/month)	11·1	8·2
n	667	583

(b) Girls

Non-	27·2	36·7
Light (1−2/month)	28·1	37·7
Moderate (3−4/month)	25·3	17·6
Heavy (5+/month)	19·4	8·0
n	545	586

Here, too, if we compare non- and light book readers on the one hand against moderate and heavy book readers on the other, we find that there are fewer non- and light book readers in the 'school library only' category; but this time the difference is not statistically significant for boys, and is significant at the 0·1% level for girls, and also at the 0·1% level if both sexes are taken together. This finding (that there is less book reading in schools which provide class libraries to supplement the school library) was contrary to our expectation, and must inevitably call into question the suggestion made in our Interim Report that secondary schools ought to provide class libraries that are available for borrowing at least during English lessons.

This recommendation arose primarily out of impressions formed during our visits to schools for follow-up interviews (see Chapter 4); and it may be that the composition of our sub-sample of schools for this purpose made it untypical, and led us to underestimate the amount that can be achieved in the secondary school by a school library which is well housed, suitably stocked, and administered in an enlightened way by trained and qualified librarians or teacher-librarians. It must be said, however, that our visits certainly gave us ground for believing that there are a number of secondary schools where the school library provision leaves much to be desired; and we still hesitate to accept the findings from Tables 42 and 43 straightforwardly at their face value.

In the first place it must be remembered that the data in these tables are contaminated to a certain (though probably slight) extent because the figures for the columns headed 'school and class libraries' include some schools which in fact provided class libraries for only a few of their classes, other classes in the age range being dependent wholly on the school library. In the second place it is natural to ask whether the schools which provided class libraries did so as a compensation for the recognized inadequacy of the school library. Unfortunately the information available on this point from the school questionnaires was not very satisfactory. Schools were asked to answer a question (see Question 5 in Appendix V(b)) about the accommodation in which the school library was housed, indicating whether it was 'in a room designed specially for the purpose', 'in a room adapted for the purpose but adequate', or 'in a room adapted for the purpose but inadequate'. With the benefit of hindsight we can see that it would have been better to ask a question about the overall adequacy of the library to the needs of the school; and in fact some schools did indicate their dissatisfaction with some features of their school library either as a footnote to their answer about library accommodation or as a response to the open-ended question about library use (question 7), which followed.

Some schools thus pointed out that, although specially designed, the library was in fact badly designed for its purpose, or that, while originally suitable for the school when it first opened, numbers in the school had subsequently grown so much beyond the original expectation that the library was now inadequate; others mentioned the inadequacy of the book stock for the numbers in the school, or the fact that, owing to an increase in number of pupils, the library now had to be used as a classroom. All in all there was reason to believe that some of the 88 schools which provided class libraries in addition to the school library at 12+ did so in part at least because of their dissatisfaction with the school library, since 21 of them mentioned that the school library was either inadequately housed or inadequately stocked; however not too much weight can be placed on this, since out of the 89 schools which relied solely on the school library for this age group 13 also mentioned similar inadequacies in their school library.

The situation in regard to 14+ pupils was not very dissimilar since for this age group 16 out of 84 schools providing both a school library and class libraries mentioned inadequacies in the school library, while 15 out of 87 schools relying on the school library alone also mentioned inadequacies in it. Thirdly we need to take into account the possibility that the schools which had taken the decision to supplement their school library by the provision of class libraries had done so because they were aware that (for a variety of reasons, including perhaps the social background and ability level of their pupils) there was a particularly urgent need to bring books to them as directly as possible and to make a special effort to overcome a reluctance to read among some of their pupils; in this case the provision of class libraries would be not a contributory cause of the relatively low amount of book reading in the school, but a response on the part of the school to this situation and a commendable attempt to counter it. Perhaps our rather extended discussion of this point can now be seen as a demonstration of the difficulties attendant upon any attempt to explore such matters by means of a written questionnaire. What we can presumably say with fair confidence is that the relative merit of the two types of provision (school library alone versus school library plus class libraries) remains an open question and that, on the whole, class libraries in the secondary schools were not at the time of our survey fulfilling satisfactorily the purpose for which they were presumably intended.

Type of book provision in English lessons

The last school variable which we shall mention related to the approach to English teaching practised within the secondary schools, and in particular to differing types of book provision for use in English lessons. In question 1 of the Secondary School Questionnaire (see Appendix V(b)) the school was asked to tick any of the following statements which applied to the school's English teaching with (a) 12+ and (b) 14+ pupils:

A Class sets of coursebooks or comprehension books are used.
B Class sets of English thematic or topic-based anthologies are used.
C Class sets of novels, short stories or other prose books are used.
D Small sets (say 5–10 copies) of novels, short stories or other prose books are used within the class.
E A class library of miscellaneous titles is provided for pupils to read.

F   The school provides a reading list of titles which pupils are expected
to obtain from sources outside the classroom (e.g. school library,
public library).

We tried three different ways of analysing the answers to this question, but
the only one to differentiate consistently in regard to amount of book
reading was the categorization of schools into two groups: the vast majority,
which ticked either A or B or both and those — relatively few in number —
which ticked neither A nor B. The interesting feature to emerge was that the
amount of voluntary book reading was lower (both at 12+ and at 14+) in the
schools that used class sets of either course books, comprehension books or
thematic anthologies. The relevant figures are shown for the 12+ group in
Table 44.

Table 44   Type of book reader as percentage of 12+ age group by
two types of book provision for English lessons

(a) Boys

Type of book reader	Course books, comprehension books, or thematic anthologies	
	In use	Not in use
Non-	34·0	26·9
Light (1–2/month)	33·6	36·2
Moderate (3–4/month)	21·2	24·1
Heavy (5+/month)	11·2	12·8
n	1184	141

(b) Girls

	In use	Not in use
Non-	24·4	16·6
Light (1–2/month)	34·4	28·9
Moderate (3–4/month)	28·5	33·6
Heavy (5+/month)	12·6	20·9
n	1023	211

We find from this table that there is a higher proportion of non- and light
book readers in the schools which use course books, comprehension books
or thematic anthologies, and while the difference is not statistically significant

for boys on their own, it is significant at the 0·1% level of probability for girls, and at the 0·1% level for both sexes taken together.

Similar figures for the 14+ group are shown in Table 45.

Table 45   Type of book reader as percentage of 14+ age group by two types of book provision for English lessons

(a) Boys

Type of book reader	Course books, comprehension books, or thematic anthologies	
	In use	Not in use
Non-	40·3	35·6
Light (1−2/month)	30·1	25·4
Moderate (3−4/month)	20·7	25·4
Heavy (5+/month)	8·9	13·6
n	1167	118

(b) Girls

Non-	34·8	18·4
Light (1−2/month)	31·9	38·5
Moderate (3−4/month)	20·8	23·0
Heavy (5+/month)	12·5	20·1
n	979	174

At this age again there is a higher proportion of non- and light book readers in the schools which use course books, comprehension books or thematic anthologies, and this time the difference is significant at the 5·0% level of probability for boys, at the 2·5% level for girls, and at the 0·1% level for both sexes taken together.

How are we to interpret this finding? We must be clear that what is in question is a difference in emphasis rather than a clear-cut polarization, since almost all schools, whichever of our two groups they fell into in regard to course books, comprehension books and thematic anthologies, also made use of one or more of the other four categories under question 1 mentioned above. We would suggest, however, that the use of course books, comprehension books or thematic anthologies implies the investment of a considerable amount of time and energy in the study of extracts in English lessons. We encountered English teaching of this kind during our follow-up visits, and in some cases we noted that, good or even enlightened though it might be in its own way, it could be curiously insulated, cut off from and indifferent to the pupils' reading (or lack of reading) outside English lessons. The implication for the English teacher would seem to be that, if the development of wide independent reading is a central or important goal of English teaching (and surely this should be axiomatic), then this objective is most effectively attained by a concentration in English lessons upon the reading of 'real' books (novels, stories and other complete prose books) rather than by the study of extracts, whether these be embedded in the traditional course book or comprehension book or in the more recently fashionable thematic anthology.

Difficulties associated with the investigation of school variables

If we review now the analysis we have been able to make in the preceding pages of the influence of school variables, we can perhaps see that, while we have been able to demonstrate an association between amount of book reading and certain school characteristics (most notably type of school and streaming), the total picture presented remains regrettably fragmentary — especially when we recall the very considerable amount of data which we amassed from the two school questionnaires. There are in any case within our data strong indications of considerable variation in amount of reading between schools of the same type, and even if we accept that to some extent these may have been associated with differences in the social composition of the schools' intake, we cannot claim to have gone as far as we would have wished in accounting for these differences. Why has this been so? It could be suggested, of course, quite bluntly that our school questionnaires were badly designed and proved to be inefficient instruments for the purposes for which they were intended. Although we tried out our schools questionnaires before-hand with a number of schools and made many modifications to them, it is true that in retrospect we can now see a number of ways in which they might have been improved.

We would argue, however, that this is only a small part of the explanation, and that the true reason for our relative failure in this part of our investigation is the fact that the features of school life which are most important in regard to reading are singularly resistant to probing by means of a written questionnaire. There are several reasons for this. In the first place it is very difficult to frame questions in such a way that they do not contain within their wording certain indications as to which answer would be most in accordance with the current 'conventional wisdom' about school organization, approaches and methods of teaching. Thus, although we are convinced that the head-teachers and heads of department who completed our questionnaire did their very best to be honest in their replies, we suspect that in certain respects a number of them tended to present a picture of their school as they would like it to be rather than as it actually was. In the second place (and this seems far more important), we would argue that those aspects of a school which matter most in the context of reading are, by their very nature, likely to slip through the relatively coarse mesh of a written question-naire, however skilfully this has been designed. Thus, although we can obtain information by this means about the accommodation in which a school library is housed, about the size of its book stock, and about the times of its opening or the arrangements under which books can be borrowed, we cannot find out anything about the far more important issue of how recent and attractive are the books on the shelves or how far they are suited to the needs and abilities of the pupils who use them. Similarly we can obtain information about whether or not class libraries are provided, but we cannot find out anything about the quality and kind of the books which are included in these collections. Yet our subsequent follow-up visits to a sub-sample of schools suggested strongly that it is often the kind, quality and suitability of the books provided that is one of two crucially vital factors.

Thus — to anticipate briefly points that will be made more fully in Chapter 4 — we often felt that primary schools, in their class libraries, laid too exclusive an emphasis on the book as a source of information, spending much money on reference books and on expensive non-fiction, but being content with a fiction collection that was dated, dowdy and rather vapid. By contrast, some of the secondary schools we visited seemed to be setting their sights rather too high on the kind of fiction they included in the school library and in their class libraries, stressing above all fiction that was good by adult standards and failing to cater for the need some of their pupils evidently felt for reading which was relatively simple, immature and thin in quality. Again we were unable in our written questionnaire to find any satisfactory way of gauging the equally vital factor of the human quality of the teachers and librarians who mediated between the book stock and the pupils who might use it — their insight into children's needs and stages of development, the warmth of the personal relations they formed with their pupils, the tact, knowledge and appropriateness of the guidance they provided, the strength of their own enthusiasm for books and their devotion to the task of developing the reading progress of their children. Yet here again, in our visits to schools, we repeatedly formed the impression that it was the presence of such qualities as these in individual teachers or librarians that accounted above all for the success of a school in developing its pupils' voluntary reading. For some of the most important issues raised by the written questionnaire we are forced therefore to rely in the end upon the relatively subjective evidence which is set out in Chapter 4.

The relative importance of the different variables (two computer programmes)

One final section now completes our statistical treatment of the question-naire survey as far as amount of book reading is concerned. In this section so far we have been able to demonstrate an association between amount of book reading and a considerable number of variables associated essentially with the child and the home and a more limited group of variables associated with the school. What we lack is any measure of the relative importance of those variables (of either type) which have been shown to be relevant. In order to gain some insight into this we used two different computer programmes, AID (Automatic Interaction Detector) — described by Sonquist and Morgan in *The Distribution of Interaction Effects* — and the General Linear Hypothesis from the BMD package (a biomedical programme developed at the University of California and described by Scheffe in *The Analysis of Variance*, Wiley, 1959). Both programmes, given a dependent variable (in our case the number of books read by each child during the month of the survey) and a number of independent variables (in our case such factors as ability and attainment rating, social class, etc.), pick out the best set of predictors from these variables. However because each programme operates by different criteria of 'best', they are liable to produce different configurations.

We look first at AID which operates in the following way. Suppose any one of the independent variables can take four values: A, B, C or D. Then the population can be split into two groups on the basis of this variable in seven different ways, as follows:

A	B or C or D
B	A or C or D
C	A or B or D
D	A or B or C
A or B	C or D
A or C	B or D
A or D	B or C

If the order of the values must be preserved, then only three different divisions are possible:

A	B or C or D
A or B	C or D
A or B or C	D

AID considers all independent variables in turn, and all possible divisions for each variable (the user can specify whether or not the order of the variable values must be preserved), and each time calculates the mean and sum of squares for the two resultant groups. That division for which the total sum of squares (or variance) is a minimum is then selected and the population is split into two groups on this basis. These two groups are in turn divided by the same procedure in respect to another variable, and the process continues until none of the groups can be divided further. A group may be regarded as indivisible for any of the following reasons:

a   Further subdivision would produce groups containing fewer than a specified minimum number of cases.
b   The best division fails to reduce the variance by a specified minimum.
c   The group contains less than a specified minimum variance.

We used the AID programme for each of our three age groups, and the following points are relevant to its use with our data. First, all variables, both home and school, were included in the exercise regardless of whether or not the tables had suggested that they were relevant to amount of reading. The reason for this was that our tables merely pick out trends for the whole sample, and it was thought possible that when interaction effects were considered other trends might become apparent. Secondly the analysis requires that all unknown values of variable are excluded. Consequently the sample considered for each age group embraces only those children who answered all the relevant questions, so that for every age group the n is smaller than that for most of the tables shown earlier in this chapter. Thirdly, because we contemplated using the BMD programme also, ability and attainment grading E — a small group — was omitted for the sake of consistency between the two programmes. (The exclusion of this group was recommended for the BMD programme because its inclusion would have resulted in too many empty cells.)

For the 10+ group the following independent variables were fed into the AID programme:

Sex of child
Social class of child's father
Ability and attainment rating
School type (junior/junior-with-infants)
Emphasis on teaching methods (see question 7 in Appendix V(a))
Timetable organization of school (structured/integrated/a mixture)
Organization of classes (streamed/mixed ability/vertical grouping)
Hours per week spent in teacher reading stories aloud
Whether books can/cannot be taken home from school library
Whether parents read/do not read library books
Presence/absence of quality newspapers among those taken by family
Family size

Child's attitude to school, as rated by teachers
Expressed liking for school

The outcome of the AID analysis is shown diagrammatically in Table 46.

Table 46   Diagrammatic representation of AID analysis for 10+ age group

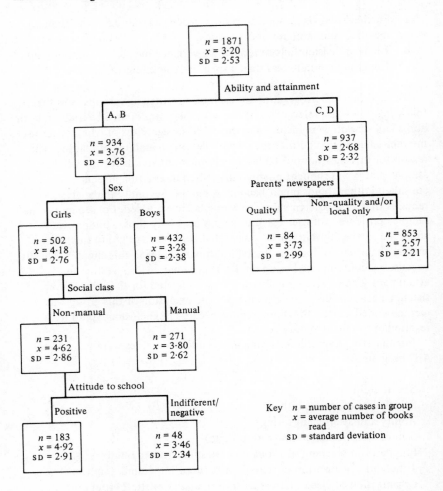

From Table 46 we see that at 10+ the best single predictor of amount of reading is ability and attainment. We then find that for children graded A or B the next most important factor is sex, but for children graded C or D it is the parents' newspaper. Then, following through to the end of the analysis, we see that the highest reading group found by the programme consists of girls of ability and attainment A or B whose fathers are in non-manual occupations and who have a positive attitude to school. The lowest reading group on the other hand are children of ability and attainment C or D whose parents take non-quality and/or local newspapers only.

We turn next to the AID analysis for the 12+ age group for which Table 47 shows a diagrammatic representation. The variables fed into the programme for this group were:

Sex
Social class of father
School type
Emphasis on teaching methods in English (see question 2 in Appendix
    V(b))
Expressed liking for English lessons
Expressed liking for school
Organization of school (streams/sets/mixed ability)
School on split site or on single campus
School library accommodation adequate/inadequate
Access to school library/class libraries/both
Use/non-use of course books, comprehension books or thematic
    anthologies in English lessons
Age at which child expects to leave school
Whether parents read/do not read library books
Presence/absence of quality newspapers among those taken by family
Family size
Child's attitude to school, as rated by teachers
Ability and attainment rating
Sex of school (single-sex/mixed)

From Table 47 we see for the 12+ age group the best single predictor of amount of reading is again ability and attainment, though this time the sub-division is into grade A on the one hand and grades B, C and D on the other. This time the highest reading group consists of children (both sexes) who are of ability and attainment A, who like school very much or quite a lot, come from small families (not more than one sibling) and attend schools in which the classes are either streamed or mixed ability. The lowest reading group are — rather surprisingly — children also of ability and attainment A, but in this case those who do not like school, are attending secondary modern or comprehensive schools, and have fathers who are in a manual occupation.

For the 14+ age group the same list of variables was fed into the AID analysis as for the 12+ group. Table 48 shows a diagrammatic representation of the analysis for this age group. Here we see that the most important single

Table 47 Diagrammatic representation of AID analysis for 12+ age group

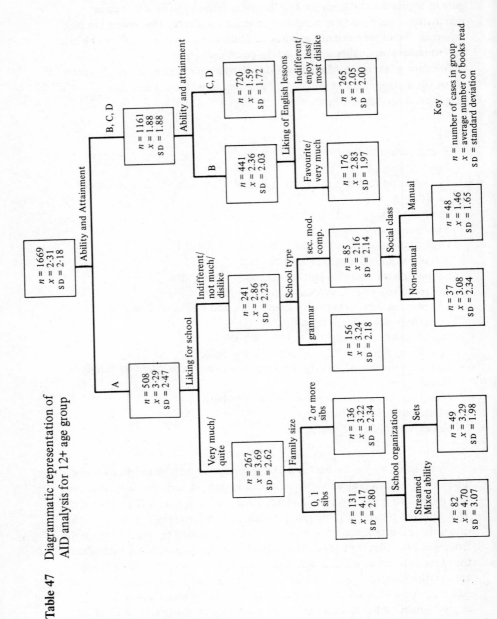

Key

n = number of cases in group
x = average number of books read
s D = standard deviation

variable is the age at which the child expects to leave school. (Presumably at 12+ this is an issue on which the child is less likely to have made up his or her mind.) The highest reading group at this age were those who liked English lessons and expected to stay on at school to age 18. The lowest reading group were children of ability and attainment grading C or D who expected to leave school at ages 15, 16 or 17.

The disadvantage of the AID programme from the point of view of our own data is that, because some of our independent variables are interrelated, this form of analysis does not necessarily produce the best overall set of predictors. Thus, once a division has been made using a particular variable, those of the remaining variables which are highly correlated with it will be 'weakened', and this may in the long term result in unsatisfactory divisions

Table 48   Diagrammatic representation of AID analysis for 14+ age group

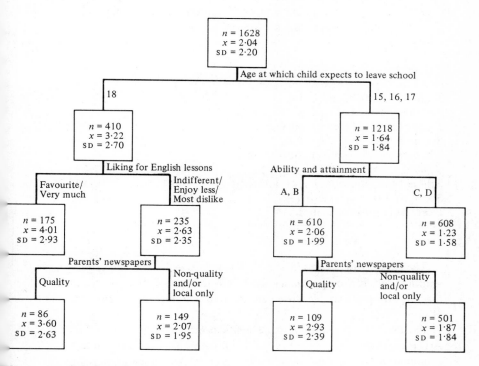

Key n = number of cases in group
       x = average number of books read
       SD = standard deviation

at later stages of the analysis. For this reason we also tried out the General
Linear Hypothesis programme for each age group. This is rather simpler
in concept and fits a model of the form

$$P = \mu_0 + \mu_1 + \mu_2 + \mu_3 + \ldots \mu_n + \text{error}$$

where P is the predicted variable (in our case number of books read); μ_0 is
the average number of books read; and $\mu_1, \mu_2 \ldots \mu_n$ are contributions made
by the predicting variables. For example, if we take a variable V which takes
four values A, B, C or D, then a quantity μ_a, μ_b, μ_c or μ_d will be added into
the total depending on whether the child takes value A, B, C or D for that
variable.

The same fourteen variables that were fed into the AID programme were
given to this programme for the 10+ age group, and different combinations
of variables were tried to give the best model. The group of variables which,
taken together, constituted the model giving the best prediction is shown in
Table 49.

Table 49   Independent variables specified by General Linear Hypothesis
programme as giving, in combination, the best prediction of
amount of reading for the 10+ age group

Variable	Degrees of freedom	F-ratio
Ability and attainment rating	3	15·25
Presence/absence of quality newspapers among those taken by the family	2	5·25
Sex of child	1	12·78
Whether parents read/do not read library books	2	5·49
School type (junior/junior-with-infants)	1	10·10
Social class of child's father	1	14·73
Expressed liking for school	4	7·64

Error = 1887   Mean square = 5·82

The F value for the model was 9·46 which is well above the 0·1%
significance value of approximately 2·7 for this model; and this indicates
that the group of variables listed are undoubtedly highly relevant to amount
of book reading.

For the 12+ age group the same eighteen variables that were fed into the
AID programme were given to the GLH programme, and again different
combinations of variables were tried to give the best model. The group of
variables which, taken together, constituted the model giving the best
prediction for this age group is shown in Table 50.

Table 50 Independent variables specified by General Linear Hypothesis programme as giving, in combination, the best prediction of amount of reading for 12+ age group

Variable	Degrees of freedom	F-ratio
Ability and attainment rating	3	13·91
Sex of child	1	23·84
Whether parents read/do not read library books	2	6·11
School type	2	17·64
Social class of child's father	1	5·89
Expressed liking for school	4	12·00

Error = 1904   Mean square = 4·11

The F value for the model was 12·84 which is well above the 0·1% significance value of approximately 2·7 for this model; and this again indicates that the group of variables listed are undoubtedly highly relevant to amount of book reading.

The same twenty variables that were fed into the AID programme were given to the GLH programme for the 14+ age group, and different combinations of variables were tried to give the best model. The group of variables which, taken together, constituted the model giving the best prediction is shown in Table 51.

Table 51 Independent variables specified by General Linear Hypothesis programme as giving, in combination, the best prediction of amount of reading for 14+ age group

Variable	Degrees of freedom	F-ratio
Quality of newspaper taken/not taken by family	2	58·21
Access to school library/class library/both	2	22·20
Degree of liking for English lessons	4	12·87
Attitude to school, as assessed by school	2	35·16
Emphasis on different methods of English teaching	3	8·73
Sex	1	4·13
Organization of school classes (streamed/ mixed ability/sets)	3	7·56
School on single campus/divided site	1	5·45

Error = 2117   Mean square = 4·2

The *F* value for the model was 18·95 which is well above the 0·1 significance value of about 2·5 for this model; and this indicates that the group of variables listed are undoubtedly highly relevant to amount of book reading.

It will be seen that this programme carries the analysis of the relative importance of the different independent variables rather further than did the AID programme for this age group, and enables us to say that the highest amount of book reading among the 14+ children can be expected to arise in the case of girls whose family take quality newspaper(s), who like their English lessons, are assessed as having a favourable attitude to their school, and attend a school on a single campus where the classes are un-streamed, where the emphasis in English teaching falls upon reading from a wide selection of books but at the same time a small number are reserved for class discussion and reading, and where they have access to a school library only.

C – THE QUALITATIVE FINDINGS

Diversity of book reading

When we turn to the kinds of book read by our sample, the most important feature to mention is the extraordinary diversity of book reading under-taken by these children. Thus out of our achieved sample of 7839 children 25·4% had read no book during the previous month; the remaining 74·6% made up a total of 5846 book-reading children and these children proved to have read no fewer than 7557 separate and different books according to the titles mentioned in their questionnaires. Of course, these titles included some which had been read by a number of children and we were able to list and follow separately 246 titles which had been read by ten or more children during the month. There were however a very considerable number of titles which had been read by one, two or three children only. Individual titles ranged in difficulty from *Silly Simon* by Molly Clarke to *The Return of the Native* by Thomas Hardy, and in maturity from *Sam Pig Goes to Market* by Alison Uttley to *Such Darling Dodos* by Angus Wilson and *Women in Love* by D. H. Lawrence; while the spread of interests revealed embraced on the one hand *Stamps* (a Ladybird book) and *Show Jumping* by Pat Smythe, on the other *Silent Spring* by Rachel Carson and *The Social Psychology of Industry* by J. A. C. Brown.

A fuller sense of the diversity we encountered can perhaps be conveyed by mentioning some of the more unusual titles for each age group. Thus the narrative reading of the 10+ children encompassed at one end of the spectrum Dr. Seuss's witty primer *The Cat in the Hat* and P. Krasilowsky's charming picture-story book *The Cow Who Fell in the Canal*, at the other *The Little*

Grey Men by B. B. and *Little Lord Fauntleroy* by F. H. Burnett; while there was also the occasional 10+ poetry reader who mentioned such books as *Old Possum's Book of Practical Cats* by T. S. Eliot and *A Book of Nonsense* by Edward Lear. The 12+ group was remarkable for the range of its non-narrative titles; these included, for example, *Better Table Tennis*, *Cheeses of the World*, *Hair Care*, *Haydn* by Rosemary Hughes, *The Hidden Persuaders* by Vance Packard, and *Ventriloquism for Beginners*. At this age, too, some surprisingly mature fiction was read — for example, Gogol's *Dead Souls* and Mark Twain's *Pudd'nhead Wilson*. At 14+ the non-narrative range was also wide, stretching from *Home-made Beer and Wines* to Machiavelli's *The Prince* and Pevsner's *South Lancashire*; while the fiction read at this age included Trollope's *Barchester Towers*, Ivy Compton Burnett's *Brothers and Sisters*, Zola's *Germinal*, Conrad's *Lord Jim* and *Nostromo*, Mailer's *The Naked and the Dead*, E. M. Forster's *A Passage to India*, Camus' *The Plague* and Henry Miller's *Tropic of Capricorn*.

Perhaps we should not omit mentioning also the two 14+ readers who had engaged during the month with (respectively) *Blake's Complete Writings* and *The Complete Works of Edgar Allan Poe*. In part, no doubt, this enormous range in children's book reading reflects the vast proliferation of books specially published for children, often in attractive format, and readily available to them through school or public libraries or paperback bookshops; it is noteworthy that the 1969 edition of *Children's Books in Print* listed over 14 000 books specially published for children and actually in print in that year. As the titles listed above make clear, however, the older age ranges also reported reading a great many books that were adult books and not children's books. It seems likely that the diverse nature of children's book reading these days has also been influenced by the increasing tendency of both primary and secondary schools to provide for their classes either a library reading list or a class library made up of individual copies of assorted titles. (In this respect school practice in the 1970's contrasts with that reported by Jenkinson in 1940, when the English syllabus in senior and secondary schools normally provided its reading in the form of a class set, all of the same book.) However, it seemed clear (and our later interviews tended to confirm this impression) that children greatly value the opportunity given to them by book reading to exercise their own choice and to pursue highly individual interests and tastes through books. This opportunity for individual choice is one advantage which the book has over the television programme, since at any one time television offers at most the choice between three channels, and the programmes available on these channels tend in any case to converge towards a common denominator of appeal. The great and continuing strength of the book in its competition with the audio-visual media is, in fact, its unrivalled ability to give the individual the chance to follow his own particular bent at any one particular time, to engage actively rather than passively with the medium, to take the printed word at his own pace, to return to and re-read a particular passage or even to skip if the mood takes him. The opportunity for self-discovery and self-realization opened up by books seems to us an integral and central component in any conception of education which takes personal growth as its goal.

Classification of books into seven categories

To return to our questionnaires, it will be clear that the attempt to handle such a diverse array of individual book titles inevitably presented our research team with an almost Herculean task of classification. In a certain number of cases we were led to conclude that the title had been obligingly 'made up' by a well-intentioned child out of a desire to please. Discounting these cases, however, it was natural that some of the titles should have been either garbled or misremembered, and we were not always in a position to correct the errors which had crept into reports of either titles or authors. (Some of the errors in regard to authors which we were able to correct were curious enough to be worth recording. We were able to put right, for instance, the mistaken belief of various children that *Wuthering Heights* had been written by H. G. Wells, *The Thirty-Nine Steps* by John Bunyan, *Tom Sawyer* by R. L. Stevenson, *The Wind in the Willows* by Edith Nesbit, and *Stig of the Dump* by C. S. Lewis. Enid Blyton's industry, remarkable enough in all conscience, was overestimated by some children who credited her with responsibility for *Treasure Island*, *King Solomon's Mines* and *The Bible*. Perhaps the most bizarre mis-attribution of all, however, was made by the child who claimed to have read — this in days long before any TV vogue for the Pallisers — *Pip the Pixie* by Anthony Trollope. On the whole we learned from experience that it was advisable to trust titles rather than authors in a good many instances. Not, of course, that titles could be regarded in any sense as sacrosanct; thus we thought it probable, after appropriate research, that the girl who said she had very much enjoyed Enid Blyton's *The Naughtiest Girl in the Monastery* was really thinking of the same author's *The Naughtiest Girl is a Monitor!*) For three months we pursued as many titles as we could, with the aid of bibliographies, catalogues and helpful children's librarians, trying to identify doubtful cases, and gain as much information as we could about titles that were not known to us. In the end we had to discard as unclassifiable a total of 855 titles, which made up 11·3% of the total.

From the beginning we decided to set our face against the kind of classification by topic, setting or subject matter used in many previous studies of children's reading. Jenkinson, for instance, categorized his sample's books under the headings 'school stories', 'detective stories', 'stories of home life', 'adventure stories', 'love stories', 'historical stories' and 'technical'.

Except in the case of books written to a standard formula for the commercial market, the boundaries between such categories are hard to establish at all unambiguously, and the rationale for such classification is so uncertain that there is some doubt as to what benefit it achieves. Thus R. L. Stevenson's *Treasure Island* and Enid Blyton's *Five on a Treasure Island* would presumably fall within the same category, yet a cursory reading of the two books is enough to establish that the differences between them are in every way far more significant than the fact that they can both be termed 'adventure stories'.

We started instead to develop our own mode of classifying, aiming at a system which arose naturally out of the data in front of us but which was at the same time simple enough to be operated effectively over a vast range of titles, not all of which we were able actually to handle and examine. The first split which demanded to be made was between narrative and non-narrative. Our category of 'narrative' consisted predominantly of fiction, but we also included biographies, autobiographies and memoirs, largely on the grounds that whether a story is true or invented seems to make little difference to a child's motives for reading it or to the kinds of satisfaction to be taken from it. (Compare from this point of view *The Dam Busters* by Paul Brickhill and *The Wooden Horse* by Eric Williams with *The Cruel Sea* by Nicholas Monsarrat and *Where Eagles Dare* by Alistair Maclean.) Except for titles about which we had not enough information, the only ones which resisted categorization into either narrative or non-narrative were the annuals such as *Beano Annual* or *Blue Peter Annual*. However, these formed an insignificant proportion of the whole, since − although there was a perceptible number of listings for them at 10+ − this dwindled rapidly at 12+ and had vanished almost entirely at 14+.

The next step was to subdivide our narrative category into books written specifically for children (juvenile narrative) and those intended originally for adults (adult narrative). There were a few difficult borderline cases here, of a kind exemplified by our uneasy decision that *Tom Sawyer* was juvenile narrative while *Huckleberry Finn* was adult narrative. We also acquired an uncomfortable awareness that, although a certain number of books from the past (for example, Alexandre Dumas' *The Three Musketeers*) were written in the first instance mainly for adults they have by now been largely, if not exclusively, appropriated by a juvenile readership. Nevertheless, despite certain anomalies, we felt satisfied that this breakdown into juvenile narrative and adult narrative was a meaningful one.

The final step was to make a further split within our two narrative categories, this time into 'quality' and 'non-quality'. Our decision to incorporate a discrimination of this kind followed careful study of a large number of juvenile narrative books, as a result of which it became evident that such books polarize themselves into two fairly distinct groups − on the one hand those whose production has been essentially a commercial operation, a matter of catering for a market; and on the other hand those in which the involvement of the writer with his subject matter and his audience has been such as to generate a texture of imaginative experience which rises above the merely routine and derivative. We were satisfied that the distinction we were making at this point was a real one, even though its application in given instances brought into play an element of subjective judgement. For this reason we would have liked ideally to draw upon a wider body of expert opinion than that commanded by the three members of the research team. Could a similar distinction be made within the adult narrative category? Here the borderline is admittedly less clear cut. Nevertheless, inspection of our lists certainly revealed a broadly similar polarization and we were encouraged to persist in our sub-categorization by the recollection that a judgement of this kind (to buy or not to buy?, to recommend or not to recommend?) has continually to be made by practising teachers as part of their day-to-day responsibilities. In the end, therefore, the question we were asking ourselves as we applied this quality/non-quality discrimination was roughly of the following kind: is this book one that we can imagine a responsible teacher justly recommending to pupils at a certain stage of development on the ground that they are likely to take from it some imaginative experience valuable to them at their own level, over and above the mere practice of reading skills? We are conscious that the labels 'quality' and 'non-quality' are not really satisfactory, in that they may easily suggest a narrow and exclusive set of standards quite other than those we actually applied. We have therefore made public our criteria by listing in alphabetical order in Appendix VI all the authors of the books assigned by us to the two 'quality' categories (see pp. 330–333).

It should be added that there remained one fairly small group of narrative books which could not be classified under either the juvenile/adult or the quality/non-quality dichotomy. These were the ones we had to be content to call 'fairy tales, myths and legends' — re-tellings sometimes by known writers (and ranging in that case from Enid Blyton's flat-footed versions of Brer Brbbit to Roger Lancelyn Green's sensitive re-working of the Arthurian romances) but often by writers unspecified. They were certainly narrative but beyond that they remained obstinately miscellaneous.

In the end, then, we had seven workable categories, and Table 52 shows the percentage representation of each of these categories in the total list of 7557 titles.

Amount of book reading by categories

Table 53 shows the amount of book reading for the sample as a whole (all ages combined) subdivided into these same categories.

Table 52   Categories of book as percentage of all book titles listed

Type of Book	% of total
Juvenile narrative	
quality	6·6
non-quality	36·2
Adult narrative	
quality	6·9
non-quality	16·5
Fairy tales, myths and legends	2·2
Annuals	0·8
Non-narrative	19·5
Unclassified	11·3

Table 53   Categories of book as percentage of all book reading (age groups combined)

Type of Book	% of all book reading		
	Boys	Girls	Both sexes
Juvenile narrative			
quality	12·8	20·6	17·0
non-quality	26·6	39·6	33·4
Adult narrative			
quality	12·4	10·5	11·4
non-quality	13·0	11·2	12·1
Fairy tales, myths and legends	2·7	3·5	3·1
Annuals	1·8	1·0	1·3
Non-narrative	23·1	6·9	14·5
Unclassified	7·6	6·8	7·2

If we compare Table 52 with Table 53, it is some consolation to find that although 11·3% of the total number of book titles proved unclassifiable, this category accounts for no more than 7·2% of the total number of book-mentions. Table 53 also makes unmistakably clear the relatively small part played by non-narrative in children's book reading (no more than 14·5% of our sample's book reading as a whole). It is clear that narrative (predominantly though not exclusively fiction) accounts for the overwhelming majority of children's book reading in this age range. Indeed, if we include the relatively small category of fairy tales, myths and legends, we can say that at least 77% of the reading of the sample consisted of narrative. It will be noticed, however, that much of this narrative reading is of little value by adult standards (over 45% of the sample's total book reading was judged to be non-quality narrative), and in this respect at least our findings are not very dissimilar from the conclusion reached by Jenkinson in 1940.

Table 54 enables us to study the same set of phenomena in greater detail, since it shows the percentage of book reading in each category broken down by both sex and age.

What is noticeable first of all from this table is that the very high proportion of narrative book reading already mentioned remains remarkably steady from 10+ through 12+ to 14+. There is however a difference between the sexes which is also remarkably consistent. Thus at each of the three age levels about two-thirds of the boys' reading consists of narrative books. For the girls, the proportion of narrative reading is invariably much higher, standing at more than four-fifths of the whole for each age level. Correspondingly there is also a very consistent and unvarying pattern in regard to the amount of non-narrative book reading. If we take both sexes combined, the non-narrative reading accounts for 14·4 per cent of the whole at 10+, 13·9 per cent at 12+ and 15·3 per cent at 14+. However, within this stable pattern there is also a very consistent tendency for girls to read remarkably little non-narrative, whereas boys read considerably more. Thus for each age range, non-narrative accounts for very nearly one-quarter of the total book reading of the boys, whereas for girls it is never more than one-twelfth. This difference was also commented on by J. J. Taylor in his study of the reading of 2000 pupils in two grammar schools and two secondary modern schools (Taylor, 1972, 1973 and 1974).

As far as narrative reading is concerned Table 54 shows a marked movement towards more adult books as the children grow older. This stands out more clearly in Table 55 where we have extracted the figures for juvenile narrative and adult narrative books, at the same time conflating the quality and non-quality subdivisions within each of these categories. Looking at Table 55 it is noticeable that at 14+ there is a sizeable minority (as much as one-quarter of the girls) who are still reading books written specially for children. At a time when the press tends to portray all teenagers as precociously sophisticated in their attitudes and behaviour, it is perhaps of some importance to note that their self-chosen reading shows a number of them to be still, even at 14 or 15, children at heart.

We can also, by extracting data from Table 54 in a slightly different way, examine the percentage of quality and non-quality narrative reading by children at different age levels. Thus in Table 56 we have conflated juvenile and adult narrative reading to give the two categories of quality narrative and non-quality narrative, and quality narrative is seen to form a higher

Table 54 Categories of book reading as a percentage of all book reading for each age-and-sex grouping

Book category	10+ Boys	Girls	12+ Boys	Girls	14+ Boys	Girls
Juvenile narrative 'quality'	15·2	22·5	15·2	25·9	6·1	10·8
Juvenile narrative 'non-quality'	37·8	51·5	26·6	43·0	8·6	14·7
Adult narrative 'quality'	5·6	2·6	10·9	9·1	25·2	25·9
Adult narrative 'non-quality'	3·3	1·6	13·9	8·3	27·6	31·5
Fairy tales, myths and legends	4·3	6·7	2·0	1·6	1·0	0·4
All narrative combined	66·2	84·9	68·6	87·9	68·5	83·3
Annuals	2·9	1·8	1·2	0·6	0·7	0·1
Non-narrative	22·8	7·3	23·4	5·2	23·3	8·2
Unclassified	8·0	6·1	6·9	6·4	7·6	8·5
n	3766	4403	2685	3110	2326	2528

(Note: in the above table n for each column represents the total number of book-mentions for the age-and-sex grouping concerned.)

Table 55 Narrative and non-narrative book reading as percentage of all book reading

Book category	10+ Boys	Girls	12+ Boys	Girls	14+ Boys	Girls
Juvenile narrative	53·0	74·0	41·8	68·9	14·7	25·5
Adult narrative	8·9	4·2	24·8	17·4	52·8	57·4

Table 56 Quality and non-quality book reading as percentage of all book reading

Type of narrative (juvenile and adult)	10+ Boys	Girls	12+ Boys	Girls	14+ Boys	Girls
Quality	20·8	25·1	26·1	35·0	31·3	36·7
Non-quality	41·1	53·1	40·5	51·3	36·2	46·2

proportion of total book reading as children grow older, though it should be remembered of course that the 14+ children are in general reading fewer books than the 10+ children. More than one interpretation of these figures is possible and it is not easy to decide at all confidently between them. It may be that at 10+ there is more undiscriminating reading which ranges around among different levels, and that as a result of this exploration some children at any rate begin to refine their tastes and choose books with more judgement. On the other hand it may be that the readers of non-quality books are the ones who discard the habit of reading with increasing age, and at 14+ become content to take their imaginative satisfactions solely from comics or television. (Another possibility is that we unwittingly applied more rigorous standards in categorizing the juvenile narrative books than in categorizing the adult narrative books, in which case the tendency would be an artefact created by our own procedures.) It should be said at once that the design of our survey does not permit really definitive answers to the questions raised here. The kinds of change which occur in children's reading over a period could only be traced with any confidence by a longitudinal study of the same individual children. Even from our own data, however, we can infer certain pointers as to the type of explanation which is most likely to be the true one, and we shall attempt to do this in the paragraphs which follow.

First we must note that, while Tables 54, 55 and 56 set out the variations with age of the proportions of the differing types of book read, they do not reveal the changes which take place in absolute terms. Thus if we take as our example non-narrative reading by boys, we can see (from Table 54) that as a proportion of the total number of books read this increased from 10+ to 12+; however, between these ages the total number of books read by boys declines, so that we cannot be sure whether or not there has been an actual increase in the number of non-narrative books read.

It is open to us, however, to present the same data in terms of the average number of books read per child during the month of the survey; and this we can see in Table 57, where each 10+ boy reads on average 0·61 non-narrative books per month, while each 12+ boy reads on average 0·47 non-narrative books. Thus in this case there has been an actual decline in the number of non-narrative books per head read by boys over these two age levels. In general this table makes clear the way in which the amount of reading of each type of book declines with increasing age. In these circumstances it is perhaps encouraging to note that, from 10+ through 12+ to 14+, the amount of quality narrative reading holds up rather better than the amount of non-quality narrative reading. The decline in the amount of reading of annuals and of fairy tales, myths and legends is only what we would expect, but in the light of the trends revealed in Table 57 the decline in absolute terms in the amount of non-narrative reading is more surprising, particularly in the case of boys. A possible explanation may be that the non-

Table 57 Average number of books of each type read by children in different sex and age groups

Book category	10+ Boys	10+ Girls	12+ Boys	12+ Girls	14+ Boys	14+ Girls
Quality narrative	0.56	0.82	0.52	0.87	0.56	0.79
Non-quality narrative	1.10	1.74	0.80	1.27	0.64	0.99
Fairy tales, myths and legends	0.12	0.22	0.04	0.04	0.02	0.01
Annuals	0.08	0.06	0.02	0.01	0.01	0.00
Non-narrative	0.61	0.24	0.47	0.13	0.41	0.18
Unclassified	0.22	0.20	0.14	0.16	0.13	0.18
TOTALS	2.69	3.28	1.99	2.48	1.77	2.15

Table 58 Distribution of children in different narrative/non-narrative book-reading categories, by age and sex (in percentages)

Type of book reader	10+ Boys	10+ Girls	12+ Boys	12+ Girls	14+ Boys	14+ Girls
Non-book-readers	15.8	9.4	33.2	23.3	40.0	32.4
Narrative only	46.6	71.6	38.5	65.5	36.0	55.3
Non-narrative only	9.6	1.1	10.1	1.4	8.1	1.6
Narrative and non-narrative	24.0	15.7	16.5	8.8	14.5	9.4
Unclassifiable books only	4.0	2.2	1.7	1.0	1.4	1.3

narrative books read by the older children are more serious and demanding ones which therefore take longer to read.

Classification of children into five types of book reader

We can gain a different perspective again, if we tabulate our data not in terms of types of book but in terms of types of book reader. Thus, if we take the narrative/non-narrative division first, we can classify our children into the following five types of book reader:

(i)   non-book-readers
(ii)   readers of narrative books only
(iii)   readers of non-narrative books only
(iv)   readers of both narrative and non-narrative books
(v)   readers none of whose books could be classified as either narrative or non-narrative.

(Note: for the purposes of this classification, fairy tales, myths and legends were treated as narrative, while annuals were treated as unclassifiable. It was also necessary to include under (ii), (iii) and (iv) some children who read also some books which were unclassifiable; the numbers involved were not so great however as to distort our table to any marked extent.)

Table 58 shows the distribution of children in each of the five categories, for each age-and-sex grouping.

The most striking feature of this table is the confirmation it provides of the existence of a very high proportion of girls who read narrative books only. Among the boys, readers of narrative books only form a much lower (though still fairly large) proportion, while we can also see that among the boys there is a higher proportion than among the girls of readers who mix narrative with non-narrative book reading. It is also noticeable that, while there are very few girls indeed who read non-narrative books only, there is a significant proportion of boys (ranging between 8% and 10%) who restrict their reading in this way. Moreover, the proportion of readers of non-narrative books only remains quite steady from 10+ through 12+ to 14+, and this fact tends to lend weight to our impression that the decline with increasing age in the absolute number of non-narrative books read is illusory, and should be seen in terms of longer and more demanding non-narrative books being read in fewer numbers but without a significant reduction in the amount of time devoted to them.

The same strategy of tabulating our data in terms of types of book reader instead of in terms of types of book can be applied to the quality/non-quality dichotomy. In this case we again have five types of book reader:

(i)   non-book-readers

(ii) readers of quality narrative books only

(iii) readers of non-quality narrative books only

(iv) readers of both quality and non-quality books

(v)   readers none of whose books could be classified as either quality or non-quality.

(Note: in this case the books which could not be classified as either quality or non-quality included non-narrative, Fairy tales, myths and legends and annuals. Again it was necessary to include under (ii), (iii) and (iv) some children who also read books which were unclassifiable in terms of the quality/non-quality dichotomy, and clearly in this case the element of distortion thus introduced into our table is more serious — though unavoidable.)

Table 59 shows the distribution of children in each of these five categories, for each sex-and-age grouping. Clearly in this table the persistent disparity between the sexes in regard to the proportion of readers whose books are unclassifiable in terms of quality is produced mainly by the much higher proportion of boys who were shown (in Table 58) to be readers of non-narrative books only. However the most striking feature of Table 59 is the decline, from 10+ through 12+ to 14+, in the proportion of children reading non-quality books only. By contrast there is very little change in the proportion of children reading quality books. (Indeed, in the case of the girls, the proportion of quality only readers actually increases a little with increasing age.) We note moreover that the proportion of children who read both quality and non-quality books diminishes a little with increasing age, though not very markedly. We can say therefore that this table lends support to our hypothesis that it is mainly the readers of non-quality narrative who discard the habit of book reading with increasing age.

Amount of book reading and reading of quality books

Before we move on to a discussion of individual books, there are three further aspects of our data which deserve attention. First we may ask whether there is any relationship between amount of book reading and the type of books read in terms of quality. In Table 60 we show the distribution of light book readers, moderate book readers, and heavy book readers who in each of our quality/non-quality categories.

It should be evident from scrutiny of Table 60 that no very simple or obvious relationship can be inferred. We may look first at the two columns for heavy readers (5 or more books per month). Clearly rather a high proportion of these, particularly among the girls, are reading both quality and non-quality books. This is only to be expected since the more books a child reads during the month the more chance there is of these books

Table 59 Distribution of children in different quality/non-quality categories by age and sex (in percentages)

Type of book reader	10+ Boys	10+ Girls	12+ Boys	12+ Girls	14+ Boys	14+ Girls
Non-book-readers	15·8	9·4	33·2	23·2	40·0	32·4
Quality only	14·1	11·4	13·8	17·4	13·8	16·0
Non-quality only	33·7	39·8	23·6	27·2	19·1	22·5
Quality and non-quality	21·8	34·5	17·0	29·3	17·1	25·8
Unclassifiable books only	14·8	4·9	12·4	2·8	10·0	3·2

Table 60 Quality of book reading by amount of book reading

Type of book reader	Boys Light (1–2)	Boys Moderate (3–4)	Boys Heavy (5+)	Girls Light (1–2)	Girls Moderate (3–4)	Girls Heavy (5+)
	%	%	%	%	%	%
Quality only	25·4	16·4	10·1	28·7	15·1	5·3
Non-quality only	38·8	36·8	28·2	47·7	36·9	22·5
Quality and non-quality	9·6	35·4	56·2	15·0	45·6	71·8
Unclassifiable books only	26·2	11·5	5·5	8·6	2·4	0·5
n	1402	960	507	1289	1025	663

(Note: in interpreting the figures given for n at the foot of each column it should be remembered that non-book-readers have been excluded from this table.)

including more than one type. From these same two columns, however, we can see that the proportion of non-quality only readers is not particularly high — something like a quarter, or — to be more accurate — 28·2% for the boys, 22·5% for the girls. This is in itself enough to rule out as an inaccurate any stereotype which sees the heavy reader as a child who ploughs steadily through a pile of Enid Blytons; for the most part the heavy reader is one who reads voraciously but undiscriminatingly. If he can identify this group the teacher would perhaps be justified in seeing them as children whose reading could comparatively readily be influenced by tactful guidance towards better books. If we turn, on the other hand, to the two columns for light readers (1—2 books per month) we see that the largest proportion here consists of children who are reading non-quality books only. Possibly these children need this kind of reading in order either to consolidate their reading skills or to establish a firm enthusiasm for the activity of self-initiated reading; if so, the teacher may need to proceed cautiously in any attempt to wean them towards more worthwhile types of book. At the same time we should note that there is also a quite high proportion of these light readers who read quality books only (25·4% in the case of boys, 28·7% for girls). Perhaps these children are those who tackle lengthy and time consuming books, and therefore read only a small number of them in the course of a month; if the teacher can identify this group, it may be suggested that all they need is encouragement and discreet commendation.

Quality and narrative book reading (boys only)

We look next at the relationship between 'quality' and 'non-quality' book-reading on the one hand and narrative and non-narrative book-reading on the other. Since the girls read such a small number of non-narrative books in any case this relationship is worth examining only in the case of the boys. The relevant data are set out in Table 61 which divides boys at each age into those who read narrative only and those who read a mixture of narrative and non-narrative, and shows the percentage in each category who read quality only, non-quality only and a mixture of both quality and non-quality. We can see that among the boys who confined their reading to narrative only, there is a higher proportion of quality only readers and a lower proportion of non-quality only readers, and if we take all ages together this difference is significant at the 2·5% level.

Social class and type of book

We turn finally to the relationship between social class and the type of book read in terms of quality. The basic data here are set out in Table 62.

We have already commented on the higher proportion of non-book-readers among social class M children as compared with social class NM. Apart

Table 61 Distribution of boy readers according to their choice of books (in percentages)

Type of book reader	10+ Narr. only	10+ Narr. + Non-narr.	12+ Narr. only	12+ Narr. + Non-narr.	14+ Narr. only	14+ Narr. + Non-narr.
Quality only	21·9	18·4	26·5	23·7	28·5	25·4
Non-quality only	46·0	49·5	41·4	46·0	35·8	43·2
Quality and non-quality	32·1	32·1	32·1	30·2	35·6	31·4
n	630	321	514	215	466	185

Table 62 Type of book reader (quality/non-quality) by social class

	10+ Boys		10+ Girls		12+ Boys		12+ Girls		14+ Boys		14+ Girls	
Type of book reader	NM	M	NM	M	NM	M	MN	M	NM	M	NM	M
	%	%	%	%	%	%	%	%	%	%	%	%
Non-book-readers	8·9	17·8	5·3	10·0	24·7	36·9	11·8	27·0	28·2	45·2	21·4	37·4
Quality only	13·4	14·2	11·7	11·1	12·8	14·2	18·8	17·0	15·8	13·2	16·4	15·9
Non-quality only	38·0	32·2	36·3	41·2	27·2	22·5	30·8	25·9	22·6	17·2	23·7	22·5
Quality and non-quality	29·6	20·1	45·1	31·6	25·9	13·3	37·8	27·2	25·7	12·9	35·7	20·7
All books read unclassifiable	10·1	15·7	1·6	6·1	9·4	13·2	1·0	2·9	7·6	11·6	2·8	3·5
n	358	839	375	772	437	775	400	718	393	768	359	692

from this, the impression we gain from Table 62 is that, although social class NM children are undoubtedly reading more books than social class M children, they are not necessarily reading books of higher quality. Thus the proportion of children reading quality only books does not differ markedly as between social class M and social class NM; indeed in two sub-groups (10+ boys and 12+ boys) social class M actually has a higher proportion of quality only readers. However, the proportion of children reading non-quality only is in general lower among class M children than among class NM children (the only exception being the 10+ girls); and the proportion reading a mixture of quality and non-quality is for all groupings considerably lower for social class M children than for social class NM children. It seems likely, of course, that this phenomenon is related to the fact (already commented on) that social class M children contain a higher proportion of non-book-readers than do social class NM children. Another related feature of the data set out in Table 61 is perhaps the fact (unexpected and also rather intriguing) that there is a higher proportion of children reading only books which are unclassifiable in terms of quality among social class M children than among social class NM children. It must be remembered for the purposes of this table unclassifiable books include not only annuals and fairy tales, myths and legends (both quite small categories) but also non-narrative books; and this may lead us to hypothesize that social class M children are more inclined to read non-narrative books than social class NM children. This hypothesis seems to be confirmed if we extract figures showing, for the two social class groups, the non-narrative book as a percentage of total book mentions. These figures are shown in Table 63. (It should be noted that this table is concerned with types of book and not with types of reader.)

Table 63   Non-narrative books as a percentage of total book mentions for social clases M and NM, by sex and age

Social class	10+ Boys	Girls	12+ Boys	Girls	14+ Boys	Girls
M	24·1	8·3	26·7	5·4	27·4	7·3
NM	18·7	5·7	17·7	4·6	19·4	9·3

We can see from this table that non-narrative books form a higher proportion of books read among social class M than among social class NM for all sub-groups, and this difference is significant beyond the 0·1% level for boys, and at 0·5% level for 10+ and 12+ girls when taken together, but it is not significant for 14+ girls. While this finding is certainly of interest, it should perhaps be qualified by the reminder that we are dealing here with proportions and not with absolute numbers — as previously pointed out the total amount of book reading is less for social class M children than for social class NM children.

The 246 widely read books

We move on now to a consideration of some of the individual books which are relatively widely read; but it is in place to utter the reminder that we do so within the context of an enormously diverse pattern of book reading, in which the overwhelming majority of titles receives only single or infrequent mentions. It will be recalled that, out of the 7557 book titles mentioned in the answers to the questionnaire, only 246 were listed by ten or more children as having been read during the previous month. These widely read books are shown in List A arranged alphabetically under each of the seven categories. (To avoid misunderstanding it should be explained that these 246 titles accounted for a little under 31% of the total book mentions by the sample.)

List A   Book titles mentioned more than ten times in completed questionnaires

Juvenile quality narrative

Alice in Wonderland (Lewis Carroll)
Alice through the Looking-Glass (Lewis Carroll)
Anne of Green Gables (L. M. Montgomery)
Around the World in 80 Days (Jules Verne)

Ballet Shoes (Noel Streatfeild)
Bambi (Felix Salten)
A Bear Called Paddington (Michael Bond)
The Black Arrow (Robert Louis Stevenson)
Black Beauty (Anna Sewell)
The Borrowers (Mary Norton)

The Children of the New Forest (Frederick Marryat)
Coral Island (R. M. Ballantyne)

Doctor Doolittle (Hugh Lofting)

The Eagle of the Ninth (Rosemary Sutcliff)

Elidor (Alan Garner)
Emil and the Detectives (Erich Kästner)

The Family from One End Street (Eve Garnett)

The Goalkeeper's Revenge (Bill Naughton)
Good Wives (Louisa M. Alcott)

Heidi (Johanna Spyri)
Heidi Grows Up (Charles Tritten)
Heidi's Children (Charles Tritten)
The Hobbit (J. R. R. Tolkien)
The Hundred and One Dalmatians (Dodie Smith)

I am David (Anne Holm)

Jo's Boys (Louisa M. Alcott)
A Journey to the Centre of the Earth (Jules Verne)
The Jungle Book (Rudyard Kipling)

Kidnapped (R. L. Stevenson)

The Last Battle (C. S. Lewis)

The Lion, the Witch and the Wardrobe (C. S. Lewis)
Little Men (Louisa M. Alcott)
Little Women (Louisa M. Alcott)
The Lost World (Arthur Conan Doyle)
The Magician's Nephew (C. S. Lewis)
Mary Poppins (P. L. Travers)
Moonfleet (J. Meade Falkner)
My Friend Flicka (Mary O'Hara)

The Otterbury Incident (C. Day Lewis)
The Owl Service (Alan Garner)

Paddington at Large (Michael Bond)
Peter Pan (J. M. Barrie)
Pinocchio (Carlo Collodi)
Prince Caspian (C. S. Lewis)

The Railway Children (E. Nesbit)

The Secret Garden (Frances Hodgson Burnett)
The Silver Chair (C. S. Lewis)
The Silver Sword (Ian Serraillier)
Snow Cloud, Stallion (Gerald Raftery)
Stig of the Dump (Clive King)
Swallows and Amazons (Arthur Ransome)

The Swiss Family Robinson (J. D. Wy
Tarka the Otter (Henry Williamson)
Tom Brown's Schooldays (Thomas Hughes)
Tom Sawyer (Mark Twain)
Tom's Midnight Garden (Philippa Pearce)
Treasure Island (R. L. Stevenson)
Twenty Thousand Leagues under the Sea (Jules Verne)

The Voyage of the 'Dawn Treader' (C. S. Lewis)

The Water Babies (Charles Kingsley)

The Weirdstone of Brisingamen (Alan Garner)
What Katy Did (Susan Coolidge)
What Katy Did at School (Susan Cool
What Katy Did Next (Susan Coolidge
The Wind in the Willows (Kenneth Grahame)
The Wizard of Oz (L. Frank Baum)

Young Mother (Josephine Kamm)

Juvenile non-quality narrative

The Adventurous Four (Enid Blyton)

Bedtime Stories (Enid Blyton)
Biggles (W. E. Johns)
Biggles Flies South (W. E. Johns)
Biggles of 266 (W. E. Johns)
Billy Bunter (Frank Richards)
Bobby Brewster (H. E. Todd)
The Boy Next Door (B. Cavanna)

The Castle of Adventure (Enid Blyton)
The Circus of Adventure (Enid Blyton)
Claudine at St Clare's (Enid Blyton)

The Famous Five Big Book (Enid Blyton)

Fifth Formers at St Clare's (Enid Blyt
First Term at Malory Towers (Enid Blyton)
Five Fall into Adventure (Enid Blyton
Five Get into a Fix (Enid Blyton)
Five Get into Trouble (Enid Blyton)
Five Go Adventuring Again (Enid Bly
Five Go Down to the Sea (Enid Blyto
Five Go Off in a Caravan (Enid Blytor
Five Go Off to Camp (Enid Blyton)
Five Go to Billycock Hill (Enid Blytor
Five Go to Demon's Rocks (Enid Blyt
Five Go to Mystery Moor (Enid Blyto

Five Go to Smugglers' Top (Enid Blyton)
Five Have a Wonderful Time (Enid Blyton)
Five Have Plenty of Fun (Enid Blyton)
Five on a Hike Together (Enid Blyton)
Five on a Secret Trail (Enid Blyton)
Five on a Treasure Island (Enid Blyton)
Five on Kirrin Island Again (Enid Blyton)
Five Run Away Together (Enid Blyton)

Holiday House (Enid Blyton)
Hollow Tree House (Enid Blyton)

In the Fifth at Malory Towers (Enid Blyton)
The Incredible Adventures of Professor Branestawm (Norman Hunter)
The Island of Adventure (Enid Blyton)

Jennings and Darbishire (Anthony Buckeridge)
Jennings As Usual (Anthony Buckeridge)
Jennings' Diary (Anthony Buckeridge)
Jennings Follows a Clue (Anthony Buckeridge)
Jennings Goes to School (Anthony Buckeridge)
Jennings' Little Hut (Anthony Buckeridge)
Jill Enjoys her Ponies (Ruby Ferguson)
Jill Has Two Ponies (Ruby Ferguson)
Jill's Gymkhana (Ruby Ferguson)
Jill's Pony Trek (Ruby Ferguson)
Just William (Richmal Crompton)

Last Term at Malory Towers (Enid Blyton)
The Mountain of Adventure (Enid Blyton)

The Mystery of Banshee Towers (Enid Blyton)
The Mystery of Tally-Ho Cottage (Enid Blyton)
The Mystery of the Burnt Cottage (Enid Blyton)

The Mystery of the Disappearing Cat (Enid Blyton)
The Mystery of the Invisible Thief (Enid Blyton)
The Mystery of the Missing Man (Enid Blyton)
The Mystery of the Missing Necklace (Enid Blyton)
The Mystery of the Pantomime Cat (Enid Blyton)
The Mystery of the Secret Room (Enid Blyton)
The Mystery of the Spiteful Letters (Enid Blyton)
The Mystery of the Strange Bundle (Enid Blyton)
The Mystery of the Vanished Prince (Enid Blyton)
The Naughtiest Girl in the School (Enid Blyton)

Pony Jobs for Jill (Ruby Ferguson)

The Rilloby Fair Mystery (Enid Blyton)
The Ring o' Bells Mystery (Enid Blyton)
The River of Adventure (Enid Blyton)
The Rockingdown Mystery (Enid Blyton)
Round the Clock Stories (Enid Blyton)
The Rub-a-dub Mystery (Enid Blyton)

The Sea of Adventure (Enid Blyton)
The Second Form at St Clare's (Enid Blyton)
The Secret Island (Enid Blyton)
The Secret Mountain (Enid Blyton)
The Secret of Killimooin (Enid Blyton)
The Secret of Moon Castle (Enid Blyton)
The Secret of Spiggy Holes (Enid Blyton)
The Secret of Terror Castle (Alfred Hitchcock)
The Secret Seven (Enid Blyton)
Secret Seven on the Trail (Enid Blyton)
Shadow the Sheepdog (Enid Blyton)
Six Bad Boys (Enid Blyton)

Six Cousins Again (Enid Blyton)
Son of Black Beauty (Philip Briggs)
Sue Barton, Student Nurse (H. D. Boylston)
Summer Term at St Clare's (Enid Blyton)

Those Dreadful Children (Enid Blyton)

The Treasure Hunters (Enid Blyton)
The Twins at St Clare's (Enid Blyton)

Upper Fourth at Malory Towers (Enid Blyton)

The Valley of Adventure (Enid Blyton)

Well Done, Secret Seven (Enid Blyton)

Adult quality narrative

Animal Farm (George Orwell)

Ben Hur (Lew Wallace)

The Call of the Wild (Jack London)
A Christmas Carol (Charles Dickens)
The Chrysalids (John Wyndham)
Cider with Rosie (Laurie Lee)

The Dam Busters (Paul Brickhill)
David Copperfield (Charles Dickens)
The Day of the Triffids (John Wyndham)
The Diary of Anne Frank
Dr Jekyll and Mr Hyde (R. L. Stevenson)

The First Men in the Moon (H. G. Wells)

Great Expectations (Charles Dickens)
Gulliver's Travels (Jonathan Swift)

The Hound of the Baskervilles (Arthur Conan Doyle)
Huckleberry Finn (Mark Twain)

The Invisible Man (H. G. Wells)
Ivanhoe (Sir Walter Scott)

Jane Eyre (Charlotte Brontë)

King Solomon's Mines (H. Rider Haggard)
The Kraken Wakes (John Wyndham)

Lady Chatterley's Lover (D. H. Lawrence)
The Last of the Mohicans (J. Fenimore Cooper)
Lord of the Flies (William Golding)
The Lord of the Rings (J. R. R. Tolkien)
Lorna Doone (R. D. Blackmore)

The Man in the Iron Mask (Alexandre Dumas)
The Memoirs of Sherlock Holmes (Ar Conan Doyle)
The Midwych Cuckoos (John Wyndham)
Moby Dick (Herman Melville)
My Family and Other Animals (Gerald Durrell)

Nineteen Eighty-Four (George Orwell)

Of Mice and Men (John Steinbeck)
Oliver Twist (Charles Dickens)

The Pearl (John Steinbeck)
The Pied Piper (Nevil Shute)
Pride and Prejudice (Jane Austen)

A Ring of Bright Water (Gavin Maxwell)
Robinson Crusoe (Daniel Defoe)

Shane (Jack Schaefer)
Sherlock Holmes Stories (Arthur Conan Doyle)
Sons and Lovers (D. H. Lawrence)

A Tale of Two Cities (Charles Dickens)
The Thirty-Nine Steps (John Buchan)
Three Men in a Boat (Jerome K. Jerome)
The Three Musketeers (Alexandre Dumas)
The Time Machine (H. G. Wells)
To Sir With Love (E. R. Braithwaite)
A Town Like Alice (Nevil Shute)
The Tunnel (Eric Williams)

The War of the Worlds (H. G. Wells)
White Fang (Jack London)

The Wooden Horse (Eric Williams)
Wuthering Heights (Emily Brontë)

Adult non-quality narrative

Born Free (Joy Adamson)
Cry Apache (John Robb)
Doctor No (Ian Fleming)
Goldfinger (Ian Fleming)
The Guns of Navarone (Alistair Maclean)
The Haunting of Toby Jugg (Dennis
  Wheatley)
Ice Station Zebra (Alistair Maclean)
Jamaica Inn (Daphne du Maurier)
Love Story (Erich Segal)
Mystery of the Green Ghost (Alfred
  Hitchcock)

On Her Majesty's Secret Service (Ian
  Fleming)
Reach for the Sky (Paul Brickhill)
Sex and Savagery of Hell's Angels (Jan
  Hudson)
Skinhead (Richard Allen)
Ten Little Niggers (Agatha Christie)
The Virgin Soldiers (Leslie Thomas)
When Eight Bells Toll (Alistair Maclean)
Where Eagles Dare (Alistair Maclean)

Fairy tales, myths and legends

Bible (and Bible stories)
Brer Rabbit
Cinderella
Grimms' Fairy Tales

Hans Andersen's Fairy Tales
King Arthur
Robin Hood
Snow White

Annuals

Beano
Blue Peter
Bunty

Dandy
Diana

Non-narrative

Guinness Book of Records

The most widely read books in each age group

More detailed information about the most widely read books in this list is
presented in Tables 64, 65 and 66. In each table the books are listed according
to the number of times they were read by one of the three age groups, and
the first column of figures shows the percentage of the age group which read
each book. Thus 114 children aged 10+ claimed to have read *Black Beauty*
during the previous month, and this figure constitutes 4·5% of the age group.
On the questionnaire each child was asked to tick against each book one of the
following five statements:

It was one of the best I have ever read.

I liked it very much.

I quite liked it.

I did not like it much.

I did not like it at all.

Table 64   Most widely read books in the 10+ age group ($n = 2784$)

Most widely read books	% of age group	Mean liking score		
		Boys	Girls	Combined
Black Beauty	4·5	4·0	4·0	4·0
Treasure Island	2·8	4·1	2·7	3·7
The Secret Seven	2·7	4·1	3·8	3·9
Little Women	2·6	—	4·0	—
Alice in Wonderland	2·2	—	3·7	—
The Lion, the Witch and the Wardrobe	2·0	3·8	4·2	4·1
Heidi	1·6	—	4·2	—
Robin Hood	1·6	3·9	—	—
Brer Rabbit	1·3	3·6	3·7	3·7
Tom Sawyer	1·3	3·8	3·9	3·8
Robinson Crusoe	1·1	3·9	—	—
The Three Musketeers	1·1	3·9	—	—
Five on a Treasure Island	1·0	—	4·4	—
Oliver Twist	1·0	*	4·1	—
Swiss Family Robinson	1·0	4·1	—	—
The Borrowers	0·9	—	3·2	—
Five Go Down to the Sea	0·9	—	4·2	—
Five Go Off to Camp	0·9	—	4·3	—
The Wind in the Willows	0·9	*	3·4	—
Dr. Doolittle	0·8	*	*	—
Five Go Off in a Caravan	0·8	—	4·3	—
Grimms' Fairy Tales	0·8	—	4·1	—
Kidnapped	0·8	4·0	—	—
Mary Poppins	0·8	—	3·2	—
The Secret Island	0·8	—	3·9	—
A Christmas Carol	0·7	—	*	—
Five on a Hike Together	0·7	—	4·5	—
Five Run Away Together	0·7	—	4·2	—
Island of Adventure	0·7	—	4·2	—
Snow White	0·7	—	3·7	—
The Silver Sword	0·7	—	4·3	—
What Katy Did	0·7	—	3·4	—

— Read by fewer than 10 boys or 10 girls

* Insufficient ratings to yield meaningful liking score although read by 10 or
  more boys or 10 girls

These statements were scored 5, 4, 3, 2, 1 respectively, and from the answers it was possible to compute for most books a mean liking score which ranged theoretically from 5 (very favourable) to 1 (very unfavourable). Where appropriate these liking scores are shown in the right-hand columns of Tables 64, 65 and 66.

Table 65 Most widely read books in the 12+ age group (*n* = 2664)

Most widely read books	% of age group	Mean liking score Boys	Girls	Combined
Little Women	3·0	—	4·0	—
Black Beauty	2·6	3·7	4·1	4·0
Treasure Island	2·1	3·9	3·3	3·8
The Lion, the Witch and the Wardrobe	1·3	—	4·4	—
Jane Eyre	1·2	—	4·0	—
Heidi	1·2	—	3·9	—
Oliver Twist	1·2	3·8	3·9	3·8
The Secret Seven	1·1	*	4·1	—
The Silver Sword	1·0	4·2	4·2	4·2
Tom Sawyer	1·0	*	3·4	—
What Katy Did	1·0	—	3·7	—
Good Wives	1·0	—	3·8	—
Kidnapped	1·0	3·1	—	—
Journey to the Centre of the Earth	0·8	3·8	—	—
Alice in Wonderland	0·7	—	3·9	—
Little Men	0·7	—	3·8	—
The Railway Children	0·7	—	*	—
What Katy Did Next	0·7	—	3·9	—
Great Expectations	0·6	—	3·7	—
The Hobbit	0·6	—	—	—
The Naughtiest Girl in the School	0·6	—	4·2	—
Robin Hood	0·6	3·8	—	—
Robinson Crusoe	0·6	*	—	—
The Wind in the Willows	0·6	—	—	—

—Read by fewer than 10 boys or 10 girls
* Insufficient ratings to yield meaningful liking score although read by 10 or more boys or 10 girls

If we look first at Table 64, which lists the books most widely read by children aged 10+, we cannot fail to be struck by the remarkable predominance of such old favourites as *Black Beauty, Treasure Island*, and *Little Women*, and the relatively thin representation of more recent writers of books for children. Indeed among twentieth century children's writers the only two to achieve the distinction of having written a book which is read by 1% or more of this age

Table 66   Most widely read books in the 14+ age group ($n = 2527$)

Most widely read books	% of age group	Mean liking score Boys	Girls	Combined
Little Women	1·7	—	3·8	—
Skinhead	1·7	4·3	4·1	4·2
Day of the Triffids	1·4	3·8	4·2	4·0
Jane Eyre	1·4	—	3·9	—
Animal Farm	1·3	3·9	3·3	3·5
Oliver Twist	1·1	*	3·6	—
Lord of the Flies	1·1	3·7	3·8	3·7
Love Story	1·0	—	4·0	—
Nineteen Eighty Four	1·0	3·8	—	—
Where Eagles Dare	0·9	4·5	—	—
The Chrysalids	0·9	—	4·3	—
Cider with Rosie	0·8	—	3·2	—
Treasure Island	0·8	3·4	—	—
Hell's Angels	0·8	3·6	—	—
War of the Worlds	0·8	4·1	—	—
Black Beauty	0·7	—	*	—
Wuthering Heights	0·7	—	3·2	—
Ten Little Niggers	0·7	—	4·5	—
A Town Like Alice	0·7	—	4·2	—
Diary of Ann Frank	0·6	—	3·8	—
The Pearl	0·6	—	—	—
Goldfinger	0·6	—	—	—
Heidi	0·5	—	3·7	—
The Hobbit	0·5	—	4·3	—
My Family and Other Animals	0·5	—	4·2	—
Pride and Prejudice	0·5	—	3·2	—
Sherlock Holmes Stories	0·5	—	—	—
To Sir With Love	0·5	—	3·9	—

—Read by fewer than 10 boys or 10 girls
* Insufficient ratings to yield meaningful liking score although read by 10 or more boys or 10 girls

group are C. S. Lewis with *The Lion, the Witch and the Wardrobe* and Enid Blyton with *The Secret Seven* and *Five on a Treasure Island.* It is true that further down the list there are more titles by Enid Blyton, together with Mary Norton's *The Borrowers* and P. L. Travers' *Mary Poppins* (the rather low liking score for which may perhaps be explained by the fact that these books are really intended for a slightly younger age group); and one should also add in Hugh Lofting's *Dr. Doolittle,* which had insufficient ratings to yield a meaningful liking score and Ian Serraillier's *The Silver Sword* which, although it only just scrapes into the list in terms of number of readers, is so highly enjoyed by those who do read it as to have a liking score of 4·3. These exceptions are certainly not enough, however, to alter the overwhelmingly nineteenth-century flavour conveyed by the list as a whole. Similarly redolent of the past is the corresponding list for the 12+ age group (Table 65), where *Little Women* takes the lead over *Black Beauty* and *Treasure Island,* and the only representatives of the last half-century of children's books are C. S. Lewis's *The Lion, the Witch and the Wardrobe,* Enid Blyton's *The Secret Seven,* Ian Serraillier's *The Silver Sword,* and (much lower down the list) Enid Blyton's *The Naughtiest Girl in the School.* It is only with the 14+ age group (Table 66) that we encounter a list where past and present mingle together on more equal terms.

The influence of book availability in school on 10+ book reading

So marked was the bias among the 10+ and 12+ age groups towards the familiar children's classics that we were naturally led to wonder how far these lists might be an indication not so much of what children truly prefer but rather of what is available to them. At an early stage in the processing of the questionnaire answers we had been alerted to the unexpectedly sparse occurrence of many of the most highly regarded writers of children's fiction from the past two or three decades. Thus writers such as Joan Aiken, L. M. Boston, Meindert DeJong, Leon Garfield, Cynthia Harnett, William Mayne, Philippa Pearce, K. M. Peyton, Catharine Storr, Henry Treece, E. B. White and Laura Ingalls Wilder have been highly (and surely justly) praised by critics and children's librarians, and have even, in some cases, given rise to the suggestion that the present day may come to be regarded as a 'golden age' of children's literature. Yet their books figured infrequently on the questionnaires, nor was there evidence of very wide reading even of the more firmly established children's writers such as Alan Garner, Rosemary Sutcliff or Arthur Ransome. We therefore selected 67 highly regarded but infrequently read children's books of fairly recent date and were able to keep in view the number of times these were read, in the same way as we traced the mentions of those books which had been read ten times or more. Armed with this information about the number of times certain titles had been read, we next compiled a list of 65 quality narrative books which we judged to be suitable in difficulty and level of appeal for the 10+ age group and which included both widely read and infrequently read titles (see List B).

List B Quality narrative books for the 10+ age group

Alice in Wonderland (Lewis Carroll)
Around the World in 80 Days (Jules Verne)

Bambi (Felix Salten)

A Bear Called Paddington (Michael Bond)
Black Beauty (Anna Sewell)
Black Hearts in Battersea (Joan Aiken)
The Borrowers (Mary Norton)

Charlotte's Web (E. B. White)
The Children of Green Knowe (L. M. Boston)
A Christmas Carol (Charles Dickens)
Coral Island (R. M. Ballantyne)

Doctor Doolittle (Hugh Lofting)

The Eagle of the Ninth (Rosemary Sutcliff)
Earthfasts (William Mayne)
Emil and the Detectives (Erich Kästner)

The Family from One End Street (Eve Garnett)
Finn Family Moomintroll (Tove Jansson)
Five Children and It (E. Nesbit)

Good Wives (Louisa M. Alcott)
Gulliver's Travels (Jonathan Swift)

Heidi (Johanna Spyri)
The Hundred and One Dalmatians (Dodie Smith)

Jo's Boys (Louisa M. Alcott)
A Journey to the Centre of the Earth (Jules Verne)
The Jungle Book (Rudyard Kipling)

Kidnapped (R. L. Stevenson)

The Last of the Mohicans (J. Fenimore Cooper)
Legions of the Eagle (Henry Treece)
The Lion, the Witch and the Wardrobe (C. S. Lewis)
Little House in the Big Woods (Laura Ingalls Wilder)
Little House on the Prairie (Laura Ingalls Wilder)
Little Women (Louisa M. Alcott)

Marianne Dreams (Catherine Storr)

Mary Poppins (P. T. Travers)
Moominpapa at Sea (Tove Jansson)
The Moon of Gomrath (Alan Garner)
Mrs Pepperpot (Alf Prøysen)

Oliver Twist (Charles Dickens)

Paddington Abroad (Michael Bond)
Peter Pan (J. M. Barrie)
Pinocchio (Carlo Collodi)
Prince Caspian (C. S. Lewis)

The Railway Children (E. Nesbit)
Robinson Crusoe (Daniel Defoe)

The Secret Garden (Frances Hodgson Burnett)
Secret Water (Arthur Ransome)
The Silver Sword (Ian Serraillier)
Smith (Leon Garfield)
Stig of the Dump (Clive King)
Swallows and Amazons (Arthur Ransome)
The Swiss Family Robinson (J. D. Wyss)

Thimble Summer (Elizabeth Enright)
The Three Musketeers (Alexandre Dumas)
Tom Sawyer (Mark Twain)
Tom's Midnight Garden (Philippa Pearce)
Treasure Island (R. L. Stevenson)
Twenty Thousand Leagues under the Sea (Jules Verne)

The Viking's Dawn (Henry Treece)

The Water Babies (Charles Kingsley)
The Weirdstone of Brisingamen (Alan Garner)
What Katy Did (Susan Coolidge)
The Wheel on the School (Meindert DeJong)
The Wind in the Willows (Kenneth Grahame)
The Wolves of Willoughby Chase (Joan Aiken)
The Woolpack (Cynthia Harnett)

Table 67 65 quality narrative books judged suitable for 10+ children, their availability in schools (spring term 1972), and number of times read by 10+ children, March 1971

Order of availability	Book title	Number of schools in which available	Number of times read
1	Treasure Island	174	72
2	Heidi	172	43
3	Black Beauty	171	119
4	The Wind in the Willows	156	24
5	Alice in Wonderland	154	60
6	Little Women	154	70
7	Gulliver's Travels	153	16
8	Robinson Crusoe	147	28
9	The Silver Sword	147	17
10	Doctor Doolittle	145	17
11	The Lion, the Witch and the Wardrobe	143	56
12	The Swiss Family Robinson	142	26
13	Coral Island	140	17
14	The Borrowers	139	25
15	A Bear Called Paddington	137	19
16	Mary Poppins	137	21
17	Tom Sawyer	135	33
18	What Katy Did	135	18
19	Kidnapped	134	20
20	The Jungle Book	133	16
21	The Water Babies	132	17
22	Pinocchio	131	11
23	A Christmas Carol	130	19
24	Emil and the Detectives	128	10
25	The Family from One End Street	126	8
26	Peter Pan	124	8
27	Stig of the Dump	122	17
28	The Secret Garden	121	8
29	The Railway Children	116	13
30	Oliver Twist	113	26
31	Paddington Abroad	111	8
32	The Hundred and One Dalmatians	107	13
33	Around the World in 80 Days	102	12

Table continued overleaf

Table 67 (continued)

Order of availability	Book title	Number of schools in which available	Number of times read
34	Swallows and Amazons	101	8
35	Good Wives	93	13
36	Twenty Thousand Leagues Under the Sea	91	17
37	Prince Caspian	85	14
38	Mrs Pepperpot	83	10
39	Bambi	82	7
40	A Journey to the Centre of the Earth	78	13
41	The Three Musketeers	78	25
42	The Weirdstone of Brisingamen	77	4
43	The Wheel on the School	76	2
44	Jo's Boys	72	7
45	The Last of the Mohicans	71	15
46	Tom's Midnight Garden	71	5
47	The Eagle of the Ninth	67	3
48	The Children of Green Knowe	65	2
49	The Woolpack	63	2
50	Finn Family Moomintroll	62	4
51	Charlotte's Web	58	5
52	Little House in the Big Woods	55	7
53	Moon of Gomrath	53	4
54	Five Children and It	51	2
55	Smith	46	3
56	The Viking's Dawn	40	2
57	Little House on the Prairie	36	8
58	Legions of the Eagle	35	1
59	Moominpapa at Sea	34	3
60	Secret Water	33	3
61	The Wolves of Willoughby Chase	26	1
62	Marianne Dreams	23	4
63	Black Hearts in Battersea	19	4
64	Earthfasts	18	2
65	Thimble Summer	14	2

After adding a further 14 non-quality narrative titles to act as 'distractors', we circulated this list in January 1972 to all the primary schools in the sample asking them to tick each title which was actually available to 10+ pupils during the spring term 1972, either as part of a class library, a school library or a public library collection on loan to the school. This supplementary questionnaire in the form it was sent out to the schools is reproduced as Appendix VII (p. 334). No fewer than 188 out of 193 schools responded to this further request for help, and as a result we were able to construct Table 67, which shows the number of schools in which each of these 65 titles was available alongside the number of times the same titles had been read in March 1971 by the 10+ children in these same schools. In this table the titles are listed in descending order of availability.

There proved to be a positive and quite high correlation betwee the number of times a book had been read and the number of schools in which it was available (product moment correlation coefficient = +0.66, with $t = 6.9$, significant at the 0·01 level of probability) which strongly suggests that at this age level availability in school plays an important, though not exclusive, role in determining which books children read. It should be noted that in this inquiry we have left out of account the influence of the public library, which is an important further source of availability (at 10+ public library borrowing amounts to 16% of total book reading, whereas school sources — school library and class library combined — account for 34%). We did not find it practicable to pursue a similar line of inquiry in our secondary schools, but it seems likely that, at the older age levels too, availability in school is an important factor influencing the choice of books. Thus several of the titles most widely read by 14+ children — *The Day of the Triffids, Jane Eyre, Animal Farm, Lord of the Flies, Nineteen Eighty-Four* and *The Chrysalids* — seem likely to have been suggested or provided by the school; and, although at 12+ and 14+ public library borrowing has increased to 21% of all book reading, books borrowed from school sources continue to account for a considerable proportion of all books read (21% at 12+ and 22% at 14+).

Sources of books read

We were, in fact, able to carry a little further our study of the influence of the school upon pupils' reading by tabulating the information the children had supplied about the sources from which they had obtained their books. For each book mentioned as having been read during the month the children in the sample answered the question, 'Where did you get the book from?', by ticking one of the following statements:

I got it from the class library.
I got it from the school library.

I got it from the public library.
It belongs to me.
I borrowed it from a friend.
I borrowed it from someone in the family.
I got it somewhere else.

Since the numbers in our sample differed slightly as between the three age groups, we have made the raw figures comparable by adjusting them to show the number of books from each source that would have resulted had there been 1000 boys and 1000 girls in each case (see Table 68).

Table 68   (a) Number of books from each source per 1000 boys

Source of books	Age group 10+	12+	14+
Family	102	102	125
Friend	71	98	141
My own	721	693	646
Public library	435	453	340
School library	344	255	275
Class library	644	138	95
Other (or not stated)	368	250	158
All sources	2685	1989	1780

Table 68   (b) Number of books from each source per 1000 girls

Source of books	Age group 10+	12+	14+
Family	118	118	237
Friend	139	163	211
My own	1033	920	565
Public library	496	467	509
School library	385	382	363
Class library	640	147	133
Other (or not stated)	464	282	133
All sources	3275	2479	2151

Some interesting features emerge from this table. We notice in the first place that children read fewer books of their own as they get older, and though this decline is slow and steady in the case of the boys, it is quite marked and dramatic in the case of the girls. It may be that as children grow older parents, aunts and uncles are inclined to discontinue the practice of giving them books as presents (though one can only speculate as to why this should apply more to girls than to boys). To some extent the older pupils make up the resulting deficit by reading more books that belong to either friends or to other members of the family, and this tendency is again particularly marked in the case of the girls. On the other hand the number of books which have been obtained either from a public library or from the school library remains comparatively stable as between the three age groups. It is true that the reading of books from the public library drops among 14-year-old boys, and that boys in secondary schools are less inclined to read books from the school library than are primary school boys; but on the whole these figures suggest that, as far as the minority who borrow from public or school libraries are concerned, once this habit has been formed there is a good chance of its persisting, at any rate up to age 15. The most striking feature of Table 68, however, is the way in which the class library (one of the most important sources of books in the primary school) dwindles to insignificance in the secondary school. Thus at 12+ the reading of class library books drops sharply to less than a quarter (girls) or less than a fifth (boys) of what it was at 10+, and it continues to fall away even further at 14+. The change here is large enough to go some considerable way towards accounting for the overall diminution of book reading among the older age groups, though we should perhaps beware of forming an oversimplified picture of what is happening.

We can be fairly confident that the most important factor at work here is that primary schools almost invariably provide a class library for their pupils (181 out of 188 primary schools in the sample provided such a library for their 10+ pupils) whereas only a minority of secondary schools do so. Nevertheless, according to the heads of English departments, rather more than two-fifths of the secondary schools in our sample provided a class library for pupils (93 out of 188 schools for 12+ pupils, and 87 out of 188 schools for 14+ pupils). Even where class libraries are available, therefore, the older pupils seem inclined to make less use of them. No doubt the continual presence of books in a classroom which is used as a 'home base' favours their maximum use, particularly by pupils who are not disposed to go out of their way in search of reading matter; and there is clearly a contrast here with the typical secondary school pattern, in which the pupil's day is often spent on the move between different classrooms, and the class library is only accessible during English lessons. It seems also, however, that the role of the class library may be differently conceived in the two types of school. Thus it was noticeable that among the 10+ pupils non-quality narrative books were much the largest category among the class library books read (indeed, among the 10+ girls, more than half of all the class library books read were in this category), whereas at 12+ and 14+ quality narrative books were more predominant. We may surmise that primary schools see the class library as an instrument for enticing pupils to read, regardless of the quality of the material read, whereas the secondary schools envisage the class library as a means of inducing pupils to read good books. Some of the non-quality narrative titles included in primary school class libraries will of course be relatively short and easy to read (as is the case with the Enid Blyton stories made available in about a third of our primary schools), so that comparison between the age groups in regard to the number of books read may be deceptive.

Social class and book source

We may next ask whether or not social class has a bearing upon the sources from which children obtain their books. The relevant data are set out in Table 69; in this case the number of books from each source is shown as a percentage of the total number of book mentions for the age-and-sex grouping concerned.

Table 69   Book source as a percentage of total number of book mentions for each age-and-sex grouping, by social class

(a) Boys

Source of books	10+ NM	M	12+ NM	M	14+ NM	M
Family	5·6	3·8	7·2	4·7	8·3	7·3
Friend	3·9	2·4	5·9	5·0	8·8	8·1
My own	36·8	28·6	41·0	38·0	41·7	34·0
Public library	16·6	18·0	24·8	26·0	21·3	20·8
School library	11·5	16·1	11·5	15·2	15·3	18·0
Class library	24·5	29·7	7·6	7·3	2·6	8·4
Other	1·1	1·3	2·0	3·8	1·9	3·3
n	1060	1879	1037	1208	875	1089

(b) Girls

Source of books	10+ NM	M	12+ NM	M	14+ NM	M
Family	4·7	3·8	7·1	4·0	13·6	9·9
Friend	6·0	4·1	6·8	7·9	11·9	9·3
My own	39·6	35·1	39·5	43·0	24·9	27·8
Public library	17·0	17·5	23·6	18·6	27·9	23·6
School library	10·6	14·7	16·7	16·4	14·7	20·4
Class library	20·7	23·3	4·6	7·9	5·5	7·0
Other	1·4	1·4	1·8	2·2	1·6	2·0
n	1360	2035	1234	1399	1016	1178

We have already had evidence (in Table 68) that the children's own stock of books forms the largest single source from which they draw the books they read. This fact is naturally a feature also of Table 69; but we note, in addition that there is a consistently higher proportion of children reading their own books among boys in social class NM than among those in social class M, and this is true also of girls at 10+. On the other hand among girls at 12+ and 14+ the reverse is true, and this aspect of Table 69 is slightly surprising since we know that social class NM children in all age-and-sex groupings claim to own more books than their counterparts in social class M. Another feature to note is that, among the boys, social class M children are more dependent on the libraries (whether class, school or public) for their supply of books than are children in social class NM, and we find that this higher proportion of books obtained from these three sources is significant at 0·1%, 1·0% and 0·1% level of probability for 10+, 12+ and 14+ boys respectively. The comparable pattern among the girls is not so clear cut, but it seems that in this case social class NM girls are more likely than social class M girls to use the libraries provided by the school, and this difference is in fact significant at the 0·1% level for both 10+ and 14+ girls.

Liking scores and book source

It will be recalled that we have for each book-mention (except in cases where the child failed to answer this question) a 'liking' score ranging between 5 (highly favourable) and 1 (highly unfavourable). The 'liking' scores awarded by children in different age-and-sex groupings are shown in Table 70.

Table 70   Liking scores of children in different age-and-sex groupings as percentage of total n book mentions)

Liking score	10+		12+		14+	
	Boys	Girls	Boys	Girls	Boys	Girls
1	4·0	3·5	2·2	3·1	2·6	3·0
2	8·1	8·0	6·6	7·0	7·8	8·4
3	22·6	23·8	25·1	22·7	27·6	25·9
4	38·0	37·3	40·0	42·2	40·7	40·6
5	27·2	27·4	26·1	24·9	21·1	22·2
n	3094	3589	2315	2709	2118	2366
% of books given a liking score	82·2	81·5	86·2	87·1	91·1	93·6

Note: In interpreting Table 70 it should be remembered that the key to the liking scores is as follows:

1 = I did not like it at all
2 = I did not like it much
3 = I quite liked it
4 = I liked it very much
5 = It was one of the best I have ever read.

It will be noted that children were more prepared to give a liking score to a book at the older ages than at the younger. It is more important that at all ages children proved reluctant to tick the more unfavourable statements, so that, although in theory the mid-point on the scale should have been 3·0, in the event the mean liking score for all books rated was in fact 3·76. It seems reasonable therefore to group together scores 4 and 5 as favourable and scores 1, 2 and 3 as relatively unfavourable. We can then construct a table for liking score by source of book, and if we do so we find that for every age-and-sex grouping the books owned by the child are given a more favourable liking score than books obtained from other sources. (This difference is significant beyond the 0·1% level of probability when all children are combined together.)

In Table 71 we have omitted 'my own' from the book sources listed in order to make possible a clearer comparison among the other sources.

Table 71   Book source by liking score ('my own' omitted)

(a) Boys

Source	10+ Liking score		12+ Liking score		14+ Liking score	
	1, 2 or 3	4 or 5	1, 2 or 3	4 or 5	1, 2 or 3	4 or 5
	%	%	%	%	%	%
Family	5·1	7·6	11·8	9·1	12·4	13·5
Friend	3·1	5·1	9·2	10·2	14·1	14·6
Public library	22·3	29·5	37·2	46·8	34·2	35·3
School library	24·0	20·8	26·8	22·9	28·6	27·8
Class library	45·5	37·1	15·0	10·9	10·8	8·7
n	800	1217	500	822	518	711

(b) Girls

Source	1, 2 or 3	4 or 5	1, 2 or 3	4 or 5	1, 2 or 3	4 or 5
Family	5·1	7·5	9·6	9·1	14·9	17·2
Friend	6·8	8·5	14·2	12·2	14·0	15·3
Public library	25·4	30·1	30·2	40·0	31·9	36·2
School library	23·6	20·3	31·9	28·7	27·7	23·8
Class library	39·1	33·6	14·1	10·0	11·4	7·5
n	923	1272	562	977	656	995

We see at once from Table 71 that books which are obtained from school sources receive consistently fewer favourable liking scores in contradistinction to books obtained elsewhere. A 2 x 2 table of books obtained from school and class libraries by books obtained from other sources against liking scores 1, 2 or 3 by liking scores 4 or 5 reveals lower liking scores for school books significant at the 0·1% probability level for both boys and girls. (It should perhaps be added that if we take social class M children and social class NM children separately the same difference is shown at significance levels of at least 0·1% for both boys and girls in each social class grouping.) This finding gives particular reason for concern when we remember the very heavy dependence of many social class M children on school sources for their books; we may conclude that there is urgent need for much greater effort to ensure that school libraries and class libraries are stocked with books which really suit the preferences of children at all age levels under study, and that this is especially important in the case of boys.

If we attempt to pursue a little further the responses children made in general to the 'liking' question, it seems more convenient and more meaningful to present the data in terms of mean liking scores for different groupings. Thus in Table 72 we show the mean liking scores for each age-and-sex grouping.

Table 72   Mean liking scores for all books for each age-and-sex grouping

Age group	Boys	Girls
10+	3·76	3·77
12+	3·81	3·79
14+	3·70	3·68

We can see from Table 72 that although the 12+ age group were inclined to give rather higher and the 14+ age group rather lower liking scores than the sample as a whole, the differences between sub-groups were not really very marked.

Liking scores and book type

We can also show the same liking scores for each book type, and we present this information in Table 73 both for each age-and-sex grouping and for the whole sample. Several rather diverse points emerge from examination of Table 73. First, the unclassified books are the ones which fairly consistently receive the most unfavourable liking scores; presumably this group included a number which were reported in terms of inaccurately remembered titles because they had left no very marked impression in the minds of their readers. Fairy tales, myths and legends also received unfavourable ratings particularly from the 12+ group (both sexes) and to a lesser extent from the 14+ boys and the 10+ girls; it is noticeable however that the very small number of girls who either persisted in or returned to this type of reading at 14+ were highly enthusiastic in their attitude towards it. In view of the general reluctance of girls to undertake non-narrative reading it is not surprising that they should return a considerably more unfavourable liking score than the boys towards

Table 73 Mean liking score for different book types

Book type	Boys 10+	12+	14+	Girls 10+	12+	14+	Whole sample
Juvenile quality	3·80	3·78	3·61	3·73	3·81	3·68	3·76
Juvenile non-quality	3·74	3·81	3·73	3·88	3·84	3·68	3·81
Adult quality	3·92	3·80	3·63	3·71	3·68	3·67	3·70
Adult non-quality	4·11	3·96	3·79	3·69	3·88	3·77	3·83
Fairy tales, myths and legends	3·79	3·32	3·58	3·59	3·50	4·40	3·63
Annuals	3·88	3·52	3·87	3·66	3·89	3·67	3·75
Non-narrative	3·77	3·87	3·71	3·48	3·60	3·70	3·73
Unclassified	3·44	3·58	3·63	3·57	3·59	3·63	3·57
All quality books	3·83	3·79	3·63	3·73	3·77	3·67	3·73
All non-quality books	3·77	3·86	3·77	3·88	3·84	3·74	3·82

the few non-narrative books that they did read. The boys' ratings of non-narrative books are not particularly favourable, however, with the exception of the 12+ age group. It may be that there is still a need for there to be made available more non-narrative books which are genuinely suited, in format, style and language complexity, to the tastes and capacities of this age range.

If we turn finally to the broad category of narrative which accounted for the overwhelmingly largest proportion of our sample's book reading, we find that there is a very persistent tendency for non-quality narrative to gain more favourable liking scores than quality narrative. (Indeed the only exception to this tendency occurs in the case of the 10+ boys who gave a higher mean liking score to juvenile quality narrative than to juvenile non-quality narrative.) This is a somewhat disappointing finding, but it should perhaps be interpreted with a certain amount of caution. In the first place the differences between the various liking scores are not in general very large, and it has perhaps to be accepted that, although this question yielded some interesting information about differences in liking score for certain individual widely read books, it did not discriminate particularly well between either groups of children or categories of book. In the second place, there seems to be a distinct possibility that the liking scores for quality narrative books have been depressed by a tendency on the part of schools to make available a rather high proportion of quality books which are either too difficult or too mature for the age groups for which they are recommended. This possibility seems particularly relevant in the case of the rather low liking scores for adult quality narrative recorded by the 14+ boys and by the girls in all age groups.

Books left unfinished

We turn next to a consideration of unfinished books — those narrative books which children underlined because they 'decided not to finish them'. The overall proportion of narrative books left unfinished was 9·8%, which seems quite high, and the variation in this figure for difference age-and-sex groupings is shown in Table 74.

Table 74   Percentage of narrative books left unfinished

	10+	12+	14+
Boys	10·2	10·0	9·8
Girls	9·9	9·7	9·5

We see that there is a steady decrease in the percentage of unfinished books among the older children, and also that boys seem more likely than girls to leave their books unfinished. Although these differences are not statistically significant, the regularity of the trend gives them a certain interest. It should be noted that quality narrative books are more likely to be left unfinished than are non-quality narrative — a further reflection perhaps of the tendency we have suspected on the part of adults to recommend or provide unsuitably difficult quality books. Of some interest in this connection is the information shown in Table 75 as to the proportion of books from different sources left unfinished.

Table 75   Proportion of narrative books from different sources left unfinished (percentages)

Source	10+ Boys	Girls	12+ Boys	Girls	14+ Boys	Girls
Family	8·4	10·7	15·2	14·2	12·8	7·9
Friend	9·1	7·5	13·6	6·4	12·0	6·9
My own	7·1	5·4	8·0	6·5	7·1	6·8
Public library	8·5	11·1	7·4	9·6	10·1	10·7
School library	12·7	12·4	12·8	13·4	10·8	12·2
Class library	11·8	12·4	14·0	17·3	14·5	14·1
Other	17·1	13·2	14·5	9·3	17·2	10·0
All sources	10·2	9·9	10·0	9·7	9·8	9·5

It is noticeable that for both boys and girls the school and class libraries tend to yield a rather higher proportion of unfinished books than other sources, though at 12+ the family is also markedly unsatisfactory from this point of view. If we construct 2 x 2 tables of finished/unfinished books against books obtained from school sources/books obtained elsewhere we find that the proportion of unfinished books is significantly higher for all age groups among the girls (at least 0·1% level of probability) and also for the 10+ boys (0·1%) and the 12+ boys (0·5%); the difference is not significant, however, for 14+ boys. Once again the appropriate conclusion would seem to be that there is a need to weed out from school and class libraries — and particularly from class libraries in the secondary schools which provide them — a certain number of books which are unsuitable in terms of difficulty and/or maturity. (It is perhaps worth noting also that, with the exception of the 14+ girls, children in social class M are more likely to leave books unfinished than children in social class NM, and when the whole sample is taken together this difference is significant at the 0·5% level of probability.)

Books re-read

Another point which has some interest relates to the proportion of book mentions which were re-readings (indicated as such by a cross against the title on the questionnaire). These data are shown first in Table 76 as a percentage for all book mentions for each age-and-sex grouping.

Table 76 Book mentions which were re-readings as a percentage of all book mentions

	10+	12+	14+
Boys	19·7	20·4	18·9
Girls	20·8	23·2	18·2

Very striking here is the high proportion of re-readings; indeed overall about one book out of five read by each child has been read previously. We note also that there is an increase in the percentage of books which are re-readings between 10+ and 12+ (not significant for boys, significant at 2·5% level for girls). It might be tentatively suggested that this is associated with the tendency for 12+ children to cling to their juvenile narrative reading, while at the same time experimenting to a modest but increasing extent with adult narrative books, which are new and untried. This interpretation would fit in with the fact that the percentage of books which are re-readings drops again between 12+ and 14+, by which age more experience of adult authors has been gained.

It should be remembered however that Table 76 shows re-readings as a percentage of the total book mentions for each age group, and that these percentages are difficult to interpret since as we know the total amount of book reading decreases with increasing age. It may be more appropriate therefore to present the data in terms of the average number of re-readings per child, and this is shown in Table 77.

Table 77   Average number of book mentions which were re-readings for each age-and-sex grouping

	10+	12+	14+
Boys	0·53	0·41	0·34
Girls	0·68	0·57	0·39

Viewed in this way we find that there is a steady decrease in the absolute number of re-readings with increasing age, and also that there is more re-reading by girls than by boys.

We may pursue the matter a little further by looking at the percentage of book mentions which are re-readings for each of the different book categories.

Table 78   Percentage of book mentions which were re-readings in each book category, for each age-and-sex grouping

Book category	10+ Boys	Girls	12+ Boys	Girls	14+ Boys	Girls
Juvenile quality narrative	17·9	21·6	22·6	25·7	17·0	31·3
Juvenile non-quality narrative	19·0	22·4	24·0	27·2	23·4	27·8
Adult quality narrative	17·5	18·4	16·3	14·8	15·6	13·9
Adult non-quality narrative	18·5	12·5	14·2	14·3	16·8	15·7
Fairy tales, myths and legends	20·4	19·8	14·5	20·4	20·8	30·0
Annuals	33·3	39·7	45·1	38·9	23·5	33·3
Non-narrative	23·2	15·9	20·7	15·3	25·0	13·5
Unclassified	13·2	8·6	15·1	14·6	14·2	11·2

For its proper interpretation Table 78 needs to be read in conjunction with Table 54 which shows the increasing shift at the older ages from juvenile narrative to adult narrative books. It may be suggested that there is some confirmation in Table 78 of a tendency for 12+ children to direct their re-reading particularly towards favourite juvenile narrative books, and that this

tendency persists at 14+ among the minority (particularly girls) who continue
to read juvenile narrative.

School stories, detective stories, historical stories, pony stories and science fiction

We will conclude our section on the qualitative aspects of children's book
reading with references to three subsidiary investigations which have a certain
interest. In the first place, although at an early stage we had decided against
adopting a system of classification into the rather amorphous story types
favoured by earlier investigators of children's reading, we remained aware that
children's librarians and others concerned with choosing books for children
have an understandable curiosity about the breakdown of children's reading
between such categories at different ages. We therefore selected from Jenkinson's twelve categories three (school stories, detective stories and historical
stories) which we thought we could identify fairly unambiguously from our
records. To these we added two more categories which were not apparently in
evidence in 1938 but which seemed to us to form recognizable groupings in
our 1971 lists — namely pony stories and science-fiction. We then rescrutinized
our questionnaire answers to produce a count of the number of book readings
in each age group which could be assigned to one of these five categories.

Even though we had restricted ourselves to categories which seemed
relatively clear cut, we found that in practice the boundaries were sometimes
shadowy and hard to define. Thus detective stories merge at one end of the
spectrum into the vaguer category of 'crime stories'; but we decided that for
our purposes the detective story must be limited to the 'who dunnit' in which
the central focus of interest is on the efforts of a detective to solve a mystery
by processes of either logic (Sherlock Holmes) or intuition (Father Brown).
Also we rejected from this category stories in which children play at being
detectives, believing that the appeal of these stories (e.g. *William the Detective,
Bobby Brewster Detective* or *Emil and the Detectives*) is essentially rather
different in kind. Again in defining to ourselves historical stories we insisted
that a recognizable element in their appeal to the reader must be the attempt
to recreate either historical events or historical personages (as in Scott, Dumas
or Rosemary Sutcliff) or a historically located way of life (as in Cynthia
Harnett) — a definition excluding a few romantic stories which use their
period setting only as a source of perfunctory exotic atmosphere. In the case
of pony stories, we were inclined to be a little more liberal. Strictly speaking,
one could perhaps confine this category to those stories in which the central
character is a girl who either owns, tends, rides or yearns for one or more
ponies. (The 'Jill' stories by Ruby Ferguson provide an obvious and popular
example). Rightly or wrongly, however, we decided to admit under this head
a certain number of other stories in which the central character is a horse or

pony; since the widely read *Black Beauty* is one of these, the decision was one that was taken only after careful deliberation.

Table 79 shows the number of readings in each category as a percentage of the total number of book readings for each age group. (In this section of our analysis it was not practicable to differentiate between the sexes, and the percentages therefore relate to boys and girls taken together.) As might be expected, school stories are read mainly at 10+ and 12+, and their popularity has waned markedly at the age of 14+. Jenkinson found a similar trend among his boys and girls, though his percentages were much higher — for boys 14·0% at 12+ dropping to 6·7% at 14+, and for girls 22·3% at 12+ dropping to 12·4% at at 14+. A considerable proportion of the school stories read in 1971 belonged either to the *Malory Towers* or *St. Clare's* series by Enid Blyton or the *Jennings* series by Anthony Buckeridge; *Tom Brown's Schooldays*, described as 'remarkably popular' by Jenkinson, seems to have lost most of its appeal by now, and it is perhaps surprising (a tribute to its continued presence in outdated school libraries?) that it collected as many as 27 readings among our 1971 sample. Historical stories seem to appeal these days only to a comparatively small minority of child readers, though they are rather more widely read at 12+ and 14+ than at 10+. Noticeable here is the almost complete disappearance of Scott's novels from the 1971 lists. Detective stories are rather little read at 10+ and 12+ and only come into their own at 14+, at which age a variety of titles by Agatha Christie were much in evidence. This trend, too, replicates the trend found in Jenkinson, though here again Jenkinson's percentages were much higher — 27·6% for boys at 14+ and 10·0% for girls at 14+. As far as our two new categories are concerned it turns out that the reading of pony stories is quite extensive (mainly, we may surmise, among girls) at 10+ and 12+, but falls away markedly at 14+. Science-fiction on the other hand plays only a small part in children's reading at 10+, but increases steadily at the older age ranges, until at 14+ it becomes the only one of these categories to claim, at any age range, more than 5% of total book readings. Much of this science-fiction reading is attributable to the popularity of three authors — Jules Verne and H. G. Wells as pioneers of the genre, and John Wyndham as its modern exponent.

Table 79   Number of readings of five types of fiction as percentage of total book readings for each age group

Book category	10+	12+	14+
School stories	3·6	4·4	1·0
Detective stories	0·2	2·0	4·1
Historical stories	1·5	2·6	2·6
Pony stories	4·0	4·8	1·3
Science-fiction	1·3	2·5	5·4
n	8199	5864	4920

The non-narrative books

Secondly, a brief note on the category of non-narrative books, which it will be recalled accounted for only 14·5% of the total book reading of the sample, but in the case of boys amounted to the rather higher proportion of approximately 23%. This category is remarkable for the large number of different titles mentioned and the infrequency with which each is read; most of the 1400 titles given appear once only. The range in both kind and quality is enormous. A. J. P. Taylor, Mao-Tse-Tung, Donne and *The XYZ of Love* appear in the 14+ lists; Ladybird books on *Oil*, the *Police* and *Space* in the 10+ and 12+ lists; while *Up With United* and the sporting enthusiasms of television pundits figure in the lists for all three age groups. How to play the game, take photographs, fish, watch birds, and cook are topics which jostle with evidence of serious interest in art, music and religion. Classification of such disparate material is difficult indeed.

Nevertheless certain trends and patterns emerge. Naturally the overall decline of the book reading habit between 10+ and 14+ is reflected in this category as well. 10+ readers account for 41% of non-narrative books read, 12+ readers for 31·8%, and 14+ readers for 27·2%; while the average number of non-narrative books read per child declines from 0·39 at 10+ through 0·31 at 12+ to 0·28 at 14+. There appears to be slightly less general interest in science and technology (taking these to include machines and locomotion) among older children than among the 10+ group; 14·9% of the latter's reading in the non-narrative category comes under this heading, 13·0% of the 12+ group's, and 12·7% of the 14+ group's. Interest in animals (including pets) declines sharply between 12+ and 14+; it accounts for 20·4% of non-narrative reading at 10+, 19·8% at 12+ but only 13·7% at 14+. Interest in history, geography and nature (including animals in general but excluding pets) declines markedly after 10+, the percentages being 37·9% at 10+, 26·6% at 12+ and 25·6% at 14+. Interest in 'flora and fauna' also declines in the same direction, the respective percentages being 31·8%, 28·2% and 21·2%. On the other hand, 32·4% of 14+ non-narrative book reading may be classified as 'creative hobbies' (including pets and active sport), the comparable percentage at 12+ being 31·5% and at 10+ only 21·2%; while 'interest in George Best' and the *watching* of sport declines slightly from 11·5% at 10+ through 11·1% at 12+ to 10·7% at 14+. Interest in poetry, music and painting is noticeably higher among the 14+ group than among younger children. It is our general impression that, among the rather small minority of children (approximately one-tenth) who confine themselves to non-narrative book reading, this category would repay rather more nurture, encouragement and guidance than it receives from teachers at present.

Favourite writers

Finally, we report briefly what emerged from the question which invited children to name their favourite writer. The question, it will be recalled, took the form: 'Do you have a favourite writer, one whose books you like reading more than anyone else's?'. In response to this 49·9% of the sample named a favourite writer, but it was noticeable that the younger age groups were more inclined to do so than the older. Thus 58·1% of the 10+ group named a favourite writer as compared with 50·2% of the 12+ group and only 40·4% of the 14+ group. This trend is no doubt linked with the reduced amount of book reading by the two older age groups, but it may also suggest a greater readiness among the younger children to attach their enthusiasm and allegiance to a single author. There was also a consistent tendency for girls to be more inclined to name a favourite writer than boys. Thus, at 10+, 69·9% of the girls named a favourite writer as compared with 47·9% of the boys; at 12+ 60·4% of the girls as compared with 41·8% of the boys; and, at 14+, 46·3% of the girls as compared with 38·0% of the boys. This sex difference seems to be too marked to be explicable wholly in terms of the heavier book reading of girls, as set out in Table 12 and 13.

When we tabulate the individual favourite writers named by the different age-and-sex groupings some interesting features emerge. In Table 80 we list in descending order of frequency the most often-named favourite writer, giving in each case the number of mentions as a percentage of the total number of children in the particular age-and-sex grouping.

The most striking feature of Table 81 is surely the overwhelming predominance of Enid Blyton, particularly among the girls. Indeed, taking the sample as a whole, no fewer than 1604 children named Blyton as their favourite writer, and some measure of the extent to which she led the field is given by the fact that the runner-up, Charles Dickens, was named by only 158 children in all. It is of some interest, however, to compare the number of times an author is named as 'favourite writer' with the number of books by the same writer which had been read during the month of the survey. Comparative figures for the 'Top 13' favourite writers are given in Table 81.

It will be noted that most of these authors have been read much more frequently than they have been named as favourite writer, Louisa M. Alcott being the most striking example, though followed fairly closely by Anthony Buckeridge and C. S. Lewis. In the case of Enid Blyton it is undoubtedly the case that a considerable number of children, particularly girls, have been induced to regard Enid Blyton as their favourite writer, but that many of them do not in fact read a great many of her books — short, easy to read, and readily available though they undoubtedly are. Charles Dickens is also named more frequently as favourite writer than the number of his books actually read might lead us to expect; and we may suspect that in this case some

Table 80 Named favourite writers as a percentage of all children in each age-and-sex grouping

(a) 10+

Author	Boys	Girls
E. Blyton	19·5	50·1
R. L. Stevenson	3·7	0·9
C. Dickens	2·2	1·6
W. E. Johns	2·4	–
C. S. Lewis	0·9	1·0
A. Buckeridge	1·4	0·2
M. Bond	0·5	0·6
A. Sewell	0·5	0·5
L. M. Alcott	–	0·8
Lewis Carroll	0·1	0·7
A. Ransome	0·6	0·1
H. E. Todd	0·7	–
n	1403	1344

(b) 12+

Author	Boys	Girls
E. Blyton	10·3	31·2
C. Dickens	2·4	2·2
R. L. Stevenson	1·9	1·5
W. E. Johns	3·0	–
A. Hitchcock	1·6	0·9
A. Christie	0·9	1·4
M. Saville	0·4	1·5
I. Fleming	1·3	0·2
L. M. Alcott	–	1·5
N. Streatfeild	–	1·5
J. Verne	1·3	–
C. S. Lewis	0·2	1·0
A. Buckeridge	1·0	–
A. Conan Doyle	0·8	0·3
H. G. Wells	0·8	0·2
L. Carroll	0·1	0·7
W. Price	0·7	–
A. Sewell	–	0·8
n	1350	1255

(c) 14+

Author	Boys	Girls
E. Blyton	3·1	9·0
A Christie	2·2	5·7
C. Dickens	1·7	2·4
A. Maclean	3·2	0·7
H. G. Wells	2·4	0·9
I. Fleming	1·9	0·7
J. Wyndham	1·3	1·4
N. Shute	1·1	1·2
A. Conan Doyle	1·6	0·2
W. E. Johns	1·5	–
A. Hitchcock	0·4	0·9
D. Wheatley	0·7	0·8
J. Plaidy	–	1·2
R. L. Stevenson	0·8	0·3
J. Verne	0·9	0·2
G. Heyer	–	1·0
L. M. Alcott	–	0·9
G. Durrell	0·6	0·2
H. Innes	0·6	0·2
G. Orwell	0·5	0·3
J. Steinbeck	–	0·8
n	1307	1107

Table 81   Number of times authors were named as favourite writer compared with the number of their books read during the month

Author	Number of children naming as favourite writer	Number of books read per month
Enid Blyton	1604	1944
Charles Dickens	158	205
Agatha Christie	121	195
R. L. Stevenson	120	239
W. E. Johns	96	241
Alistair Maclean	57	100
Ian Fleming	56	138
C. S. Lewis	54	205
H. G. Wells	51	84
A. Conan Doyle	45	93
Anthony Buckeridge	43	179
Louisa M. Alcott	43	310
Jules Verne	41	143

children may have written down his name either because it came most readily to mind or because his was felt to be a 'safe' name and likely to please. In general, we must conclude that, although a question of the 'name your favourite writer' type yields interesting information about children's attitudes towards specific authors, it is no substitute for questions seeking factual information about the books which have been actually read; and that results from the two types of inquiry do not in the event correlate very closely, for a number of reasons.

Classification of periodicals into six categories

We turn now to an analysis of the different types of periodical read by our sample. A very large number of different titles were named as read regularly, and to classify them satisfactorily proved to be no easy task. After study of all those periodicals of which we could obtain specimens, we decided in the end on the following six categories:

(i) Comics which consist wholly or mainly of stories told by means of picture-strips: juvenile and pre-adolescent comics such as *Dandy*, *Beano*, *Wizard*, *Victor* and *Judy*, and also teenage pop and romance comics such as *Jackie*, *Mirabelle* and *Valentine*;

(ii) Fiction magaines in which the stories are told in continuous prose; teenage magazines such as *Loving*, and adult women's magazines such as *Woman* and *Woman's Own*;

(iii) Non-fiction magazines of general interest such as *Look & Learn* and the Sunday paper colour supplements;

(iv) Non-fiction magazines dealing with specific interests, such as animals, motor-cars, hobbies, etc.;

(v) Non-fiction magazines dealing with sport (*Shoot*, for example);

(vi) Miscellaneous and otherwise unclassifiable magazines (for example *Reveille* and *Radio Times*).

Amount of periodical reading by category

In terms of these categories it should be said at once that by far the greatest proportion of periodical reading (more than two-thirds) consist of comics, the proportion for girls being rather higher than for boys. In Table 82 we set out the percentage of periodicals of each category read regularly by the boys and girls in each age grouping.

Table 82 Types of periodical as percentage of total number of periodicals read

Type of periodical	10+ Boys	Girls	12+ Boys	Girls	14+ Boys	Girls
Comics	76·4	86·2	63·2	78·1	38·5	55·5
Prose fiction magazines	2·8	5·8	3·2	12·0	5·0	32·0
Non-fiction magazines – general	3·4	1·9	6·0	2·7	8·6	3·7
Non-fiction magazines – specific	1·7	0·8	7·1	1·7	21·1	2·4
Non-fiction magazines – sport	10·3	0·4	15·3	1·0	18·2	1·3
Other	5·3	4·8	5·2	4·5	8·6	5·2
n	4389	4728	3959	4081	3504	3741

Several interesting features emerge from Table 82. In the first place we notice the very high proportion of girls' periodical reading at 10+ and 12+ which is devoted to comics; this reduces at 14+, where stories told in picture strips are replaced to some extent by stories told in continuous prose, a shift which beings to show itself slightly at 12+. The boys also devote a high proportion of their periodical reading to comics at 10+ and at 12+, although even here the percentages are markedly lower than in the case of girls. At 14+ there is a dramatic slump in their comic reading (to a mere 38·5%), but in their case it is non-fiction magazines which tend to replace comics. Indeed at 14+ the boys' reading of non-fiction magazines (47·9% in all) amounts to a higher proportion of their periodical reading than does their reading of comics and prose fiction magazines combined (43·5%); This change appears to be due very largely to the marked increase in their reading of non-fiction magazines dealing with specific interests, supplemented by a more modest increase in their reading of non-fiction magazines concerned with both sport and general interests. Very noticeable is the difference between the sexes in regard to interest in sport as expressed in terms of periodical reading; periodicals concerned with sport play a negligible part in the girls' periodical reading at all ages, whereas for boys the non-fiction sport magazines account for about one-tenth of their periodical reading at age 10+, and this proportion increases steadily at the later ages. To some extent the slump in comic reading among 14+ boys is no doubt attributable to the fact that no publisher has found a formula to appeal to their interests in comic form in the way that *Jackie*, for instance, scoops the market for girls of the same age. It does seem clear however that some boys at this age are particularly interested in using their periodical reading as a means of extending their interest in and knowledge about hobbies, things mechanical, and sport.

It needs to be remembered, however, that for boys and girls there is a steady decline from 10+ through 12+ to 14+ in the average number of periodicals read (see Table 14), so that Table 82 does not by itself tell the whole story. In some ways it is more revealing to present the data in terms of the average number of periodicals per head in each category which are read regularly. In Table 83 we present first the figures for the sample as a whole.

Table 83   Average number of periodicals in each category per head

Type of periodical	Boys	Girls	Boys and girls
Comics	1·9	2·5	2·3
Prose fiction magazines	0·1	0·6	0·4
Non-fiction magazines – general	0·2	0·1	0·1
Non-fiction magazines – specific	0·3	0·1	0·2
Non-fiction magazines – sport	0·4	0·0	0·2
Other	0·0	0·0	0·0
TOTALS	2·9	3·3	3·1

In Table 84 we present in fuller form the data summarized in Table 83, giving this time the average number per head of each type of periodical for each age-and-sex grouping; the increase in non-fiction reading among the 14+ boys is a real one, and not merely a larger share of a smaller total. It is noticeable that, even so, the 14+ boys are reading on average one comic per head, and this is perhaps surprising in view of the relative paucity of comics aimed particularly at this age group; it may be of course that they are con-

Table 84   Average number of periodicals per head in each category, for each age-and-sex grouping

Type of periodical	10+ Boys	Girls	12+ Boys	Girls	14+ Boys	Girls
Comics	2·39	3·03	1·85	2·54	1·03	1·77
Prose fiction magazines	0·09	0·21	0·09	0·39	0·13	1·02
Non-fiction magazines — general	0·11	0·07	0·18	0·09	0·23	0·12
Non-fiction magazines — specific	0·05	0·03	0·21	0·05	0·57	0·07
Non-fiction magazines — sport	0·32	0·01	0·45	0·03	0·49	0·04
Other	0·17	0·17	0·15	0·15	0·23	0·16
TOTALS	3·13	3·52	2·93	3·25	2·68	3·18

tinuing to read the comics bought in the family mainly for their younger brothers. The comic reading of the 14+ girls stays fairly high in absolute terms (1·77 per head), and this is supplemented also by the reading of approximately one prose fiction magazine per head. (As we shall see later *Loving* and other teenage magazines such as *Lover, Petticoat* and *Nineteen* account for much of this, though a good deal is also contributed by the girls' reading of such magazines as *Woman* or *Woman's Own* which are probably bought primarily by and for their mothers).

Classification of children into five types of periodical reader

In the same way that we developed earlier a classification of children in terms of their type of book reading (see Tables 58 and 59) we thought it might be useful to attempt a similar classification into types of periodical reader. For this purpose we combined comics and prose fiction magazines into a single category of 'fiction periodicals'; while at the same time we merged all non-fiction magazines, whether concerned with general interests, specific interests or sport, into a single category of 'non-fiction periodicals'. We then had the following five types of periodical reader:

(i)   children who read no periodicals;
(ii) children who read fiction periodicals only;
(iii) children who read non-fiction periodicals only;
(iv) children who read a combination of fiction periodicals and non-fiction periodicals;
(v)   children who read unclassifiable periodicals only.

Table 85 shows the distribution of these five types of periodical reader as a percentage of all children for each age-and-sex grouping.

Table 85   Types of periodical reader as a percentage of all children for each sex-and-age grouping

Type of periodical reader	10+ Boys	Girls	12+ Boys	Girls	14+ Boys	Girls
None	17·0	12·1	18·8	12·6	20·8	12·3
Fiction only	50·8	78·7	33·0	74·8	17·5	69·7
Non-fiction only	5·1	0·8	11·1	1·6	24·6	2·0
Both fiction and non-fiction	27·2	8·4	37·0	10·9	36·8	15·5
Unclassifiable only	0·0	0·0	0·2	0·1	0·3	0·4
n	1402	1345	1353	1259	1307	1173

What is particularly striking about Table 85 is the very high proportion of girls who confine their periodical reading to fiction periodicals — either comics where the stories are told in picture strip form, or prose fiction magazines, or a combination of both. By contrast the boys are much less inclined to restrict their periodical reading in this way; at 10+ about a half of the boys (50·8%) are readers of fiction periodicals only, but at 12+ this percentage has declined to 33·0%, and at 14+ it declines even further to only 17·5%. Again, whereas there are very few girls indeed who confine their periodical reading to non-fiction periodicals, there is in each age group among the boys a by no means negligible minority who are readers of non-fiction only, and at 14+ this minority increases to almost a quarter of the whole (24·6%). And again, if we turn our attention to those who combine fiction periodicals with non-fiction periodicals, we find that this group forms quite a considerable proportion of boys at all ages, rising from 27·2% at 10+ to 37·0% at 12+ and 36·8% at 14+, and these figures are in each case markedly higher than for the girls in the same age group. In general the sex difference revealed here in regard to type of periodical reading may be said to parallel to some extent the sex difference in regard to book reading as revealed in Table 58.

It is perhaps worth mentioning that there is a social class difference in regard to the amount of non-fiction periodical reading undertaken by children. Even in the 10+ and 12+ age groups, boys in social class NM are inclined to read rather more non-fiction periodicals than boys in social class M, but at 14+ this class difference becomes very much more marked, so that social class NM boys are reading per head 0·4 non-fiction periodicals of general interest as compared with 0·2 for social class M boys, and they are also reading 0·7 non-fiction periodicals dealing with specific interests as compared with 0·5 for social class M boys. Among the girls there is also a slight tendency for

Table 86 Percentage of children regularly reading named periodicals

(a) 10+ age group

Boys (n = 1403) Periodical	%	Girls (n = 1344) Periodical	%
Dandy	38·4	Dandy	32·7
Beano	38·0	Beano	30·0
Beezer	16·8	Bunty	27·2
Topper	16·2	Mandy	23·4
Victor	14·7	Judy	21·9
Shoot	13·3	Diana	17·3
Cor	12·6	Tammy	16·7
Sparky	10·5	Sally	13·8
Tiger	10·0	Princess Tina	13·2
Look In	9·8	Beezer	13·1
Lion and Thunder	9·6	Topper	12·1
Scorcher	9·4	Jackie	11·9
Whizzer and Chips	9·1	June	11·5
Wizard	8·9	Cor	11·2
Goal	7·4	Look In	8·5
Score 'n Roar	6·9	Sparky	8·5
Buster	6·3	Whizzer and Chips	7·5
Countdown	6·0	Woman's Own	5·4
Hotspur	4·7	Woman	4·2
Look and Learn	4·3	TV Times	3·7
Striker	4·3	Romeo	2·9
TV 21	4·2	TV Comic	2·9
Valiant	4·2	Twinkle	2·9
TV Comic	3·5	Buster	2·7
TV Times	3·2	Look and Learn	2·2
Smash	3·1	Woman's Weekly	2·2
Hornet	3·1	Woman's Realm	2·1

social class NM girls to read more non-fiction periodicals than social class M girls but, as we have seen, the amount of such reading is at all times very small indeed among the girls.

Percentage reading named periodicals in each age group

A fuller picture of the periodical reading of boys and girls at each age level is given in Table 86. In this table we have listed for each age-and-sex grouping all the periodicals which are read by 2% or more of the boys or girls of the given age range.

If we study Table 86 we find that (except in the case of the 14+ boys who need to be considered separately) the periodicals at the top of the list for each age-and-sex group are almost invariably comics — i.e. periodicals which

(b) 12+ age group

Boys (n = 1350) Periodical	%	Girls (n = 1255) Periodical	%
Beano	27·0	Bunty	28·9
Dandy	24·4	Jackie	25·7
Shoot	17·3	Mandy	21·0
Victor	15·3	Judy	18·5
Goal	13·0	Beano	17·2
Tiger	12·3	Dandy	15·1
Beezer	11·3	Diana	12·2
Scorcher	10·6	June	10·1
Topper	10·4	Tammy	9·6
Lion and Thunder	8·7	Romeo	9·2
Valiant	8·4	Sally	8·4
Score 'n Roar	7·6	Princess Tina	8·0
Sparky	7·3	Woman's Own	7·7
Cor	7·2	Valentine	7·6
Look and Learn	6·9	Beezer	7·3
Hotspur	6·7	Mirabelle	6·7
Buster	6·2	Woman	6·4
Countdown	5·7	Topper	5·8
Look In	5·7	Lover	5·4
Wizard	5·3	Loving	5·3
Smash	4·9	Sparky	5·1
Hornet	4·6	Fab 208	4·9
Football Monthly	4·5	Cor	4·5
TV Times	4·3	Look in	4·5
Whizzer & Chips	4·1	TV Times	3·2
Striker	3·1	Weekend	3·2
TV 21	3·0	Whizzer & Chips	2·9
Angling Times	2·9	Petticoat	2·6
World of Wonder	2·1	Woman's Weekly	2·6
		Woman's Realm	2·2
		Look and Learn	2·1
		Buster	2·0

consist wholly or mainly of stories told by means of picture-strips. Naturally the comics themselves vary with the age and sex of the reader. Thus for the 10+ boys *Dandy* and *Beano* head the list by a comfortable margin, followed some way behind by the not very different *Beezer* and *Topper,* and also by *Victor* which emphasizes adventure rather than comedy in its picture-strips. Surprisingly, perhaps, *Dandy* and *Beano* also head the list for 10+ girls — surprisingly because their rather crude humour does seem, on the face of things, to be directed towards boys rather than towards girls. In this case, however, the top-runners are followed rather more closely by a number of comics

Table 86 Percentage of children regularly reading named periodicals – *con.*

(c) 14+ age group

Boys (n = 1307) Periodical	%	Girls (n = 1175) Periodical	%
Shoot	16·7	*Jackie*	58·0
Goal	14·5	*Loving*	19·4
Beano	12·5	*Mirabelle*	18·8
Victor	12·5	*Valentine*	18·4
Dandy	11·0	*Romeo*	13·8
Football Monthly	6·9	*Woman's Own*	13·6
Scorcher	6·3	*Woman*	12·3
Lion and Thunder	5·8	*Bunty*	11·2
Hotspur	5·6	*Lover*	10·5
Tiger	5·4	*Fab 208*	10·4
Hornet	5·3	*Mandy*	8·1
Score 'n Roar	5·1	*Judy*	7·7
Valiant	5·1	*Petticoat*	7·3
TV Times	4·7	*Beano*	6·0
Topper	4·4	*Nineteen*	4·9
Angling Times	4·4	*Dandy*	4·4
Weekend	4·1	*Weekend*	4·4
Beezer	3·4	*Honey*	4·3
Look and Learn	2·9	*Woman's Weekly*	4·1
Anglers' Mail	2·8	*Woman's Realm*	3·8
Striker	2·8	*TV Times*	3·7
Wizard	2·8	*Diana*	3·1
Observer Supplement	2·6	*June*	3·0
Melody Maker	2·5	*Rave*	2·2
Motor	2·5	*Sally*	2·1
Radio Times	2·5	*New Musical Express*	2·0
Sunday Times Supplement	2·4	*My Weekly*	2·0
Buster	2·3	*Tammy*	2·0
Daily Telegraph Magazine	2·3		
Hotcar	2·3		
New Musical Express	2·3		
Smash	2·2		
Motor Cycle News	2·1		
Sounds	2·1		

specifically designed for pre-adolescent girls – *Bunty, Mandy, Judy, Diana, Tammy, Sally* and *Princess Tina.*

Among the 12+ boys *Beano* and *Dandy* still head the list, though their lead has been reduced; it is perhaps a little surprising that *Victor* does not appear to have increased its following at all significantly among this age group as compared with the 10+ boys. Among the girls *Beano* and *Dandy* are still read by a surprisingly high percentage of the 12+ age group, but the lead has been taken decisively this time by the girls' pre-adolescent comics notably *Bunty, Mandy* and *Judy*; while the girls' comic *Jackie*, which is very much a teenage affair, is already being read by no fewer than a quarter of the age group. By the time we reach the 14+ girls, teenage interests have asserted themselves decisively; indeed *Jackie* has achieved an astonishing predominance, being read regularly by no fewer than 58%. The other comics which tail behind it (*Mirabelle, Valentine, Romeo*) are quite similar in their range of subject matter and type of appeal. Quite a number of these 14+ girls also read magazines which are aimed mainly at older teenagers and in which the love stories are told mainly in continuous prose; thus 19·4% read *Loving* and 10·5% read *Lover*, while further down the list we may also notice *Petticoat, Nineteen* and *Honey*. In addition, the 'adult' women's magazine now have a certain following; thus 13·6% read *Woman's Own* and 12·3% read *Woman*.

If we now turn to the 14+ boys, we find that it is non-fiction magazines concerned with football that have the largest following. Thus *Shoot* is read by 16·7% of the age group, *Goal* by 14·5% and *Football Monthly* by 6·9%. As these figures indicate, the periodical reading of these boys is not only smaller in amount than that of the other age-and-sex groupings, it is also dispersed among a much wider range of different publications. Indeed, apart from the football magazines, the most widely read periodicals are mainly comics designed for younger boys; thus *Beano, Victor* and *Dandy* come third, fourth and fifth in the 14+ boys' list, although even so they only attract 12·5%, 12·5% and 11·0% of the age group respectively. It is perhaps a little surprising that there is no comic which attempts to corner the market among the 14+ boys in the same way that *Jackie* does among the 14+ girls: perhaps however the boys' interests at this age have become too miscellaneous to be catered for by a single publication.

What can we say about the non-fiction magazines which deal with topics other than commercialized sport? Clearly they are very little read *except* by the 14+ boys. *Look and Learn*, the only periodical concerned to present a miscellany of information in a form digestible by children, is very little read by girls, and achieves its highest readership among the 12+ boys, where its 6·9% share of the age group is still only a relatively modest one. The football magazines have been read to some extent by the younger boys — indeed, *Shoot* is read by 13·3% of the 10+ boys and by 17·3% of the 12+ boys; but it is only among the 14+ boys that other specialized interests begin to show themselves in the form of periodical reading. On the evidence of Table 86, moreover, these interests are strictly limited, being confined to fishing (*Angling Times* and *Anglers' Mail*), pop music (*Melody Maker, New Musical Express* and *Sounds*), and engines (*Motor, Hot Rod* and *Motor Cycle News*).

In general, however, it is evident that comics are the most potent form of periodical reading for the majority of the age group we are concerned with. We have presented here evidence as to which of them are read at particular ages; we shall discuss their nature and their likely influence in a subsequent chapter.

4 The follow-up interviews

SUB-SAMPLE, PROCEDURE, AND PURPOSES

From the beginning our research programme embraced not only the written questionnaires, but also a series of individual follow-up interviews with a small proportion of the children who had completed the written questionnaires in March 1971. We had hoped originally to interview approximately 10% of the children in the larger sample but, owing to staff changes within the research team at a crucial time, and unforeseen problems with the computer programmes which preoccupied us a good deal during 1971/72, we were unable to achieve quite as much as this. In the end, five members of the research team interviewed a total of 576 children in 34 different schools spread throughout the country. Wherever possible we interviewed during the school year 1971/72 the same children who had completed our written questionnaire in March 1971. Even in the case of the secondary schools this inevitably involved some loss in numbers where children had either left or moved to a different school or were absent at the time of interviews.

A more radical problem arose, however, in regard to the 10+ children who, in March 1971, had been in their final year at a primary school. By the time we started out interviews they had, of course, moved on to a variety of different secondary schools, and it would not have been practicable to trace them and arrange interviews with them in the time available to us. As far as the junior schools were concerned, therefore, we decided to visit a selection of the same schools in which our written questionnaire had been answered, but in this case to interview a randomly chosen sample of the children who were in their final year during 1971/72. Although these were different children from the ones who formed part of our main sample, we felt that valuable information would be gained from interviewing them since they would be at precisely the same stage in their school career as the ones who had answered our written questionnaire in March 1971, and in most ways closely comparable with their counterparts in the main sample.

We were aware, however, of some disadvantages to this procedure; and since, as mentioned in an earlier chapter, we had in our sample three junior schools in one city which had been transformed in September 1970 to middle schools, we decided to follow up in these three schools the same children who had answered our written questionnaire in March 1971. Our micro-sample for interviewing purposes therefore consisted of 177 children in the 10+ age group in junior schools (different children from the 10+ children in the main sample), 40 children in the 11+ age group in middle schools, 246 children in the 13+ age group in secondary schools, and 113 children in the 15+ age group in secondary schools. It should be made clear that the 34 schools visited were not a representative selection of the 381 schools which completed our main questionnaire, and were not intended to be. We did take care to ensure that all geographical regions were covered in the interviewing, but beyond that the selection of schools had to be governed by other factors, such as accessibility and the willingness of schools to accept a visit from our interviewers.

The aim of the follow-up interviews was to explore in greater depth the circumstances which influence children's reading both in nature and amount, and the attitudes and feelings they have towards the books and periodicals they read. We hoped also to gain insight into the ways in which they view the role of reading in their own lives. Originally we had hoped it might be possible to have some preliminary findings from the computer analysis to provide guidelines for our interviewing, but in fact the computerizing of the questionnaire data proved to be such a time consuming procedure that we had to embark on the interviewing in October 1971 with only an impressionistic over-view of what had been revealed by the questionnaire survey. We prepared a five-page schedule around which to structure our interviewing, and this has been summarized in Chapter 2. It will be seen that while the interviews were concerned basically with the experience of reading in the child's life, an attempt was made also to gain an impression of the family circumstances within which this reading was carried out, and in particular of the leisure-time activities both in the evenings and at weekends which either complemented or competed with reading.

The interviewer's normal procedure was to meet the interviewees as a group for a teaching period, during which each pupil filled in a copy of the same questionnaire that we had used for our main survey. An assessment sheet for the children concerned had also been filled in beforehand by the school, and in the case of some junior schools, this information was supplemented by intelligence quotients and reading ages. The interviewer then saw each child individually for about half an hour, talking in as informal a way as possible about the books and periodicals mentioned in the pupil's written questionnaire, and about topics raised under the various headings of the interview schedule. At the end of each interview the researcher summarized his impressions on the front sheet of the schedule, while his memory was still fresh. Our target was 16 interviews per age group in each school visited, but in practice some children almost always slipped through our net because of absence or other reasons, and in general we interviewed between 12 and 15 pupils per age group, taking two days on each visit. During the odd moments at lunch time and other times of the day the interviewer talked with the head or head of the English department and with members of staff concerned, visited the library, examined the classroom libraries, and gathered as much information as was possible about the social environment served by the school. On the basis of notes made, the interviewer subsequently wrote up his impressions of the school.

On the whole the children we interviewed were remarkably friendly, frank and forthcoming, but inevitably there were some children who viewed the adult stranger with a suspicion which inhibited them from giving anything but incoherent or monosyllabic replies to questions. On such occasions we sometimes formed the impression that there was some painful or distressing family circumstance (for example, a broken home) about which the child did not wish to talk. Occasionally, too, a child who was failing in school work, and particularly in reading, seemed to regard the interview as an inquisition against which he had to defend himself by guarded replies. (We always went to great lengths to stress that our inquiries were not in any sense to be regarded as a test, but in one or two schools this intention seemed to have been thwarted by the way in which the head had talked to both staff and children about our visit.)

One minor aspect of our purpose in undertaking these interviews was the hope that we would be able to gain some impression of the extent to which written questionnaire replies could be regarded as trustworthy. Of course the interviewees had completed the written questionnaire under slightly different circumstances from those under which the questionnaires for the main survey were administered, but even so it seemed possible that by probing a little further in personal conversation one might gain some measure of the seriousness and accuracy with which children had answered the written questions. In this respect it must be admitted that the outcome of our interviews was, on the whole, inconclusive. That in the majority of cases the children had seriously attempted to give honest and truthful answers to the written questionnaire seemed above question. However, there was certainly some indication that when children came to list the books which they had read during the previous four weeks their conception of this period was hazy or elastic. We found that some children (particularly at 10+) had included here books which had been read at an earlier period than that specified, and occasionally indeed there was a child who, out of helpfulness or defensiveness, had listed a book which he was so blank about that the interviewer was forced to doubt whether he had ever read it at all.

However, these instances of over-claiming were counterbalanced by an almost equal number of children who proved at the interview to have overlooked one or more of the books which they had in fact read during the previous four weeks, so that one had to conclude that while there must certainly have been some inaccuracies in the questionnaire data, there was no good reason to suspect a consistent bias towards either over-claiming or under-claiming. It did seem clear, however, from our interviews that with the 10+ children that we were operating just on the edge of the age at which reasonably reliable replies to a written questionnaire had become possible. Some of the 10+ children we interviewed (those interviewed between October 1972 and March 1973) were, of course, a few months younger than the sample of 10+ children who participated in the main questionnaire survey. The able and intelligent children of this age seemed perfectly capable of giving sensible and accurate questionnaire answers, but one felt less confident when one came to children of lower ability and attainment in this age range.

THE 10+ INTERVIEWS

The most striking impression left by our interviews with this age group, as indeed with the others, is of the extent to which the amount, nature and quality of a child's reading is intimately and inextricably bound up with his attainments, interests, personality, and total life situation. The point can be made by listing a few individual cases.

Let us start with two girls who seldom read books. Sharon, a bright and cheerful ten-year-old, has been assessed as B in ability and attainment and, although she is insistent that she never watches TV, she tells the interviewer that she has been a regular reader of *Jackie* for years. She is at the time of the interview in train of reading a narrative book borrowed from the school library, but it seems that she does not usually succeed in finishing the books she starts reading. Her life is far from being an empty one, however; she spends one evening a week at the Girl Guides, and one evening at First Aid, and her spare time is spent either helping her mother in the house, or in active hobbies which include crocheting, knitting and making dolls' clothes (which she then sells). She tells the interviewer that her father, a manual worker, had a heart attack last year, and it seems perhaps fair to guess that both saving and earning money have assumed greater importance since then. The impression the interviewer takes away is of a child who is busily and bravely doing her best, alongside the rest of her family, to cope with a situation which is not without its strains and anxieties. Is it surprising really that books do not figure largely in her life at present?

Next, there is Sarah, aged eleven, the second child in a family of five, with divorced parents and a stepfather who is at present unemployed. She goes every Saturday to see her 'real' dad, and a certain sense of strain is apparent even in this brief interview, for though she is an alert and brisk child, there is a nervous and wary look which comes over her whenever a question comes near to her home life. She is graded D on ability and attainment, reads an enormous number of comics, but has read only one narrative book during the previous four weeks. She likes fairy stories, and watches a great deal of television, but her dominant preoccupation in life is her wish to become as much like a boy as possible. She spends most of her leisure time dressed in trousers, playing football, or engaged in other tomboyish activities, with her brother and his friends. Her comics include a number of boys' comics, as well as the obligatory *Judy, Mandy* and *Bunty*. It seems clear that the drives which govern her living do not at present lead her to attach much value to reading, though this is not to say that they could not be channelled in this direction by a percipient teacher.

Alongside these two we may place Brian, also aged eleven, the second in a family of four boys. His father is a skilled manual worker, and he attends an inner-city school which missed classification as an educational priority area by the barest of margins. He is a lively, engaging lad, who is graded C by the school for ability and attainment, and who regularly reads eight comics, ranging from *Dandy* to *Superman*. Although he does find some time for other pursuits (fishing, TV-watching and occasional roller skating) his consuming passion is for bird-watching, an enthusiasm which he has caught from his father. He spends all his weekends with his friends bird-watching in the country just on the fringe of the city; all his school projects are about birds, and the only books he reads are non-narrative bird books (four of them during the past four weeks). He is a child whose dominant interest is to some extent pushing him towards reading, albeit on a narrow front as yet.

A different instance of the way in which an obsessional interest may interact with reading patterns is provided by Karen, a tall willowy ten-year-old whose whole life revolves around horses. Her particular life-style (weekends and holidays spent almost exclusively either riding or helping to look after horses at a nearby stables) is one we learned to associate more usually with girls from middle class and upper-middle-class homes, but Karen's father is a skilled manual worker, though the suburb they live in is predominantly middle class in character. Karen announces frankly that she prefers being with horse to being with people, that the occupation she takes up will be one concerned with animals, and that she will be getting her own pony before very long. The school tells us that she is only a little above average in IQ, but that she has the very advanced reading age of 14·4. She sees only one periodical, a pony magazine, but she has read six narrative books during the month, four of which were pony stories (her favourite writer is Ruby Ferguson). Clearly the only problem about her reading is whether its scope can be extended eventually to take in human beings as much as horses.

It would be wrong to give the impression, however, that children's dominating interests always fall into the easily recognizable patterns exemplified by bird-watching or pony-riding. There is Simon, aged ten, the son of a skilled manual worker, graded B for ability and attainment by his school, a school for which incidentally he expresses the utmost dislike. Simon watches much television, reads innumerable comics, and spends his time on a miscellaneous range of activities which include pop records, drawing, football and swimming; but his real passion is his intense and informed interest in marine flora and fauna, which he follows up whenever he can by collecting specimens on the beach, and which impels him to the confident declaration that he intends to become a marine biologist when he leaves school. Apart from reading in non-narrative books, this interest has led him towards Jules Verne's *Twenty Thousand Leagues under the Sea* and thence to the reading and re-reading of other books by Jules Verne, plus a developing absorption in a wider range of science-fiction. Equally individual and self-motivated is David's fascination with war and the techniques of war, past and present. This is by no means an exclusive interest, since David (also the son of a skilled manual worker, and also graded B by his school) learns the violin, is a keen stamp-collector, and spends much time on the hobby of aeroplane modelling. It is his interest in warfare, however, which motivates much of his reading, and has impelled him for instance to plod on right to the end of an unabridged edition of Scott's *Ivanhoe*, even though he found it at times heavy going. David, incidentally, when asked what he intends to do when he leaves school, answers with quiet certitude, 'go to university'.

As further instances of individual diversity we may cite two girls, both avid readers, from the same small rural school, a school remarkable not only for its friendly relationships and civilized atmosphere but also for its intelligent emphasis on the fostering of good quality narrative reading. Yvette, aged eleven, is an exceptionally able and articulate child whose father is in a professional occupation. She has a reading age of 14+, and though her everyday life at home embraces many other activities besides reading, she has read no fewer than 12 narrative books during the month. These range from 'trash' through *Heidi* and Noel Streatfeild to Jules Verne and *Lorna Doone*; moreover, she is able to talk about her reading with sensitivity and discrimination. The support she takes, in this respect from her home background can be gauged by the fact that her mother (an infant school teacher) is at present reading *Lord of the Rings* to Yvette and her younger brother every evening. Jean is only a little less able than Yvette (her reading age is 13·3), and she too names reading as her favourite activity. She spends a good deal of her time 'playing out' with her brother's gang or with her own friends, but she also watches TV a good deal, reads four comics regularly, and goes roller skating. She has read five narrative books during the month, but four of these were by Enid Blyton (her favourite writer); her class teacher says that she is capable of reading at a far more mature level than this (and she has in fact read both *Black Beauty* and *Swiss Family Robinson* in the fairly recent past) but that she continually reverts to her more babyish favourites. Perhaps beneath the veneer of sophistication conferred by her much-travelled life (her father is in the R.A.F.) there lurks a childish need for security and regression. At any rate for whatever reason it does seem to be true that, as her teacher puts it, she 'consistently under-achieves', and this judgement is possibly in line with her own expressed aspiration to become a hairdresser when she leaves school.

One final example from the other end of the spectrum: Michael is the eleven-year-old son of an unskilled manual worker, and the middle child in a family of nine. His headmaster says that the family is undernourished, and just on the verge of 'problem' status. Michael didn't in the least mind being kept at school after 4 p.m. by the interviewer; as he explained, his brothers and sisters would simply sit on the couch at home waiting for their mum to come home with her pay packet and put some money in the TV set. Michael is graded E by the school, and the answers he has written on his questionnaire are either undecipherable or unintelligible; despite his enthusiastic but incoherent spoken comments on a book he says he has read, we feel compelled to classify him as a non-reader. Yet Michael (to quote the interview report) 'is intensely fond and proud of his family, speaks warmly and familiarly of siblings and parents, their fun and their problems'. Some readers will perhaps see this case as a chastening reminder that there are other things in life besides reading; certainly we can agree that for the school his failure in reading is only part of a wider and more daunting problem.

In general then the dominant impression left behind by a review of these interviews is a sense of the uniqueness of each individual child. It is of the utmost importance to stress this fact since it has crucial implications for the kind of guidance which can helpfully be given by teachers, librarians and other interested adults.

Yet, as we sift through the records, there do emerge from the enormous diversity of specific cases some recurring patterns which deserve attention. The best authenticated of these is an association between ability and attainment (as assessed by the school) and amount of book reading. The extent to which our interview sample replicated in this respect the finding of the questionnaire survey can be brought out by examining the anomalous cases — the quite small number of children, that is, who appeared to contradict the general trend. Thus, among the 177 junior school children interviewed, there were only 5 who read neither books nor comics, and of these two had been assessed E, and two had been assessed D. The sole anomalous case was that of Steven, a ten-year-old boy who had been assessed A by his school but who read no magazines or comics and had read no book during the month, nor indeed, as far as could be discovered, for a good many months previously. Steven described his mother as someone who read a great deal in bed ('one book after another in her spare time'), and his father (also described as fond of reading) was in a non-manual occupation, so it did not seem plausible to attribute Steven's disinclination for reading to home influence. It emerged however that the boy's twin passions were gymnastics and football and that, apart from some television-watching, he spent almost all his free time kicking a ball about with his friends on the recreation ground near his home.

If we move one step further along the scale, we find that there were only 9 children among our 177 who read comics only, and that 5 of these had been assessed C by their schools, and three of these were reported to have reading ages distinctly below their chronological ages. Thus it seems a fair statement of the position to say that among the 10+ children we interviewed virtually all the non-book-readers were children to whom the mechanical difficulty of reading represented a powerful disincentive against involvement in a book. We can in fact assert with some confidence that these 13 junior schools had been remarkably successful in establishing in their children the habit of voluntary reading since only 14 out of the 177 children (16 if we add in two doubtful cases) had read no book during the previous month. (It will be recalled that in the larger questionnaire sample the proportion of non-book-readers among the 10+ children was a little higher, at 13%.)

It was certainly our impression that in all the junior schools we visited the development of reading was given a high priority among the educational objectives which were being pursued, and that the teachers' high valuation of reading, together with the universal provision of readily available classroom collections of books, had an important influence on the children's attitudes. Further confirmation of this is provided in our interview records by the presence there of a not inconsiderable number of low-ability children who claimed nevertheless to have read a higher-than-average number of books. Thus among the 177 there were four children graded D who came into the 'high' book-reading category (5 or more books during the month) and 6 children graded D together with 2 children graded E who came into the 'moderate' book-reading category (3 or 4 books during the month). At first sight these claims naturally invite scepticism, and it must be agreed that where reading is a prestigious activity (as it clearly was in all these junior schools) the weak reader will inevitably be tempted to inflate his prowess when confronted with a questionnaire. Nevertheless our interview reports show that for the most part these children displayed enough recall of the books they had named to allay the interviewer's suspicions. What is noticeable, however, is that most of the books they had mentioned were very short and sometimes very simple ones — Ladybird books, simple re-tellings of well known stories, books really intended for a younger age range, sometimes even stories which seemed to be 'supplementary readers' with simplified vocabulary designed to give additional practice to backward readers. The children concerned had complied with the rubric of the questionnaire, in that they had themselves 'chosen to read' these mini-books and had not read them under compulsion; but the effect of their perfectly honest answers was to be slightly misleading. (If the phenomenon was present to the same degree in the much larger sample of the questionnaire survey, then it is arguable that we ought perhaps to discount by one or two decimal points the high figure of 3·0 books per month for the 10+ group.) The aspect which deserves stressing, however, is the additional evidence provided here of the esteem attached to reading in these schools even by the pupils who were not very good at it.

Another recurrent pattern which became noticeable in the course of the interviewing was that of an association between a non-manual paternal occupation and amount of reading, though this was perhaps rather less conspicuously in evidence than it had been in the questionnaire survey, partly because the interviews brought to the forefront of our consciousness the fact that there are philistine middle class homes as well as working class ones, partly because in a good many cases it seemed clear that the decisive parental influence was that of the mother whose occupational or social status did not form part of the data available to us. Yet, when this qualification has been made, there can be no doubt that a home background in which books are valued often gives a child a flying start in his reading career, and can be one of the influences which guide a child towards satisfying books of high quality. Here, for instance, is Carolyn, a busy ten-year-old with both an interest in and talent for music, who has read six titles from Arthur Ransome's *Swallows and Amazons* series during the month, in addition to one other juvenile quality narrative title. Both her parents are teachers, and she explains that Arthur Ransome is now her favourite author because he used to be her mother's favourite, and she has the complete series on the bookshelves at home. (It is interesting to note that a year ago she was enjoying reading Enid Blyton, and that she has moved on from there not because she had tired of Blyton, but because she had read them all!) Instances of this kind could be duplicated a good many times, yet even so the dominant impression left by the interviews was that at the 10+ stage the influence of the school was even more massive in its effect upon both amount and type of reading than that of the home.

Before we look in more detail at the schools' influence, however, there are two other lines of thought which seem worth mentioning. First, our interviews lent little support to the stereotype sometimes offered of the bookish child as one who is immersed in books to the exclusion of all other interests. On the whole, the children in the 10+ group who read a large number of books seemed also to be children who were busily engaged in reading comics, watching television, playing games, and pursuing a variety of hobbies and interests, both active and sedentary. Occasionally, it is true, one did come across the heavy reader of non-quality fiction who seemed to have few other interests, but such children were very much the exception. Indeed we were led at times to feel that our interviewees tended to polarize themselves into two groups, those who were hyperactive in a great many directions, including reading, and those who were in general somewhat lethargic or apathetic and displayed a low level of involvement in any of their activities. To press this generalization too far would merely be to perpetuate another unjustifiable stereotype; we mention the impression merely to underline the extent to which voluntary book reading seems for most children of this age to fall into place as one among a vast number of normal and natural leisure activities.

The second line of thought is more speculative. One of our interviewers formed the impression that the children tended to fall into three main groups — those whose leisure time was spent mainly with other members of the family, those who were mainly solitary in their use of leisure, and those whose leisure activities centred around the peer group. The other interviewers were more sceptical about the possibility of forming a reliable classification of this kind upon the basis of a half-hour interview; and even the advocate of this typology did not claim to be able to assign all his interviewees to one of the three categories. Nevertheless he recorded the categories wherever they seemed to him unambiguous, and a review of these cases (spread across all age levels) indicated that the 'peer-group children' read significantly fewer books than the other two types. This small subsidiary investigation is reported here merely as an exploratory study of an area which might warrant more sustained and rigorous inquiry.

We have already mentioned that each of the 13 junior schools visited had a classroom collection or form library available to the 10+ children. It seemed to us regrettable that in a number of schools the children were either not encouraged or not allowed to take home the books they read, particularly since there were other schools which found that no particularly alarming book losses resulted from their more liberal borrowing arrangements; nevertheless the more restrictive schools did provide time within lessons for reading books from the form library so that even here quite good, if necessarily fragmented, use was made of what was available. The composition of these form libraries varied enormously from school to school, however. Thus in one urban school there was a small central library, well equipped with recently purchased non-fiction and with expensive reference books, but the fiction in the form libraries had a dilapidated appearance, was heavily weighted with old and unattractive stock, and contained very few recent titles. Another urban school in an area of terrace housing which was running to seed had its scanty provision of fiction spread out among class libraries, only one of which our interviewer judged to be even adequate; this school catered for quite a high proportion of immigrant children, and there was undoubtedly a social dimension to the poor level of reading revealed by our interviews, but it seemed evident that poor book provision was another contributory factor (this school provided as many as 5 out of the 16 non-book-readers interviewed). In yet another urban school in a different part of the country the meagre class libraries were supplemented, in theory at least, by a generous and varied School Library Service loan collection which amounted in all to some 2000 books; this collection was stored, however, in lock-up cabinets in the corridors and, as these were opened only after school, the amount of borrowing seemed to be in practice a good deal less than might have been hoped.

Understandably the amount and type of book provision often seemed to be closely related to, and even a function of, the school's more general ethos and objectives. Thus in one rather traditionally oriented school serving an area of neat and well kept artisan housing the school day was dominated by daily tests which seemed to be a legacy from the days of the vanished 11+ examination. There was no reading aloud by the teachers, no library time, and no conversations about books, and the staff seemed wholly unaware that there was anything to deplore in the scantiness of the class libraries: the only mitigating feature was that children were allowed to take home fiction books from the dismally equipped school library (though not from the class libraries) and that some clearly did so.

In another school in a mixed suburban area there was generous provision of books both in a central library and in classroom libraries, and there was much emphasis on expanding reading lists, on library periods, and on the setting aside of time for reading silently within lessons. Here, however, the dominant emphasis was upon the development of the children's reading ages, and the experiential value of what was read seemed to have no place in the teachers' thinking; Enid Blyton was deplored, not because of the vapidity of her narrative and characterization, but because 'she only raised their reading age to 9+'. In this school the amount of book reading was commendably high, but it consisted very largely of rather poor and feeble non-quality fiction. In another tightly streamed school the books themselves were also streamed according to a carefully organized colour coding system; yet another school had an excellent reading list, which had clearly influenced some of our interviewees' reading quite extensively, but which was designed only for the A stream.

By contrast we may mention the more comprehensive concern for the development of children's reading which seemed in evidence in one rural school, where the children who completed their questionnaires ahead of the others quietly brought out their books (mainly Puffins) and went on with reading them quite unprompted. In this school there was a minute central library, but plentiful and varied classroom provision of books, which were clearly well used. In addition the school's book resources had lately been supplemented by a weekly visit from an excellent School Library Service van, and the staff commented that the stimulus of this, together with the increased choice of books it made available, had already had a marked impact on both the quantity and quality of the children's reading, an observation which we were able to confirm in a number of our interviews.

Finally, one instance of a different type of book-influence from a pleasant school in a village now absorbed into the outskirts of a large town. Here the well stocked though small reference library was much used for 'research' and topic work, and there were also quite reasonable collections of fiction in the classroom libraries, and the teachers did a good deal of reading aloud to the children which they reckoned to be valuable not only as an experience in itself but also as an introduction to books and authors which some children would go on to read for themselves. However, the most pervasive influence disclosed in our interviews was that of the nearby branch of the public library, to which almost all the children belonged, and which ran for its child members a carefully thought out and well organized scheme of 'Good Reader's badges', with book tokens awarded according to a points scheme based on both length and quality of books read.

This seems an appropriate point at which to include a note on the part played by quality narrative in the reading of children in these schools. We have already mentioned (p. 133) the doubts that arose in our minds about the availability of recent children's fiction of high quality in the junior schools in our main questionnaire sample, and we have reported the inquiry which led us to the conclusion that such books are relatively little read because they are rather thinly represented among the books available to children at 10+ in general. Our first hand observation of the micro-sample of 13 schools tended on the whole to reinforce this conclusion. There were exceptions, of course, but broadly speaking these schools tended to lay a heavy emphasis on the book as a source of information, and to spend a high proportion of their available funds on reference books and on expensive non-fiction books. Invariably fiction of a sort was also provided (usually in classroom libraries, sometimes in a central collection as well), but the volumes available were often old and rather tatty, and it seemed in a number of schools that little care had been given to their choice and that the teacher's guidance in regard to these books was somewhat perfunctory. To a regrettable extent it seemed that teachers were inclined to set store by the reading of fiction and narrative as a means of ensuring practice in reading, rather than as an important source of intellectual and emotional development or as a valuable and satisfying experience in its own right — and in a certain sense of course this approach might be said to have paid off. With very few exceptions the 10+ children we interviewed were forming the reading habit, and showed every appearance of enjoying the exercise of their relatively new found reading skill. We suspected, however, that the reality was less simple than this, and that our 10+ interviewees included a number of children who would later discard the habit of book reading in part at least because their experience of book reading at this age had never become sufficiently enthralling or rewarding to establish a durable intrinsic motivation towards books. The issues raised here are complex, of course, and it was by no means the case that high liking scores invariably went hand in hand with quality reading. Nevertheless it remained our impression that the children who had found their way forward from the vapid standardized and repetitive 'series' books to fiction of more intense imaginative power were the ones whose reading interest was most likely to endure into the secondary school.

A crucial test instance in this area of controversy is, of course, the fiction of Enid Blyton; and we found that our 13 schools varied a good deal in their attitude towards this writer, and also in the extent to which they were or were not prepared to include her books within their classroom libraries. There is no denying that many 10+ children find Enid Blyton's stories (and especially the 'Famous Five' series) highly enjoyable, far more so than the wincing adult reader might expect; and their attraction is only partially explained by the fact that they are easy to read, simple and straightforward in their language, and relatively short. Let Ivan, an intelligent middle class Blyton-lover who started on her at the age of eight, speak for himself, for he is more articulate than most of his fellow enthusiasts. 'I like Enid Blyton', he says, 'because she usually writes about children and you can imagine it is you.' Alongside this we can place the comment of the eleven-year-old girl who chooses Enid Blyton as her favourite writer because (as she puts it) 'she can really imagine our children's minds'.

We could perhaps accept that, as a stage to pass through on the way towards fiction which is more intensely imagined and more vividly realized, there is no great harm in Enid Blyton; and certainly some children do leave her behind without difficulty or regrets. We may quote, for instance, Maria, a bright eleven-year-old with varied interests and an active family life, who reads a varied diet of quality and non-quality fiction and whose favourite authors at the moment are Malcolm Saville and William Mayne; of Enid Blyton she remarks 'they are all basically the same adventure . . . I got sick and tired . . .'. Or, alternatively, as John puts it, 'I tried another Enid Blyton after C. S. Lewis, but I didn't like it any more.' For both these children the experience of reading more widely has enabled them effortlessly to place Enid Blyton's limitations, and to move on from her.

What however of the equally able children who get stuck, as it were, in a single groove? Here is Rachel, for instance, an able ten-year-old with an IQ of 140 and a reading age of 14·6, whose reading is confined almost exclusively to Blyton, or Stephen, an almost equally able ten-year-old with a reading age of 13+, who reads nothing but comics and Blyton. We cannot but feel that these children are missing experiences from which they would benefit because their respective schools are failing to harness their potential. We do not suggest that non-quality fiction (such as Blyton) should be excluded from junior school classroom libraries, since at a certain stage of development for certain children it may have a role to play; but we do urge that it should always be complemented by ample provision of appropriate quality fiction. Our visits to the interview schools convinced us that most junior schools need to update the narrative element in their classroom libraries, to weed out any titles that are too vapid, tedious or dated to deserve shelf room, and to spend much more money on children's fiction of high quality, particularly that which has been written specially for children of this age range during the past quarter of a century.

This is not to suggest, however, that the task of the school can be regarded as complete when the right books have been made available. There is still a need for great tact, sensitivity and judgement on the part of the teacher in bringing child and books together at the right moment. Instances of mistaken or ill-judged guidance were not lacking in our interview records. There was Douglas, for example, a ten-year-old who had only just graduated from 'readers' to the class library, and whose first choice, a re-telling of *Moby Dick*, had proved sadly unrewarding. (At this point, it must be admitted, even an Enid Blyton would probably have done more for his future development.) Or Gareth, an able eleven-year-old, who found little encouragement at school, where class library books could not be taken home, and who had not been helped by the good intentions of his older brother (a university student) who had bought him *Treasure Island* as a Christmas present, a book which Gareth started, found too difficult for him, and did not finish. If mistakes of this kind are to be avoided — and their effects can be long lasting — two conditions must be fulfilled. First, teachers need to have a much wider knowledge of the full range of children's fiction now available. Second, there is a need for smaller classes so that out of his knowledge of each child as an individual the teacher may be enabled to bring forward at the right time the book which uniquely matches that child's reading capacity, interests and current stage of development.

THE 11+ INTERVIEWS

Three of the junior schools selected for our main questionnaire survey had begun in September 1970 to be transformed into middle schools catering for the 9–13 age range, a metamorphosis we did not learn about until the planning of our questionnaire administration was too advanced to permit us to substitute alternative junior schools. There seemed to be no good reason, however, to exclude these 10+ children from out sample, since their schools were still only at the beginning of the process of transition; and we could even see, *post hoc*, some advantage in including them, since this made it possible for us to interview the same children in the same schools at the beginning of the following year. As it turned out, of the 48 children who answered our questionnaire in these schools in March 1971, 3 had left and 5 were absent in the following autumn, so that our interviewees in this group made up a total of 40.

The three schools were all situated on post-war council housing estates on the fringe of a large city, and the children we interviewed were predominantly from comfortably-off working class homes in which the breadwinner was a skilled or semi-skilled manual worker. Possibly because we interviewed them early in the school year, our general impression was that this group was reassuringly similar to the 10+ interviewees described in the previous section. Here was a similarly diverse range of interests and life-styles, interacting, in ways not always entirely predictable, with reading patterns quite similar to those of the 'top juniors'. We were indeed able to add to our catalogue of highly individual obsessions two fresh instances: first, Jeffrey, at the younger end of a large and chronically hard-up family, who was totally absorbed in the fascination of helping the local ice-cream man make and sell ice-cream, an activity which ate up all his spare time and earned him 50p a day, half of which he contributed to the family kitty; second, Marilyn, who was completely wrapped up in her passion for her neighbour's two small babies, spending all her waking hours looking after them and playing with them. (Both these children were too preoccupied to do much reading, or even much television watching.) Only occasionally did we encounter a shift towards more 'teenage' interests. Lorraine was one of those who were exceptional in this respect — a mature eleven-year-old, much taken up with clothes, boys, and pop music, who liked to spend her time sewing and dressmaking, dancing, or going round shops with her friends, keeping up with the fashions. Interestingly, however, Lorraine's reading, of which she still did quite a bit, had stayed on a more juvenile level. As well as *Jackie* and *Woman's Weekly*, she still read *Dandy* and *Beano*, and the three narrative books she had read during the month were all by Enid Blyton.

In this group of 40 children we found a rather higher proportion of non-book-readers than among the 10+ interviewees. Thus there were three children who had read neither books nor comics (including one boy graded A whose interests seemed to centre wholly round football and sport) and four more who read comics only. The numbers involved are too small to permit us even to guess whether or not this represents the first manifestations of a drift away from book reading which will show itself unmistakably at the older ages. However, at one of the three schools some teachers voiced their disquiet at the difficulties they encountered trying to foster book reading within the particular social environment served by their school, and expressed their feeling that, since books played no great part in the lives of these children's prosperous working class homes, the onus lay on them as teachers to devise ways of inducing the children to persist in reading a book all through. Thus, with the 10+ children the previous year, one teacher had bought a class set of Paul Berna's *1000 Million Francs* which was read together in English lessons in ways designed to demonstrate how enjoyable the reading of such a book could be. Pupils were also required to keep book records of their out-of-school reading on a simple form which provided space for brief statements about the setting of story, the main events, the most interesting part, and the main characters. With the three classes of 11+ children, the teachers concerned had organized a carefully structured scheme of individualized reading based upon a collection of twenty-odd children's fiction titles each of which was available in a small set of four or five copies. The books were mainly paperbacks, by modern authors of high quality such as Philippa Pearce, Alan Garner, Catherine Storr, Ian Serraillier and Henry Treece; and each title had an individually constructed worksheet to go with it.

The children chose a book on the basis of a short summary, and then read it on their own in lesson time, making up afterwards an illustrated folder containing their answers, drawings, and reactions. In that English lessons were now centred not on textbooks or exercises but on 'real' books, self-chosen within certain limits, the scheme seemed to represent a real advance; and our interviews provided evidence that it was already persuading some children of the satisfactions to be obtained from reading good quality fiction. Thus Christopher, though his favourite author was still Enid Blyton, had rated Philippa Pearce's *A Dog So Small* as one of the best books he had ever read, while Anita, also a Blyton-lover, had been captivated by *A Dog So Small* and *Children on the Oregon Trail* (both read under the school scheme), had been influenced by the recommendations of her classmates to read an E. Nesbit story on her own initiative, and thought that her public library borrowing in future would include more books by authors introduced to her by the school reading scheme. On the other hand, there were some signs that the scheme was proving more successful in influencing those who had already formed the reading habit (albeit with a penchant for inferior material) than in converting non-readers into readers.

Perhaps because the books were read 'in school' rather than taken home, children were inclined to see the scheme as part of school work, and so to miss its potential bearing upon their leisure time activity. Richard, for instance, an able boy who did not read books in his spare time, had clearly gone along with the scheme only to the extent that there were 'marks' for it; other children had not listed in their questionnaires books read under the scheme because they regarded them as 'compulsory reading' rather than as 'chosen from a class library' — an instance of the difficulty, in these days, of drawing an unambiguous boundary line round the concept of voluntary reading. Perhaps these objections point only to the teething troubles of a scheme still in its infancy. Thus the teachers were aware of the need to include in their list both some easier books for the weaker readers and some more taxing and rewarding books for their more mature pupils, and additional volumes meeting these criteria were already being added to what was available.

However, the difficulty of making such a scheme sufficiently flexible to meet pupils' real needs was highlighted by the case of Gillian, a pleasant if slightly immature eleven-year-old, graded B for ability and attainment, whose interview showed her to be wholly absorbed in an overwhelming interest in wild life, which channelled much of her leisure time into bird-watching and restricted her reading to non-narrative books for young naturalists. She had abandoned fiction reading because it no longer interested her, and the class scheme so far had failed in her case — *Children on the Oregon Trail* she had found 'a bit boring' and had not really enjoyed. Clearly there were narrative books she could be directed to which would impinge upon her current obsession (*Chang*, Henry Williamson, Konrad Lorenz, Gerald Durrell?), but what she needed was individual guidance which took her own current situation as its starting point. Nevertheless, when these reservations have been mentioned, this school's reading scheme provides an outstanding example of what can be achieved when a school makes a concerted and organized attack upon the problem posed by an environment which is discouraging towards book reading.

THE 13+ INTERVIEWS

In this age group we interviewed 246 children spread between 18 different secondary schools. Inevitably there was much more diversity among these schools than among the primary schools or the middle schools discussed above, and in fact our micro-sample here comprised 9 comprehensive schools (8 of them mixed, the other one boys' only), one mixed junior comprehensive school for the 11–14 age range, 4 secondary modern schools (1 mixed, 3 girls' only), and 4 grammar schools (1 mixed, 1 boys' and 2 girls'). This heterogeneity makes it more difficult to discern generalized patterns with confidence, and though we shall risk some generalizations in the account that follows we are aware that these deserve to be received with some caution.

One fact that is indisputable, however, is that our 13+ interviewees were reading distinctly fewer books than their counterparts at 10+ and 11+. This manifested itself most strikingly in the much higher proportion of children who had read no book during the four weeks preceding the interview. Thus, out of the 246 children interviewed, as many as 51 were non-book-readers according to this definition – a proportion which, even so, is rather lower than the 29% of non-book-readers recorded among the 12+ group in the main sample. (This difference may be due in part to the fact that, as compared with the main sample, our interviewing sample had too few secondary modern schools and was correspondingly overweighted with comprehensive schools.)

However the number of children who read neither comics nor books remained quite small – only 8 in all, of whom 2 had been assessed E for ability and attainment, 3 had been assessed D, and 3 assessed A. Of these three anomalous cases two were grammar school girls from middle class homes who appeared to be rebelling against pressure from academically and culturally ambitious parents; in reaction they spent as much time as they could with a gregarious and intellectually frivolous peer group, frequenting discos and youth clubs, playing pop records, and taking part in a variety of sporting activities. The third anomalous case was that of an able boy from a working class home who had a similarly active social life with his peer group, playing football, listening to pop records, and watching a great deal of TV; he named his favourite spare time activity as 'dressing up and going out'.

Clearly the great bulk of the increase in non-book-reading (as compared with the 10+ group) was accounted for by an increase in the proportion of children who were reading comics only. These 'comics only' readers numbered 43, of whom only 16 had been graded D or E; the remainder comprised 7 children graded A, 15 graded B, and 5 graded C, thus making up a total of 27 children who must be deemed perfectly capable of reading a book but who did not in fact choose to do so during the month under review. In a few cases it seems possible that this abstinence from books was only temporary. Thus Arthur, graded C by his school, who regularly read 5 periodicals, including *Look and Learn* and *Aeromodeller* as well as *Dandy* and *Beano*, explained that more usually he would have been reading either westerns or Sexton Blake stories but that during the past month he had been too busy to do so because he had been engaged in preparing for a first aid examination. Until a few months ago he had been a reader of Enid Blyton, a number of whose books he owned, and there seemed to be a fair possibility that in the future he would again take up book reading of an unambitious kind, particularly since in the village where he lived (previously served only by a library van which visited during school hours) a new branch library had opened during the week of the interview. In a similar way it seems doubtful whether books had dropped permanently out of the life of Lynn, an able grammar school girl, unusually mature (in one sense) for her age, and evidently quite fully occupied by a life which included spending all Saturday working at a hairdresser's and Saturday evening and Sunday evening at a disco or a cinema. Lynn regularly read six romantic comics ranging from *Jackie* to *Lover*, and during the past year her awakening sexual curiosity had led her to read several novels by Edna O'Brien whom she named as her favourite writer.

When we review the interview records of those able 'comics only' children who seem less likely to resume the book reading habit in the near future, it is difficult to perceive a clear and uniform pattern among the influences which have caused them to abandon books. Some are compulsive TV-watchers, some are much absorbed with a gregarious teenage social life, some have a passion for sport (football most usually, but table tennis, wrestling and athletics also appear in the records). Others have developed obsessive interests in hobbies, which seem at present to be channelling their energies into practical activities which do not involve reading; examples of these are woodwork, electronics, astronomy and railways among the boys, cooking, baby-minding and bell ringing among the girls. (It seems possible that judicious guidance from a knowledgeable librarian or schoolteacher might succeed in engaging some of these children with non-narrative books which treat their interests at an appropriate level; thus the railway fanatics already read *Railway Magazine* regularly, while elsewhere among the interviewees there are enthusiasts for astronomy who have found their way to books by Patrick Moore and others.) The only features which almost all this group have in common is that at some stage in the fairly recent past they have given up reading children's fiction because it no longer satisfied them, and that there has been no effective influence from the school to direct them toward fiction reading of a more adult kind. It should

be made clear, moreover, that this deficiency in reading guidance is not confined to a few schools only; the non-book-readers of average or above average
ability were in fact distributed among no fewer than 12 out of the 18 schools
visited.

We shall return in a moment to a somewhat critical discussion of the extent
and nature of the schools' influence on pupils' reading at 13+. In the meantime
it seems appropriate to mention a few of the features of our interview records
which suggest that in any case there are bound to be peculiarly difficult and
delicate problems in providing effective reading guidance at this age. The
central point is that for most children this is an uneasy transitional stage in
their lives. They still have many childish attributes, yet in some area or other
most of them are reaching forward tentatively to an exploration of more adult
interests and attitudes. The contradictory tastes and unresolved conflicts which
seem to be characteristic of the 13+ group show up very clearly in the miscellaneous levels of reading which many of them engage in simultaneously. A
fairly typical instance is that of Deborah, a grammar school girl who is still
reading juvenile fiction such as *Heidi Grows Up* and *What Katy Did*, but who
has recently formed the ambition to become an air hostess and whose romantic
interests now find expression in her regular reading of *Jackie*. A similar but
more extreme divergence is shown in the reading of Catherine, an able comprehensive school girl whose books for the month consist of Enid Blyton and
Billy Bunter, but who names as her favourite comics the disparate conjunction
of *Beano* and *Lover*. Or, to take a slightly different example, there is Paul,
an articulate likeable boy of average ability who has read during the previous
month an Enid Blyton story, a non-narrative book about pond life, and the
lurid paperback *Hell's Angels*, the latter essentially, it seems, out of curiosity,
Perhaps the most bizarre conjunction of all, however, is to be found in the
record of Bernadette, an avid and eclectic reader whose list of nine books for
the month started with *White Boots* by Noel Streatfeild and finished with
Boot Boys, an unsavoury paperback from the salacious and sadistic *Skinhead*
series.

To some extent, of course, the shift of interest away from 'childish things'
is reflected in the choice of comics at this age; the boys are now more inclined
to name as their regular or favourite reading an adventure comic such as
Victor or a football comic such as *Shoot*, while a considerable number of girls
now take *Jackie* either as a supplement to or a substitute for the more juvenile
girls' comics such as *Mandy, Bunty* or *Judy*. In a more general way the same
movement shows itself in the appearance of a new range of authors' names
attached to adult fiction reading. Thus William has found his own way to an
enthusiasm for the adventure stories of Alistair McLean which he now buys in
paperback editions, Jennifer has taken up horror stories and ghost stories and
expresses a liking for the volumes imprinted with the brand-name of Alfred
Hitchcock, Michele has graduated to the romantic fiction of Georgette Heyer

which she borrows from the public library but which is also her mother's favourite reading. Sometimes these changes seem to come about almost by chance; Janet, for instance, an able comprehensive school girl who used to read Enid Blyton, has now become addicted to Agatha Christie, largely apparently because a schoolfriend who emigrated gave away her collection of Christie's detective stories before going away.

Sometimes a more positive and self-directed process of choice seems to be at work, as in the case of Ann who a year ago was reading career books and stories by Elfrida Vipont but now borrows science fiction by John Wyndham from the public library and names John Wyndham and Walter Macken as her favourite authors. It often seems to be the case, however, that in the process of sampling fiction which deals with more adult characters, themes or situations these children gravitate towards novels which display a sensibility somewhat cruder than that of the juvenile quality writers they have grown away from. Thus, in what sense can we regard it as a step forward for Mary that she has left behind her the *Swallows and Amazons* series by Arthur Ransome and taken up instead the historical novels of Jean Plaidy? In this particular case, since Mary is an avid and wide reader, it seems likely that she will move on in due course to historical fiction of higher quality (she has already tried and enjoyed one novel by Rosemary Sutcliff). But in any case we perhaps have to accept that at this stage the child has his own criteria of choice which are not the same as the adult's, and that these may necessarily involve some vacillation in respect of quality. Certainly it seems to be true that these children are often determined to try out new writers for themselves, and are inclined to disregard school guidance or provision, preferring to assert their own individuality by borrowing from friends or from relatives or from the public library or by buying their own paperbacks. School guidance has in fact at this age to face more competition from other extra-school influences and needs therefore to become both more tactful and (though in the nature of things this may be an almost impossible prescription) more surefooted.

In fact, however, what our interviews suggested above all was a striking lack of school guidance for this age range as compared with the pervasive emphasis on such guidance for the 10+ children. We suspect, admittedly, that in a number of schools the staff concerned would not have agreed with this diagnosis, and certainly it is difficult to make a fair assessment on the basis of a brief visit to a school. We formed the impression, however, that in this matter of reading guidance there can sometimes be a startling discrepancy between the theory and the practice. Thus it was undoubtedly in good faith that the headmaster of one school assured our interviewer that every pupil in the school carried with him at all times a book borrowed from the school library which he could bring out to read whenever the teacher or the lesson left him without other occupation; in talking to the children, however, our interviewer found it impossible to locate a single pupil who even knew of the existence of this admirable arrangement.

In any case there was a group of seven schools (more than a third of our micro-sample) which expressed only minimal pretensions to a concern about their pupils' voluntary reading. Two of these (one grammar and one comprehensive) were schools with an exam-oriented ethos in which, predictably enough, the development of the children as individual human beings took second place to the attainment of GCE or CSE grades. (In the comprehensive school one might have expected some enlightening influence from the CSE syllabus, with its emphasis on wider reading, but it seemed clear that this did not reach down as far as the 13+ group.) What was more surprising was the emergence of at least three schools (one grammar, two comprehensive) in which the English teaching was evidently lively and enterprising according to its own lights, using the fashionable thematic framework, and embracing a good deal of classroom talk, dramatic improvisation, and creative writing, but in which nevertheless there was remarkably little attempt to forge a link between English lessons and out-of-school reading. As a typical example we may cite a pleasant and orderly comprehensive school, in a fairly new building and with a socially mixed intake, where the English lessons were clearly much enjoyed by the pupils. A thematic framework was the norm, with lessons centring around carefully chosen extracts, but reaching out into work with tapes, improvised situations, dramatizations, and creative writing. Yet there was no discernible attempt to link up these extracts with the pupils' own reading — or even, in some cases, to ensure that the extracts (however relevant thematically) were pitched at an appropriate level of difficulty for the pupils' own reading skills.

Thus in the first two years English was part of an interdisciplinary scheme, sharing a joint timetable with humanities and religious education, and one of the first-year themes had been 'survival', with extracts chosen from Golding, Steinbeck, Wyndham, Bradbury and Jack London; the only author included whom these 11+ children could plausibly be expected to go on to read for themselves at their own level was Clive King. The school library, though copiously stocked and said to be readily available with easy borrowing arrangements, was little used, and the head of the English department, while aware of this, seemed to be unperturbed by it. (In fact about a third of the children interviewed were non-book-readers, while the others were reading books at a level distinctly below their true potential and taking them almost exclusively from sources other than the school.) In schools such as this our interviewers felt that the English teaching, for all its apparent progressiveness lacked an important dimension, in that it remained curiously insulated and sealed off from the ongoing development of the children's lives and in particular from the development of their reading tastes and enthusiasms. Moreover the prevalence in these classrooms of trendy and lavishly illustrated thematic anthologies only served on the whole to underline the fact that the content of this

English teaching was essentially adult-centred rather than genuinely child-centred.

In schools that did take seriously their responsibilities towards their pupils' voluntary reading, the attempts at influence were more likely to be exercised by means of the school library than by classroom libraries. In fact only 3 of our 18 schools provided class libraries (one grammar school, one comprehensive school, and one secondary modern school); but it seems profitable to discuss them first, if only to bring out the practical difficulties attendant upon this mode of provision in the average secondary school. It will be recalled that all the junior schools we visited provided classroom libraries for the 10+ children, and that despite some regrettable limitations in the quality of the books provided this system proved in its own way remarkably successful. Of course this success must be due in part at least to the fact that in the junior school children spend most of their school day in the same classroom; the classroom library can therefore be available continuously and uninterruptedly, and there is no need for children to make any special effort to go in search of books. The class teacher, armed with a close knowledge of his children, can be on hand at all times to prompt, advise and recommend as occasion requires. Moreover the range of reading ability and taste present within a 10+ class is not as a rule too wide to be catered for by a class collection of moderate size.

None of these conditions prevails as a general rule in the secondary school. The most one can hope for is that the English teacher has his own teaching room to which his different English classes come in turn and where the classroom libraries can therefore be stored and borrowed from during English lessons. As a consequence of these difficulties the provision of class libraries, even in the few secondary schools that attempted it, seemed to be partial only, dependent on individual teacher initiative, and sometimes a little half hearted. Thus in the grammar school there was a class library for only one out of the two teaching groups; and three of our interviewees had borrowed from it during the month, reading as a result *Jim Davis* (rated 'One of the best books I have ever read') and four other books (including *The Old Man and the Sea* and *The Thirty-nine Steps*) all of which were 'liked very much'. Since our interviewees at this school included three non-book-readers, and since the general level of the book reading of the remainder was, at best, undistinguished and, at worst, confined to *Hell's Angels* and *Skinhead*, it seemed to us that an extension of the class reading scheme could well have had a beneficial effect.

In the comprehensive school the classroom libraries were small (fewer than two books per pupil) and consisted mainly of rather mediocre paperbacks. They were, however, only one element in a three-pronged attack on the reading problem, the other two consisting of library periods for the younger forms, and an extensive and well judged set of reading lists (one for the junior school, one for the middle school, and one for the upper school) which some pupils at least valued and made use of. It turned out that hardly any of the children we interviewed had read class library books during the month, preferring to take their very miscellaneous book reading either from the school library or from the public library or from their friends' collections (the ubiquitous *Skinhead* series was circulating around this school as well at the time of the visit). It was in the secondary modern school that the class library seemed to have had the greatest visible impact, though here too it had apparently been in operation only for one of the three streams. Five of the girls interviewed had read books introduced to them by the class library, and had recorded very favourable reactions to *Old Yeller, Little Women, 101 Dalmatians* and *The Railway Children* (*The Red Pony* had also been read, but had gone down less well, being seemingly too mature in its appeal for this particular group, none of whom were graded more than C by their school). In this school quite a creditable amount of reading had been achieved, and the existence of the class library was clearly only one manifestation of the staff's concern to develop and foster reading; the school ran a scheme under which children regularly bought paperbacks from Scoop Club, and some children had also been influenced by the discussion circle run on two evenings a week by the local public library.

In general, however, the secondary schools we visited clearly found that it suited their circumstances better to work through the medium of the school library, and at least 7 our of the 18 had made serious attempts to do so, though (so far as we could judge) with rather varying success. The libraries themselves varied a good deal both in the size and amenity of their accommodation and in the extensiveness and suitability of their book stock; but at least in these schools the library was readily accessible at convenient times and book borrowing was encouraged. Where the use made of these opportunities was disappointing, it often seemed fair to apportion some of the blame to the social environment served by the school. Thus three large urban comprehensive schools with well equipped libraries lamented the very limited amount of book borrowing which resulted from their efforts, and were inclined to feel that what hampered them above all was the low esteem in which books were held in the predominantly working class homes from which their pupils were drawn. (Nevertheless in two of these schools quite a considerable amount of book reading was in fact done, though most of it was trashy in quality, and very little was drawn from school sources.)

Of course the obvious objection to a central library in a large school is that it is likely to be visited and used only by those children who are already committed to book reading, so that it is clearly a *sine qua non* that regular library periods for browsing and borrowing must be provided in the timetable during the earlier years at least. Such arrangements were in force in the three comprehensive schools we have mentioned; but we suspect that what was lacking was the tailor-made guidance which can only come from a teacher who knows his pupils individually and which cannot in the nature of things be supplied by a professional librarian (however well qualified) who meets the children only on infrequent occasions in the setting of the library. Certainly in the two (admittedly much smaller) schools where the school library was being used with real success, the outstandingly significant factor seemed to be the personal knowledge and enthusiasm of the English teachers involved.

Thus in one secondary modern girls' school our interviewer was enormously impressed by the zeal and dedication of the senior English mistress who was also in charge of the library. This school was in a small rural town within travelling distance of a large city, and there had developed there within recent years both a slum-clearance estate and some middle class commuter housing estates, so that the school's catchment area was quite mixed socially. However, about 35% of the age group was creamed off to selective schools, so that even the most able pupils in this school were by no means exceptionally promising material. The library was small, having been built up laboriously from scratch during the five years of the school's existence, and the emphasis on book selection had been largely (though not exclusively) on better quality fiction. Access and borrowing arrangements were very easy; although these were no class libraries as such, a pile of library books was always to be seen on the English teachers' desks, and the senior English mistress devoted much of her energy to 'selling' books to the children by means of her own informed enthusiasm. The effects of this policy were even more in evidence with the 15+ group, but it was clearly beginning to pay off already with the 13+ girls, among whom the favourite writers named ranged from Enid Blyton and C. Pullein-Thompson through Louisa M. Alcott and J. R. R. Tolkien to Charlotte Brontë (named twice). Thus Marie's obsession with pony stories (she had read eight of them during the month) had been directed via the school library to an enthusiasm for *My Friend Flicka*, and thence to other books by Mary O'Hara also borrowed from the school library.

What was noticeable in this school, too, was the way in which the enjoyment of quality books read in class had in several cases extended its influence into private reading; thus Fiona, who mentioned having also enjoyed *Day of the Triffids*, *Jane Eyre* and *Wuthering Heights* in English lessons, had been so taken by *Animal Farm* when read in class that she had gone on to buy *1984* for her leisure-time reading and had rated it as 'liked very much'. It must be freely admitted that this approach did not work equally well for all children (and perhaps could never be expected to); Diana, for instance, had also read *Animal Farm* in class and told our interviewer that she had thought it 'a bit daft' (though graded B by the school Diana was a comic reader only). Moreover to pin one's hopes too much on the enjoyment of good books read together with the teacher does risk the possibility that such satisfactions may be accepted rather too passively as something that belongs to the classroom situation only. Thus Tina had enjoyed reading under her English teacher's guidance *Lord of the Flies, A High Wind in Jamaica* and *Jane Eyre,* but even so (and despite her ambitions to become an infant teacher) book reading had not yet come to be numbered among her leisure-time activities. In general, however, this school was aware of the need to move forward on a broad front, taking care to include non-quality fiction among the library stock, and several children had made use of this provision during the month, in addition to reading similar books which were either their own or had been borrowed from friends. Even so the assiduous and impressively sustained efforts made by the school had not succeeded in influencing all the 13+ girls we interviewed; of Rachel, for instance, who lived a busy aimless but perfectly happy life on her father's small farm, our interviewer had to record as a summing-up: 'School has not touched this child.'

A similar commitment to fostering reading was evident among the English staff at a small rural mixed comprehensive school. Here, though there was some mixture of social classes, the children's parents were predominantly working class, mainly factory workers together with some agricultural labourers and poor farmers. The library was not large, but it was particularly well stocked with a wide range of fiction; there was no Enid Blyton on the shelves, but non-quality fiction was adequately represented, and mixed in with a generous well chosen collection of quality juvenile fiction and adult classics from both the 19th and 20th centuries. The extent to which children made use of the widely ranging opportunities offered them can be indicated by mentioning a few individual cases. Take, for example, Wayne who has read during the month books by Geoffrey Trease, Henry Treece and Agatha Christie, all borrowed from the school library; or Jacqueline, whose two books (both from the school library and both 'liked very much') were *Walkabout* by James Vance Marshall and *The Reaction,* a story about a pop group; or Malcolm, whose four books (all from the school library) were three Arthur Ransome books together with Alfred Hitchock's *Sinister Stories*; or Beverley, whose five books included, at opposite poles, a story by Anthony Buckeridge and *Young Mother* by Josephine Kamm; or Susan, whose five books ranged from *Amanda in Floristry* (a re-reading) to Poe's *Tales of Mystery and Imagination* (rated 'one of the best books I have ever read'); or Norma who has read a mystery story and a Gerald Durrell book from the school library together with *Skinhead* borrowed from a friend; or Nicola, whose five school library books included ones by H. E. Bates, K. M. Peyton and Monica Dickens, but who has also read *Skinhead* from an unspecified source and found it unattractive. Most of the children interviewed named a favourite author, and these ranged from Enid Blyton through Joy Adamson, Eric Knight and Dodie Smith to C. S. Lewis, Henry Treece, Gerald Durrell, K. M. Peyton and Conan Doyle.

Most striking in this school was the fact that there were no non-book-readers at all among our 13 interviewees. In part this must be credited to the efficiency of the school's remedial teaching; backward readers were withdrawn during practical lessons for intensive coaching, and this had worked so well that the 15 backward readers identified on entry had been reduced to 5 by the end of their second year. It was clear, however, that the intelligent and concerted use made of the school library by the English staff had also played a large part. Thus our interviewer commented of Jacqueline, who had read and much liked *Walkabout,* that she would almost certainly have been a non-book-reader in other schools; and was able to adduce also the case of Glenys, who two years ago read nothing, but during the previous month had read three school library books, including *Young Mother*, though she still named Enid Blyton as her favourite writer. The key to the school's success could be traced above all to the English staff's systematic encouragement of wide reading, with regular, tactful and unfussy checking of and discussion about the entries on a reading list record which each child kept on a standardized form in his school diary. The other foundation stone on which everything rested, however, was the judicious selection of books provided in the school library, where trash was excluded but a wide range of good or goodish books was available to demonstrate in practice that reading can be a really satisfying activity for all.

In general then our review of the records of interviews with 13+ children has suggested that, around the second and third years of the secondary school course, there is still a crucially important role for the school to play in fostering and guiding their pupils' leisure-time reading, and that a regrettably large proportion of schools are failing to fulfil this role effectively. It is true that at the 13+ age there is some evidence of an increase in the claims upon children's time made by social activities with the peer group (either organized or *ad hoc*) which take the child outside the home circle during the evening or the weekend; it is true also that for a considerable proportion of children the demands of homework are beginning to effect a regular (though not on the whole very large) reduction in the time which might be available for reading. Nevertheless the impressive success of some schools in overcoming these adverse factors was in marked contrast to the relative failure of others to do so. (Our interviews with the 13+ children suggested that the tendency of the 12+ children in the main sample to take an increased proportion of their books from sources other than the school may have been due in large part to the schools' failure to understand or to discharge satisfactorily their responsibilities in regard to children's voluntary reading.) And it was our interviewers' impression that what counted above all was the degree of concern and commitment felt, first, by the English teachers and, secondly, by those in charge of the school library; wherever this concern was strongly present, one could expect to find in operation patterns of organization appropriate to the particular circumstances of the school.

We conclude this section by mentioning, as constructively as possible, a few points which seem particularly relevant around this age level. First it should be stressed that it remains just as true for the 13+ group as it was for the younger age groups that a child's reading (or non-reading) is intimately intertwined with his total life situation; moreover the diversity among these 13+ children (in terms of interests, attainments, maturity, ambitions, family circumstances and general life-style) is unquestionably as vast as it ever was. It is this that makes it so important that adult intervention in regard to reading should be based upon close knowledge of the child's individual bent and capacities. In a large secondary school it may often be necessary to concentrate book provision in a single central library, and provided there are easy borrowing arrangements and regular library periods on the timetable we have no wish to denigrate the value of this arrangement. Nor do we wish to undervalue the contribution which can be made under these circumstances by the presence of a qualified librarian. The professional skills of the librarian cannot however be a substitute for the professional skills of the English teacher, who has close knowledge of the developmental stage and consequent needs of his own pupils. Library periods should *always*, we suggest, be under the supervision of a form's English teacher, and there should be the closest possible collaboration between the library staff and the English teaching staff over all matters of book choice and reading guidance. Where well informed individual guidance is not provided, the children most liable to suffer are those who have not yet formed the book reading habit and who consequently fail to make good use of the opportunities available to them in library periods.

This leads us on to our second point — namely that teachers must expect to find in the second and third forms of the secondary school (and particularly among children from working class homes) a proportion of children who have not yet become 'hooked on books' and in regard to whom the school needs to set high among its priorities the task of getting them thus hooked. For these children it is important to provide, either in the school library or in the class library, a certain amount of enticing fiction which is relatively undemanding both in its linguistic difficulty and in its emotional maturity. Just how far a school needs to go in compromising its own standards of quality for the sake of these non-book-reading children will need to be judged in the light of specific circumstances, but we certainly think that some degree of compromise may be necessary.

As an example of the kind of child we are thinking of we may cite Elizabeth, who until recently was reading only comics but whose craze for ponies has now led her to read nine pony stories within the period of a month, mostly either her own or borrowed from friends, but two of them borrowed from the school library. This fiction is all of negligible merit in its own right, but it does represent a step forward from her previous level of reading. In this particular case the movement forward seems to have been self-initiated rather than the result of adult intervention; but the link with the school library is surely to be welcomed, as representing a possible agent of further progression in the future. Thus in the same school other pony-mad girls have been successfully introduced by the school library to *My Friend Flicka*, while our interview records also include, in a different school, the case of Linda, another girl with a passion for pony stories who has had *Flambards* recommended to her by her English teacher and now names K. M. Peyton as her favourite writer. In general it seems important to realize that, at certain stages for certain pupils, inferior fiction may deserve a place on the school library shelves, not as an end in itself but as a bridge leading to better things.

The third point to make is that at about 12+ or 13+ some children are feeling their way forward towards fiction that deals with more adult problems and situations, and that school library provision needs to take into account the uncertain and fumbling nature of this movement. Sometimes a step backward in terms of quality seems to be an inevitable concomitant, and it is at this stage that the school library or class library needs to interpret its own standards of quality with some latitude. Even so there are some difficult decisions to be made. Probably most teachers would agree that school funds should not be spent on the *Skinhead* series, but that the inclusion of Agatha Christie and Alistair Maclean on the library shelves would be justified as a means of retaining the allegiance of some pupils who might otherwise fail to make the transition from juvenile fiction to adult fiction. To what extent, however, could one hope to reach an agreed consensus of teacher opinion about Ian Fleming?

Finally, it should be mentioned that around this age the vocational objectives of some children are beginning to take fairly definite shape and that the implications of this for reading guidance should not be overlooked. Career novels are the obvious prescription here, but it must be admitted that the ones available (mainly for girls) do not meet the requirements in all cases. Here is Jane, for instance, who wants to become a games mistress or a gym mistress, but who spends what time she has left after homework and sport either playing pop records or reading Enid Blyton; how much scope is there here for using her quite clearly formulated vocational amibition as a means of leading her on in reading? Even more intractable from this point of view is the case of Daniel, a somewhat apathetic 14-year-old who rarely reads a book, and spends most of his time either at the youth club, going out with his 'mates', listening to pop records, or watching TV. His one real enthusiasm shows when he mentions his Saturday job as assistant at a butcher's stall in the market, an occupation he intends to take up when he leaves school. Does this offer any lever for reading guidance to use, however? On the other hand, there are in our records some cases of children whose vocational interests do lead towards reading. Thus Alan, who is determined to join the navy, is 'passionately keen on ships, water sports and warfare'; and though only graded D by his school has read three books during the month which bear on these interests. Again there are two girls who intend to become domestic science teachers who have read non-narrative books about cookery and clearly see reading as something which can have relevance for their career ambitions. Perhaps the most one can say is that reading interests may take on at this age an additional vocational dimension for some children, and that teachers and librarians should be on the lookout for ways of building on this where it exists.

THE 15+ INTERVIEWS

In 12 of the 18 secondary schools where we carried out the 13+ interviews we also interviewed as many as possible of those children (now in their fifth year at school) who had formed our 14+ sample in these schools in March 1971. The 12 schools concerned comprised 3 grammar schools, 2 secondary modern schools and 7 comprehensive schools. In theory (if there had been no drop-outs at all) this should have given us the possibility of interviewing between 180 and 190 children of 15+. In practice we were able to interview only 113 children of 15+ in all. Of those who slipped through our net a few were temporarily absent from school at the time of our interviews; the overwhelming majority, however, had left school as soon as they reached the statutory school-leaving age. (It seemed clear that even had we been able to carry out our interviewing earlier in the school year this would have made only a marginal difference to the drop-out rate. Four schools, two grammar and two comprehensive schools, were interviewed during November and December 1971, yielding a total of 44 pupils of 15+; interviews took place at the remaining eight schools between January and March 1972.) Moreover a massive proportion of the children remaining in school were those of high ability. Of the 113 children of 15+ interviewed no fewer than 98 had been assessed as either A or B by their schools at the time of their completing our questionnaire in March 1971. It became clear that however widely we were to cast our net there was no prospect of securing a satisfactory number of interviews with 15+ children in the C, D and E categories; and, as we had already completed a sufficient number of interviews with children graded A and B, we decided to abandon our intention to interview 15+ pupils in the remaining six secondary schools where we were conducting interviews with 13+ children.

In effect, therefore, our 15+ interviews covered only those more able members of our 14+ sample who were staying on at school to take either CSE or GCE O-level. Before we examine their case, however, it may be worth glancing briefly at the small number of interviews (15 in all) with the less able 15+ children who were still in school, though it should be remembered of course that these are unlikely to be at all representative of the much larger number of children in the same ability gradings who had left school at the earliest opportunity. Of these 15, the one who was graded E and the three who were graded D were all, understandably enough, non-book-readers. The 11 graded C formed a much more varied group. They included some girls who were aiming at CSE in certain subjects, but who managed even so to do some book reading. Thus, Patricia had actually read 9 books during the month, mostly from the public library, and these ranged from *Love Story* and *There is a Happy Land* to books by Joan Tate and Alan Garner (her interest in whom had been first aroused by the television version of *The Owl Service*). Again Shirley, a girl from a middle class home, acknowledged that the $1\frac{1}{2}$ hours a night she had to spend on homework was reducing the amount of reading she did, yet even so she had managed to read during the month one informational book on life in the Arctic which was related to her school work, and (from the school library) one novel, *The L-Shaped Room* which she had found too slow moving for her taste. The boys, by contrast, showed very little involvement with their school work, were much preoccupied with peer-group activities, such as football, youth clubs, and discos, and were almost all either complete non-readers or readers of comics only. Indeed the only two who had read any books during the month were Peter who had read informational books about his hobbies (in his case Judo and radio) and Martin whose books were confined solely to the *Skinhead* series. Clearly, however, the numbers in the group were too small to justify any attempts at generalization.

When we revert to the main body of our 15+ interviewees, namely the 98 boys and girls assessed as higher than average for ability and attainment, the most striking feature of their records is the high proportion who have read no book voluntarily during the previous month. Thus 14 out of the 58 pupils graded A are non-book-readers in this sense; and so are no fewer than 15 out of the 40 graded B. We noted in our analysis of questionnaire data from the main sample an increase at 14+ in the proportion of able children who were non-book-readers, and the evidence from the smaller (and slightly older) interview sample clearly represents a continuation and intensification of this trend. Unquestionably the most important factor at work among the 15+ group is the increasing pressure to spend long hours on homework in preparation for external examinations at the end of the year. Thus Francis who has read no books, reads no periodicals, and watches no TV, devotes all his weekday evenings to homework, right up until 11 p.m., and most of his weekends as well. He is no doubt an extreme case (an able boy who has made up his mind that he wants to take a science degree at university), but there are clearly a great many in this age and ability grouping who give homework a high priority and spend much time on it. (Only rarely do we encounter someone like Janet who is well organized and strong-minded enough to concentrate all her homework into three evenings a week so that she can spend the rest of her leisure with her boyfriend.) Nor is it only the GCE exam which exerts this kind of pressure. Andrea, graded B, finds that her projects for CSE are singularly time consuming, and the only books she has made use of during the month are those which she has consulted for the purposes of her schoolwork: she very reasonably observes to the interviewer: 'If they made the day longer we'd all be reading.' Repeatedly our interviewers encountered boys and girls who stressed that this year was an atypical one, and that it was only temporarily and with a sense of regret that they found themselves obliged to either reduce their voluntary book reading or abandon it altogether.

For many of these adolescents, however, it is not simply a case of reading being displaced by homework in a straightforward substitution. A variety of specialized interests and hobbies (football, fishing, cycling, tennis, pop records, music making) continue to make demands on their leisure time, and may take preference over reading when it becomes clear that something has to be sacrificed. Thus for Pamela, an able girl preparing for O-level, it is only partly the heavy demands of homework that prevent her from reading; she plays the violin in a youth orchestra, puts this high on her list of priorities, and does not seem to mind that the combined pressures cut out entirely the fiction reading that she used to give some time to occasionally. In general it seems that these specialized interests do not lead to much associated reading at this stage — perhaps there simply is not enough time available now both to pursue a hobby and read about it. Thus Andrew has serious interests in both hiking and geology, and these are catered for by his school, but do not extend their influence into his reading; such reading as he does is motivated by the quest for immediate thrills, and his favourite authors are Alistair Maclean and Ian Fleming. Nor is it only highly specific hobbies and interests that now compete for the limited time available. For many pupils the increased demands of homework seem to coincide with a period of life when there is an intensified urge to take part in gregarious social activities with their peer group, so that evenings spent on homework alternate with evenings devoted to youth clubs, Boys Brigade, discos, cinema visits, boyfriends, girlfriends. Indeed many of these 15+ interviewees (particularly the girls) lead such amazingly busy lives that it is remarkable that a number of them do nevertheless manage to cram a certain amount of book reading into the interstices.

Thus it is not perhaps surprising that Barbara, a grammar school girl whose life is very much home oriented and who only goes out one evening a week to her church youth club, should have managed (as well as doing her homework) to read three not very exacting books from the school library in the course of the month. The same amount of book reading does seem, however, to be distinctly more of an achievement in the case of her classmate Lisa, who has a steady boyfriend, is much involved in the peer culture, and spends most nights of the week out either at pottery classes, youth clubs or dances; moreover, though one of her three books belonged to the *Skinhead* series, the other two (both borrowed from the school library) were novels of some substance and quality, namely Hines' *Kestrel for a Knave* and Braithwaite's *To Sir With Love*. But as an example of just how incredibly full a life one of these adolescents can lead we may cite Sarah, who only stays at home one night a week, is studying both German and cookery at evening classes, looks after a Brownie group another evening, goes out with her boyfriend, and also spends all day Saturday and half Sunday working in a shop; her weekend job permits her to afford half-a-dozen magazines, and she has also read three books during the month (pretty trashy ones admittedly, for her favourite author is Ruby M. Ayres).

For most of those who continued to read books despite the pressing demands of school work and social life it seemed that books were seen mainly as a means of relaxation and distraction, a way of escaping for the time being from the tensions associated with this examination year. Most characteristically these pupils were to be found reading contemporary or recent fiction at a level distinctly below the potential indicated by their high academic ability, and the authors whose names kept recurring in their lists were Alistair Maclean, Agatha Christie and Dennis Wheatley, alongside a variety of other writers of undemanding crime stories, adventure stories or love stories. Middlebrow writers such as Nevil Shute or J. B. Priestley also figured occasionally, as did some rather undistinguished exponents of such genres as sci-fi, horror stories or historical fiction. Sometimes trivial or escapist fiction rubbed shoulders on the same list with more arduous and rewarding novels, in a way that may suggest a need at this stage to read on different levels at different times; Judith, for instance, had read six novels during the month, and these ranged from *Chateau of Flowers* by Denise Robbins at one extreme ('liked very much') to *Pride and Prejudice* (rated 'one of the best books I've ever read') at the other. (It was perhaps as an expression of rebellion against the official school ethos that some of these able and normally percipient boys and girls descended to readings of such lurid paperbacks as *Skinhead* and *Hell's Angels*; a similar impulse was no doubt working itself out on a slightly different level in the case of Christine, a particularly bright and intelligent girl whose only books during the month had been *The Penguin Krishnamurti Reader* and *The Little Red School Book*, but who proclaimed her favourite author to be D. H. Lawrence, and who was able moreover to talk about his novels with real sensitivity.) In general the books read at this age had mostly been borrowed either from the public library or from friends or relatives; in only 5 out of the 12 schools were there indications that some pupils had made use of the school library as a source of books, though in a sixth school it seemed that a reading list provided by the English staff had had some influence on the choice of books obtained from other sources.

It was disappointing (though not unexpectedly so) to find that the O-level English literature syllabus, with its traditional set of three books to be studied in detail, bore scant relationship to these pupils' own reading enthusiasms and seemed indeed to have exercised little influence upon their private reading, except to inhibit it. Gordon, for instance, didn't care at all for his set Shakespeare play, which was *Romeo and Juliet*, and had no use for Dylan Thomas' poetry which he found 'incomprehensible', but at his own level and on his own initiative he had found his way to two novels by J. P. Donleavy and one by Nevil Shute which he was able to talk about with some critical acumen; in his case the O-level English course seemed unlikely to turn him away from reading, but would probably deter him from choosing A-level English in the sixth form.

With other pupils the boredom or distaste excited by their set books risked producing a more wide ranging adverse effect on their attitude to reading; and even where the set books were enjoyed, the myopic concentration demanded by the prescribed mode of study ensured that this enjoyment remained sealed off within its own compartment of school work, and seldom overflowed into any 'reading-around' of other books by the prescribed authors. One would hope for a more enlightened and beneficial influence from some of the CSE English syllabuses where the list of books to be read is often both wider and more nearly related to the pupils' own tastes; and in a few cases there were encouraging signs of this, though where it was in evidence it seemed to be due not so much to the syllabus itself as to the enthusiasm and perceptiveness of the English teachers who were operating it. Thus in one secondary modern school there were several girls whose appreciation of authors studied for CSE had spread over into enthusiastic private reading (guided by the teacher) of such authors as Emily Brontë, D. H. Lawrence, John Steinbeck and H. E. Bates; while at the same school Alison's disclaimer, in her questionnaire, of any 'voluntary reading' proved to be a little misleading, since she had in fact been reading at home during the month as part of her work for CSE both *Silas Marner*, which she much enjoyed, and *Great Expectations* with which she had persevered although she confessed to finding it 'a bit boring in places'. Of Alison the interviewer wrote 'she is really a book reader, able to talk intelligently about John Wyndham (her favourite author), influenced by the CSE syllabus which stresses wide reading, and likely to continue reading serious books as an outcome from it'.

Although in general both schools and examination syllabuses seemed to do disappointingly little at this stage to foster reading of good fiction, it would be misleading to omit mention of the minority of highly gifted pupils who were finding their own way to reading of remarkably high quality. Thus in one grammar school there was Joanna (favourite author Emily Brontë) who, despite the claims of her nine O-levels, had found time during the month to read both *Cancer Ward* and *One Day in the Life of Ivan Denisovitch*, and commented, with justice, that 'both books were hard to understand and needed a lot of concentration'. In another grammar school there was Jocelyn who was enthusiastic about her recently concluded reading of Maxim Gorky's *My Childhood* (this one a teacher's recommendation), and had also got a long way into *Dr Zhivago* but had found herself obliged to abandon it because of the pressure of school work. Nor was it only the girls who were thus ambitious; in one comprehensive school there was Alan who had read during the month

James Vance Marshall's *Walkabout* (rated 'one of the best books I have ever read'), Nevil Shute's *A Town Like Alice,* Orwell's *Animal Farm,* and Hemingway's *The Old Man and the Sea* (all 'liked very much'). As a rule, however, it was certainly the girls who set their targets highest; and we may appropriately conclude by referring to three girls in a single grammar school whose lists of books read during the month were really remarkable. On the same day our interviewer encountered Teresa who had read books by Alan Paton, J. B. Priestley and Jane Austen (both *Pride and Prejudice* and *Emma*); Kathryn who had read books by John Wyndham, Anne Frank, Thornton Wilder, Graham Greene and Françoise Sagan (as well as re-reading parts of Tolkien's *Lord of the Rings*); and Lillian who had read books by Simone de Beauvoir, John Wyndham, Evelyn Waugh, Alexander Solzhenitsyn, and D. H. Lawrence. All these books had been obtained from sources other than the school, though it is possible that the school reading list had had some influence (not explicitly disclosed) upon their selection; since in the same school there were a number of equally able girls who had read only thrillers or mediocre romantic fiction it seems fair to attribute the impressiveness of these lists above all to the girls' own exploratory self-directing initiative.

To sum up our 15+ interviews, then, we can say that there seems to be a marked reduction at this age in the amount of voluntary reading undertaken, together with, for most pupils, a perceptible deterioration in its quality. It is impossible to avoid the conclusion that this must be attributed above all to the harmful affects of the external examination system; both schools and pupils are inclined to narrow their horizons and to concentrate their efforts on the attainment of good examination grades. Particularly regrettable is the influence of the O-level English literature syllabus, which is unduly constricting in its emphasis upon a small number of set texts and which bears too distant a relationship to the natural tastes and interests in reading of adolescents at this stage in their development. There is surely a need for a radical rethinking of the purposes of this aspect of the GCE O-level examination.

The 15+ interviewees were not a representative sample of the age range so that extrapolation backward from these interviews to the full range of abilities represented in our 14+ questionnaires is hazardous. Nevertheless it seems a fair guess that the reduction in amount of reading at 14+ could be attributed to two circumstances in particular: first, the onset of an increased burden of homework in anticipation of the external examinations to be taken the following year; second, increased pressure upon leisure time resulting from the adolescent wish to engage more fully in peer-group social activities. Where these influences combine they are unfortunately quite likely to result in a permanent turning away from reading by a number of young people.

POSTSCRIPT (AND INTERVIEW SUMMARY SHEETS)

The follow-up interviews were costly both in the demands they made upon staff time and in terms of travelling expenses, since journeys were made to all areas of England and Wales. We felt in the end nevertheless that they had been justified because they added flesh to the bare bones of our statistical analysis of the questionnaire data, and because they furnished certain insights which could not have been obtained by any other means.

We conclude this chapter by printing nine examples of the completed interview summary sheets to convey something of the 'feel' of the interviews and to indicate the nature of the material upon which this chapter has been based. As in all other references to interviews the names of the children have been changed, to avoid identification of individuals, but otherwise the material is presented in the form in which it was written up by the interviewer at the time.

Interview summary sheet 1

School type: Junior mixed   *Child's name:* Margaret Brown   *Age:* 11

Father's occupation: Engineer   *Older siblings:* 6 (Boys 2, Girls 4)

Mother's occupation: —   *Younger siblings:* —

Occupation of siblings if at work: 3 married women with children
                                       1 cook

Attitude to school: 5 <u>4</u> 3 2 1

School ability grouping: High   Middle   Low   <u>Unstreamed</u>

Ability and attainment: A <u>B</u> C D E

Reading age: $13\frac{1}{2}$ years

TV hours watched: 2–3   *No. of comics and magazines:* 0

No. of non-narrative books: None

No. of narrative books: 12

> *Bedknobs and Broomsticks; The Homework Machine; Heidi;*
> *Heidi Grows Up; Heidi's Children; Lorna Doone; Much too Much Magic;*
> *River of Adventure; The Secret Seven; Go Ahead, Secret Seven;*
> *Ballet Shoes; What Katy Did*

No. of newspapers taken: 5

Interviewer's report

Although 7th in line, it looks as if Margaret isn't the least intellectually. Reads an enormous amount, varying her diet with TV, and her TV with reading — satiety with the one throws her back to the other. An impressive list of books, and not exaggerated. She was one of five in the sample who started reading (Puffins mainly) as soon as they had finished the questionnaire, and the book she was starting then she has <u>now</u> (four or five hours later) almost finished. She will read 2 or 3 a week always, but *Lorna Doone* (half-finished) took her three days. Recently, by re-reading old favourites, she has got through more than usual.

Interview summary sheet 2

School type: Junior mixed   *Child's name:* John White *Age:* 11

Father's occupation: Lorry Driver   *Older siblings:* 3 (Boys 2, Girls 1)

Mother's occupation:—   *Younger siblings:* 5 (Boys 3, Girls 2)

Attitude to school: 5̲ 4 3 2 1

School ability grouping: High Middle Low Unstreamed

Ability and attainment: A B C̲ D E

Reading age: 9½ years

TV hours watched; 2–3

No. of comics and magazines: 9
      Dandy; Beano; Mandy; Victory; Hotspur; Sparky; Whizzer and Chips;
      Score; Shoot

No. of non-narrative books: None

No. of narrative books: 2
      The Happy Fisherman; The Goalkeeper's Revenge (Naughton)

No. of newspapers taken: 3

Interviewer's report
In the middle of an enormous family; does a great deal of helping about the
home, from making the breakfast to clearing the pots, every day and especially
at weekends. His passion is football, but his interest in books is now largely
in fantasy — e.g. *Alice, The Happy Fisherman, Hans Anderson.* His reading
suggests he has more about him than merely football.

Reading age has advanced by one year in the last four months.

Interview summary sheet 3

School type: Junior Mixed   *Child's name:* Joan Black *Age:* 11

Father's occupation: Ill, off work for   *Older siblings:* 2
                            4 years   *Younger siblings:* 0

Mother's occupation: Home-help

Intended age for leaving: 18

Attitude to school: 5 4 3 2 1

School ability grouping: High   Middle   Low   Unstreamed

Ability and attainment: A B C D E

TV hours watched: 3—4

No. of comics and magazines: 6
        Beano; Dandy; Judy; Sparky; Whizzer and Chips; Beezer

No. of non-narrative books: None

No. of narrative books: 4
        Black Beauty; Florence Nightingale; Snow White and Rose Red;
        Cinderella

No. of newspapers taken: None

Interviewer's report
A pretty, composed child. Father very ill and things at home difficult - not
enough money, anxiety over illness. Plucky child, keeps herself well occupied.
Likes fairy stories and comics and cinema. Keen swimmer. Active helper in
home — needs to be. Obliging, chatty — careful to describe exact routines and
jobs that she does. Quite intelligent, I'd say. Heavy TV. Retells stories from
film, TV and books clearly and vividly; enjoys fantasies.

Interview summary sheet 4

School type: Secondary modern (girls)   *Child's name:* Mary Gray   *Age:* 13

Father's occupation: Bus driver

Mother's occupation:—

Older siblings: 2

Younger siblings: 1

Occupation of siblings if at work: 1 married
1 chiropodist

Intended age for leaving: 18

Attitude to school: 5 <u>4</u> 3 2 1

School ability grouping: <u>High</u> Middle Low Unstreamed

Ability and attainment: A B <u>C</u> D E

TV hours watched: 1—2

No. of comics and magazines: 6
   Beano; Dandy; June and Schoolfriend; Diana; Woman; Woman's Own

No. of non-narrative books: None

No. of narrative books: 6
   The Red Pony; 101 Dalmatians; Malory Towers; one St. Clare's Book;
   Story of Jane Seymour; Story of Elizabeth I

No. of newspapers taken: 4

Interviewer's report
Clearly there is some 'upward striving' in this working-class family — parents
would like her to 'do well' and go to college. But she also revealed a wide
variety of activity within the home — a busy active life, reading comics and
books, swimming (with dad sometimes), drawing, taking dog for walks, making jewellery (for financial gain!), playing with friend which includes acting
and miming, helping elder sister with her new house and garden, etc. (Not
much time for TV.)
   There was a confiding, slightly 'old-fashioned' quality about her disclosures
(juvenile in a charming way rather than mature — no self-consciousness), but
I felt that this was a busy child in whose life reading played a part along with
other activities. Varied interests in reading too (Blyton, historical, Hitchcock),
but she didn't like the realistic gore of *The Red Pony* — too much for her to
take.

Interview summary sheet 5

School type: Comprehensive (mixed)   *Child's name:* George Smith   *Age:* 13

Father's occupation: Factory worker   *Older siblings:* 0

Mother's occupation: Factory worker   *Younger siblings:* 3

Intended age for leaving: 18

Attitude to school: <u>5</u> 4 3 2 1

Attitude to English lessons: 5 4 <u>3</u> 2 1

School ability grouping: <u>High</u> Middle Low Unstreamed

Ability and attainment: <u>A</u> B C D E

TV hours watched: 1−2

No. of comics and magazines: 4
       Beano; Beezer; Birds of the World; Animal Life

No. of non-narrative books: None

No. of narrative books: 1 *A Christmas Carol*

No. of newspapers taken: 5

Interviewer's report
Incredible interest in entomology. Has vast collection of moths and butterflies
− keeps them at grandpa's for quiet. Is very interested in animals − has large
collection of reference magazines; reads books on animals etc. Certainly
orientated towards non-fiction and books on animals in particular (2 of
periodicals are encyclopaedic magazines). Reads encyclopaedias when interested
in something. Involves himself passionately. Dickens' *Christmas Carol* read in
2 nights 'I couldn't put it down'. Very adult turn of phrase: 'I'll be frank: I
don't watch much TV . . .'. Interested in art. One close friend, and brother.
A loner. Motivated to do well. Grandpa ex-university.

Interview summary sheet 6

School type: Secondary modern (girls)   *Child's name:* Helen Green   *Age:* 13

Father's occupation: Mechanic   *Older siblings:* 2

Mother's occupation: Shop assistant   *Younger siblings:* 0

Occupation of siblings if at work: Bank clerk
                                       Mechanic

Intended age for leaving: 16

Attitude to school: 5 4 <u>3</u> 2 1

Attitude to English lessons: 5 4 <u>3</u> 2 1

School ability grouping: High <u>Middle</u> Low   Unstreamed

Ability and attainment: A B <u>C</u> D E

TV hours watched: 3—4

No. of comics and magazines: 5
      Jackie; Judy; Mandy; Bunty; June and Schoolfriend

No. of non-narrative books: None

No. of narrative books: 1 *Old Yeller* by F. Gipson

No. of newspapers taken: 4

Interviewer's report

A pleasant but not very forthcoming girl. Reads a lot of comics. Has been encouraged to read in class library. Owns a number of Blytons. Her elder sister has evidently 'got on' — works in a bank and lives away from home — the member of the family who buys books for her. The parents don't really bother about reading, though mother vaguely thinks that to read would be good for her schoolwork. She reveals no marked interests or hobbies — does much TV watching. Clearly books play no part in the life of the home. Yet school (class library) has encouraged her to read *Old Yeller*, which she is really enthusiastic about — she <u>could</u> be hooked on books.

Interview summary sheet 7

School type: Secondary modern (girls)   *Child's name:* Catherine Jones *Age:* 13

Father's occupation: Inspector in   *Older siblings:* 4
                       factory   *Younger siblings:* 2

Mother's occupation: —

Intended age for leaving: 16

Attitude to school: 5 4 <u>3</u> 2 1

Attitude to English lessons: <u>5</u> 4 3 2 1

School ability grouping: <u>High</u>   Middle   Low   Unstreamed

Ability and attainment: A B <u>C</u> D E

TV hours watched: 2—3

No. of comics and magazines: 1 *Valentine*

No. of non-narrative books: None

No. of narrative books: 3
         The Red Pony; 101 Dalmatians; The Railway Children

No. of newspapers taken: 1

Interviewer's report
At the young end of a large family. Father now off work with arthritis. A
small, lively, vivacious child. Quite forthcoming. Reading plays quite a large
part in her life, and she regularly attends the local public library discussion
circle (2 nights a week) with her friend. Doesn't like to have to write about
the class library books after reading them — 'it spoils the enjoyment'. Is
expected to play with her younger brothers. Uses TV selectively. Shows
intelligence and discrimination in her reaction to books, and has read and
enjoyed *David Copperfield, Jane Eyre* and *The Railway Children* — under the
influence of school English teaching. Has inherited a number of books from
her older sisters.
     Difficult to see quite why books should loom larger in her life than in other
girls of the group — family 'skilled manual' but not otherwise remarkable.

Interview summary sheet 8

School type: Secondary modern (mixed)

Child's name: Peter Roberts   *Age:* 16

Father's occupation: Civil engineer

Older siblings: 0

Mother's occupation: Nurse

Younger siblings: 0

Intended age for leaving: 16

Attitude to school: 5 <u>4</u> 3 2 1

Attitude to English lessons: 5 4 <u>3</u> 2 1

School ability grouping: <u>High</u> Middle Low Unstreamed

Ability and attainment: A <u>B</u> C D E

TV hours watched: 1–2

No. of comics and magazines: 3
        Shoot; Car Mechanics; Hot Car

No. of non-narrative books: 1 *The Waste Makers* by Vance Packard

No. of narrative books: 1 *Brothers in Law* by H. Cecil

No. of newspapers taken: 3

Interviewer's report
A large, bear-like figure, with more brain than immediately apparent. Casual manner belied seriousness — he 'likes to spend at least three hours on homework', he takes magazines that 'teach him something' (except for *Shoot*?), and he reads H. G. Wells with enthusiasm. His non-fiction book, *The Waste Makers,* he found heavy going but carried on because he was interested. He intends to go to Technical College when he leaves school.

Interview summary sheet 9

School type: Comprehensive (mixed)   *Child's name:* Carol Robinson *Age:* 16

Father's occupation: Shop foreman   *Older siblings:* 4 girls

Mother's occupation:—   *Younger siblings:* –

Occupation of siblings if at work: 2 married, 1 wages clerk, 1 office worker.

Intended age for leaving: 17

Attitude to school: 5 4 3 2 1

Attitude to English lessons: 5 4 3 2 1

School ability grouping: High   Middle   Low   Unstreamed

Ability and attainment: A B C D E

TV hours watched: 1–2

No. of non-narrative books: None

No. of comics and magazines: None

No. of narrative books: 5
  The Devil Rides Out, Strange Conflict, The Satanist, The Golden
  Spaniard (all by Dennis Wheatley); The Last Frontier (Alistair Maclean)

No. of newspapers taken: 2

Interviewer's report
Her main interest is riding, and with her general interest in pets (she used to
have 10) she wants to be a vet's assistant — having decided she is capable of
the requisite O-levels. Her sisters have achieved something distinctive, and it
seems likely she will do so too. Surprising that such a quiet, well groomed girl
should not be a little more enthusiastic about school — but at least she is
determined to stay until she has the qualifications she needs for a vet's
assistant.
    Her reading is limited in range, but there is plenty of it. She gets encourage-
ment from her sisters, who are continually recommending this or that. She
doesn't read magazines, because she 'prefers books'.

5 The books children prefer

SOME THEORETICAL CONSIDERATIONS

One of the stated aims of the research programme as originally put forward
was 'to explore the qualities inherent in the most popular books which lead
children to prefer them'. This way of putting it does in itself highlight the
difficulty of what was proposed. When we try to clarify our conception of
what it is that children take from their reading of books or periodicals we
inevitably move into an area which is much more speculative and impressionistic than anything that has gone before. The young reader seldom finds
it possible to be articulate in any very specific way about what he has liked or
valued in his reading (a fact that we were able to confirm repeatedly in our
follow-up interviews with individual children). In essence, therefore, we are
limited to hypothesizing on the basis of our own reactions to the books or
reading matter which is widely read or favourably commented on by children
of given ages. We can have no certainty that our own adult reactions are
congruent with, or even necessarily similar to, the reactions of the child
reader; and the interpretations we place on the evidence need therefore to be
cautious and tentative.

Nevertheless from an early stage in the history of research into children's
voluntary reading, investigators have put forward such interpretations with
varying degrees of confidence, and we may take as our starting point one of
the earliest of such comments, namely, that of J. A. Green writing in 1913
about the reading of evening school pupils in the West Riding of Yorkshire.
The purpose in reading which Professor Green found most thoroughly acceptable was evidently that of information-seeking, and he refers with regret to
the existence of only 'a very small proportion of boys whose reading is allied
to some practical interest – their daily work or their hobbies, and an equally
small number who take pleasure in History, Travel, and the like'. As we have
seen, our survey enables us to say with certainty that in the 1970s also there
are some children (almost always boys) who turn to books and periodicals as
a source of information or knowledge.

In our own sample, however, the vast majority of the boys and almost all the girls confined their book reading to the narrative form, and of their counterparts in 1913 Professor Green had this to say: '. . . the great majority live in quite a different world from their teachers. Here are dwarfed little selves whose emotional life is bound up with local gossip, the excitement of football, and a humour so crude that their teachers find it difficult to see any fun whatsoever in it . . . They sink into reading as a dissipation. Anything will do if it will only carry them out of the world that is theirs. Fiction and fun! Fun and fiction! And what strange fiction it is! Wild adventure, impossible school stories, sentimental novels, the merest melodrama, make up the main account.' It is clear that underlying these observations is the belief that the main motive for reading in these boys and girls was the desire to escape from a drab and unsatisfying real world. The notion of escape in fiction and entertainment has been subjected to careful and somewhat critical examination by D. W. Harding in recent years, but it may be doubted whether in Professor Green's outburst it represents more than − to borrow Harding's phrase − 'just a brickbat to be thrown at something we condemn'.

A more serious and responsible attempt to describe the characteristics of popular children's books and to analyse their appeal is to be found in one of the earliest American surveys, that by Terman and Lima first published in 1925. These authors write:

There are certain elements in literature that children always desire, the first is action; the second is human interest; and the third is imaginative appeal. There are other things that help to make a book interesting, but children do not always demand them as they do these three. They prefer direct discourse to indirect. They like colourful descriptions and names for everything. They like to have the place and time of the story or incident clearly indicated so that they may easily picture the scene in their own minds. They like humour, but it must be of the 'funny incident' kind . . . They will not tolerate preaching or moralising unless it is so successfully concealed as not to be easily recognisable as such. Finally they demand sincerity − a genuine un-affected treatment of whatever subject is chosen.

Terman and Lima go on to express the view that children are motivated to read by one or more of the following: (a) curiosity; (b) desire for wish-fulfil-ment; (c) the tendency to imitate, and they follow this up with a memorable and quotable formulation: 'The child does not read as the adult does for an hour's entertainment or instruction; he reads himself by a process of empathy into the book and finds there a satisfying fulfilment of his sub-conscious wishes.'

Alongside this we may place the following rather similar conclusions arrived at quite independently by another US investigator, Marie Rankin, in 1944. After studying the records of library withdrawals, Rankin read and analysed the ten books of fiction shown to be the most popular with adolescents or near-adolescents. She found that in these books the action was fast moving and unimpeded by paragraphs of pure description, and that characterization was conveyed by relating the activities of the persons in the story rather than by detailed delineation. The plots were not complex, but interest was sustained by a sequence of mysterious or highly adventurous incidents, and the endings were conventional with 'happiness ever after' implied if not actually stated. Frequently a young person was the centre of interest in the story, and the story was set in scenes in which the young American reader could easily imagine himself. Rankin sums up her analysis by writing 'the findings suggest that children who select these books often do so because they are able to identify themselves with the characters and thus vicariously live a life that might conceivably lie ahead of them.'

From these quotations it can be seen that some of the earlier studies of children's reading preferences led to the conclusion that a major motive leading children to prefer their favourite books is the desire to obtain vicarious imaginative satisfaction of a wish-fulfilment kind, often by means of identification with a hero or heroine not too unlike themselves. The most extended exposition of this interpretation is the paper published in 1942 by the distinguished psychoanalyst Kate Friedlaender. Dr. Friedlaender describes her material as partly drawn from cases in analysis, partly from first hand observation of children, and partly from the findings of Jenkinson's 1940 survey *What Do Boys and Girls Read?* Her paper covers the stages of latency (which would include our 10-year-olds) and pre-puberty (which would correspond roughly to our 12-year-olds and 14-year-olds); but she starts by referring to other psychoanalytical studies of younger children and the attraction fairy tales hold for them.

The main conclusions of these studies she summarizes as follows: 'One reason, therefore, for the child's love of the fairy tale is that he finds in it his own instinctual situation and meets again his own phantasies which explains the pleasure in reading or listening to fairy-stories; moreover, the fairy-tales' particular solutions for these conflicts appear to be a means for alleviating anxiety in the child.' At the older ages, too, Friedlaender claims, children's favourite books 'exercise their power of attraction . . . through their emotional content.' Thus in favourite stories of the latency period (the examples quoted are *The Prince and the Pauper, Little Lord Fauntleroy, The Little Princess, Heidi,* and *Emil and the Detectives*) she finds 'a few particular themes . . . repeated over and over again . . . with extraordinarily slight variations'. Particularly noticeable is the theme of a sudden change in the child protagonist's environment or family circumstances — from cottage to castle, or vice versa. Friedlaender sees this recurrent theme as a version of what Freud called the 'Family-Romance' — the child's fantasy that his 'real' parents will turn out to be other and more distinguished in some way, a fantasy said to be very widespread among latency-period children and believed to be generated at this stage in development by a growing disillusionment with parents who have hitherto been idealized as infallible and omnipotent. Other themes mentioned as typical of latency-period books are those of a distinctive family situation in which the child replaces a deceased parent; the 'taming' of bad and intractible grownups through 'the child's goodness and innocence, and its fearlessness and belief in the excellence of the adult'; and the character drawing of the child heroes and heroines who are invariably represented as exaggeratedly good, brave and moral. Friedlaender claims that in these themes we can recognize 'some universal phantasies and defence-mechanisms which are characteristic in the child's development at the beginning of latency'.

When Friedlaender moves on to the slightly older age range which she characterizes as 'later latency and pre-puberty' she draws upon Jenkinson's lists of the most widely read books, and selects for detailed comment *David Copperfield* and *Treasure Island*, said to be the most popular books for boys between 12 and 15, and *David Copperfield* and *Jane Eyre*, said to be the most popular books for girls of the same age. We shall return later in our argument to examine more closely Friedlaender's account of *Treasure Island* and *Jane Eyre*, since these books also came high up in our own lists. For the moment it is enough to say that for this age range, too, Friedlaender contends that the most popular books are ones which offer children fantasies corresponding to those characteristic of their own instinctual life and 'in the least disguised manner'. In general we may summarize Friedlaender's argument by quoting her belief that at the ages she is concerned with 'the function of reading is still not concerned with acquiring knowledge, but . . . looks for gratification of the instinctual life'.

It must be admitted that in the working our of her thesis Friedlaender displays at times a somewhat cavalier attitude towards detail which makes one wonder how closely or how recently she has read the books concerned. Nevertheless her paper does valuably extend our conception of the wish-fulfilment motive in children's reading, making it clear that the instinctual satisfaction the child reader gains from fiction may often be concealed from conscious awareness, and may in fact come not directly but in disguised or symbolic form. Her account does raise for us sharply, however, the question of how far the motivations for reading she describes are peculiar to children, since it has frequently been suggested, particularly by writers with a psychoanalytic orientation, that all reading of fiction is similarly motivated.

Thus Simon O. Lesser in *Fiction and the Unconscious* (1960) quotes various studies of reading and the circulation of library books which indicate that in pre-adolescence and adolescence about three-quarters of all leisure-time book reading is devoted to fiction, but then goes on to add that 'in adulthood the percentage is evidently not a great deal lower'. In his generalized account of the role of fiction in human life, Lesser builds up a picture quite similar to that painted by Friedlaender. Starting with a striking quotation from Freud, 'the meagre satisfaction that man can extract from reality leaves him starving', Lesser lists at some length the inherent and inescapable deficiencies of real experience, deficiencies which result in part from man's biological nature and in part from the inevitable concomitants of culture and civilization, and concludes as follows:

It is to make good some of the deficiencies of experience that people read fiction. A perfectly satisfied person, Freud declares, would not day-dream, nor would a perfectly satisfied person feel any compelling need to read stories. We read because we are beset by anxieties, guilt feelings and ungratified needs. The reading of fiction permits us in indirect fashion to satisfy those needs, relieve our anxieties, and assuage our guilt. It transports us to a realm more comprehensible and coherent, more passionate and more plastic, and at the same time more compatible with our ideals than the world of our daily routine, thus providing a kind of experience which is qualitatively superior to that which we can ordinarily obtain from life.

Elsewhere in his book Lesser makes more explicit the psychoanalytic view of the relationship betwen fantasy (daydreaming) and fiction. He ranges fiction, play, fantasy and wit along a continuum, seeing them as 'alike in that they all represent substitute gratifications . . . (and) alike, too, in that they all rearrange the facts of reality to mold phantom worlds more harmonious, more gratifying and less fearful than the world of experience'. Daydreaming differs from the reading of fiction, however, in that it is a solitary and therefore guilt-ridden activity, whereas the social dimension of fiction ensures that when we read we can (in Freud's words) 'enjoy our own day-dreams without reproach or shame' because we know that they are shared by others — in the first place by the author and additionally by other readers.

Closely allied to this viewpoint, though not perhaps wholly congruent with it, is the argument advanced by another psychoanalytic writer, Hans Sachs (1942). For Sachs the majority of daydreams aim openly and directly at the satisfaction of wishes which, though frustrated by reality, are perfectly harmless, and may be typified at the simplest level by the thirst that produces the fantasy of drinking or by ambition which is satisfied by a daydream of success. But if 'immediate wish-fulfilment in the fantasy-way is the general character of daydreams', Sachs points out that we are well acquainted with a class of literature ('not a very high class sort of art, but an immensely popular one') of which almost the same could be said.

All those works which are building up a 'happy end' solution and would have either no effect at all or become positively distasteful without it, belong in this category . . . Even here, trying, painful, or sad episodes are by no means entirely absent: the hero or heroine hangs over a precipice or falls into the hands of gangsters and is rescued at the very last moment, or one of them comes very close to marrying the villain or the adventuress. But nobody can entertain any serious doubts that all this sort of thing is introduced only to serve as a foil or contrast, or rather for the purpose of heightening the tension so that the final happiness might be enhanced by a keen feeling of relief. The basic structure of these works is, in spite of all complicating factors, one of great simplicity, and this is one reason why they please mostly the simpler minds of children, adolescents, and of the great unsophisticated multitude. The more obvious the tendency to serve as 'entertainment' — i.e. momentary wish-fulfilment — becomes, the greater the resemblance to a typical daydream. Indeed, some of them would be indistinguishable from the common or garden variety of daydreams if it were not for one decisive factor: they retain their social function. They give pleasure not only to their author, if to him at all, but to an indeterminate number of people. It cannot be doubted that this pleasure is based on the fact that each person in the audience or each reader identifies himself with the hero and in this way transforms, without knowing or intending it, a story that thousands share with him into his own private daydream. The better and more readily the audience succeeds in doing that — and the shrewd author uses all sorts of tricks to facilitate it — the better they will be pleased. These works of art or borderline art resemble the photographs made at fairs and amusement parks, where every one can have his likeness taken as a mountaineer, cowboy, or sailor, by placing his head in position over a dummy provided for the purpose.'

By contrast with this 'entertainment' type of fiction, Sachs characterizes the great works of literature as ones in which the driving force comes from wishes which have been rejected and repressed by the conscious personality and which thus give rise to guilt feelings and to deep psychic conflict. The strategies whereby the creative artist achieves, in his work of fiction, a recon-ciliation between the repressed and the repressing forces in his own psyche constitute an area of discussion to which we shall return later, together with the allied question of the extent to which the social bond between author and reader may contribute to the alleviation of guilt feelings in each of them. It is worth noticing however that Sachs supports his overall contrast between day-dream and work of art by reference to some rather uncommon instances, intermediate between the two, of shared daydreams in which two individuals are for a time brought together by a strong suppressed wish which they have in common. Though such mutual daydreams seem to be very rare indeed, Sachs is able to cite from his case studies two episodes which suggestively illustrate the part which sharing can play in giving social sanction to a fantasy which neither of the partners could have produced or enjoyed separately.

Clearly but unsurprisingly, then, our consideration of children's motivations for reading can only proceed as part of a more wide ranging examination of reading in general. At this point, however, we may reasonably ask what col-lateral evidence we have, apart from adult impressions gained from reading children's books, to support the kind of interpretation outlined by Terman and Lima, Rankin, and Friedlaender. Some anecdotal observations of identification and wish-fulfilment processes at work in the reading patterns of individual children will probably form part of the stock of experience of many readers. It is seldom possible, however, to observe these processes at work in any depth, and it therefore seems worth quoting Bruno Bettelheim's account of one small boy's response to a particular story. Bettelheim (1949) provides in his article a lengthy, detailed and fascinating account of the application of a 'total therapeutic environment' to a delinquent 7-year-old boy whom he calls Harry. Harry's delinquency took the form of truancy, stealing and violence, and arose from a home with an alcoholic father and a domineering unloving mother. Bettelheim comments that his truancy was basically a counter-phobic defence in that he was running away from a fear-producing situation, and goes on to relate:

One evening . . . an illustrated story was read to him. It concerned a little chick who was accidentally hatched out with some ducks, and told of the chick's return to his own yard and his own kind. The chick had many adventures and frights on the way over the hill to the barnyard, but the last picture showed him in the presence of a whole group of chicks exactly like himself. When the counselor got to this point, Harry looked at the picture and said with delight, 'He's home! There they are, all those others are just like him. He's with them now.'

Harry asked to have this story read to him over and over again. It was his favourite for a long time, and he stopped requesting it only after had had virtually stopped running away. To him, it obviously meant that, like the little chick, his long series of fearful adventures were over, and that he was safely at home among people to whom he belonged.

It would be hard to deny that in this instance Bettelheim's exceptionally well informed account of the child reader's life-situation provides persuasive circumstantial evidence for the identification-cum-wish-fulfilment hypothesis.

In a more general way it seems likely that children's predilections for their 'favourite story' may often be an illuminating indicator of their dominant reading-motivations, and this line of thought provided the basis for an interesting and original approach adopted by Collier and Gaier in research described in three articles (1958a, 1958b, 1959). 264 College students (80 men and 184 women) were asked to summarize their favourite childhood story, to report the circumstances of their first encountering it, and to compare past and present impressions of it. The underlying assumption was that the passage of time would have highlighted the memory of those reading experiences which had played a most crucial role in the individual's development. As far as the women were concerned, a majority reported on fairy tales which had first been heard at an average age of $4\frac{3}{4}$, and whose themes reflected intensely felt oedipal conflicts, particularly ones between a young, naïve and helpless heroine and an older malevolent woman such as a wicked stepmother, a witch, or a bad fairy. In these stories good and bad characters were vividly contrasted, and the heroine was protected from her persecutor not by her own actions but by an outside agent such as a fairy godmother, a good fairy, or dwarfs, or a rescuing prince. The only other large group among the women students reported on realistic fiction encountered first between the ages of 7 and 10. In these stories the leading characters were children rather than adults, but they might be either boys or girls. The themes of the stories were concerned chiefly with human relationships as such, with the mastery of impulses and feelings, and with moral valuations. The authors reasonably comment that in each case the theme and atmosphere of these favourite stories correspond rather closely to the emotional preoccupations dominant at the age when the story was first encountered.

As far as the male students were concerned, 40% reported realistic fiction first encountered between the ages of 7 and 10, and in these stories there was an absence of any leading female characters, and a pronounced emphasis on one male character and on themes of adventure, or self-assertion, and of overcoming physical obstacles. 30% of men reported on fairy tales, and 18% on animal stories, and here the central figure tended to be a male or animal character threatened by giants or by impersonal physical dangers, and resolution of the action was encompassed not by magical agencies but through physical daring, strength or ingenuity. As far as the men's stories were concerned, the authors concluded that their findings were consistent both with Ruth Benedict's hypothesis that popular stories reflect cultural role-expectancies, and also with Otto Rank's theory that hero myths embody the fulfilment of universal human wishes. It is perhaps uncertain how much weight should be attached to evidence of this kind, but Collier and Gaier's work does seem to provide further indirect confirmation for an interpretation of children's reading of the type first outlined by Terman and Lima.

A more rigorously empirical methodology was attempted by Whitehead (1956) in a study of the attitudes of 1870 pupils in fourteen grammar schools towards twelve novels which had been read during the previous nine or ten months as part of the school English syllabus. A specially constructed Thurstone-type attitude scale was used to measure the favourableness or unfavourableness of the children's attitude towards each novel, and it was found that for ten out of the twelve books (the exceptions being *Pride and Prejudice* and *Jane Eyre*) differences in sex, age, teacher and school had been unimportant in determining attitude as compared with the qualities inherent in the novel itself. For these ten novels therefore (the titles in question were *Prester John, The Pilgrim's Progress, A Christmas Carol, A Tale of Two Cities, Silas Marner, The Trumpet Major, The Cloister and the Hearth, Kidnapped, Treasure Island* and *Gulliver's Travels*) a children's order of preference was deduced, and an attempt was made to interpret the result by making use of the assessments of a small group of adult judges. Thus nine graduates with honours degrees in English were asked to rank the ten books for each of the following five qualities, drawn up on the basis of previous research studies:

(i) Simplicity of language
(ii) Ease of identification with hero or heroine
(iii) Degree of emotional immaturity of the theme handled in the novel
(iv) Openness of the 'wish fulfilment' element (i.e. the extent to which the reader's satisfaction seems recognizably to derive from the imagined gratification of his own wishes or daydreams)
(v) Degree of imaginative coherence (i.e. the extent to which the inter-connections between character, motives, actions and consequences of actions are consistently maintained within the novel's chosen convention).

The coefficients of concordance for the rankings were all highly significant, and the adult judges' ranking for each quality was then correlated with the children's order of preference, yielding high positive correlations for qualities (ii), (iv), (iii) and (i) (in that order) and a low negative correlation for quality (v). The conclusion drawn was that grammar school children of this age range (11–16) prefer novels in which they find it easy to identify them-selves with the hero or heroine, and in which the element of wish-fulfilment is comparatively open and undisguised; it is an added recommendation if these novels also deal with themes that are relatively immature emotionally, and are written in comparatively simple language. In this study the number of books dealt with was small, and the age span of the subjects was rather wide and was variable as between individual books. Nevertheless the investiga-tion broke new ground in its attempt to move beyond purely subjective impressions in the interpretation of children's reading preferences, and it must be accepted that the evidence assembled corroborates, in some measure, the importance of identification and wish-fulfilment in children's responses to fiction.

Some indication that children's ability to tolerate realistic rather than wish-fulfilment outcomes in fiction may increase with age is provided in a Canadian study by Douglas who used a 'story completion' test with 261 children aged between 8 and 10. Douglas told the children stories in which the hero (or heroine) was looking forward to an important event when this became impossible owing to some accident, and asked them to choose one of three alternative endings. The endings available involved either wish-fulfilment, pessimism or a compromise. The tendency to choose wish-fulfil-ment and expect a happy ending was less common in the older children who were more likely to suggest accepting some form of compromise. Age may not be the only factor at issue here, however, since in a similar but more open-ended test, used with 116 children, there was an indication that realistic story endings were more often supplied by children with higher IQs. In this connection it seems appropriate to refer to Wolfenstein's (1944) study of the story preferences of adult subjects of differing personality types. Wolfenstein prepared six stories each having two alternative endings: one which sacrificed plausibility to wish-fulfilment, the other the reverse. The stories were presented to eleven psychotics, eleven neurotics, and fourteen 'normal' subjects. Subjects were then asked which ending they preferred and questioned as to the basis of their preference; and they were classified in two main groups according to whether their responses were predominantly realistic or predominantly unrealistic. The psychotics were found to be mainly unrealistic, in contrast with both the neurotics and the normal subjects. The latter two groups did not appear to differ significantly. In both the neurotic and the psychotic groups realism was found to be positively correlated with age, with intelligence, and with amount of education.

Of more uncertain relevance is another study by Wolfenstein (1946), which nevertheless seems worth mentioning at some length on account of its original and ingenious experimental method. Wolfenstein arranged for a children's story to be specially written by a professional author to a 'prescription' formulated by a panel of child-psychologists. Starting with the belief that the birth of a second child is in some ways traumatic for the older child, the intention was that the story should deal with the experience of the first child during the time when the second child was expected and ending with the birth and homecoming of the new baby. It was to be shown that the older child already experiences a sense of deprivation during the mother's pregnancy, as the mother becomes less able to lift the child etc., and that the child has very mixed feelings towards the coming baby, often wishing it were not there. The prescription required that various devices should be introduced into the story by which the mother could help the child through this experience, such as letting the child help with preparations for the baby.

In the writing of the story the major artistic problem was to find means of expression for the child's ambivalence which would not arouse undue guilt. The outcome was a story entitled 'Sally and the Baby and the Rampatan' in which the author solved this problem in two ways. First he had the child in the story develop a fantasy in which her feelings were expressed in disguised form. Secondly he provided the child in the story with a series of abrupt concise verbal retorts ('Ohs', 'uh-huhs', and 'I knows') which expressed ambivalence acceptably because they were also funny. The child's fantasy in the story is summarized by Wolfenstein as follows:

After her parents have told her about the coming baby, Sally goes to bed and puzzles about how they don't know whether it will be a boy or a girl. When she grows up she will manage things better. She'll have just what she wants.

Suddenly the image of a strange new animal comes into her mind, an animal that is part duck and part bunny and part pussy-cat, an animal that she can make anything she likes and that is equipped with a wonderful name — 'Rampatan'. The little girl thinks how funny it would be if mother had a Rampatan instead of a baby, and no one but she would know what it was. Next morning she teases her mother, telling that she has thought of a Rampatan, but refusing to tell what it is.

and on this feature of the story Wolfenstein makes the comment:

The Rampatan fantasy expresses with the ingenious condensation of a dream-image the wishes of the child in the given situation, the wish to create something as the parents have created something, the wish to determine what the baby will be, the wish to outdo the mother, to destroy the mother's baby and at the same time to make restitution, to substitute her own baby for the mother's baby, to have a secret from the parents just as they have secrets from her, and to take an active role in relation to happenings which she has suffered passively. The Rampatan fantasy . . . is the attempt of the child in the story to find an outlet for wishes unrealizable in reality by means of imaginative creation.

The main subjects with whom this story was used were ten 4-year-old children (5 boys and 5 girls) and their mothers. First, the children's fantasy life was investigated in two or three individual play sessions. The mothers then read the story to their own child and reported on their own and the child's reactions, both individually and in a group discussion. In addition, the child's reactions were explored in further play interviews, and the story was also re-read to the children in a group. Supplementary studies were also made of the reactions of five pregnant mothers and eight fathers to the story.

It is not easy to summarize at all concisely Wolfenstein's lengthy analysis of the reactions obtained, particularly since these varied considerably from one individual subject to another. It was very noticeable, however, that mothers tended to identify with the mother in the story rather than with the child, so that to them it seemed to be essentially a story of a pregnant woman expecting her second child. Correlated with this was the mother's tendency to disregard or object to any expression of ambivalent feeling by the child in the story, in particular to either disregard or reject the Rampatan fantasy or to deny the relevance of this fantasy to the story as a whole. The children, on the other hand, enjoyed the Rampatan element much more than their mothers.

Wolfenstein comments that in the story there are portrayed two forms of compensation for Sally's frustrations. On the one hand there are the compensations provided by the mother, such as presents, telephone calls from hospital, or the suggestion that the baby is also Sally's baby. On the other hand there are the compensations in which Sally helps herself, primarily by creating the Rampatan fantasy but also by releasing ambivalance in her abrupt retorts. It was clear that the first type of compensation was much more favourably regarded by the mothers, who wanted to provide all the compensations themselves, whereas the second type of compensation appealed more to the children. Wolfenstein takes this to indicate that in dealing with undesirable impulses the mothers in general preferred 'repression' to 'sublimation'. Thus most, though not all, of the mothers were inclined to dissociate the Rampatan fantasy from the result of the story, and this Wolfenstein regards as a defence against recognizing the origin of the fantasy in the child's hostility. Particularly striking by contrast was 'the ability of the children to assimilate the Rampatan fantasy and to connect it with the baby story'. It may be felt that Wolfenstein's discussion of her findings remains somewhat diffuse and lacking in clarity of focus, but the study is certainly one which opens up new perspectives and uncovers layers of response which seldom come to light. Her material would seem to confirm the highly important part which identificatory and wish-fulfilment elements play in the response to a story, at any rate for small children, and to suggest also that the specific life circumstances within which the story is read may strongly condition the ways in which both children and adults respond to such elements. The discordance between the mother's response to the Rampatan fantasy and that of their children may also suggest one source for the conflicting valuation often put on books by adults and children, a kind of diversity which has been noted earlier in our references to the work of Shuttleworth and Norvell (see Chapter 1), and which was also commented on explicitly by Friedlaender.

Our discussion so far has been conducted mainly in terms of substitute gratification, wish-fulfilment and identification. In recent years, however, these terms have been brought into question in a quite fundamental way by D. W. Harding's penetrating analysis of the processes involved in the reading of fiction (Harding, 1962). Thus Professor Harding suggests that the concept of wish-fulfilment or vicarious satisfaction in the reading of fiction 'stands up poorly to serious examination' since the desires are not in fact, of course, satisfied. Harding rejects as inconceivable the implied suggestion that the reader of fiction 'temporarily gets a delusive satisfaction through what amounts to hallucination while he reads'; and takes the view that it would be more proper to see fiction as a conventional device whereby wishes or desires can be formulated, acknowledged of defined — a process in the course of which the reader joins with the author in the social act of affirming a set of values. 'It seems nearer the truth, therefore, to say that fictions contribute to defining the reader's or spectator's values, and perhaps stimulating his desires, rather than to suppose that they gratify desire by some mechanism of vicarious experience. In this respect they follow the pattern, not of the dream with its hallucinated experiencing, but of waking supposition and imagination — "Wouldn't it be wonderful if . . .", "Wouldn't if be sad if . . ." '

Again Harding suggests that 'identification' is a blanket term which is far too loosely used. Does it mean that the reader sees resemblances between himself and a fictional character? Does it mean that he admires the character and wishes he could be like him (though recognizing that he is actually unlike)? Does it mean that he adopts the character as a model for imitation? Or does it refer to the process of empathy by means of which a reader may enter into a character's feelings and experiences? Harding's conclusion is that '. . . we can avoid all this uncertainty and describe each of the processes accurately by speaking explicitly of empathy, imitation, admiration or recognition of similarities', and he goes on to say: 'The onlooker's observation of other people or of personae in fiction and drama may be accompanied by a preference for some, by specially sensitive or full insight into some, by awareness of likenesses between himself and some (not necessarily those he admires), and by a wish that he resembled some. These processes, occurring with all degrees of clear awareness or obscurity, form part of the tissue of ordinary social intercourse as well as entering into the enjoyment of fiction.'

As this last quotation will indicate, Harding's own view of fiction stresses much more its continuity with the role we adopt in real life when we are onlookers or spectators. In an earlier article (Harding, 1937) he had described the onlooker role as one of four distinguishable modes of human activity (the other three being operative response, intellectual comprehension, and perceptual enjoyment) and had characterized the onlooker as one who is engaged in a detached evaluative response to an event in which he does not actively participate and is not directly involved. 'Part of everyone's time is spent in looking on at events, not primarily in order to understand them, but in a non-participant relation which yet includes an active evaluative attitude.' Harding suggests, moreover, that 'the events at which we are mere onlookers come to have, cumulatively, a deep and extensive influence on our systems of value . . . To obliterate the effects on a man of the occasions on which he was only an onlooker would be profoundly to change his outlook and values.' Harding emphasizes, too, that as onlookers we are continually and inevitably subject to influence from the evaluative comments of our fellow-spectators and, in a more general sense, from the cultural moulding of our own society's values. He suggests the existence of a series which links direct spectatorship of actual happenings with the indirect spectatorship of events we missed seeing, as in a vast amount of gossip and narrative, and as a further step the imaginary spectatorship either of private fantasy or of make-believe in a social setting (whether the social setting be children's play, drama, or fiction). From this point of view fiction has to be seen as 'a convention for enlarging the scope of the discussions we have with each other about what may befall'; and it is important to remember that in reading a novel we are always conscious of being at a distance from the events and outside them. Thus as interested onlookers we see the fictional happenings through the author's eyes and either take over or reject his evaluative judgments on the events described. It seems to be implicit in Harding's view that it is these evaluative judgements which affect us particularly powerfully as we read, and which form the important residue left behind in our minds from the reading of narrative.

It should be noted that, in his careful analysis of the novel reader's response, Harding does not question the fact that 'intense empathic insight into the experience of another person' or 'absorbed sympathy with some character' may often by an important component in the experience of reading fiction. He does, however, make two important points which are highly relevant to our own argument. First he contends that 'the processes that are sometimes labelled "identification" and "vicarious experience" need to be described more carefully and in more detail for psychological purposes'; and in the second place he points out that, even when these processes have been accurately defined, they are 'totally insufficient as an account of the reader's response to fiction' since 'an account based on them alone neglects the fact that the onlooker not only enters into the experience of the participants but also contemplates them as fellow-beings'. Thus Harding's main stress rests upon the evaluative judgements which accompany the onlooker component of the reader's role rather than upon the imaginative sharing of the persona's experience which has been emphasized in other accounts. He does, however, find room in his own perspective for both elements, and it may seem that the crucial issue which has to be explored is the way these two elements are related to each other in our response to different fictions or different types of fiction.

As a preliminary to this, however, it may be worthwhile to look more closely at Harding's objections to the use commonly made of the term 'identification'. It does seem to be the case that for many writers part of the attraction of the term lies in its vaguely technical-sounding associations. In particular the term suggests a link between the novel reader's experience of absorbed sympathy with a fictional character and the psychoanalytic concept of 'identification' as a central process in the formation of personality – specifically, the child's close but largely unconscious emotional bond with a parent or adult as a result of which he is enabled to take into himself certain traits from the other person and to accomplish the sublimation of some of his own instinctual drives. What recommends the analogy is perhaps its covert implication that fiction can exert a powerful influence upon the reader's value system, but as an explanation of this influence the analogy itself is not one that can be pressed very far, since it unhelpfully blurs the distinction between a feeling relationship with someone in real life and an imagined sympathy with a fictional character who exists only as a distillation of the reader's contact with words on a page.

Nevertheless we must register a doubt as to whether Harding's alternative formulations – empathy, imitation, admiration, recognition of similarity – add up to a wholly satisfactory account of that aspect of the fiction reading experience towards which the term 'identification' points. Perhaps the best way of indicating where they may fall short is to take a specific example. *Northanger Abbey* is a novel which would seem, at first sight, to lend itself particularly aptly to a discussion in terms of 'evaluative judgements'. Initially, at any rate, the author's scheme is to mock the reader's expectations by presenting Catherine Morland as a very ordinary girl who has none of the attributes of the conventional heroine, and to satirize the sensationalism of the Gothic novels by contrasting the extravagant anticipations aroused in Catherine by her reading with the more sober actualities of English social life as she comes to experience them. And as the novel develops, this element of detached evaluative comment continues to play an important part in the reader's response, alongside Henry Tilney's 'placing' of the artificialities and pretensions of conventional society, and the author's overt representation of John Thorpe as an impudent 'rattle' and Isabella Thorpe, as a 'vain coquette'. In the opening chapters, moreover, the reader's consciousness remains quite distinct from that of Catherine herself; we view the characters and events through the author's eyes rather than through those of the heroine, and there is a persistent ironic contrast between our own insight into the reactions, attitudes and motives of the minor characters and Catherine's innocently imperceptive vision of them.

Of course it would be an exaggeration to claim that the reader does not empathize with Catherine at all; once the satiric stance of the opening two chapters has been relaxed, we are to a limited but increasing extent led to enter into her feelings and her point of view, though this empathic relationship with the heroine remains relatively undeveloped by comparison with Jane Austen's other novels, and is accompanied always by an ironic and distancing detachment. Indeed it seems to be the case that this dual perspective (at once inside and outside the heroine's consciousness) plays a crucial role in directing the reader's flow of sympathy towards Catherine, as the narrative unfolds. By it we are steadily won over to a respect for the honesty and genuineness of feeling which is the obverse of her unworldly innocence and ingenuousness, so that when we encounter Henry Tilney's ironic characterization of Isabella as 'Open, candid, artless, guileless, with affections strong, but simple, forming no pretensions, and knowing no disguise' we immediately join with Eleanor in recognizing these words as a truthful description of Catherine herself. And whatever the devices by which the novelist brings it about, there can be little doubt that in our reading of the second half of the novel the dominant response is one of absorbed emotional involvement with Catherine, a state of mind in which our sympathetic feelings have become attached to a concern about her fortunes and an intense wish that the outcome of events may be favourable to her. This response comes most fully into the open at the point when General Tilney causes her to be turned out of Northanger Abbey so unceremoniously, and has het sent home unattended at the shortest possible notice. Throughout her stay with the Tilneys we have been given a fuller entry than before into Catherine's feelings; though simultaneously aware of her self-deception, we have nevertheless gone along with her in her fantasies about the heavy wooden chest in her bedroom and about the old-fashioned black cabinet with its roll of laundry bills, and we have even empathized with her suspicions about General Tilney's treatment of his dead wife. After each of these escapades we have shared her sense of guilt and self-recrimination, and this new-found consciousness of error on her part gives rise to a closer affinity than before between the points of view of the reader and of the heroine. At this point in the novel it is a hardened reader indeed who does not feel closely linked with Catherine in the distresses of her journey and in the ignominious-ness of her return home, does not hope intently that her desolated 'loss of spirits' will be short lived, or does not experience relief and rejoicing (on his own behalf as well as on Catherine's) when Henry Tilney makes his appearance at Fullerton two days later.

This gathering together of sympathetic feeling around a favoured character may be dependent on empathy, but does not seem to be identical with it. (In reading Conrad's *The Secret Agent,* for instance, we empathize extremely vividly with Mr. Verloc, but only to a very limited extent does our sympathy flow along with him.) Whether or not we continue to call it identification, it seems hard to resist the conclusion that a response of this kind is a very central component in our reading of most fiction, and that it is moreover one of the most important means by which we attain emotional satisfaction from such reading. Perhaps we can define this component a little more precisely by careful scrutiny of Harding's other alternatives. A reference back to the example con-sidered in the previous paragraph might suggest that recognition of similarity is by no means an indispensable prerequisite for the response we have in mind. Unquestionably an absorbed sympathy with Catherine Morland may be experienced by readers who are elderly and male as well as by those who are young and female. Nevertheless it does seem to be true that identification (in the sense we are trying to pinpoint) may often be facilitated by recognition of points of resemblance, and we may perhaps hazard a guess that this factor operates with particular force in the case of the relatively unsophisticated reader. Certainly the predominance of youthful heroes or heroines in the books widely read or highly liked by our sample seems too marked to be accidental. Conspicuous, too, in our lists are some stories with girls as central characters (*Little Women, Heidi, Jane Eyre*) which are widely read and much liked by girl readers, but virtually unread by boys; while there are also some books centring around male characters which are either read exclusively by boys (*Robin Hood, Robinson Crusoe, The Three Musketeers*), or are much more favourably rated by boy readers than by girl readers (*Treasure Island*).

It might be argued, however, that in our discussion of this matter so far we have concentrated too exclusively upon points of resemblance that are overt, obvious, unmistakable. Perhaps, in a rather more subtle and inward sense, empathy itself becomes possible only when some facet of the self resonates in response to a corresponding feature which is perceived as inherent in the other person, whether real or fictional. On this view, such resonance would necessarily be triggered off by a subjective perception of likeness, but there is no compelling reason why the resemblance should always be apparent to the external observer. The rather diffuse conception of recognition of similarity that we have now arrived at seems however to exhibit more congruence with empathy than with identification as such. To make the point in specific terms we may empathize with Mr. Verloc because we recognize in ourselves a certain human kinship with (say) his laziness, stupidity and egocentricity; but our sympathetic involvement with the fate of Catherine Morland has a distinctive quality which goes beyond empathy and which seems to demand a different type of explanation. Is it then admiration (another of Harding's alternative formulations) that will provide the key to our understanding of this distinctive quality which differentiates identification from empathy? Certainly some measure of admiration is present in our response to Catherine (the term we used in an earlier paragraph was 'respect'), and it is hard either to recall or to envisage an identificatory reading-response entirely lacking in some such feeling-tone. Nevertheless our attitude to Cathrine is undoubtedly a mixed one, and it could be suggested that her follies (more accurately perhaps her recognition of her folly conjoined with our recognition of it) contribute at least as much to our sympathetic involvement with her as as do her good qualities. Don't we, in fact, feel most closely identified with her at that point in the novel when she sits in the carriage which conveys her away from Northanger Abbey, feeling guilt at her own outrageous misconceptions about General Tilney, bewilderment and resentment at the disproportionate retribution meted out to her, and suspense as to the future prospects of her relationship with General Tilney's son? If this is conceded, it must also be admitted that neither admiration, nor recognition of similarity, — nor even a combination of the two — seems adequate to account for this particular instance of identification.

In our somewhat abortive attempt to clarify the confused notion of identification in the reading process, there is one line of thought which we have not so far pursued. Very central to the psychoanalytic concept of identification in real life is the idea of an endeavour, largely unconscious, to 'mould a person's own ego after the fashion of the one that has been taken as a model'. We may quote Freud's own considered way of putting it in his *New Introductory Lectures*: 'Identification ... is a very important form of attachment to someone else, probably the very first, and not the same thing as the choice of an object ... If a boy identifies himself with his father he wants to be *like* his father ...' (*Freud's Complete Psychological Works*, **XXII**, 63). Clearly this bears some relationship to the alternative formulation of Harding which we have not yet seriously considered, namely, 'adopting the character as a model for imitation'.

Now, at first sight, it seems inherently implausible that a moulding or modelling of this type (undoubtedly very important in real-life relationships) can play a significant part in our response to the reading of fiction. Surely it cannot reasonably be maintained that in 'identifying' with Catherine Morland the middle-aged male reader wants to become like her. Yet, on reflection, we can see that this difficulty arises from a failure to differentiate clearly enough between the real world and the fictional world. The reader who is in his right mind is fully aware that what he is doing is reading a novel, and that in whatever ways this activity may influence – either in the short term or the long term – the balance of forces within his own psyche, it cannot in the real world transform him into someone other than himself. Nevertheless, within the fictional world constructed for him by the words of the novelist, he may for a time be caught up by the wish to be some particular character in imagination, to share the consciousness, feelings and experience of this character, and to gain emotional satisfaction from the absorbed imaginative sympathy which accompanies this sharing. In this sense the identification experienced by a reader of fiction seems to be very intimately bound up with the kind of emotional satisfaction which others have described as wish-fulfilment. It is true that the wishes are gratified only in imagination, but the gratification can be intensely pleasurable nonetheless, and it is attained by an emotional attachment which encompasses not only empathy and recognition of similarity, but also the wish to be temporarily like the chosen character. To return to our specific instances, we can say that the main emotional satisfaction which the reader derives from the relevant sections of *The Secret Agent* is that of joining with Conrad in his authorial evaluative judgement (compassionate, empathic, but ultimately disapproving) of Mr. Verloc, whereas the main emotional satisfaction which the reader takes from the latter part of *Northanger Abbey* is that of joining with Catherine in her own experiences of alarm, distress, suspense and, ultimately, relief.

If we are right in thus reinstating wish-fulfilment accomplished by means of identification to a position quite near the centre of the fiction reading process, there is still one puzzle about it which needs disentangling. If the dominant motivation of the reader of fiction is the pleasure principle, why is it that novels and stories so regularly include the presentation of experiences which are unpleasurable, painful, even deeply distressing? On one level, of course, this question can be answered easily enough. If the reader is to enjoy vividly in imagination the satisfaction of, say, triumph, vindication or relief, it is necessary that this dénouement should have been preceded by a contrasted imaginative experience of anxiety, suspense, or other kinds of unease. We have already seen that this introduction of 'trying, painful, sad episodes . . . to serve as a foil or contrast' was mentioned by Hans Sachs as an obvious characteristic of the class of literature which he called 'entertainment' fiction. The point we have to make now is that Sachs' sharp dichotomization of all fiction into the 'entertainment type' on the one hand and 'great works of literature' on the other is not justified, at least in regard to this characteristic.

In all fiction, if we look carefully enough, we can find unpleasurable episodes whose role is in part to prepare for, heighten and enhance a subsequent wish-fulfilment gratification. In this respect, at any rate, popular and serious, trivial and great, must be seen as ranged along a continuum; and the main difference seems to be that in the case of great literature one needs to examine the episodes more closely before one can identify the presence of the kind of mechanism we have been talking about. Furthermore, it may be suggested that one function of the unpleasurable element is to disguise from consciousness the fact that wish-fulfilment gratifications are being attained, particularly in cases where the wish in question has been repressed or has guilt feelings attached to it. The way in which disguise of this kind works in fiction can perhaps be suggested by quoting Virginia Woolf's perceptive account of her protagonist's daydream about herself ('a pleasant track of thought, a track indirectly reflecting credit upon myself') in her short story 'The Mark on the Wall'. As her narrator puts it, 'all the time I am dressing up the figure of myself in my own mind lovingly, stealthily, not openly adoring it, for if I did that I should catch myself out, and reach my hand at once for a book in self-protection. Indeed, it is curious how instinctively one protects the image of oneself from idolatry, or any other handling that could make it ridiculous or too unlike the original to be believed in any longer.' Clearly the extent to which an individual may need to cover up with a disguise his instinctual gratifications either in daydreaming or in fiction reading must vary from one person to another; but it may be suggested that as we move towards the more serious and the more complexly structured end of the fictional continuum, we shall meet works in which the underlying wishes are both more deeply rooted in the human psyche and more strongly repressed by the conscious personality, and in which as a corollary the satisfaction of these wishes is more elaborately disguised by a realism which accords due weight to the unpleasant or distressing aspects of human experience.

However, even if we agree that the unpleasurable experiences in fiction are often there either to enhance or to disguise the more pleasurable wish-fulfilment satisfactions, it must be said that there are also occasions when the painful element seems to be present more for its own sake than as a foil to something else. As an example, one might point to moments in *Jane Eyre* which seem to involve a masochistic enjoyment, on the part of the reader, of imagined experiences of persecution, humiliation or subjection to injustice. Now it is well known that under certain circumstances experiences which are normally painful may become a source of pleasure and be actively sought after as such; we need only to make the points: (a) that this psychic mechanism may operate in regard to imagined experience as well as in regard to actual experience, and (b) that in its less extreme forms it is more widespread than the pathological label for it might suggest. One aspect of the complex phenomenon known as masochism may, however, deserve further comment. What leads us to welcome painful experience may often be an unconscious feeling that we deserve punishment in payment, as it were, for pleasures which would otherwise awaken in us a sense of guilt. It seems likely that a similar 'balancing of the accounts' may often operate in our reading of fiction, so that a painful or distressing episode in a novel may serve to alleviate the guilt which would otherwise have marred for us the enjoyment of an associated or subsequent wish-fulfilment gratification. If this is so, we may claim, on this second level, to have indicated two further ways in which the presence of unpleasurable elements in fiction may be accountable for without requiring us to abandon the dominance of the pleasure principle.

Even so, it may be asked whether there are not still some instances of painful or disturbing experience in fiction which are more properly thought of as manifestations of the reality principle, and which it would be more natural to approach in terms of Harding's view of fiction as 'a convention for enlarging the discussions we have with each other about what may befall'. Certainly we shall be right to insist that all the data we have examined reinforces our conviction that any satisfactory account of the fiction reading process must embrace both of these two elements: on the one hand, the imaginative sharing of a character's experience which we have continued to call 'identification' and which is very closely linked with wish-fulfilment motivations in reading, on the other hand the evaluative judgements which go hand-in-hand with the reader's spectator role and which may include the realistic acceptance of unwelcome and unwished-for aspects of human experience. At this point, however, what needs stressing is that in most fiction these two elements are much more intimately and intricately bound up together than our discussion has so far managed to bring out. In considering *Northanger Abbey* we found it perfectly natural to talk about the two strands separately since in this early work which the author never fully revised for publication they do not really become integrated. If we turn however to *Emma*, a late work in which the same author employs her mature powers as novelist, we shall find that identificatory satisfactions and evaluative judgements are fused together to such an extent that they have become difficult to discuss in isolation from one another.

The painful acquisition of self-knowledge which constitutes the theme of the book involves both the heroine and the reader in a re-exploration and redefinition of the criteria by which we judge conduct and people, and this reshaping of our values comes about essentially through our close sympathetic engagement with Emma in her day-to-day living, in the course of which we see events both through her eyes and also with the author's more far-seeing vision — a further development of the dual perspective, at once inside and outside the heroine's consciousness, which we observed in its embryonic form in *Northanger Abbey*. It is true that the ultimate outcome in this novel too is a happy ending, but on the way there we are compelled to an unusually full and inward recognition (this is surely the core to the novel) of the reality of human fallibility; the point to be underlined here however is that the realistic evaluative judgement has been accomplished by means of an identificatory relationship between the reader and the heroine, and it may be claimed that this close interweaving of the two elements is peculiarly characteristic of the way fiction works at its best level. It is perhaps in place to recall D. H. Lawrence's way of putting it: 'It is the way our sympathy flows and recoils that really determines our lives. And here lies the vast importance of the novel properly handled. It can inform and lead into new places the flow of our sympathetic consciousness and it can lead our sympathy away in recoil from things gone dead.'

One final comment of a more tentative kind may suggest, from a different point of view, how inevitable it is that there should regularly be a close link between illusory experience (fantasying, daydreaming, fictional wish-fulfilment) and the ability to recognize reality. In his attempts to understand the way in which the small child develops the ability to construct a sense of the objective reality which is outside himself, D. W. Winnicott has devoted a good deal of attention to the 'transitional objects' which form the first link between inner and outer reality and which are the precursors of all subsequent cultural experience, starting with children's creative play and going right through to the worlds of art and literature. Winnicott sees the infant's early relationship with his mother as the key to his ability to proceed from the pleasure principle to the reality principle, and he suggests that the infant's first experience of the breast is itself an illusion which is the necessary foundation for his later knowledge of the breast as an object, the role of the mother being to wean him away from illusion towards a grasp of objective reality by a process of gradual disillusionment. If we are prepared to give any credence to this admittedly difficult concept, we should perhaps see the whole span of the individual's cultural development as an extended process of spiritual weaning, a fitful and uncertain progress away from illusion towards an increasing ability to accept the full reality of human experience, yet at the same time a progress which is itself inescapably based upon and rooted in the experience of illusion. The ultimate goal of such a progress would no doubt be that clear-eyed capacity to tolerate and embrace the full complexity of the human lot which we associate with the greatest works of Shakespeare or Tolstoy; but it must be admitted that, at the present stage of our civilization, relatively few of us are destined to proceed that far along the road. For most of us the spiritual weaning remains partial and incomplete, but the contribution which fiction can make towards helping us on our journey should never be underestimated.

SOME WIDELY READ BOOKS EXAMINED

With these theoretical considerations in mind it may be appropriate now to look in detail at some of the specific books which were most widely read by the children in our sample. Before we do so it is proper to remind ourselves that in many cases these books may have been 'widely read' because of their ready availability in schools, public libraries, bookshops or newsagents, rather than as the unfettered choice of children who had a wide range of suitable alternatives open to them. However, we have usually for each widely read book a mean 'liking score' which represents the opinion of those children who read it, and we can therefore confine our detailed comments to books which were greatly liked and enjoyed by a substantial group of children at one or more of our three age levels.

Let us begin by looking at the most widely read of all children's books. In the month of the survey *Black Beauty* was read by no fewer than 2·7% of our total sample, and although its massive and ubiquitous availability must have accounted for much of this reading, it also achieved a very high overall liking score of 4·0. (In terms of readership figures *Black Beauty* reached its peak at 10+, where it was actually read by as many as 4·5% of the age group; at 12+ it was still the second most widely read book, having been read during the month by 2·6% of the age group, and at this age its liking score among the girls who read it actually increased from 4·0 (at 10+) to 4·1, although at the same time the enthusiasm for it among its boy readers dwindled to the slightly below average liking score of 3·7.)

At first sight the enduring pre-eminence of a book published in 1887 may seem surprising, particularly since its language is stiffly Victorian and makes few concessions to the juvenile reader. Anna Sewell wrote *Black Beauty* with a clear didactic 'prevention of cruelty to animals' purpose. Much of the technical detail invoked to this end (about bearing reins, for instance, or about the necessity for removing stones from horses' hooves, or the enormity of failing to put the drag on the wheels when the carriage is going downhill) is now so out of date as to make little contact with current experience, but it may be assumed that the humane anti-cruelty sentiments continue to make a strong appeal to children. One doubts, however, whether this is in itself enough to account for the book's continuing vast popularity. Clearly the child reader identifies (in some sense) with Black Beauty, but it seems that this identification bears a specific feeling-tone which can be localized in the persistent references to the folly, blindness, insensitivity, selfishness or cruelty of the adult human beings who are responsible (in one way or another) for the sufferings endured by the horses. We note that the horses themselves are never to blame for any of the accidents or mishaps which befall them; if their own actions have been a contributory cause, these are invariably due to the way in which their tempers or constitutions have been ruined by ill-treatment. The real blame always attaches to their owners, grooms or drivers, and the horse is in the hapless position similar to that often occupied by the child — able to perceive the folly of adult behaviour and to predict its likely consequence, but unable to speak of it; forced to submit, yet all the while conscious of rectitude and superior insight. The characteristic feeling-tone we have in mind may be represented by the following passage from Chapter 32 ('A Horse Fair') where Black Beauty himself is speaking:

There was a great deal of bargaining, of running up and beating down, and if a horse may speak his mind so far as he understands, I should say, there were more lies told, and more trickery at that horse fair, than a clever man could give an account of.

A further instance may be cited in the following conversation between two horses in Chapter 34, where the incomprehensible human folly or wickedness in question is war:

'Do you know what they fought about?' said I.
'No,' he said, 'that is more than a horse can understand, but the enemy must have been awfully wicked people if it was right to go all that way over the sea on purpose to kill them.'

Does it seem then that the main emotional outcome of the book is to justify the child reader's self-complacency *vis-à-vis* the adults? In its structure the book consists of a sequence of short episodes, most of which are highly moralistic, and these are finally drawn together by a wish-fulfilment ending, in which Black Beauty enjoys in old age a comfortable retirement out at grass. The detailed observation of human behaviour which informs the separate episodes is often quite shrewd. In addition to this, however, the overall pattern formed by the episodes, with their variousness and their cumulative record of Black Beauty's ruin and only partial recovery, does embody a haunting vision of the irresistible march of events which make up equally an equine or a human life in its progression from infancy to old age. Over and above the instinctual gratifications which surely make up the book's lasting appeal, these features constitute an uncontracted-for bonus, which seem to us fully to justify the inclusion of *Black Beauty* in our list of quality narrative.

The instinctual gratifications afforded by *Treasure Island* are less easy to separate from the author's evaluative judgements and the expression of his deeper purposes: Stevenson's judgements are not imposed upon the narrative but enacted, created through and contributory to the developing story. Nevertheless, at the age when the book is most widely read and liked (10+, when the mean liking score for the boys in our sample is 4·1), the reader seems unconsciously to make the distinction by responding consciously to the instinctual appeal rather than to the judgements. In 'R. L. S.: Inspiration and Industry' (1960) Douglas Brown remarks that *Treasure Island* is 'ordinarily read by children a year or two too young for it' — by which he means that a true response to Stevenson's evaluation of Jim or of Silver is beyond the reach of the normally endowed ten- or eleven-year-old. The child at that age, Brown maintains, takes from the book

the ingredients it has in common with ephemeral yarning: even (so discussion with teachers suggests) elements of violence and coarseness abstracted from the imaginative handling of them and made to seem unpleasant (and relished for it) by isolation and over-emphasis . . .. The younger the reader — the less able to perceive, or be helped to perceive, what Stevenson actually does — the more vulnerable to such distortion must be the impressions from the book.

Granted that the elements of violence and coarseness are imaginatively handled in *Treasure Island*, appreciation of them nevertheless requires the kind of submission to their power that the ten-year-old boy Brown has in mind naturally makes. The death of Blind Pew, the murder of poor Tom (and Allen's last cry a moment earlier), Job Anderson 'cut down' in the stockade, the plunge of Israel Hands to his watery grave, George Merry's death throes in the empty treasure pit — these and similar incidents awaken sadistic or vengeful passion in the reader; and much of the attraction of the book for the 10+ boy must lie in the 'isolated' enjoyment he derives from indulging the passion. Yet such enjoyment is necessary to the larger understanding of the incidents, their place in the tale, and may therefore not be so regrettable as Brown suggests it is.

We are arguing of course from a presumption of the declining power of *Treasure Island* to affect the growing boy today. 2·8% of the 10+ age group read it in the month of the survey, 2·1% of the 12+, and only 0·8% of the 14+ — the figures correspond to the shrinking liking scores from 4·1 at 10+, through 3·9 to a mere 3·4 (a below-average rating) at 14+. It seems from the figures that between the ages of 12 and 14 the book loses much of its attraction for the normally endowed individual and voluntary reader; and we may be tempted accordingly to discount the importance of Brown's contentions in an effort to justify the introduction of *Treasure Island* to the age range that will read and like it, in the hope that something of Stevenson's imaginative handling of routine excitements and attractions will rub off on the young reader before he is too old to enjoy the book.

In defence of our enterprise, however, we would say that the title itself promises ephemeral satisfactions of the kind advertised in *Five on a Treasure Island*, and that both title and satisfactions are of a sort quickly to pall upon the modern adolescent. The flag waving ('we weighed anchor . . . the same colours flying that the captain had flown and fought under at the palisade'), the robust commitment to law and order ('If you'll come up one by one, unarmed, I'll engage to clap you all in irons, and take you home to a fair trial in England' — Smollett to Silver, under the flag of truce at the stockade), 'Flint's Pointer' and 'Flint's Fist', the romance of buccaneers and the fearful thrills attached to the 'seafaring man with one leg' — such elements appeal essentially to the pre-adolescent child, who is young enough to accept them without irony. By the time the reader is as old as Stevenson envisaged him, certain adult books of a more sophisticated nature are nowadays competing for his attention (*Skinhead, Lord of the Flies*, the works of Alistair Maclean and Ian Fleming), and *Treasure Island* may seem to offer him relatively wholesome gruel.

The appeal of the book to the prepubertal boy, by Dr Friedlaender's account (1942), goes deeper than we have so far suggested. She observes a 'typical adventure story . . . whose phantasies answer to a definite phase in the dissolution of the Oedipus complex'.

The boy . . . leaves his mother to be taken on by a party of men in their hunt for treasure. Owing to good luck, bravery, disobedience to orders, no matter what, he learns of the treasure's whereabouts, discovers the conspiracy among the pirates, comes repeatedly to the rescue of his fellows, and outwits the most dreaded of the pirates. He saves his own life by intimidating the pirate ringleader . . . with the news of how he, the youngest of them all, has been the one, right from the start, to see through and to foil his plottings. The boy, in these ways, measures his strength with his father's, the father image being represented by various good and bad characters in the story, and so becomes acknowledged by all as a rival on an equal footing. This phantasy overshadows everything else, the original cause of the rivalry, the competition for the mother, getting altogether pushed into the background. The homosexual attitude to the father, which constitutes a significant phase in the dissolution of the Oedipus complex, seems to be the unconscious content of many adventure stories.

Perhaps it is Dr Friedlaender's interest in the 'unconscious content of many adventure stories' that allows her to rearrange the specific qualities and details of *Treasure Island* to suit her thesis. Nevertheless, her account stands, despite signs that she has not read the book closely or recently enough. Stevenson does provide, in his own way and expressed with variously elaborate qualifications, food for the child reader's self-assurance *vis-à-vis* the adults that we have suggested is also part of *Black Beauty*'s appeal. The rivalry of the boy with the grown men appears in Jim's 'envious' emulation of the Doctor in taking French leave from the stockade, in his private knowledge and use of Ben Gunn's coracle, in the way he measures his strength against Israel Hands in the collaborative task of beaching the schooner. The homosexual attitude to the father, present to some degree in each of those moments, is expressed most powerfully after the special relationship of Jim with the Sea Cook ('to me he was unweariedly kind') has been snapped, and we see the captive Jim and Silver tied as it were by a lifeline on the mutineers' expedition to the treasure pit.

At each point Stevenson's inspiration and industry make of the 'unconscious content' something that invites closer examination than the young reader will normally be willing or able to give, his identification with Jim being so urgently provided for. But it is worth drawing three further strands from the book to illustrate Stevenson's simultaneous provision of wish-fulfilment material and creation of art: (i) 'Narrative continued by the Doctor' is more than a mechanical device to report events beyond Jim's ken: it indicates a leap towards the adult that Jim and the young reader will become; the reader, for a season, 'plays at being the Doctor'. (ii) When Jim hands 'Flint's Fist' to the Doctor at the beginning he is rewarded, as befits his station, with pigeon pie at a side table; when he reports what he has heard in the apple barrel he is rewarded with a kindly seat at the same table as the grown-ups, who listen to him and share their raisins with him; but at the end, having beached the ship and disposed of Hands, he eats as an equal with his friends in Ben Gunn's cave, and it is Silver, now treated like a dog, who jumps up to serve his masters. (iii) The title is fully realised: Jim becomes a wealthy man (and writes like one, we might say); but dreams afflict him at the end, as they do at the beginning, and both sets of dreams have their waking equivalents in the narrative. The roots of *Treasure Island*, for writer and reader alike, may lie in the 'unconscious content of many adventure stories', but the flower is a unique imaginative experience for them both.

If we were rigidly to follow the order of listing in our table of 'most widely read books in the 10+ age group', the next book to be examined would be *The Secret Seven* by Enid Blyton. However, we have reason to believe that this eponymous volume in a widely read series attracted to itself a number of fortuitous mentions which should strictly have accrued to later volumes in the series, the specific titles of which were not remembered. We will return to the 'Secret Seven' series briefly later; meanwhile, since the same author's 'Famous Five' series is in fact more widely read at 10+ if its fifteen titles are treated as a group, it seems more appropriate to take the most frequently mentioned of these as our next text for discussion, particularly as this happens to be *Five on a Treasure Island*.

Not even *Five on a Treasure Island*, we should stress, is read as often at 10+ as *The Three Musketeers* (30 mentions) or *Robinson Crusoe* (31); but together the 'Five' books are mentioned 297 times, a figure which puts *Black Beauty*'s 125 mentions into somewhat meagre perspective. Moreover, the generally enthusiastic verdict delivered by the children is unmistakable from the liking scores; the 67 boy readers gave us a mean liking score for the series of 4·0, while the 230 girls provided the even higher one of 4·2. It may also be significant that of the 297 mentions, 98 are re-readings while 160 are of copies personally owned. There can be no doubt that children have easy access to Enid Blyton's books and that — 20% of the sample naming her as their favourite author — a high proportion prefer them to other books, the preference persisting among a number of girls as late as 14+. The phenomenon of their success, despite the refusal of many public libraries to tolerate them on their shelves, their general denigration in colleges of education and the lukewarm support they get from the schools (two-thirds of the primary schools in our sample would not stock them), does suggest something approaching addiction.

'It's as though she's writing about us,' answered one of the children inter-viewed. Generally, however, the comments rely on 'exciting' to account for the admitted attraction of 'adventures' — two words which appear with in-sistent frequency in the Blyton tales themselves — and only the exceptional child answers the question 'What books did you enjoy a year ago?' in this illuminating way: 'Enid Blyton — not now. Tried another after C. S. Lewis but didn't like it any more.'

Miss Blyton's reliance on the explicit language of excitement is of a piece with her formula for excitement. A detached (if not remote) cottage, an uninhabited island conveniently accessible by rowing boat, a castle with dungeons, gold and a deep well, four pre-adolescent children evenly distributed between the sexes, and parents whose principal functions are to provide food and to be left in peace — that summarizes *Five on a Treasure Island* and might with minor alterations serve to indicate the scope of other books in the series. The only adults to impinge upon the world of the Famous Five are crooks; the dungeons that in the first tale contain the gold in another house 'a poor little rich girl'; and provided 'the mystery deepens' within the context of an impregnable fortress Kirrin Island itself is dispensable; the base remains the same, 'at Kirrin Cottage again'. Enid Blyton rings her minor changes book by book, not in order to be original with the minimum of alteration but to assure us that her world is still what we have always taken it to be, a perpetual holiday, child-centred, well fed and spiced with superable problems. That the formula is attractive even the brightest children will testify; books which pro-vide just the expected kind of adventure and degree of excitement, and which make no linguistic demands, appeal to children in much the same way as do fish fingers and minced meat.

What Dr Friedlaender would have made of this material is hard to say. It is too crude and callow for discussion in terms of the homosexual attitude to the father (or the mother), or of the measurement of the children's strength against the adults'. The Famous Five do not grow up in the course of their career through the fifteen books, though from time to time a 'Golly, how you've grown' makes a perfunctory gesture towards the facts of physical development (in the reader, really, rather than in the *dramatis personae*). Nor are they psychologically interesting as a group of Peter Pans; ability or inability to come to terms with life is not an issue that exists for Enid Blyton. If we leave her values and judgements on one side for the moment, we might say that no issues at all exist for her; her literary activity resembles a donkey on a treadmill, knowing or desiring no other kind of mill.

We are reduced, then, to 'identification' and 'wish-fulfilment' as elements in the appeal of Miss Blyton's books; but when we ask what kind of child (what tasks and prospects) the reader is invited to identify himself with, or of what sort of wishes he may seek vicarious fulfilment, we necessarily move into the area of the author's implicit moral assumptions about the world and its inhabitants. There is of course a numerical and sexual variety in the four (the fifth is a dog), as in the Seven: and the reader is theoretically free to find his specially sympathetic figure among the group. But there is no real room for manoeuvre: the stereotypes of character, elocution and situation eliminate all but the cardboard differences between the Janets and the Johns. And the conformity of Enid Blyton's children to each other's and their author's notions of propriety in behaviour and attitude is of a piece with her unthinking or unconscious propagation of philistinism.

The philistinism takes various forms, some of them inert expressions of dominant values and interests in society today, all of them to some degree at odds with the imaginative purposes of education. Exploration, whether physical or metaphorical, involves a willing encounter with the unknown, with the not entirely predictable; Miss Blyton invokes it frivolously as the inevitable activity of children loose on 'a treasure island', reducing 'explore' to a synonym for 'go to'. Ruined castles are peculiarly fascinating monuments of our history; Miss Blyton, in offering to present one, shows a degree of ignorance that effactually insults her young readers. The discovery principle of modern primary education, the reconstruction in scrap materials of a medieval castle, the study of rabbits through the discipline of keeping and feeding them, or the business of learning to row without getting blisters — such things do not concern Miss Blyton, for whom rowing is 'fun', a castle is 'ruined' and rabbits 'lollop', and whose fundamental sense of the purposes of life appears to be that of possession, acquisition and commerce. The value of the tin box the Five recover from the wreck beside the island is not that it may be intrinsically interesting (cf. the oilskin packet Jim Hawkins removes from the Captain's chest) but that it represents wealth: 'the other things don't matter much — they are only that old diary, and a few letters.' *Treasure Island* has not touched Enid Blyton. Ben Gunn expresses the value of Flint's treasure as not worth a piece of English cheese to one marooned without it; and Jim, kneeling in the firelight before the massed coins in the cave, evinces an interest in their various sources and histories that, along with his imaginative understanding of Ben's achievement in finding and transporting the treasure without map or carrier, enlarges our sense of the significance of the book's title. But for Enid Blyton, in her concern *merely* to realize the dream of the jack-pot, happiness is gold-block-shaped, and it is the adult characters' ignorance of *how much* is there for the taking on Kirrin Island that is represented as the fault to be made good by the children. (Compare Stevenson's treatment of that 'issue' — between mother and son — in the Admiral Benbow Inn.)

That the young are apparently unaffected by Miss Blyton's assumptions and attitudes may mean no more than that her values are not unique but derived from the values of the acquisitive society in which, whether we will or no, we all live — or merely that her language is so impoverished as to excuse the reader from any more exacting task than the rapid perusal required to follow the story. Nevertheless, in making use of Enid Blyton in schools — with backward readers, early readers, slow-reading readers who want the fillip of a number of books mastered, and other individual cases — we need to be aware of what we are actually exposing the children to, and aware too of the ease with which the normally endowed and advanced readers may allow themselves to slide into a Blytonian vest from which extrication may, for some of them, prove an unnecessarily difficult operation.

The Secret Seven can scarcely be said to inhabit a different moral world from that of the Famous Five, but there are certain more or less adventitious differences which need to be mentioned, the more so since they may have some bearing on the fact that the 'Seven' series has distinctly more attraction for boy readers than the 'Five' stories, which are very much the preserve of the girls. (At 10+ about a fifth of the readings of 'Five' books are by boys, but about two-fifths of the mentions of *The Secret Seven*.) A possible reason for this sex difference may lie simply in the Secret Seven's tacit assumption that it's a boy's world, that females are eunuchs at any rate during the hours of darkness when the mystery deepens, and that girls are to be given only the less dangerous tasks. By contrast the 'Five' books seem to cater both for the orthodox doll-loving, table-laying girl and also for the girl who regrets not having been born a boy.

In some obscure way a superficial 'sociological' difference may also be at work: the Seven are day-school children who meet in a greenhouse, while the Five, gathering in their holidays from their super boarding schools, bear a certain relationship to the *Malory Towers* and *Naughtiest Girl* characters whose appeal is explicitly angled towards girl readers. A third reason may lie in the criminals, crime and crime-detection of *The Secret Seven*, compared with the romance of islands, woods and castles more characteristic of the Five's world; the former being more 'down to earth' may perhaps appeal more strongly to boys than the latter. It must be stressed, however, that the similarities between the two series seem more significant than the differences; and the Department of Relevant Studies must be baffled by the eagerness with which children of both sexes, not only from One End Street and the council estate backing on to Acacia Avenue, but from Greenland's icy mountains and India's coral strand, press for further adventures of the Five or the Seven. Readability at the simplest level may account for Miss Blyton's popularity in the United Kingdom, but the strength of her international following is harder to understand.

Moving down the 10+ list we come next to two books which though ignored, understandably, by the boys are widely read by the girls. *Little Women* is better left on one side for the moment since though the 10+ girls like it, it is no less well liked by the 12+ girls and actually heads the 12+ list in terms of number of mentions. *Alice in Wonderland* on the other hand is not much liked by the girls who read it at 10+; perhaps its frequency of mention is a hangover from a genuine popularity at an earlier age, or perhaps it is simply one of those books which adults insist on buying for children even though most of them find it beyond their reach when they actually read it. The next book to be discussed, *The Lion, the Witch and the Wardrobe* (the first of C. S. Lewis's 'Chronicles of Narnia'), is genuinely popular at any rate with its girl readers. With the 10+ girls it achieves the high liking score of 4·2, while among the 12+ girls it moves up to fourth place in the list and gains the exceptionally high liking score of 4·4. (At this age, it is worth noting, 50% of its mentions are re-readings.)

The Lion, the Witch and the Wardrobe's basic appeal is not unlike that of the characteristic Blyton adventure. Four children, uprooted from their normal environment and placed in the remote 'house of an old Professor . . . in the heart of the country', are free as the Five to pursue their own interests. Having been told to keep out of the way when the housekeeper is showing visitors around, they hide in an old wardrobe which opens upon 'the land of Narnia' — 'behind them were coats hanging on pegs, in front of them were snow-covered trees'. The strange country to which the wardrobe gives them access is ruled by the White Witch, an image of the mythical snow queen. Opposed to the Witch is Aslan, who after a long absence during which Narnia has known winter but no Christmas is now reported to be 'on the move — perhaps has already landed'. Aslan's arrival is heralded by a visit from Santa Claus, the emergence of the crocuses and the great thaw, which at a critical moment immobilizes the White Witch's sledge. The children — and here an important distinction is to be made between the characteristic Blyton adventure and what Lewis offers us — are implicated in the struggle between the Witch and Aslan; they do not stumble upon trouble, or get mixed up in an affair unrelated to them, but are necessary figures in the magicians' trial of strength. Aslan and the Witch alike require the four children, 'Sons of Adam and Daughters of Eve', to occupy the four thrones of Narnia — the Witch, however, for her own ill purposes, Aslan for good and disinterested reasons. Aslan's personal withdrawal, after the annihilation of the Witch's forces, gives the four crowned heads the absolute authority of a benevolent oligarchy, until they feel themselves obscurely pulled towards what proves to be the wardrobe; the magical sequence then contracts to a moment, and the four children re-enter the spare room.

Lewis's handling of the magic is as directly simple as are his vocabulary and sentence structure; there are no problems of style, morality or human relations too difficult for a ten-year-old. Lewis provides too, however, for the reader whose interest extends beyond the minimal satisfactions of an exciting tale and justice done to good and bad. The simplest of adult injunctions, 'Never shut yourself up in a wardrobe', is employed as the key to the story — Edmund's failure to observe the rule is related to his moral turpitude, both in Narnia and in the house, while the other children's 'sensible' precaution to hold 'the door closed but not shut' is related to moral rectitude and their ability to elude the White Witch. Of the same order is the appearance of Father Christmas. More is represented by him and his largesse than Blytonian awards to good children: the gifts are for responsible use in subsequent crises, and the benevolent dispenser is himself the harbinger of ultimate victory over the snow queen. The more alert young reader, or the re-reader, is thus invited to think about the significance of the incident without being explicitly told what to think, and that is a reason for categorizing *The Lion, the Witch and the Wardrobe* as juvenile quality.

Lewis is of course essentially a man with a message, his propaganda on behalf of Christianity being (at any rate to the adult reader) distastefully unorthodox in places. But the children interviewed seemed unaware of the author's doctrinal-didactic purposes and disposed to accept the accompanying moral advice — priggish, nagging and self-regarding though it may be — without reluctance or resistance, the appeal for them of *The Lion, the Witch and the Wardrobe* resting apparently on more fundamental elements in the book than the intellectually imposed allegory or the gratuitous finger wagging. Lewis presents his tale with such care for detail and significance that we may presume he consciously entices the readers towards the pill by way of their unconscious taste for the sugar.

The fundamental appeal seems to be that through the wardrobe the children have access to a world denied to ordinary adults — access that is a form of compensation for having been 'driven' from the normal world by the 'denied' (and disliked) housekeeper. Narnia is a child-centred world, and yet 'in play' the children rehearse adult responsibilities and challenges, coming back to the wardrobe when the normal world has once again been cleared for them of intrusive grownups. We have suggested in discussing *Black Beauty* that the personal association of child reader with 'human' horse depends to some extent on the tone of knowing disenchantment with adult motives and behaviour. In *The Lion, the Witch and the Wardrobe* the children enter a world in which 'human' animals are subject to the vicious and corrupting tyranny of the differently 'human' White Witch, who in turn is to be defeated by the alliance of the children with a friendly lion and other loyal animals. Aslan the Lion, as Christ-figure, combines lovable animal qualities with those of a truly respectable adult, thus satisfying in the child reader what Dr Friedlaender diagnoses as an unconscious wish for parents without clay feet; and, again in his Christ-rôle (but the doctrinal aspect here is enabled to meet another and less unconscious wish in the young reader), Aslan after the 'Harrowing of Hell' leaves the children in charge of Narnia, putting his trust in their will and ability to rule. Though the Lion and the Witch may be sensed, despite their opposed spirits, as somehow *in loco parentis* to the children, they are nevertheless figures ultimately to be displaced by the children, whose assumption of authority is the kind of fantasy the young reader may be expected to find especially attractive.

If *Heidi* had not first appeared as early as 1880, it might have been written to illustrate a Freudian view of the satisfactions yielded to the child reader. Certainly it suits Dr Friedlaender's purposes, even to her awareness 'how the richness and colourfulness of the fairy tale are gone out, and instead what an expression of monotony one now gets' from the well trod themes. The themes are there in abundance — the frequent switches in the child's environment, fortunes and happiness, the child's characteristic life with a relative or friend, the taming of intractible adults, the 'triumph of the heroine's ethical qualities' — and they compose the enabling material for the desired wish-fulfilment.

The point to stress, however, in attempting to explain what is actually the declining popularity of *Heidi* between the ages of 10 and 12 (for although it is no less well liked than Lewis's book at 10+ by its predominantly girl readers our figures suggest that Puffins are right to advise 12 as the upper age limit), is not the familiarity of the themes but the form they are couched in. The story opens with Heidi, an orphan, being transferred from the ordinary life she has known in a village to the mountain hut and goats of a disaffected recluse. The change in her circumstances seems to herald a tale 'of an *unwanted* child, *dumped* on her strange grandfather . . . when her young aunt *could no longer be bothered with her*' (Puffin blurb; our italics). But the potential trauma is never realized: 'unwanted', 'dumped', 'couldn't be bothered' come across as routine ideas, not as felt experience through the narrative. Heidi, we feel, is better apart from her aunt; her grandfather proves more amiable than strange; her 'rough little bed in the loft' (Puffin blurb) is in fact a comfortable heap of hay in a room with a view; and the only nigger in the woodpile is the occasional pressure upon idyllic remoteness of Calvinist civilization in the valley below.

Heidi's second transfer makes her homesick for the hut, despite her kindly treatment. The orphan is placed as companion to a poor little rich girl in a distant town, where she longs to exchange her soft bed for the hay loft, her balanced diet for goat's milk, *urbs* for *rus*. However, during her spell there Heidi learns to read, so making a painless concession to education and civilization.

Her favourite story, which she constantly re-read, was about the shepherd whose picture had brought the tears to her eyes when she first saw it. Now she knew it showed him happily tending his father's sheep and goats in sunny meadows, like those on the mountain. In the next picture he had left his good home and was minding a stranger's pigs in a foreign land. Here the sun was not shining and the countryside was grey and misty. The young man looked pale and thin in that picture, for he had nothing but scraps to eat. The last one showed his old father running with outstretched arms to greet him as he returned home sorrowful, and in rags.

Identification of herself with the Prodigal (for she too is 'pale and thin' by the time she is found sleep-walking to 'the door of the mountain hut') involves just the sort of exclusion of what is irrelevant to her own imagined condition that the child reader is generally assumed to make in fantasy-fulfilment of a wish: the Elder Brother has been excised; 'minding a stranger's pigs' seems to be registered as the symbolic equivalent of her office as companion; while the Prodigal's 'scraps' may provide her with the unconscious motive for not eating — to run to the outstretched arms in real fulfilment of fantastic identification.

Being free 'constantly to re-read' the story, Heidi thereby accentuates rather than alleviates her homesickness; and the kindly townsfolk return her to her grandfather. Back in the mountain hut, ironically, she begins to want her urban friends around her, and to want for herself and her rural friends the marks of civilization and wealth she has unconsciously grown to accept in the town. The potential trauma is again averted, however, the two worlds of the book being amalgamated for Heidi in a series of happy compromises. The sting has been drawn from the orphan myth and its associated themes. There is no little Dick or Helen Burns to point the starker aspects, not even the relatively controllable problems presented in *Thursday's Child*, *A Little Princess* or *Anne of Green Gables*. If the popularity of Enid Blyton's work (which *Heidi* uncomfortably resembles at the more cosy moments) did not present contradictory evidence, we might argue that by the age of twelve the child reader feels let down by sugar that proves to contain not even the most palatable pill. At any rate we can offer the suggestion that the peculiar appeal of the orphan myth to girls seems to demand from the writer something tougher than Spyri creates in *Heidi*.

Little Women is most appropriately considered in relation to the 12+ group, since at this age it is the most widely read book, achieving a readership of 3·0% of the age group, and it also gains a mean liking score of 4·0. We should remember, however, that its appeal extends both upwards to the 14+ girls and downwards to the 10+ girls. At 10+ its mean liking score is again 4·0, and it is read by as many as 2·6% of the age group, even though this brings it only up as far as fourth place in the popularity list. At 14+ it tops the list alongside *Skinhead* as far as number of readings is concerned, but its mean liking score has declined to the average level of 3·8. Nevertheless there can be no getting away from the fact that, taking all ages together, it is by far the most widely read book among the girls, and that the predominant rating they give to it is highly favourable. The wide reading may be attributed in part to its ready availability, to recommendations from mothers, teachers and aunts for whom it was in earlier decades a much-loved book, and to the fact that it has been frequently adapted for film and television presentations. (It should be noted however that no film or television version had been in circulation during the twelve months prior to the completion of our questionnaire.) The almost uniformly favourable rating is less easy to account for at all confidently.

First published in 1868, *Little Women* is of course the archetype of the 'family story', and although much of it is relatively uneventful by comparison with modern examples of the genre, it does contain a sufficient body of incident (father away at the war, the four daughters struggling to carry on and help out the family finances in his absence, the formation of a friendship with the lonely rich boy next door, the severe illness of the father necessitating the mother's departure to help in nursing him, the attack of scarlet fever which brings one of the four girls near to death, followed by a dramatic recovery coinciding with her mother's return home, father's reunion with the family on Christmas Day, the eldest daughter's romantic engagement to the tutor at the house next door) to suggest that vicarious living with a strong element of wish-fulfilment plays an important part in the appeal of the book. But the language is often difficult, the family recreations thought up for themselves by the four girls (The Pickwick Club for instance) are often ones that would surely need elaborate annotation before they could begin to have much meaning for the modern child, while the pervasive Victorian ethos of moral struggle (and of recourse to daily bible reading to assist in the battle) seems to have little contact with typical family living today. Some of the 10+ readers may have been spared these complexities by reading a re-told version; for the most part, however, *Little Women* seems to have been available in versions which were either complete or only very slightly cut, so that one has to suppose that any difficulties encountered have been outweighed by the intrinsic appeal of those aspects of the book which are still of living interest to girl readers in the 1970s.

We may start perhaps with the characterization of the four March sisters, and begin by admitting that the traits which differentiate them are fairly obvious and indeed somewhat mechanical. Thus Meg is the pretty elder sister who hates her work as governess and aspires to be a young lady, Jo is the headstrong tomboy who wants to be an author, Beth the musical one whose only weakness is her excessive shyness, while Amy has hopes of being a great artist, makes fitful attempts to overcome her childishly self-centred disposition, and has a habit of misusing long words which derives rather too obviously from Sheridan's Mrs Malaprop. Nevertheless on this crude framework Louisa M. Alcott does succeed in building up for us by the end of the novel an unmistakable sense of the four girls as rounded individuals, largely by the way in which they have interacted in a variety of family situations, both important and trivial. One distinction of the book is indeed its success in communicating something of what it is like to live in a family — the constant conflicts, compromises and accommodations no less than the satisfactions of togetherness. In the early stages it may be felt that the reader has a good deal of choice as to which of the four sisters she associates herself with emotionally; later on it seems clear that the strongest invitation to identification is with Jo and that the reader's rôle in relation to the other three is more characteristically in the 'spectator' mode. But the sense of 'family' — of fun enjoyed together, of hardships and difficulties overcome together, and of strong emotions experienced together — must surely make up a large part of the book's enduring appeal. Nor can it be denied that in its most affecting parts the book comes very close to sentimentality, and that this quality too may be part of what endears it to the girl reader.

When all this has been said, is it quite enough to account for the book's pre-eminence in appeal over such a long period of time? It seems to us that one can detect at a number of points throughout the book a specific emotional tone which distinguishes it from its successors and imitators and which may well be the feature in it which strikes a particularly responsive chord in the feelings of the pre-adolescent girls for whom it has been a favourite book for more than a century. This specific tone is not obtrusive enough to be called a theme exactly, but it does recur repeatedly though variedly in the experience of each of the four sisters. Characteristically the situation is one in which the girl is tempted to give way to an impulse which she knows to be wrong but which is insistent in its appeal to her own inward disposition: the temptation is usually, though not always, resisted after intense inner struggle, and the emotional satisfaction results from the discovery that self-mastery can be achieved, despite the strength of the temptation. The note is struck early in the book when the girls' mother reads to them their absent father's letter which ends with the injunction: 'I know they will remember all I said to them, that they will be loving children to you, will do their duty faithfully, fight their bosom enemies bravely, and conquer themselves so beautifully, that when I come back to them I may be fonder and prouder than ever of my little women.'

To this the girls react as follows:

Everybody sniffed when they came to that part; Jo wasn't ashamed of the great tear that dropped off the end of her nose, and Amy never minded the rumpling of her curls as she hid her face on her mother's shoulder and sobbed out, 'I *am* a selfish girl! but I'll truly try to be better, so he mayn't be disappointed in me by-and-by.'

'We all will!' cried Meg. 'I think too much of my looks, and hat to work, but won't any more, if I can help it.'

'I'll try and be what he loves to call me, "a little woman", and not be rough and wild; but do my duty here instead of wanting to be somewhere else,' said Jo, thinking that keeping her temper at home was a much harder task than facing a rebel or two down South.

Beth said nothing, but wiped away her tears with the blue army-sock and began to knit with all her might, losing no time in doing the duty that lay nearest her, while she resolved in her quiet little soul to be all that her father hoped, when the year brought round the happy coming-home.

As this extract may suggest, it is in Jo's history that the struggle with the 'bosom enemy' vibrates most intensely, even though much of her tomboyish impulsiveness is represented as morally innocuous, and the 'freak' which leads her to sell her 'abundant hair' for twenty-five dollars as a help towards the expenses of her father's illness actually gains commendation from the rest of the family because of the unselfishness of her motives. (She has indeed a subsequent subdued struggle with 'the vain selfish part' of her which leads her to make 'a little private moan' for her 'one beauty'.) Jo's real private 'cross' however is her hot temper, and we see the magnitude of her temptation when (in the chapter characteristically entitled 'Jo meets Apollyon') she learns that Amy has maliciously destroyed the manuscript volume of fairy stories which represented for her the irreplaceable work of several years. On this occasion she defies her mother's gentle urging not to 'let the sun go down' upon her anger, and as a result Amy nearly drowns while skating on the ice of the frozen river, and it is only Laurie's presence and prompt action which save Jo from the potential consequences of her perverseness. In the aftermath of this episode Jo learns that her mother, too, though outwardly 'never angry' has in reality a 'quick temper' just like her daughter's which she has been trying to cure for forty years. Subsequently the degree of success Jo is helped to achieve in her struggle with her 'bosom enemy' is made real to us in her quarrels with Laurie and in the self-control she shows at 'Camp Laurence' in face of the provocations of the English boy Fred who cheats at croquet. Throughout the book numerous small incidents combine to keep alive for us the reality of Jo's moral conflict; we will confine ourselves to recalling a sentence from the letter which her mother transmits to her through the tree 'post office' in the garden: 'I write a little word to tell you with how much satisfaction I watch your efforts to control your temper.' But similar struggles, with varying degrees of success, to overcome a 'bosom enemy' form an important strand in the inner history of each of the other sisters.

In the case of Meg we may cite particularly the temptation to indulge her vanity and frivolity which she gives way to during her stay with the Moffats and her subsequent shamed repentance. Appropriately it is for Amy, as the youngest of the quartet, that the outcome of her conflict remains most prolongedly in suspense, though at the very outset we are shown an example of self-conquest in her independent decision to change the small bottle of cologne she had bought for her mother's Christmas present for the largest one she can afford (a decision brought about, however, by not wholly admirable feelings of shame, and qualified by the childish self-satisfaction of her comment: 'I'm *so* glad, for mine is the handsomest now'). Later Amy succumbs to the temptation to court popularity at school through largesse in the distribution of the forbidden 'pickled limes', and suffers for it, even though she gains a limited degree of support from her family against the excessive punishment meted out to her. But it is particularly in her enforced stay with Aunt March during Beth's illness that Amy faces her most prolonged experience of self-struggle, and the equivocal success she attains is well represented by her explanation of herself to her mother at the end of it:

'I've thought a great deal lately about my "bundle of naughties", and being selfish is the largest one on it: so I'm going to try hard to cure it, if I can. Beth isn't selfish, and that's the reason every one loves her, and feels so bad at the thought of losing her. People wouldn't feel half so bad about me if I was sick, and I don't deserve to have them; but I'd like to be loved and missed by a great many friends, so I'm going to try and be like Beth all I can . . .'

The quotation may perhaps serve to demonstrate that the moral wholesomeness which is so characteristic of Louisa M. Alcott's ambience (and so unlike that of Enid Blyton) is accompanied by insight into children's feelings that goes a long way towards keeping sentimentality at bay.

In general, however, we have said enough to suggest that an important part of the appeal of *Little Women* may be its insistent preoccupation with a certain strenuousness of moral struggle against impulses which are felt to be both dangerous and difficult to control. In offering the opportunity of identification with young heroines who are engaged in inner struggle of this kind the book seems to be touching on instinctual conflicts which are particularly characteristic of girls at the pre-adolescent stage, and we may hazard the guess that the book's function for its readers is in part at least to assuage the need to believe in the possibility of controlling one's dangerous impulses, however difficult this may sometimes be felt to be. And if the book falls some way short of being quite the great 'children's classic' which many adults presumably remember it as, we can nevertheless respect it for the qualities which it does possess and be glad that it continues to retain a justified popularity.

'It is a curious comment on Victorian civilisation,' writes Arnold Kettle of *Oliver Twist*, 'that this was considered suitable reading for children' — to which we might retort that it is an even curiouser comment on the present that the book should continue to be widely available to children in schools and presumably voluntarily read. Actually, although it is among the most frequently read books at each of our sampled ages, its popularity diminishes among its older readers, who are the most likely group to have encountered it undiluted; and its combined liking score of 4·0 has been reached through including the 4·1 rating given by the 10+ girls (the largest single group of readers), who are the most likely to have read it in an abridged version. Nevertheless, however dubious the form in which the children may have met it, *Oliver Twist* remains clearly among our front-runners, and there is point accordingly in attempting to account for its generally favourable rating.

When we consider the material that occasions Professor Kettle's remark — 'the workhouse, the parochial baby-farm, Mr Sowerberry's shop, the funeral, the Artful Dodger, Fagin's lair' — we will agree with him that the book has 'the haunting quality, but nothing of the unreality, of a nightmare', and that such material is at least as likely to distress a young reader as the starker version of *Little Red Riding Hood* may trouble the more sensitive at story time in the infants' school. *Oliver Twist* can play upon a child's fears, as indeed may the early chapters of *Jane Eyre*, but the loneliness of Oliver is fixed in peculiarly ugly and frightening circumstances. His solitary confinement for 'asking for more', his apprentice's bed on a shelf among the coffins, his imprisonment in the dust-cellar, his abandonment by Sikes after the attempted robbery of the Maylies' house, all express the savage humiliation of the unwanted child that Dickens determined to draw the adult reader's attention to; while his picaresque journey to London and his public recapture by Nancy show, in their extremely different forms, the terrifying impotence of Oliver's isolation. Nothing there, one might feel, for the child reader to derive satisfaction from.

And yet it is against such a background that Oliver is established, not simply as representative and titular *persona*, but as hero. We recall Oliver asking for more and the immediate impression his request makes on the 'bad and intractible grown-ups' —

The master . . ., a fat, healthy man, . . . turned very pale. He gazed in stupefied astonishment on the small rebel for some seconds, and then clung for support to the copper . . .

— much more readily than we recall the grownups' brutal revenge upon him. Similarly, when he has been locked up by Mrs Sowerberry and 'continues to kick, with undiminished vigour, at the cellar-door', and the Beadle has to be called to address this latter-day David 'in a deep and impressive tone':

'Do you know this here voice, Oliver?' said Mr Bumble.
'Yes,' replied Oliver.

'Ain't you afraid of it, sir? Ain't you a-trembling while I speak, sir?' said
Mr Bumble.
  'No!' replied Oliver, boldly.
An answer so different from the one he had expected to elicit, and was in the
habit of receiving, staggered Mr Bumble not a little. He stepped back from the
keyhole . . .

— we register the spirited opposition to Bumble, whose bluff has been called
(so early in the book) through the utterance of the least equivocal words in the
language, and sense that the Beadle has taken his first significant step backwards. In each case we read or recall the incident with the mind of a child
reader, applauding the blow as one for the cause of children's demonstrable
rights *vis-à-vis* adults who are equally demonstrably unworthy of their position. Dickens's social purposes make themselves felt through a presentation
of the child's predicament that appeals, willy-nilly, to the child reader or the
adult as child reader. The affecting picture of little Dick hoeing the garden
before breakfast may be intended for social reformers' eyes; but in fact it is the
weary sense of impotence in the child under his adult masters — an appealing
theme to the younger minor — that gets the message stated. The grownup's
book, *pace* Arnold Kettle, is also the child's.
  'Hero-as-victim' does not quite cover the picture of the child presented in
Oliver Twist. He is also shown to have special qualities of perception that
operate at a disconcertingly different level from the grownups', or the grownup reader's. In the 'large whitewashed room' which is Oliver's first experience
of the workhouse and its 'board', 'a gentleman in a white waistcoat' repeatedly
draws the boy's attention by 'surly' remarks; but it is not the spoken hostility
that is impressed upon us so much as the 'white waistcoat', which becomes
an inculcated symbol of unapproachable and unappeasable oppression. (When
the 'white waistcoat' eventually dies, Bumble's reign is over too, and Oliver is
safely befriended.) 'Dickens catches that acute visual awareness of children,'
writes Peter Coveney (1959), 'that grotesque other dimension of reality which
children have', and cites as one of his examples Oliver standing a second time
before the workhouse board and 'wondering, with his eyes fixed on the
magistrates' powder, whether all boards were born with that white stuff on
their heads, and were boards from thenceforth, on that account'. How far the
'eye of childhood' passages appeal directly to the child reader, and how far
they fascinate rather the adult with an interest in children, is hard to determine; but it seems arguable to us that the child respond to Dickens's understanding of the 'eye', as well as to his warm championship of the adults' victim,
and that this quality in the writing tempers to some extent the stark facts of
helpless isolation in a hostile world.
  The true palliative of the terror lies of course in Oliver's rescue from Fagin's
clutches first by Mr Brownlow and then by the Maylies, and in this the book

exemplifies some of the general characteristics of popular children's books. Dr Friedlaender, writing without *Oliver Twist* specifically in mind (though *Heidi* is one of her examples), remarks

how constantly the child's environment, in the story, suddenly changes. All at once, from impoverished circumstances the child goes to live in a castle, or vice versa; it leaves home, nursery or guardians for a school life, or leaves a kind relation to be with other people who treat it badly, and, again, the other way about.

Other themes emphasized by Dr Friedlaender as particularly attractive to 'latency-period children' are also associated with the Brownlow-Maylies parts or written from a Brownlow-Maylies consciousness. The 'taming of bad and intractible grown-ups through the child's goodness and innocence' gets its most deliberate expression in the despair and conversion of Nancy (if, that is, we find Nancy as 'bad' as Nancy herself says she is). The 'very good, very brave, very moral . . . child-hero', apart from its expression in the spirited opening, is more an idea than a realization in *Oliver Twist*; while the theme of 'disillusionment as to the infallibility of its own real parents', to be dispelled through the attachment of the fantasy to 'the new parents who figure there as omnipotent', does not appear as Oliver's *personal* disillusionment but comes across as Dickens willing the theme to its proper conclusion. It is over the Brownlow-Maylies pages that the adult reader parts company with the child. Nevertheless, even if Dickens's interests are not fully engaged there, his intentions — firmly in line with the traditionally appealing themes — make a sufficient impact upon the young reader for them to be taken as achieved.

When we turn to the 14+ list of 'most widely read books' we find *Oliver Twist* some way down and *Little Women* sharing its place at the head with *Skinhead*, whose considerable popularity among girl-readers is perhaps more surprising than its vogue among the boys. For if, as we have suggested earlier, ten-year-old boys sometimes relish the violence in *Treasure Island*, disconnecting it from any significance it may have in its context, how much more likely are their fourteen-year-old brothers to relish the violence in *Skinhead*, where it has no significance at all? The question is not merely rhetorical: there may be elements in a book which, while apparently of special appeal to a child, are yet so charged with significance of another order (the Cinderella theme in *Jane Eyre*, for instance, or Orwell's down-trodden animals, or the menacing brutality of Roger in *Lord of the Flies*, 'sharpening a stick at both ends') that our attention is compelled to move beyond general psychological considerations in determining reading motives to the power of the art displayed. *Skinhead*, however, is artless: it offers us only a masturbation fantasy, which in its various forms of politics, sex and violence caters for hungry sheep without feeding them. That it has escaped the notice of the Director of Public

Prosecutions or the Race Relations Board is due not to any compensating literary merit but to its insulation from the serious eye on the shelves of the newsagent and the motorway service station.

For *Skinhead* is not obtainable from public or school libraries (though it is known to have been used to encourage backward readers in a rural secondary modern school, and a series of 'lessons' on it in another secondary modern has enjoyed some success), nor is it generally a book that children will admit to possessing: most of its 42 readers in our 14+ sample claimed to have 'borrowed it from a friend'. *Skinhead* is an under-the-counter book today, in much the same way as *Lady Chatterley's Lover* circulated among schoolchildren in the early 1960s in a brown wrapper labelled 'Biology'. The comparison ends there, for whether Lawrence's younger readers took anything of value from his book does not affect the point that they were exposed to things of value in it, whereas the author of *Skinhead* is militantly and miserably intent (albeit incoherently, without even a show of logic or purpose) on destroying value and instilling brutal and cynical attitudes in his readers.

The general psychological factors which go some way towards accounting for the continuing popularity of *Little Women, Jane Eyre* and *Oliver Twist* among 14+ readers do not apply to *Skinhead*. The 'savage story of Britain's newest teenage cult of violence' (newest in 1970, that is) appeals to children directly by shocking them into a pre-adult illusion of reality. Violence and callousness are presented as the victorious modes of behaviour and attitude in the world today; opposition to thuggery is shown as starry-eyed, sentimentally incompetent to deal with it, cowardly, or long-haired and free-loving. Those are the terms of a book which is almost as well liked by girls as by boys and which has a combined liking score for the age group of 4·2 — higher than the comparable rating for any other book mentioned.

Skinhead himself, Joe Hawkins, seems to share many of the opinions and principles of his author, Richard Allen. Joe's fury at the mere thought of an unwashed hippie (cleanliness is next to aggro-ness for Joe, coal delivery man by day — cheating the pensioners and fornicating with the housewives), or at the sight of a Pakistani student (' "You don't deserve to be 'ere . . ." he screamed'), or in contact at the bar with 'coloured men' ('This was *his* London — not somewhere for London Transport's African troops to live'), is heatedly endorsed by the writer, who demurs only at the 'inhuman violence' shown towards the victims — and demurs while indulging himself in the fantasy beatings and rapes. The woman in the band of Brighton hippies (who are waiting for 'the Social Security Office to give them enough to take care of immediate problems') has 'taken part in practically every demonstration in Grosvenor Square, been arrested sixteen times for obstruction or disturbing the peace and, always without exception, had the Welfare State pay her fine'. She is raped on the spot (i.e. on a wintry public beach), while her companions' ribs, groins and cheekbones are subjected to the gang's 'murderous rage'; the incidents are presented in the cerebral language of a depraved sensualist who is unaware of the absurdity of his description:

. . . Joe kept kicking . . . each blow bringing him greatest satisfaction as the moans of hurt rose above the screaming (*sic*) wind . . .
It was easy, Don thought, kicking his opponent in the balls, listening to the rapturous sigh, the explosive groan. He hit the falling hippie on the head, hearing the crunch of bone against axe-handle . . .
'Me next, mate,' [Tony] yelled, watching Billy penetrate the half-stupefied girl hippie. Her jeans lay on the beach, her thighs pimpled with cold, her buttocks bruised by the relentless rocks . . .

The sex, violence and politics in *Skinhead* are difficult to disentangle: indeed their association is as deliberate as anything in this viciously mad little book can be said to be. The application of sanity to the given material would not illuminate the propaganda: in a world where the workers are idle, the police ineffective, the youth bent on 'aggro' and the general public concerned to pass by on the other side, the proper sanctions against skinheads are presented as sadistic retorts; but whenever Joe is beaten he is merely stirred to more brutal revenge, so belying his author's contention that the world is too soft towards skinheads. 'Contention', however, may seem to imply that Mr Allen has a point to make: in fact he writes a form of spicy gibberish, in which jejune prejudice and vulgar language combine to titillate the fiercest adolescent fantasies. We have Keith Bardgett's word for it, in an article on *Skinhead* in the classroom (Bardgett 1972), that his pupils responded with 'vigour and spontaneity' to his teaching of it and produced better work as a result. But the 'themes' that Mr Bardgett finds 'arising from *Skinhead*' and discussable in terms of specified real books do not (we contend) amount to anything discussable in terms of *Skinhead* itself. We deceive ourselves if we suppose that here we have an educational bridge between pornography and literature: for *Skinhead* to attract the attention of schoolchildren constitutes not an achievement on which the teacher might usefully build but a latter-day Pied Piper betrayal of them. The magnitude of the betrayal finds its measure in the widespread expression, in interviews, of the opinion that *Skinhead* (in common with its sty companions, carbon-copy sequels which have enjoyed a similar vogue among the same age group) deserves to be valued for its realism and truthfulness; when one reads on a questionnaire a comment such as '*Skinhead* is based on true facts and incidents', one finds it hard to maintain the aloofness of the sociologist or social psychologist who claims that there is no 'empirical evidence' that such fiction has any influence on its youthful readers.

As we move down the 14+ list, we find that the next most widely read book is *The Day of the Triffids*, which was once dismissed by a reviewer in *The Use of English* as 'a quick read'. It is certainly true that, even in the early pages which prepare us for the disaster and state the qualifications for survival in the hero, John Wyndham is the sort of writer to keep us up long after the fire has gone out, and his subject — the universal penalties exacted from humanity as the price of its economic greed and technological cold-warmonger-ing — has a distinctly contemporary significance. Teachers have seized on the book as the kind of thing to stir their pupils' interest in reading; and its combined liking score among the 14+ group suggests that children voluntarily read it only less eagerly than they devour *Skinhead* and with more enthusiasm than they take two other teachers' favourites, *Animal Farm* and *Lord of the Flies.*

If we separate the liking scores, however, we find that girls are distinctly more enamoured of the book than are boys; and perhaps we should ask what this apocalyptic science-fiction romance, updated Wellsian, has to offer 14-year-old girls rather than boys, who appear to like it less at 14 than at 12, and to think significantly less of it than of *War of the Worlds,* which is infrequently read by girls. Is there something in the role of women in the tale, and in the men's attitudes to women, that evokes a warmer response from girls?

When the hero, striding about the streets of the metropolis, doing what he can to help the groups of blinded people and dodging the lethal triffids (plants which have an appetite for putrescent flesh and, unattended, the power to move and strike), comes upon a sighted woman chained as a guide to a drunken brute, he does not look idly on. The rescued heroine subsequently proves to be every bit as capable as the hero, as thoughtful and wary as he in dealing with triffids or the mob or the self-appointed leaders of the incipient world that is to rise from the chaos of the old, rather more practical and realistic than the hero over the question of repopulation, and creatively feminine in her aims and objectives. A girl who can strap on a triffid-gun, drive a truck and generally show initiative and common sense while preserving her femininity (indeed, expressing her femininity through those qualities), is no hard-boiled Gwen of the liberation movement but a man's girl for girls to admire and emulate.

The basic problems for the couple are those of survival in a world devastated by a new black death, with an epidemic and incurable plague following hard upon the murder, arson, looting and unemptied dustbins of the first 'days of the triffids'. The company of sighted vigilantes to whom they attach themselves are presented with two moral questions, one of which is easily solved: how to keep the blind mob at bay is felt to be more pertinent to the present and future of the sighted minority than any notion of helping the mob; and it is at such moments — there are several, implicit and explicit — that the mentality of Hitler's 'final solution' is commended to the reader through the attitude of approved characters. The other question is less easily settled and in fact proves divisive: it is whether to preserve the sanctity of marriage and singleness of devotion in personal relations or to establish a stud farm. The heroine sees the latter course as the company's moral obligation and urges the hero to do his duty; the hero, on the other hand, is a one-woman man and bows reluctantly to his fiancée's argument and the dominant view.

Theory never becomes practice, however. The vigilantes are tricked by the leaders of the mob and scattered, and hero and heroine are separated. The hero first goes west in search of his beloved, but finds only the remnant of the 'sanctity of marriage' faction leading an incompetently monastic life in an erstwhile stately home. Irritated by grace before meals, and the remnant's failure to try seriously to survive, he resumes his quest, remembering eventually that the girl has spoken warmly of a farmhouse and friends in Sussex. Thither he goes, rescuing a small girl on the way, not a moment too soon finding the place.

Further problems beset hero and heroine, but long before their reunion we have adjusted our expectations and demands to the assumptions the author works upon – that life is to go on, with honest labour and love, and with triffids and disagreeable people kept at bay. The disappearance of our advanced and thickly populated civilization is not presented as a matter for regret, while the organic community on the farm, tiny but self-sufficient, seems a recovered idyll.

It is a sign of the power of John Wyndham's writing that when the little community is threatened with absorption into the larger authority of Brighton the reader applauds the trick played on the armed fascists and the triffids moving in for the kill, and only on reflection registers the moral doubt which the author fails to give room to. But it is a sign too of the fundamental frivolity of the tale, its 'entertainment value'. Beside *Skinhead* or the work of Ian Fleming, *The Day of the Triffids* is clearly a quality book, but its readability embraces the kind of racy satisfactions which act as a stimulating drug for repeated doses.

Rather different is the other novel by John Wyndham which figures in the 14+ list, where in terms of number of readers it reaches only eleventh place, but in terms of liking score registers the even higher figure of 4·3 from its predominantly feminine devotees. *The Chrysalids*, the story of 'a world paralysed by genetic mutation' consequent upon general nuclear devastation, is only superficially comparable with the earlier book and invites nothing like the same limiting criticism. The close and closed community which treats any deviation, human, animal or vegetable, as a blasphemy against the true image of God gives birth to a number of telepathically endowed children who realize as they grow up that society will inevitably come to regard them as deviants to be hunted and destroyed with the unswerving antagonism normally shown towards a three-legged cow or a field of irregular cabbages. Marriage will present a problem to the group, unless it can be arranged among themselves, and the irony of an heroic secret association within the larger fiercely orthodox community provides a moral and artistic dimension to the tale that we do not find in *The Day of the Triffids*.

Part of the appeal of *The Chrysalids* to the 14+ girls may perhaps lie in the beautifully presented gentleness of the boys in the group and in the unobtrusive equality of the sexes as contrasted with the patriarchal régime in their several families. The novel is fully as exciting as *The Day of the Triffids,* moreover, and if at the end there is a characterstic Wyndhamian 'slate-cleaning' (the long-armed deviants, along with the hell-bent orthodox pursuers of the group, are conveniently annihilated) the flaw is nevertheless not a fault in the seam. We suggest that for the child retarded by Enid Blyton *The Chrysalids* may offer an efficacious bridge between *The Secret Seven* and *The Crucible* which could perhaps lead him ultimately to an appreciation of *The Scarlet Letter.* (We make the suggestion having seen such a development in progress in a girls' secondary modern school, under the direction of an enthusiastic and thoughtful English teacher.)

It is surely not at all surprising that *Jane Eyre* should be among the books most widely read by girls of 12+ and 14+ or that their liking score should prove, in general, to be decidedly favourable. Nevertheless, when a book capable of engaging adult interests appeals so strongly to children (albeit girls only), it is certainly worth inquiring into the nature of that appeal. In the course of our interviews girl readers frequently expressed their fascination with Rochester — 'What did you like about the book?': 'It was *him*!' — and Kate Friedlaender (1942) sees the writer's and the reader's Oedipus-wish fulfilled in the way an 'insignificant girl wins the love of "father" '. The concentration of the child's expressed interest in the third phase of the book is considered by Dr Friedlaender in conjunction with the final phase (Jane's return to Thornfield and her consequent marriage) in terms of the girl's penis-envy. The young reader does not, of course, express her identification with Jane in such terms, although she will make explicit her 'romantic' delight in the heroine's response to Rochester's call for help and the protective rôle she is enabled to play as his wife.

The parts of the book which the interviewed child, pressed for a summary answer, does not commonly refer to include the first hundred pages as well as the intensive treatment of Jane's life under St. John Rivers's patronage. It would be absurd to suppose, whatever the centre of interest for the adolescent girl, that Gateshead and Lowood are merely phases to be tracked through on the way to Rochester's appearance in Chapter 12; some other explanation than the dark horseman's magnetism is required for the fact that so many readers actually get that far into a book whose language and subject matter read strangely today. According to Peter Coveney, 'Charlotte Brontë seeks a complete identity of feeling between her "victim" and the reader, and nothing intrudes, least of all the writer's judgment, between the reader and the heroine's psyche, as it is displayed . . . The writer wishes to attract the reader's vicarious self-pity [through] the situation of the cruelly deprived orphan and, by extension, the cruelly deprived adult'. The early chapters, Mr Coveney remarks, insist on Jane's 'victimization, loneliness, isolation'; Jane 'seems to provoke, masochistically, her self-torment', just as later she exhibits 'self-hurting, frustrating eroticism' in her 'sado-masochistic' relations with Rochester. The emotional power of the book, then, during the pages through which the young reader must go to reach what she recognizes as the heart of the novel, is inextricable from the 'vicarious self-pity' which the author indulges in herself and encourages in her readers.

Mr Coveney's account is not, however, the whole story. Q. D. Leavis (1966), while admitting that for Charlotte Brontë 'to write *Jane Eyre* must have been a great joy as well as a relief of the pressures of her inner life and aspirations', goes on to emphasize the spirit of independence she has created in the heroine. The orphan's victimization at Gateshead and Lowood is inseparable from her independence not only of the brutal figures but of the exemplary Helen Burns and the kindly Miss Temple. Jane's independence of Rochester, in conversation and behaviour, similarly qualifies the sado-maso-chistic character of their relationship: her refusal to become Rochester's mistress is of a piece with her subsequent resistance of St. John Rivers; and her ultimate marriage with Rochester, however subconsciously achieved through the fantasy of penis-envy, is explicitly the act of an independent person ('I am independent, sir, as well as rich; I am my own mistress') who proposes to be a mate rather than the beneficiary of Rochester or the ancillary of St. John Rivers. The independence Jane characteristically exhibits and grows towards has nothing of self-sufficiency about it; and if at the end Rochester feels he needs Jane more than Jane needs him, Jane nevertheless has never ceased to need Rochester and goes to him at last in her own need. But the inseparability of the pair has behind it Jane's double rejection of the 'torn veil' and St. John Rivers; the idealized marriage is imbued with a sense of independent reality ('To be together is for us to be at once as free as in solitude, as gay as in company'); and the independence Jane brings to her marriage is mirrored by Rochester's recovery of his sight and so of his own independence – 'He can find his way', remarks Jane at the end, 'without being led by the hand.'

How far is it the independence of the heroine rather than its sado-masochistic manifestations that appeals to the young reader? Dr Friedlaender declares that the book is 'not commonly thought of as a work of art but as an artless concoction of day-dreams'; and although such a confident dismissal of Charlotte Bronte's pretensions would be quite within the adult reader's com-petence to challenge, the adolescent girl might fairly be expected to respond more to the day-dreams – the husband, the income, the feminine distinction and responsibilities of one's dreams – than to the informing principles of the novelist's art whereby tempting material is controlled and directed. The important point for the teacher, knowing how good the book really is (none of the other front-runners discussed so repays the adult's re-reading of it), is that its emotional power provides a rewarding experience for the young; and it hardly matters that the rewards depend more upon the art than the responsive girl realizes.

As we turn over in our minds the detailed analyses which have been elicited by our study of a small number of the most widely read and keenly enjoyed children's books, it is natural to ask whether any generalized observations emerge which can be helpful to teachers and librarians in choosing and recommending books for the 10—15 age range. One very general point may be made at once. It seems fairly clear that instinctual satisfaction, whether thinly or elaborately disguised, is above all else the feature which these young people demand in their fictional reading, and that the types of instinctual gratification which commend themselves most strongly are those which bear some relation to the emotional desires, fears and conflicts which are most characteristic of the reader's age and stage of development. This observation seems to us to be fully borne out not only by the dozen or so books specifically examined in this chapter, but also by our experience of the very numerous and diverse well liked children's books which we have read attentively over the period of the research project. To many of our readers the point will seem too obvious to need stating. It is nevertheless in conflict with some of the simplistic assumptions that govern much current discussion about children's reading.

We cannot, for instance, endorse the widely canvassed view that the ineluctable need of the reluctant reader is for a story which recreates for him his own recognizable experience of life in comprehensive school, council estate or high-rise block. That some young readers respond with enthusiasm to naturalistic fiction about children or teenagers similar to themselves, as found in books by writers such as John Rowe Townsend, Nina Bawden or Josephine Kamm, is not in dispute; we would contend however that it is the emotional content rather than the setting that really counts (K. M. Peyton's admirable *Pennington's Seventeenth Summer* provides an illuminating case in point), and that this can be no less compelling or absorbing when it is located in characters, venues and periods utterly remote from the day-to-day living of the young reader. Equally we feel bound to reject the cognate view that would separate off fantasy from the more general experience of fictional and narrative reading; although in fantasy (or for that matter science-fiction) the writer may allow himself a more unbridled license than usual to remake the 'rules of the game', the emotional satisfactions that result for the reader do not seem to us to differ in principle or in essence from those which are gained from fiction or narrative which accepts the more normal restraints associated with a realistic depiction of human experience.

How far does it continue to be appropriate (in face of the powerful warning note uttered by D. W. Harding and discussed at length in the earlier part of this chapter) to think of these emotional or instinctual satisfactions in terms of identification, disguised wish-fulfilment and vicarious gratification? It is certainly the case that in all the 'preferred' books we have examined there is at least one character with whom the young reader could be expected to associate himself emotionally, and that this sharing of a particular character's experience normally goes hand-in-hand with that kind of transposition of the world 'according to an arrangement which is more to his liking' which Freud described as characteristic of both the playing child and the poet. It is true that the terms in which one describes this aspect of the experience of reading fiction need careful and cautious formulation; but we should deprecate any way of putting it which gave encouragement to the concerned adult to down-grade in his own scale of priorities the importance of such emotional satisfactions to the young reader.

On the other hand it is no less important to stress that (as we have seen in our detailed analyses) these identificatory and wish-fulfilment elements are normally closely intertwined with the evaluative judgements which the reader is invited to take over from the author. Inevitably a parent, teacher or librarian will view these evaluative judgements from his own adult standpoint, and where they are found to be trite, vacuous or morally objectionable there can be no excuse for deliberately exposing children to their influence. Ultimately, however, what counts is not the adult's reaction but the impact of the story and its evaluative judgements upon the child reader *at his own stage of development*, and we need to be fully aware that immature or unsubtle forms of experience may have their part to play in the young reader's movements towards reading experiences which (in the words of the Bullock Report) 'enlarge his understanding of the range of human possibilities'. This relativity of judgement we have allowed for in our own generous interpretation of what should be accorded the status of quality in our narrative categories. What is in question is not an abandonment of standards, but rather the recognition of a hierarchy of standards through which the young reader can be helped to move upwards at his own pace and in his own good time.

One final point deserves to be made. We have seen demonstrated in this chapter the remarkably varied way in which the different fictional elements may be combined within different books. Indeed, just as in our interviewing we became seized by the uniqueness of each individual reader, so in our analyses of specific books we have found incontrovertible evidence of the unique blend of ingredients which differentiates one children's book from the next. In each case generalizations can touch only part of what is at stake. The stress needs to fall in the end upon the need for the teacher to know, and respond sensitively to the individual book and the individual child, so that the two may be brought together in the right combination at the right time.

BIBLIOGRAPHY

Bardgett, K. (1972). '*Skinhead* in the classroom', *Children's Literature in Education*, 8, 56–64.

Bettelheim, B. (1949). 'Harry: a study in rehabilitation', *Journal of Abnormal and Social Psychology*, 44, 231–65, Washington D.C.

Brown, D. (1960). 'R.L.S.: inspiration and industry' in *Young Writers, Young Readers*, ed. B. Ford. Hutchinson.

Collier, M. J. and Gaier, E. L. (1958a). 'Adult reactions to preferred childhood stories', *Child Development*, 29, 97–103, Chicago.

Collier, M. J. and Gaier, E. L. (1958b). 'Preferred childhood stories of college women', *American Imago*, 15, 401–9, New York.

Collier, M. J. and Gaier, E. L. (1959). 'The hero in the preferred childhood stories of college men', *American Imago*, 16, 177–94, New York.

Coveney, P. (1959). *The Image of Childhood*, Penguin.

Douglas, V. I. (1965), 'Children's responses to frustration: a developmental study', *Canadian Journal of Psychology*, 19, 161–71, Toronto.

Friedlaender, K. (1942). 'Children's books and their function in latency and prepuberty', *American Imago*, 3, 129–50, New York.

Green, J. A. (1913). 'The teaching of English II. Literature (what boys and girls read)'. *Journal of Experimental Pedagogy*, II.

Harding, D. W. (1937). 'The role of the onlooker', *Scrutiny*, 6, 247–58.

Harding, D. W. (1962). 'Psychological processes in the reading of fiction', *British Journal of Aesthetics*, 2, 133–47.

Kettle, A. (1953). *An Introduction to the English Novel*, vol. 1. Hutchinson.

Leavis, Q. D. (1966). Introduction to *Jane Eyre*, 7–29. Penguin.

Lesser, S. O. (1960). *Fiction and the Unconscious*. Peter Owen.

Rankin, M. (1944). *Children's Interests in Library Books of Fiction.* New York: Teachers College, Columbia University.

Sachs, H. (1942). *The Creative Unconscious.* Cambridge, Mass.: Sci-Art Publishers.

Whitehead, F. (1956). 'The attitudes of grammar school pupils towards some novels commonly read in school', *British Journal of Educational Psychology*, 26, 104–11.

Wolfenstein, M. (1944). 'The reality principle in story preferences of neurotics and psychotics', *Character and Personality*, XII, 135–51, Durham, N. Carolina.

Wolfenstein, M. (1946). 'The impact of a children's story on mothers and children', *Monographs of the Society for Research in Child Development*, XI, 42, Chicago.

6 The comics children choose

'It is evident', we say in conclusion to Chapter 3, 'that comics are the most potent form of periodical reading for the majority of the age range we are concerned with'; and the point stands despite the inclination of 14+ boys towards magazines which offer information and satisfactions of a non-fiction and non-strip-cartoon kind, and despite the less obvious inclination of 14+ girls towards prose fiction magazines. The popular periodicals, even those that come nowhere near cornering the market (e.g. *Whizzer and Chips*: 9·1% of 10+ boys, or *Princess Tina*: 8·0% of 12+ girls), are — with the exception of *Loving* — all comics, as defined by our first category, and offer little in the way of continuous prose; and it would be a mistake to suppose that, while most children read a large number of comics, they are thereby reading a large number of words. In fact, that *Dandy* and *Beano* should each hold 38% of 10+ boys and 30% of 10+ girls, or that *Jackie* should have 42% of 12+ and 58% of 14+ girls, suggests rather that comics perform for many children the service of a time-consuming drug. Whether such matter may assist or restrict the development of the reading habit is difficult to determine; but certainly the satisfactions afforded by the most popular comics suggest only the thinnest relation between the two forms of reading.

THEN AND NOW

It was not ever thus. Taylor (1972) reports a remarkable decline in the verbal content of the most widely read current comics, such that the comics he studied in 1967 contained only between one-quarter and one-twelfth of the number of words in their counterparts in 1940. The 'bloods' of the 1940s are collectors' pieces, and it has not been possible to obtain any; but the television production of *Joby* in 1975, taking immense care over its period detail, gave us a glimpse of the paper the boy reads at the kitchen table — one small block picture embedded in three or four columns of close print — in fact we were shown what Taylor says of *Wizard*: 'six prose adventure stories comprising a total of some 40 000 words'. In 1940 the 7+—11+ age group was catered for by such things as *Butterfly* and *Comic Cuts*, which 'consisted of half pictorial comic reading and half fictional stories', and by *Dandy* and *Beano*, each of which carried a serial story. Today, *Bunty*'s 7500 words is nearly four times the verbal content of the modern *Beano*, page for page; while *Hornet*, which Taylor found very popular among 14+ grammar school boys in 1967, has thirty-two pages, 'four of which [are] taken up with a story in print, two with advertisements and twenty-six with stories in strip picture form with words in balloons, the total word content being around 10 000 words'.

The primary schools and the colleges of education are frequently blamed for the decline in reading standards and in the related willingness to read among children today. It is odd that some of the blame should not so readily be put where it partly belongs — on the publishers, wholesalers and retailers who for their own perfectly legal purposes have assisted in 'the crowding out of words by pictures' (Denys Thompson's phrase) and have accomplished through their ample provision of the latter a general incapacity in children to expect or demand the former. Taylor's tentative conclusion that the 'lack of the written word in comics nowadays . . . may well have affected reading standards and the power of children to "internalise" prose' is supported by his indisputable point that 'at the level of mere mechanical silent reading practice many pupils [are] missing' a pleasurable exercise that thirty years ago was voluntarily undertaken. The schools cannot make up for what the publishers do not provide.

The crowding out of words by pictures in pulp reading matter was a revolution accomplished in the 1950s, when television began to stride rapidly towards its present domination of the sitting room. It was in the 1950s that the commercial pressure for a second channel became irresistible (a general election was fought partly on the issue in 1955); and the relation between heavy television viewing and heavy comic reading in our sample can hardly be accidental. *The Men Behind Boys' Fiction* (Lofts and Adley 1970), 'a collective biography of all British authors who ever wrote for boys', provides us with an unconscious revelation:

It should be emphasised that this work is mainly intended to cover the writers of stories which appeared in boys' papers. This is, roughly, up to 1950, as after that date most boys' papers mainly consisted of picture stories . . .

In the same book, a chapter entitled 'A Tribute to the D.C. Thomson Papers and Red Circle School' adds precision to the 'roughly' and 'mainly' by providing specific dates:

There were four stages of moving upwards [viz. by different groups of pupils] in the school's history:

Stage 1	1933—35	nos.	1—106
Stage 2	1935—37		107—209
Stage 3	1937—41		210—500
Stage 4	1941—58		501—1155

New Hotspur, picture strips of Red Circle, 1959 onwards.

The remarkable thing, to a reader of the whole 'Tribute', is that the writer who praises the Red Circle for its 'style that a boy found easy to read, and that made few demands on him', should so blandly report the advent of the picture strips. In his sentimental journey backwards he compliments the D.C. Thomson editors on their 'psychology': ' . . . they seemed to know exactly what boys wanted to read and prepared their papers accordingly . . .' and claims, justifiably, that the success of the Thomson papers may be gauged by 'a survey conducted a few years before the last war *in a very large elementary school*' (our italics): it 'showed . . . that out of roughly a thousand boys about 75% were reading the Thomson papers'. Lofts and Adley find that fact 'astonishing': the real point to make, surely, is that such popularity makes nonsense of the notion that at a stroke — or within a decade — the young reader voluntarily lost his appetite for words. Demand in an industrial society is a desire created by the advertiser to match the economic capacity of the producer. There was no more demand from the young for picture strips in the 1950s than there was from the intelligentsia for the colour supplements: what determined the crowding out of words by pictures was the commercial principle that if (let us say) *Beano* could be made to attract subscribers throughout the age range there was nothing to be gained from offering children a literate alternative.

It would be helpful to have from D.C. Thomson a statement of the commercial viability of their literate papers in the early 1950s. Any large enterprise might view suddenly sagging sales, or even creeping decline, as a sign that the time had come to change, by financial decree, the demand; and we are not proposing that a publishing firm should only consider the interests of children, or that it should seek to justify itself as an honorary ancillary of the teacher of reading. Nevertheless, if 'the D.C. Thomson editors deserve the highest possible praise for contributing — by thus entertaining the young — to a part of our social history' (Lofts and Adley 1970), the firm requires a rebuke for its policy in the last twenty years.*

The rebuke is administered to Thomson's rivals, too, of course, and to society generally (including certain trend-setters in education) for more or less unconsciously conniving at the shift away from the printed word. But as Thomson is still the most successful publisher it qualifies for special scrutiny. *Dandy, Beano, Bunty* and *Jackie, Mandy, Judy* and *Diana* — by a long way the most widely read comics — are all Thomson publications. The implicit contempt for the young reader evinced by the feeble array on the newsagent's counter is more remarkable — and so more germane to a discussion of the

---

* It could fairly claim a local and social justification of its policy in the 1930s. D.C.Thomson of Dundee was a non-union house, but it was an employer and the money earned there was steady. *Beano* and *Dandy* were printed when the presses were slack, and the artist who gave us Desperate Dan also drew Oor Wullie and the Brooms for the weekly *People's Friend* and *The Sunday Post.*

place of comics in a child's life — than an attempt to determine their influence upon him. We have met, in our follow-up interviews with the children who answered the questionnaire, apparently sane and sensible girls who had read *Groupie* and *Skinhead* and who had not, so far as we could tell, gone away and done likewise. But voluntary or induced subjection to such things does not 'feed the fantasy' in the inclusive manner of *The Truth About Wilson* (see below), where the reader identifies himself with the breath-taken admirers as much as with the breath-taking hero: the fantasy in *Groupie* or *Skinhead* invites personal implication and absorption in a story which the 'Tribute to D.C. Thomson' would not describe as 'clean and entertaining' or of 'a high moral standard', but which amounts to a kind of verbal masturbation, committed by the writer and required of the reader. 'Influence' is difficult to determine — so difficult legally that it cannot be substantiated in the courts, as prosecutors of pornographers have discovered. But influence of a relatively insidious sort is had by the printed word. Just as a good book may be said to modify the reader's sensibility, so that he is not quite the person he was before he read it, so does a bad book or the feeble, exclamatory vocabulary of a modern comic condition to some extent the reader's expectations of the satisfactions and possibilities of language. The analogy of the human body applies to reading: a child's linguistic capacity depends to an indeterminate extent on his habitual exposure to the words and sentences he reads and hears. However speculative our consideration of the influence exerted upon children by their periodical reading, in that it does not answer satisfactorily to an objective test, it does lead us to support Taylor's (1972) conclusion that the lack of word power in the modern comics has contributed to our pupils' falling reading standards.

Taylor places an extract from the *Wizard* of 1940 beside one from the *Hornet* of 1967, remarking that whereas the *Wizard* piece occupied a quarter of a column the *Hornet* extract took a whole page.

The School of Deadly Secrets: Nazi Encirclement

'Psst! Roger!'

The whisper came from the dark corner under the clock in the long passage-way that led from the main hall of Pinewoods Hospice School to the dining hall.

It was late afternoon, and the boys were going into tea. The lights had been turned on in the dining hall, but not in the passage, consequently there were many dark patches.

The two boys who had just come level with the clock, Roger Martin and Jules Dumas, stopped immediately and turned their heads in the direction of the voice.

'Don't stop!' came the agonised whisper. 'Make for the door to the cellars. I'll be waiting for you there. It's urgent.'   (*Wizard*, 1940)

The Men Beneath the Ice
'We've hit a patch of rock hard ice, Chris. We need more power on the saws. I'll get through to Collins the engineer.'
'Hey, Jeff Collins says you'll burn the saws if you overload them. Better . . . Aargh! I'm falling.'
'Aargh.'
'Wow! Help! The cable's pulling me down.'
In the engineer's hut Collins heard the shout over the phone.
'What has happened? I'd better call Doctor Lessup.'   (*Hornet*, 1967)

The dilution of the prose to which the reader is exposed lies not only in the thinner spread of the butter but in the quality of vocabulary and sentence structure he is now allowed to demand. Not that the *Wizard* excerpt repays prolonged examination: the implicit and unconscious association of 'Nazi encirclement' with 'deadly secrets', whispers (furtive or 'agonised') and 'the dark' is crudely sacrificed in the explanation of the 'many dark patches'; and the clichés of expression go with the clichés of thought that the 'relevant' war story requires. Nevertheless, this undemanding prose asks three paragraphs of reading time between the first whisper and the second; not padding merely, or controlled suspense, but an attempt to provide a context for the whisperer and his audience; we are not simply *told* things, as the second piece tells us of the ice, the cable and the telephone, but are encouraged to savour the scene.

A similar case could be made for *The Truth About Wilson* (Webb, n.d.), a paperback collection of a series first printed in *Wizard* in the 1930s. It is pulp literature; no one coming to it for the first time in middle age will feel he has missed something in not having it as a boy. The incredible feats of the high-powered, ageless athlete, living on roots in the Yorkshire Moors and running at will at the White City (he is temperamental, of course), are no less silly than the exploits on ITV of the Six Million Dollar Man, whose carcase incorporates a 'complex' of machinery, electronic devices and doing-aids, by which rivals and crooks are baffled and outpaced. And yet the presentment of views and moments even in such routine passages as the following exemplifies what contemporary children have gone short of.

The starter said something, the competitors crouched. Wilson did not go down as far as the others. Murvo's back was arched like a spitting cat's as he waited for the gun.
The gaze of the Indians remained intent on the crowd.
Bang! At the crack of the gun Murvo streaked away. He did not lose a fraction of a split second. It was a marvellous start — and it must have come as a tremendous shock to him to see Wilson's back.
With a tremendous surge of power, Wilson seemed to have picked up full speed in a stride, and he pounded down the track at a pace which made the Human Express look like a freight train.
Wilson's feet hardly seemed to touch the cinders. He sustained that terrific

speed — and then, ten yards from the tape, actually accelerated. Just when he should have been feeling the strain most, he visibly put on speed, and he broke through the tape yards in front of Murvo.

Maybe there were gunmen with silencers in that crowd. I do not know. Ike Hare swears that there were, but they kept their guns away when the Shawnees took up their guard.

With black fury on his face, Belasco was already shouldering his way towards an exit as the loudspeakers boomed with the announcement that Wilson had won the hundred yards in nine seconds dead, a record likely to stand for all time.

There is a place in the account for 'Murvo's back' and his 'marvellous start', and the implicit admission that he is good enough to finish only 'yards' behind the record breaker; and written into the event is the reminder, through the Indians's non-spectator rôle, of the 'thick-shouldered Belasco . . . surrounded by a group of gum-chewing men in slouch hats' who are out to get Wilson. Murvo may be the tool of the crooks, but he is a runner, and the race is allowed to be a genuine race. However crudely done, the confrontation between Shawnees and gunmen provides a 'stationary' perspective against which to view the 'terrific speed' of the two competitors. In short there is art here, however barbarous — and words, and similes and subordinate clauses. We would not call this stuff jejune if we considered what the *Hotspur* of 1974 offered — 32 pages of strip cartoons, in which are embedded hardly distinguishable advertisements for match-box 'Skybusters', postage stamps and '3 great stories in this week's *Wizard*'.

THE FAVOURITE FOUR

We turn now to examine the most widely read magazines today, on the assumption that any analysis of the satisfactions afforded children by their ephemeral reading must take special account of the way our pupils vote with their pocket money. The nature of the influence exercised by periodicals is also more likely to be understood through an examination of what is actually there upon the most popular pages than through an attempt to get the children themselves to betray signs of that influence, for good or ill. 'But don't you think they are famously good, ma'am?' demands Captain Brown in *Cranford*, speaking of the monthly instalments of *The Pickwick Papers*. It is the same question that the publisher of *Hotspur* or *Wizard* implicitly asks of his subscriber, who with his subscription underwrites the comics, their nature, their sense of humour, their values. That their nature is ephemeral, light relief from the serious business of life and reading, tells us something about the limitations of their influence upon serious living and reading; but it tells us something too about the character and purposes of the publisher and about the society that unquestioningly accepts what the publisher offers and so can be made to appear actively to demand it. The publisher's influence, however nebulous and difficult to determine specifically, is thus (we contend) related proportionally to the financial success of his ventures. The four most successful papers are *Dandy, Beano, Bunty* and *Jackie*, and it is these to which we pay particular attention below.

If 'Korky the Cat' in *Dandy* of October 23 1971 were put into words without pictures it would offer nothing more than an example of 'How I got my own back', a humorous fantasy with which the reader may, more or less unconsciously, identify himself. Korky, selling hot chestnuts by the roadside, is deliberately splashed by the ice-cream man riding through a puddle. Korky, unobserved, then stuffs hot chestnuts into the bully's handlebars, so that the cart runs out of control and throws the bully over the hedge. Korky leaves the bully to cool his fingers on the ice-cream and makes off with the cart relabelled 'Hot Chestnuts': eager children (cf. a single child in the initial picture) 'stop [him] and buy some'.

Even the most limited reader would get little satisfaction from that. The appeal of the comic's version depends partly on the familiar assurance Korky affords us that *Dandy* is still what it has always been — our old friend has triumphed yet again — and partly on the style of the total presentation in which words at the most act as utilitarian cement for the cartoons. But the uses of the cement are more various, both in kind and in quality, than the phrase may suggest. The strictly utilitarian, in that it provides information omitted by the pictures, is exemplified by this sort of explanation in the balloons: 'That bully has left his bike, so I'll stuff these hot chestnuts into his handlebars!' or this: 'That bully needs his ice-cream to cool his hands — so I've taken over his bike!' Labelled items, such as 'Hot Chestnuts' or 'Delicious Ice-cream', perform a slightly different function, equally utilitarian but less obviously dispensable. Then there are the spoken words to correspond with the action of the pictures: 'Watch your fingers, Joey, these are hot,' says Korky unnecessarily as he hands over the bag of chestnuts, or the superfluous 'Ouch! My fingers!' from the ice-cream man as he touches the heated handlebars.

In the better picture strip stories the largely unnecessary words act as confirmation of what one sees — Korky is observed riding away on the cycle-cart, and it is observation rather than word recognition skill that detects the relabelling of the cart with 'Delicious Hot Chestnuts'. In the inferior stories the words are dragged in to do the work we might legitimately have asked of the cartoonist. *Beano*'s 'Grandpa' story of January 20 1970 introduces 'that son of mine' verbally only: we are *told* he is 'like a little kid' and that he is 'playing with rattles' before we see him — omit the words from the first two frames and no kind of 'storyline' would be detectable.

A further point to be made, with Korky the Cat before us, is that the reader is encouraged by the series of pictures to look backward as well as forward — indeed the two-way look is essential to his enjoyment, to his absorption in and of the story, his 'meditative grasp' of the whole. He is not expected immediately to notice the puddle in the first picture, where the eye is directed rather at the clever Korky, his delighted customer and a bag of chestnuts; he goes back to look for the puddle when the ice-cream man has 'cooled 'em down' in the second picture. Similarly, Korky in the final picture is shown wearing the ice-cream man's hat, and we are sent back to the penultimate sketch of a toppling cart, an airborne hat and the ice-cream man's upended legs. A dispersed attention to detail is thus invited — the reverse of a reader's attention, which is a growing sense of the drift of a passage, of its innate and characteristic movement; there does seem to be an inherent opposition between the business of 'taking' a comic strip and the ongoing and cumulative mental activity which is an integral part of the act of reading.

The striking thing about *Dandy*, however, is its pervasive conservatism. Desperate Dan, Korky the Cat and Winker Watson seem incredibly dated, and may even (we suspect) be modified reissues of earlier strips. There is one sign of the times in the Korky strip — the hairstyle and dress of one of the children shown; otherwise the hair, the dress (e.g. a 'uniform' scarf worn in the traditional external-flowing manner), the roadside chestnuts and the ice-cream cycle-cart all point to a past era. The only concession to our decade in the Desperate Dan story is a reference to the cops' Z-car; Dan's brogues and curious spurs, Aunt Aggie's curtains and bonnet are what they have always been. Winker Watson in the quad at Greytowers School wears blazer with piping, shorts and crumpled socks, the schoolmaster a mortar board, the amiable shopkeeper bow-tie, dicky and waistcoat. The boys suck bullseyes, buzz into action and call each other 'rotter'; the one intimation of the present — 'wintersports equipment fund' — is muted by the 'prize hamper for the boy who collects most money for the fund'; the creeps exeunt at the end chased by a bull.

The boy who wrote in 1964 that 'Desperate Dan has been in *Dandy* much too long and should be stopped' is exceptional: most children appear to accept their comics without question and even to be anxious to keep them as they are. From the evidence of *Dandy* alone one could indeed say that the particular appeal of a juvenile comic seems to depend on the massive irrelevance of its stories to the reader, whose fantasy of a successful resolution to a case is satisfied by comedy presented in outmoded terms. *Beano,* however, offers conflicting evidence and, since its equally strong following is fed by the same publisher, one may assume that different demands are made by different (or even the same) children. The lorry and the van shown in 'Biffo the Bear' are up-to-date models, the Rip Van Winkle figure in 'Grandpa' sleeps in front of a television set, and Billy the Cat employs a sophisticated bugging device to rescue Katie from the old mansion (in which 'no-one's lived for years'). The mortarboarded schoolmaster in 'The Bash Street Kids' is armed with a stick and 'a hundred lines', but the headmaster shows slides of a 'cold germ, a hundred times life-size'. Roger the Dodger, who has shirked tidying his bedroom, is put to cleaning up the litter in the park; and Dennis the Menace appears under a modern home hair-drier. Such signs of modernity, or relevance to the pervasive presence of hardware in our lives, are not masked by Lord Snooty's topper, the old-school scarves and the Pickwickian trousers, but appear as a legitimate part of the scene.

Dandy's conservatism may be responsible for the very slight edge the paper appears to have over *Beano* among 10+ children, while *Beano*'s awareness of the 1970s may account for its greater popularity among the 12+ group; but the swing, such as it is, from one comic to the other is barely worth remarking. It is in the ingredients the two comics have in common that we must look to determine the peculiar appeal they make to pre-pubertal boys (and their fellow-travelling sisters). Easier said than done, however. The sheer crudity of the drawing and the colour, the vulgar limitations imposed upon the imagination and sensitivity of the child (who, we know from experience of the work accomplished in primary schools, is characteristically the reverse of the moron the publisher is successfully providing for), leave us wondering what on earth the pleasure can be in exposing oneself to this stuff. And yet, that *Dandy* and *Beano* do make a very widespread emotional appeal is indisputable, and perhaps the attempt to report what we find in them will help us to understand the given pleasure. The verbal tricks of alliteration and rhyme are immediately noticeable — Korky the Cat, Biffo the Bear, Desperate Dan, Corporal Clott, or (more subtle) the Bash Street Kids. Each of these titles promises hearty tomfoolery, comic violence and table-turning in the tradition represented by the discomfiture of the schoolmaster at Speech Day in *Tom Sawyer* (a scene which Mark Twain in fact handles with an ashamed restraint, as if such sweet revenge of pupils upon teacher were safer practised than depicted). Certainly the comics draw upon a hallowed and not unwholesome hostility to the authority claimed or assumed by adult, teacher, policeman or officialdom generally. 'Education', a progressive headmaster has said, 'is a matter of saying "we" '; but for the young reader of *Dandy* or *Beano* the entrenched battle-lines of 'them and us' show no signs of crumbling. However collaborative the atmosphere in contemporary classroom or household, the child apparently delights in the manufactured opposition in the comic stories, and his delight implies a degree of emotional satisfaction that is still sought and met.

It may seem odd to speak of 'refinements' in the context of such crude and simple material, but in fact the story of a triumphant Korky recounted above is not wholly typical. In *Dandy* of January 27 1973 Korky's success is achieved too early, and the later frames show him trapped by his greedy-full stomach in a milk churn which the farmer boots and blasts around the yard. In the same issue the barge-booted Claude Hopper similarly scores early against a pair of road menders wielding ineffective sledge-hammers; the tables are turned — the workmen trap Claude in a length of land-drain piping, fill his boots with cement and use them as effective sledge-hammers. Grandpa and his 'pal Davie' in *Beano* of July 21 1973 go to the seaside, where Grandpa riding the donkey imagines himself to be a cowboy on a high-powered horse and so infects the beast that the pair race madly along the sands until the donkey drops exhausted. The final frame shows Grandpa paying for his pleasure by giving 'grandpa rides'. All three stories thus invite the reader to enjoy a series of violent and sadistic moments at the expense, ultimately, of himself rather than authority.

Of course, Grandpa, Claude Hopper and Korky, although the central figures in their stories, cater more for the spectator-mode than for the reader's vicarious emotional identification: the child reader is not a cat, a clodhopper or a grandparent, even though the attempts of these characters to cock a snook at authority strike a sympathetic chord in him. The reader more obviously identifies himself with the Bash Street Kids, who constitute a peer group ranged against the common enemy, their mortarboarded schoolmaster. Again, however, it is the refinements as much as the formula that are remarkable. In the issue of July 21 1973 the teacher has rigged up a cable-car to get him to school on time; after two early defeats the Kids manage to re-route the cable-car to 'Scotland', and so enjoy 'a free period all day'; but the final picture is of a glum row of Kids imagining the teacher wielding the 'super hawthorn whacking stick' he has acquired in Scotland. In the issue of May 18 1974 teacher and class collaborate in a fire drill, and on hearing the word 'fire' charge into action; unfortunately they soak the headmaster giving instruction on the rifle-range, and the final frame shows class teacher and Kids 'obliterated' as the headmaster turns the hose on them in revenge. The headmaster in this series appears to be a kind of third party with a roving commission — sometimes to act as a second line of teacher authority, sometimes as himself the real enemy, sometimes as the pupils' ally against the class teacher. The cold-germ story referred to briefly above shows the class teacher as usher, subject at beginning and end to the head's contemptuous will. The teacher is ordered to conduct a pre-school dip, as a result of which the Kids feel 'healthy' and 'fit' while the teacher, singled out for assault by an army of cold germs, contracts a cold and is pilloried by the head as a 'snivelling fossil'. *Beano* may be more contemporary in some respects than *Dandy*, but the given picture of the class teacher as a feeble subordinate living in a mean terraced house and facing the Kids from a high stool and ink-welled desk suggests that Dickens's account of Salem House remains the prototype for the *Beano* artist's depiction of teacher and taught.

It is something of a relief to turn to *Bunty*, which is almost as popular as *Beano* and *Dandy* among 10+ girls (27·2%) and second only to *Jackie* with 12+ girls (28·9%). Not only are the balloons furnished with more words, but the words themselves sometimes form more genuine sentences than 'Watch your fingers, Joey' and include (in the 'Meggie Miggle' story of January 27

1973) such relatively difficult words as 'remember', 'solicitor', 'executor', 'legacy', 'temporarily' and 'symbol'. Moreover, *Bunty* is not exclusively composed of comic strips; there are several pieces of continuous prose, anecdotal and ostensibly written by perfectly literate readers ('I live on a farm, and one day . . .', 'One weekend, while in town with my friend . . .', 'One Sunday afternoon, my family and I went fishing . . .'). In the murky depths of juvenile comics, where language is given no room to be anything more creative than an ancillary drudge, such faint signs of independent life bring hope with them and forward-looking thoughts: *Bunty*, if only marginally more literate than *Dandy*, does seem to be produced for children who can read and write and enjoy doing so.

The stories in *Bunty*, unlike those in *Dandy* and *Beano*, are related to the real life interests and fantasies of young girls. 'Our chum Bunty' is shown on the cover cutting out a dress. Meggie Miggle, whose father is a 'general dealer' looking for 'any old rags, old iron', saves a cat from his guard-dogs and is eventually rewarded with the loan of the cat; on another page there is a photograph of a 'cute couple' – a small girl cuddling a chimpanzee; and 'just starting' is 'the story of the struggle to save a wild stallion's life.' – girls braving danger to save a pony as spirited as St. Mawr from the grown-ups' bullets. The games played are tennis and swimming, but the stories in which they appear serve rather different purposes. 'Little Miss Frozen-Face' recounts the fortunes of 'the youngest tennis pro in the world' as she strives for recognition as 'a rival on an equal footing' (Friedlaender 1942) with the adults she plays against. 'My Sister Lee, Champion To Be' shows an aggressive, not quite straight-up-and-down girl who strides around in a full-backed bathing costume looking for a pool in which she can demonstrate her ability to break the 'world record'; accompanying Lee is her flat-chested younger sister who tries to keep her out of trouble with the authorities – matron, the swimming-pool attendant, and the toffee-nosed 'president of the swimming club'. (Consider such conscious attempts to avoid conflict beside the 'them and us' collisions in the boys' comics.) The problems of adolescence for Lee – 'idle, moody and unable to get on with people' – are presented not for the reader's sympathy but as signs of 'the mammoth task' facing her younger sister, whose job it is to 'train the champion'. The pictures feed the fantasy of the reader's crush on an older girl, tagging along helplessly behind the hoyden; the words feed the related fantasy of the younger girl being herself the heroine – 'Clare Williams had taken on the mammoth task . . . "I'll think of something. Talent like hers must get its true reward" ' – and as the final words bubble from Clare's parted lips attention is directed not towards the swimmer's budding bosom but to the visionary gleam in the wide eyes of the younger sister.

For the heroine as hoyden we have Beth Jenkins, a Jane Eyre figure, who has been 'sent to Bleakwood Hall, a school for corrective training', where the matron and the cook are shifty and cruel. Like Jane at Gateshead, Beth is put in 'solitary confinement' on grounds that to her and the reader appear flimsy; and like the Little Princess she is put to work in the kitchen. Her aggressive refusal to submit to authority is shown as the human spirit standing up to injustice – 'Don't let the bastards get you down' – and her presence in Borstal is explained as a mistake ('Though she was innocent, Beth had been in the company of three girls who had stolen goods from a car'). Her parents don't know she is in Borstal, and presumably won't know until Beth is finally declared innocent and good. The pictures show Beth sometimes as a scarecrow, sometimes as potentially pretty and civilized; the existence of good adults (her parents) as well as bad enables a satisfactory conclusion to be predicted.

In various ways, then, *Bunty* may be said to appeal more or less directly to the pre-pubertal girl, and the fact that it is read by as many as 11·2% of 14+ girls suggests the retarded development of its older readership rather than any clear concessions to adolescent fantasies (there are plenty of fathers and father-figures in *Bunty* but no one resembling a boy friend). However, when one bears in mind that *Jackie* is slightly more popular with 10+ girls (11·9%) than is *Bunty* with 14+ girls, the 'retarded development' of some children becomes less noteworthy than the 'precocity' of others.

The reason for *Jackie*'s overwhelming popularity among 12+ and 14+ girls may lie in the range of tastes and abilities it caters for combined with the representativeness of its identikit reader. The typical *Jackie* reader is presumed to work in an office or, since our sample are still at school, to intend to work in an office and realize her expectations there; if she is old enough to be married, 'we still haven't got used to thinking of her as "Mrs" '. On July 21 1973 all the office windows are open in *Jackie* editorial headquarters, where the injunction, 'Pete, take your 'orrible smelly feet off the window-sill', is offered as characteristic humour. In such an office as this, Jill of the National Westminster met Paul, who 'manages securities at a neighbouring branch': 'one can trace the romance back to Jill's first clerical assignment there', hand over hand in the foreign exchange drawers. Susan, meanwhile, is smilingly poised over her typewriter, hair gently brushing the keyboard as she conducts her 'slim-in' on behalf of 'Outline' ('which has only half the calories of butter') and Boots the Chemist (for 'a good range of low calorie drinks'). Helen's confident beauty hints, Sister Marion's discreet advice and belles not smells with Fresh & Dry Deodorant help to form the taste and the standards of the universal female: there is a 'feminine way to remove unwanted hair', and a feminine way to remove ugly spots too (back or front); and, if the feminine girl 'comes out in big red lumps' when horse-riding, *Jackie*'s Doctor will put her right.

That, give or take an ad or two, is the presumed *Jackie* reader. She has a head on her shoulders, for purposes of receiving 'deep cleansing milk' and achieving 'a lovely complexion', the *sine qua non* of success at the dance. She has depilated legs, for exposure and admiration on the beach. And she has problems – 'feminine' problems rather than the boyfriend and third-party

problems of *Loving, Valentine* and *Mirabelle.* For *Jackie* is a 'pop-teen' magazine, designed for girls who have no wish to excel at tennis or swimming and
whose romantic interest in horses has been displaced by adolescent allergies
('Many girls . . . have to give up pets such as cats, dogs and budgies because
these animals set up an allergic reaction') and the cult of David Cassidy (whose
shirt in this issue forms a decapitated two-page spread). The preoccupation
with the superficially physical and the ephemeral in *Jackie* is markedly different from the more inward interest in the younger girl evinced by *Bunty.*
Jackie, of course, is more 'real', more obviously in touch with its readership;
but it is also less 'real', in that the limitations of interest it imposes on its
readers are not the actual limitations of half the nation's adolescent girls. A
significant final 'bubble' from the gypsy whom a young couple have just
consulted gives the game away: 'For how could I tell them the truth? Sometimes there are things that should never be said.'

   Jackie's popularity 'makes it a cultural influence with adolescent girls
which cannot be ignored' (Taylor 1972). The hard facts are that of the 40
pages (160 columns) the equivalent of 19 are pictures and a further $10\frac{1}{2}$ picture
strip stories; legitimate advertisements (the distinction between editorial and
advertising matter is blurred) occupy $14\frac{1}{2}$ pages, and pictures of pop-stars (with
or without captions and forms of banal address: 'Hi, Dave') $8\frac{1}{2}$ pages; beauty
and 'personal' advice, editorial and advertised, take up 12 pages; career prospects are typing, banking and WRAC ($\frac{1}{2}$ page for each of the last two, implicit
editorial assumption of the first); of the 8 pages of continuous prose, including letters, horoscope and beauty-gossip, legitimate stories account for 3.

   Whichever way one arranges these figures, they form a low level suite.
75% of *Jackie* consists of pictures or visual aids. More than a third of the paper
is taken up by advertisements, the bulk of which are concerned with personal
grooming for the benefit (in fantasy) of the effeminate or debauched male
pop-stars whose faces and garb occupy over 20% of the space. That only 7·5%
of *Jackie* consist of legitimate stories suggests that the reader the publisher
has in mind is not accustomed to reading, or at any rate is not looking there
for reading matter. The girl who wants 'a good read' is likely to look for it in
Loving (category (ii), see p. 153), which with 19·4% of 14+ girls is the next
most popular magazine after *Jackie.* Comparative distribution of space in the
two magazines is expressed below:

	Jackie		*Loving*	
Pages	40		40	
Editorial matter	$25\frac{1}{2}$ }		{ $31\frac{1}{2}$	
Advertising	$14\frac{1}{2}$ }	40	{ $8\frac{1}{2}$	
Pictures	19 }		{ $16\frac{1}{2}$	
Picture strip stories	$10\frac{1}{2}$ }	40	{ 0	
Prose and other matter	$10\frac{1}{2}$ }		{ $23\frac{1}{2}$	

Beauty and 'personal'	12	$8\frac{1}{2}$
Continuous prose	8	$21\frac{1}{2}$
Legitimate stories	3	20

The stories in *Loving* are predictable from the title — 'He Wanted Us Both!', 'The Three of Us', 'The Mystery World of Paul Temple' (viz. Mr Francis Matthews, with his 'subtle sex-appeal'), 'It's Love that really counts', 'That Touch of Evil', 'He'll come running', and 'Night out with a stranger'. The basic fantasy is that of lying in a man's arms, being urgently kissed and gently caressed; and the person invited to indulge the fantasy is again an office girl. But *Loving*, perhaps because it addresses the post-school reader, makes no attempt to romanticize 'the office'. One of the problem letters comes from Lynne and Averil of Hull: they are 'two fed-up girls, both aged 20, and working in the same office . . . [They] would both like excitement and change.' The office is a place to escape from or to endure with patience (helped by the relief afforded by reading *Loving*). 'Most office-bound people', writes the editor, are 'pretty exhausted by the heat and stickiness of it all . . .'. Eileen, his own 'harassed and very patient secretary', has composed 'on behalf of all other secretaries everywhere', a 'prayer for the perfect secretary', expressing the sort of office humour/irritation exemplified by 'the impossible we do immediately'. The 14+ girls who read *Loving* can be under no illusions about the office: the deceptions are that the office is the normal place for a school-girl to realize her ambitions and hence that the office symbolizes the world of adult work. The limitations of vision there are of a piece with the limitations of interest assumed in the reader: *Loving*, itself the product of an office, effectually declares that release from its 'bounds' is to be achieved through indulgence in sexual fantasy.

Loving, it should be stressed, is relatively mature. Just how jejune the promoted fantasy can be in the 'pop-teen' magazines may be gauged from a characteristic article in *Mirabelle* on how to 'get one of Donny's delicious kisses'. Within the twelve column-inches of instructions we are told to 'plot out where he's likely to be every minute he's in London . . . and manage to be where Donny is . . . Simply ask him, don't demand, just ask quietly, politely, gently and sincerely.' As to the deed itself, 'Donny's different from the boys you know at school. He won't grab you roughly and give you a sloppy silly kiss . . . He's gentle and warm and sincere — and so are his kisses.'

Whether those instructions conceal a genuine (or sincere) report on experience from one who has touched the lips that roused a thousand hearts seems doubtful. The *inaccessibility* of Mr Osmond is implied in the fantasy-realization of the reader's desire: indeed his inaccessibility is surely essential to the attraction he holds for the ordinary adolescent girl. The cynical truth for such a girl is (parodying T. S. Eliot):

I have heard the Osmonds singing each to each
I do not think that they will sing to me.

And it is the writer's and the publisher's cynicism, their bland feeding upon
the girl's fantasy, that constitutes so distressing an insult to the reader.

That adolescent girls have something between their ears is no concern of
Jackie or *Mirabelle.* Indeed, intellectual interests are made to appear, by a
crude distortion of Laurentian principle, inimical to physical compatibility
with a man. In one peculiarly unpleasant strip story in *Jackie* we are shown the
pretentious but sexually inexperienced Luke happily ditching his 'highbrow
soulmate' Linda for the rather more forward Kay: 'Linda's just a friend; she
doesn't matter. I'll tell her.' Kay, however, sends him back to Linda: 'Try
kissing her like that — and maybe you'll be pleasantly surprised.' He does, and
he is, and so their relationship is restored — merely being 'soulmates' is not
enough, merely being physical is. At the end the lovers pass Kay, crying.
'Who's Kay?' — 'She's just a girl, darling,' replies Luke, 'who showed me
where love was — and maybe got her own heart broken at the same time.'
(Maybe: it's no concern of his, or of the acquiescent reader.)

It would be absurd to lay the whole blame for such a restricted vision of
life and work on *Jackie* and *Mirabelle* and similar magazines. Our civilization
is moving inexorably towards more bureaucracy, and 'the office' is increasingly the source and scene of people's jobs and income. It would be absurd,
too, for the teacher to risk a head-on collision with his 14+ girls, the majority
of whom are reading *Jackie.* However, something might be done in schools to
question the assumptions so readily made by the magazines. A general anti-
dote to the prevailing attitude might be supplied through Laura Ingalls Wilder,
whose six stories of her family life and work in pioneering days in America
are not too young for 12+ girls. And a specific question may be put to modern
children through Laura's finding herself suddenly shut out from her father's
work, when he goes to the office to write out the time-sheets for the railway
navvies: hitherto she has always been able to share work with her father or
watch him creatively at work on well or door or hayrick; now he has a job
that sometimes puts him physically apart from his family. We are no longer
pioneers or contemporaries of pioneers, and of course there can be no going
back to the log cabin on the prairie. But the younger secondary school children
could, through the 'little house' stories (which when read are apparently well
liked, and which make only the simplest linguistic demands), be given a sense
of the creative opportunities of life and work that *Jackie* shows no awareness
of. For older pupils, Penguin Books have made available in their Peacock series
books that deal sympathetically with family and boy friend relationships,
tensions between adults and children, the real world of work and youth club
and discotheque, and the predicament of the teenage mother. Such books
represent an engagement with human issues that can help the guided pupil to

place D.C. Thomson's inadequate and delusory provender.

But to talk in terms of weaning girls away from *Jackie* may seem to imply that *Jackie*-readers for the most part restrict themselves to *Jackie*. In fact, being girls, a majority of them read a good deal more than that, real books as well as other magazines. There are various reasons for deploring the success of *Jackie*, but the principal one — that it assumes the general reality of a moronic girl who in fact does not, except at her most apathetic and derivative in spirit, exist — serves to warn us that the significance of the magazine in the modern adolescent's life may not be quite what its sales suggest. The function of ephemera within her daily round may be essentially that of a teddy-bear, a familiar companion, 'a friend dropping in' (as the *Manchester Evening News* describes itself). The desire for such a drug, like the sense of TV as 'company' (the newsreader wishing us good night or a good weekend), is certainly more widespread than among school children only, and suggests that standards of entertainment and notions of recreation are a social rather than a simply educational problem.

Nevertheless, when due weight has been given to the possibly marginal impact of the magazines upon many of their purchasers, the final stress should be put on the responsibility of the producer of ephemera. Children lack, in varying degrees and for various reasons, ready access to bookshops, public libraries, school libraries; the only place all are able and willing to go to is the local newsagent's shop, and it is there that their tastes and standards in reading matter are formed, as public librarians, real booksellers and teachers know to their cost. The responsibility such a position in society entails on producer, wholesaler and retailer is enormous — and goes quite unrecognized, it seems, not only by the businessmen involved but by the society they serve. We have given the facts, as well as our judgement, of the reduced quality of the comics since the revolution of the 1950s. Perhaps we are justified in concluding with a direct challenge: if the goods delivered are as feeble, delusive and insulting to the purchaser as we have claimed they are, should we not question whether the freedom to distribute such things is a freedom we would be better without?

REFERENCES

Friedlaender, K. (1942). 'Children's books and their function in latency and prepuberty', *American Imago,* 3, 129–50, New York.

Lofts, W. O. G. and Adley, D. J. (1970). *The Men Behind Boys Fiction.* Howard Baker.

Taylor, J. J. (autumn 1972). 'The reading of comics by secondary school pupils', *The Use of English,* 24, 11–15.

Webb, W. S. K. *The Truth About Wilson.* D.C. Thomson, Red Lion Library.

7 Conclusions and recommendations

1   The main part of our investigation consisted of a written questionnaire which was administered to some 8000 children in 381 schools in England and Wales in March 1971. After excluding absentees and a small proportion whose answers had to be discarded as incomplete or unsatisfactory, we had available for analysis completed questionnaires from 2747 children aged 10+, 2612 children aged 12+, and 2480 children aged 14+, a total of 7839 children in all. 193 primary schools participated in the survey and 188 secondary schools. The sample was a stratified random sample drawn with assistance from the Statistics Division of the Department of Education and Science in such a way that for each of the three age groups every child in state schools and Direct Grant schools in England and Wales had an equal probability of selection. The overwhelming majority of the schools we approached cooperated most readily and helpfully, so that the achieved sample as a percentage of the design sample reached the remarkably high figure of 95·7% of schools. We are justified therefore in claiming that the sample was an exceptionally good one, and the result is that for the first time in the history of educational research in this country we have a questionnaire survey about children's voluntary reading conducted with a representative sample which justifies generalization of the findings to the relevant populations of children in England and Wales as a whole.

2   There are a few general characteristics of the sample which deserve mention. In the first place the class composition of the sample, as gauged by the children's description of their father's occupation, corresponded well with the class composition of the male population of the country as recorded in the Registrar General's sample census for 1966. There were rather more boys (4062) in our sample than girls (3777), but this difference is not large enough to be troubling. Schools were asked to assign each pupil to one of five grades for ability and attainment, and although the distribution of these grades was skewed in that relatively too few pupils were assigned to the lowest category, there was probably some justification for this imbalance in that special schools had been excluded from our sample and the absence rate was probably higher

271

than average for this grade of ability and attainment. It was noticeable that at each age very much higher percentages of children were allocated to the high ability and attainment grades in the non-manual social classes than in the manual social classes, and also that there was a consistent tendency to rate girls higher than boys. Schools were also asked to rate each child on a three-point scale according to his or her general attitude to school, and there proved to be a strong association between ability and attainment and favourable attitude to school. Family size was significantly smaller among non-manual families (mean family size 2·97 for girls, 2·95 for boys) than among manual families (mean family size 3·32 for girls, 3·53 for boys). Within each social class group (manual and non-manual) there was a consistent relationship between family size and ability and attainment, small families being regularly associated with high ability and attainment. Rather more than half our sample had working mothers, the proportion being higher for girls than for boys, and higher for manual families than for non-manual families. Television ownership was remarkably high among the families in the sample, ranging from 98·1% for non-manual families to 98·8% for manual families.

3　　The most important part of our questionnaire was a question which asked the respondent to name any book or books read voluntarily during the previous month, to indicate the source from which it had been obtained, and to express the reader's degree of liking for it on a five-point scale. The answers indicated that the average number of books read by each child in our sample ranged from 2·95 at 10+ through 2·21 at 12+ to 1·95 at 14+. These figures suggest a marked decline in amount of book reading by children in 1971 as compared with the children reported on by Jenkinson in 1940; however, since it remains uncertain how representative Jenkinson's sampling was, we cannot rest too much confidence on this comparison. What is certainly worrying is the marked swing away from book reading as children grow older. This becomes even more striking when we examine the percentage of children in each age group who have not read a book during the previous month. Among the girls this percentage was only 9·4% at 10+, but it rose to 23·3% at 12+ and 32·4% at 14+. Among the boys the situation is even more disturbing, since here the percentage of non-book-readers was 15·8% at 10+, 33·2% at 12+ and at 14+ had actually risen to 40·0%. If we accept that voluntary book reading is highly important for children at these ages both as a source of experience and as a means of consolidating and internalizing their reading skills, there is clearly cause for concern in these figures. Moreover, although the non-book-readers naturally include some children who are weak or backward in reading (there is indeed in the sample as a whole a statistically significant association between ability and attainment and amount of book reading), it should be stressed that most of them have the ability to read books if they choose to do so. Indeed at the two older age ranges more than two-thirds of the non-book-readers have been assessed by their teachers as average or above average in ability and attainment so that for these pupils certainly their condition is one of 'won't read' rather than 'can't read'.

It would be a mistake to concentrate too exclusively, however, on the gloomy side of the picture. Striking a more positive note we should mention that at every age there is a sizeable minority of children who show genuine commitment to book reading. Thus at 10+ nearly a half of all children have read 3 or more books in the month under study, and even at 14+ (the age group in our sample that reads fewest books) there remains a firm core of about one-third who have achieved the same amount in number of books read, an amount that seems distinctly creditable in face of the massive competition books face from television and other modern distractions.

4   In our study of our data three factors stand out as strongly linked with amount of book reading. The first of these is sex. At all ages girls read more books than boys, and at the same time there are fewer non-book-readers among the girls than among the boys. The second highly relevant factor is social class. At all ages children with fathers in non-manual occupations read more books than children with fathers in manual occupations, and there are also fewer non-book-readers in the non-manual group. The third important factor is ability and attainment as assessed by the school. Again at all ages children rated high for ability and attainment tended to read more books, and also there were fewer non-book-readers among them; it should of course be remembered that high ratings for ability and attainment were also strongly associated with membership of a non-manual family.

These three factors tend to suggest that the group most at risk in regard to non-book-reading will consist of boys in low 'ability and attainment' groupings with manual fathers, and it is certainly the case that this group is one which schools need to watch (and often do watch) with special concern. (In fact among 14+ boys of ability C, D or E as many as 54·4% were non-book-readers.) At the same time it is important to remember that what we have demonstrated is a statistical association only, and that there are also many boys and girls from non-manual homes and also many boys with high ratings for ability and attainment who are also non-book-readers. Thus, among the 14+ boys rated A or B for ability and attainment, there are as many as 29·2% who are non-book-readers, and even among the 14+ girls similarly rated there are as many as 22·1% who are non-book-readers. It might even be suggested that this group is one whose need for encouragement and help in regard to books is more likely to be overlooked by many schools.

5   We also asked the children to name the periodicals they read regularly and the answers revealed quite heavy periodical reading throughout the age range, with only a modest decline as children grew older. Thus the average

number of periodicals read regularly at 10+ was 3·29, declining to 3·07 at 12+ and to 2·91 at 14+. As in the case of books, girls read more periodicals than boys, and there are more boys than girls who do not read any periodicals (these generalizations apply to each of the three age groups). The relationship between social class and periodical reading is the obverse of that pertaining to the reading of books; in this case children from manual families tend to read more periodicals than children from non-manual families (in part this may be due to the fact that manual children are from larger families, and tend to have more siblings whose periodicals they read as well as their own). The relationship between periodical reading and ability and attainment is too complex to be summarized here; we will mention only that there seem to be two distinct groups of low ability children — those who read no periodicals and those whose periodical reading is higher than average. In case any reader should be inclined to take comfort from the persisting heavy consumption of periodicals by our sample, it should be made clear at once that the overwhelming majority (more than two-thirds) of the periodicals were comics, and that the modern comic has, in general, a remarkably low verbal content; thus it would be a mistake to suppose that our sample by virtue of their periodical reading, were for the most part engaged in reading any very considerable amount of words.

The relationship between amount of book reading and amount of periodical reading is fairly complex, but we can say that in general non-periodical-reading tends to go hand in hand with non-book-reading, and heavy periodical reading tends to go hand in hand with heavy book reading; the only sub-group to whom this generalization does not apply is that of the 14+ girls.

6   Our information about television viewing was obtained by asking each child to indicate the number of hours he had spent watching television the previous evening (which was always a weekday evening). We found that the average amount of time spent on a weekday evening in watching television was 2·49 hours for the sample as a whole, and that about three-fifths of the sample watched more than 2 hours per weekday evening, while almost two-fifths watched more than 3 hours per weekday evening. Boys watch slightly more television than girls do, but this difference is significant only at 14+. For both sexes the amount of viewing decreases as age increases, but not at all dramatically. When one remembers the other demands made upon children's time on a weekday evening during term time it seems clear that the amount of television viewing accomplished by most children cannot help but reduce the amount of time they have available for reading, and in fact we found that for each sub-group there existed an inverse relationship between amount of television viewing and amount of book reading. On the other hand we found that for all sub-groups there was a positive relationship between amount of television viewing and amount of periodical reading. It should perhaps be mentioned also that there was a consistent pattern of heavier viewing among

children graded low for ability and attainment as compared with children graded high.

7   We also found that amount of book reading was positively associated with each of the following variables: (a) smallness of family size; (b) number of books owned by the child; (c) the regularity of child's visits to the public library; (d) the parents' reading of library books; (e) the presence of quality newspapers among those taken by the family; (f) favourableness of the child's attitude to school; (g) favourableness of the child's attitude towards English lessons (12+ and 14+ groups only); (h) lateness of age at which child expects to leave school (12+ and 14+ groups only). We also found that each of these variables, except for (g), was also correlated with either social class or ability and attainment or both; and it was therefore necessary to see whether the association with amount of book reading continued to hold when these two variables were held constant. Further analysis showed that the association continued to persist, except in the case of (a) where the association remained positive only for ability and attainment groups A and B and was not significant for groups C, D and E.

8   We may summarize our argument so far by saying that our analysis identified a number of variables associated with the home which are positively associated with amount of book reading, and that there are therefore grounds for believing that family circumstances exert an important influence on the amount of a child's reading. Thus a child with a father in a non-manual occupation is likely to possess more books and to see more quality newspapers in the home, and is more likely to visit a public library regularly and to have parents who read library books. We can fairly say that this child's home is oriented towards the use of books and that this orientation is partly responsible for the fact that he is likely to have read more books than a child whose father is in a manual occupation. (Conversely the child with a non-manual father is likely to see fewer periodicals regularly, and to spend less time watching television.) We can also say that the child with a non-manual father is more likely to be assessed high by his school for ability and attainment, to express a favourable attitude to school, and to record an expectation of staying on at school to the age of 18.

9   This leads us on naturally to the other social institution which may be expected to exert an influence on the child's reading — namely the school. Our information about the schools under review was gained mainly from the school questionnaire which was completed by the head in the case of the primary schools and by the head of the English department in the case of the secondary schools. The school variable which undoubtedly proved to have most influence on amount of reading was school type. Thus at 10+ children

in junior-with-infant schools were found to read more books than children
in junior schools. This rather unexpected finding is hard to explain with confidence. It may be associated with one or more of the following: the junior-
with-infant schools were smaller and had decidedly fewer 10+ pupils than the
junior; junior-with-infant schools, having been concerned with reading from
its first beginnings, may have a more reading-oriented ethos than junior
schools; the children in these schools may have benefited from the absence
of a break in their learning of reading at 7+; there may also be an influence
attributable to the fact that junior-with-infant schools are less likely than
junior schools to have streamed classes (a feature whose bearing will be
returned to shortly).

10   In the case of the secondary schools there was a strong association
between amount of book reading and school type, with direct grant schools
reading more than grammar schools, grammar schools reading more than
comprehensive schools, and comprehensive schools more than secondary
modern schools. This finding is of course not at all surprising in view of the
positive association already demonstrated between ability and attainment and
amount of reading. However the interesting comparison arises when we
combine the grammar schools with the secondary modern schools, and find
that their amount of reading was not at 12+ significantly different from that
of the comprehensive schools and was at 14+ only marginally higher. In
interpreting this we need to take into account the fact that the 56 comprehensive schools in our sample included a number whose intake for the two
age groups under study had been creamed off to a significant extent by
selective schools. We found it could be argued that, allowing for the ability
composition of their pupils, the comprehensive schools were actually achieving
a higher level than the selective sector in regard to amount of reading at 12+
and were doing equally well at 14+.

11   An unexpected finding was that there were, for each sex considered
separately, more non-book-readers in the mixed schools than in the single-sex
schools. This finding applied, of course, only to the secondary schools, since
all the primary schools in our sample were mixed schools: in the secondary
schools it applied, however, both to the 12+ and to the 14+ age groups. No
obvious explanation for it is apparent from our data; but it may be that the
quality of book provision for reluctant readers, and the knowledgeability of
teachers about suitable books, is of a higher standard in single-sex schools,
where women teachers need to acquaint themselves only with the needs and
interests of girls and men teachers need to acquaint themselves only with
the needs and interests of boys. It seems to us that the most important
implication is that mixed schools need to be aware that their pupils include
a group which for one reason or another runs a higher-than-average risk of

becoming non-book-readers, and that specially energetic measures should be taken to combat this danger.

12   Streaming proved to be a feature of school organization which was decidedly relevant to amount of book reading. In the primary schools it was shown that 10+ children in streamed classes read fewer books than children either in mixed ability classes or in vertical grouping forms of organization. In the secondary schools streaming also had an adverse effect upon amount of reading, though here the situation is more complex, since we have to take into account not only streamed and mixed ability classes but also forms of organization in which children are put into sets for various subjects. At 12+ more books were read by children who were in mixed ability classes or were in sets for various subjects but not for English, as compared with those who were in streamed classes or were in sets for various subjects including English. At 14+ more books were read by children who were in sets for various subjects but not for English as compared with the other three types of class organization. The evidence thus seems to point towards the view that both streaming and setting for English have an adverse effect upon amount of reading, particularly at the younger ages. The most likely explanation seems to be that in a streamed or set situation any benefit gained by those pupils assigned to a high stream or set is more than cancelled out by the adverse effect on the morale of those pupils who are relegated to a low stream or set.

13   Three other school variables must be mentioned briefly. In the primary schools we found that there were more non-book-readers at 10+ in the schools where the timetable was either fully or partly structured according to the usual subject divisions as compared with those schools (only a small minority) where the timetable was fully integrated; the interest of this finding is that it tends to refute the claim sometimes made that more informal approaches to teaching in the primary school are associated with lower levels of literacy and reduced emphasis on the role of books. Among the primary schools the overwhelming majority provided class libraries for the 10+ group and whether or not they also provided a school library was not a significant differentiator in regard to amount of reading. In the secondary schools the natural comparison was between those which relied on the school library alone and those which in addition provided class libraries for some or all of their 12+ and/or 14+ pupils. Here we unexpectedly found that there was less book reading, both at 12+ and 14+, in the schools which provided class libraries to supplement their school library. In interpreting this finding we have to remember that in many schools class libraries were provided only for some and not for all of the 12+ and/or 14+ classes; and that it is possible that schools which provided class libraries may have done so either because they were aware of deficiencies in their school library, or because they were conscious of having pupils who for various reasons (including perhaps home background and ability level) were particularly liable to become non-book-readers. Our data seem to indicate however that, for whatever reasons, the class libraries in the secondary schools which provided them were not fulfilling satisfactorily the purpose for which they were presumably intended. In the secondary schools we also found a lower amount of book reading in the schools which provided for their English lessons either course books, comprehension books or thematic anthologies than in those schools which did not do so. The implication may be that if the development of wide independent reading is a central goal in English teaching this objective is more likely to be attained by reading 'real books' in English lessons than by the study of extracts.

14   So far we have reviewed findings which demonstrate an association between amount of book reading and a considerable number of home variables and a more limited number of school variables. To gain some indication of the relative importance of these variables we used two computer programmes, the first being AID (Automatic Interaction Detector). As applied to the 10+ group AID showed that the highest reading group consisted of girls assessed high for ability and attainment whose fathers are in non-manual occupations, who have a positive attitude to school, and are attending schools with mixed ability classes; the lowest reading group on the other hand were children assessed low for ability and attainment and whose parents take non-quality and/or local newspapers only. As applied to the 12+ group AID showed that the highest reading group consisted of children (both sexes) who are assessed very high for ability and attainment, who like school very much or quite a lot, come from small families, and attend schools in which the classes are either streamed or mixed ability (not in sets); the lowest reading group were (rather surprisingly) also children assessed very high for ability and attainment, but in this case they are those who do not like school, are attending secondary modern or comprehensive schools and have fathers who are in a manual occupation. As applied to the 14+ group AID showed that the highest reading group were children who liked English lessons and expected to stay on at school to age 18; the lowest reading group were children assessed low for ability and attainment who expected to leave school at ages 15, 16 or 17.

The other computer programme used was the General Linear Hypothesis programme which operates on a slightly different set of assumptions. This was applied to all groups; at 14+, it showed that the highest amount of book reading can be expected to occur in the case of girls whose family take quality newspapers, who like their English lessons, are assessed as having a favourable attitude to their school, and attend a school on a single campus where the classes are unstreamed, where the emphasis in English teaching falls upon reading from a wide selection of books but at the same time a small number of books are reserved for class discussion and reading, and where they have access to a school library only.

15   When we turn to the kinds of book read by our sample the most important feature is the extraordinary diversity of book reading undertaken by these children. Thus the 5846 children who named one or more books which they had read during the previous month mentioned in all no fewer than 7557 separate and distinct titles. 246 of these titles had been mentioned by ten or more children, and these were individually coded and followed up in the course of our computer analysis under the heading of 'widely-read books'. Taken together, these widely-read books accounted for a little under 31% of the total book-mentions by the sample. The remaining 7311 titles were each read by only a few children, often indeed only by a single child. [It seemed clear that children greatly value the opportunity given to them by book reading to exercise their own choice and to pursue highly individual interests and tastes through books. Indeed the great and continuing strength of the book in its competition with the audio-visual media (and in particular with television) is its unrivalled ability to give the individual the chance to follow his own particular bent in his own way and at his own pace at any one particular time. This opportunity for self-discovery and self-realization opened up by books seems to us an integral and central component in any conception of education which takes personal growth as its goal.] *mentioned in Hall & Coles.*

16   In handling this vast and miscellaneous array of titles we set our face against the kind of classification by topic, setting or subject-matter used in many previous studies of children's reading. Instead we developed our own mode of classifying, aiming at a system which arose naturally out of the data in front of us but which was at the same time simple enough to be operated effectively over a huge range of titles, not all of which we were able actually to handle and examine. The first split which demanded to be made was between narrative and non-narrative. Non-narrative accounted for 14·5% of all book-mentions for the sample as a whole. However this figure conceals the fact that boys read much more non-narrative than girls. Thus for the sample as a whole the percentage of non-narrative books read by the boys was 23·1 as against 6·9 for the girls, and in regard to this difference the variation between the three age groups was negligible. It also emerged that while there are very few girls indeed who read non-narrative books only, there is a steady and by no means negligible proportion of boys (ranging between 8% and 10%) who restrict their reading in this way. With increasing age there is a decline in absolute terms in the number of non-narrative books read (a decline which goes hand-in-hand with the overall diminution in book reading at the later ages); but there were indications that this should be seen in terms of longer and more demanding non-narrative books being read in fewer numbers rather than in terms of a reduction in the amount of time devoted to them. It is also noteworthy that for all sub-groups except the 14+ girls, children from manual families read a significantly higher proportion of non-narrative books than children from non-manual families.

17   The most striking point about narrative book reading is that it forms a remarkably high proportion (at least 77%) of the whole. Moreover this high proportion remains very steady from 10+ through 12+ to 14+, though here again there is a difference between the sexes which remains remarkably consistent. Thus at each of the three age levels about two-thirds of the boys' reading consists of narrative books, whereas for the girls the proportion is invariably much higher, standing at more than four-fifths of the whole for each age level.

Our category of narrative consisted predominantly of fiction, but we also included biographies, autobiographies and memoirs, on the grounds that whether a story is true or invented seems to make little difference to a child's motives for reading it or to the kinds of satisfactions taken from it. We also subdivided further this broad category of narrative, the first split being into books written specifically for children (juvenile narrative) and those intended originally for adults (adult narrative). Our final step was to make a further split within our two narrative categories into 'quality' and 'non-quality'. Our decision here was admittedly somewhat controversial, but we took it in the belief that most teachers (English teachers particularly) will find that it adds a meaningful (if rather subjective) dimension to our data. In making the discrimination between quality and non-quality narrative the criterion we used was roughly as follows: Is this book one we can imagine a responsible teacher justly recommending to pupils at a certain stage of development on the ground that they are likely to take from it some imaginative experience valuable to them at their own level, over and above the mere practice of reading skills? It should be added that there remained one group of narrative books which could not be classified under either the juvenile/adult or the quality/non-quality dichotomy. These were what we had to call 'fairy tales, myths and legends' (re-tellings sometimes by known writers, but often by writers unspecified); they were quite a small group, and account for only 3·1% of all book-mentions. For the sample as a whole juvenile quality narrative accounted for 17·0% of all book readings, while juvenile non-quality narrative accounted for 33·4%. On the other hand, adult quality narrative accounted for only 11·4% of all book reading, while adult non-quality narrative accounted for only 12·1%. Thus it can be seen that approximately 45% of the sample's total book reading was judged to be non-quality narrative, a finding which we may reasonably regard as closely matched to Jenkinson's observation in 1940 that what children chose to read in their leisure time was 'mainly trash by adult standards'.

There was naturally a tendency for children to move increasingly from juvenile narrative to adult narrative as they grew older, though it is worth stressing that even at 14+ as many as 14·7% of the boys and 25·5% of the girls were still reading juvenile narrative. There was also a tendency for quality narrative to form a higher proportion of total book reading as children grow older. On the whole, our more detailed tables tend to suggest that it is mainly the readers of non-quality narrative only who are liable to discontinue book reading between the ages of 10+ and 14+, and that those children who read some quality books are more likely to retain the reading habit over this period in their lives.

18   When we tabulated for each age group the individual titles which led the field among the 246 widely-read books we were struck at once by the remarkable predominance of such old favourites as *Black Beauty, Treasure Island* and *Little Women* among the lists for 10+ and 12+ children, and the relatively thin representation of more recent writers of books for children. Indeed so overwhelming was the nineteenth century flavour of the 10+ and 12+ lists that we were led to wonder how far these lists might be an indication not so much of what children truly prefer but rather of what is available to them. In the case of the 10+ children we were able to pursue this line of inquiry further by sending out to our primary schools a list of 65 quality narrative books including both some which had been often read and some which had been infrequently read, and asking the schools to tick each title which was available in schools for their 10+ children. There proved to be a positive and quite high correlation (+0·66) between the number of times a book had been read and the number of schools in which it was available; this strongly suggests that for this age group availability in school plays an important, though not exclusive, role in determining which books children read. It was not practicable to pursue a similar inquiry in secondary schools, but the 12+ and 14+ lists contain a large number of titles which suggest that, here too, availability in school must be an important factor influencing the choice of books. School sources are not quite so important a source of books, however, at 12+ and 14+ since at these ages the proportion of public library borrowing has increased as compared with 10+.

19   For each book mentioned as read during the previous month we also sought information about: (a) the source from which it had been obtained, and (b) the reader's degree of liking for it on a five-point scale. Except in the case of the 14+ girls the children's own stock of books forms by far the largest single source from which they draw the books they read. The public library is also an important source of books, accounting for 16% of total book reading at 10+, a proportion which increases to 21% at 12+ and 14+. Rather striking is the diminution in the proportion of books obtained from school sources;

if we take school and class libraries together these account for 36% of all book reading at 10+, but this has dropped to 21% at 12+ and 22% at 14+. It is above all in the number of books obtained from class libraries that this drop occurs, a feature associated undoubtedly with the fact that, whereas almost all primary schools provide class libraries, rather less than half of the secondary schools do so, and even then in many cases only for some of their 12+ and 14+ classes. Unfortunately this sharp reduction in the number of books obtained from class libraries is not accompanied by an increase in borrowing from school libraries; we may reasonably suppose that in a number of secondary schools (particularly perhaps those which do not provide regular library periods) it is only children who have already acquired some degree of commitment to book reading who take the trouble to make special visits to the school library in order to seek out books for borrowing. Moreover the information obtained about 'liking scores' is somewhat discouraging in this connection. Throughout the sample books owned by the child are given a more favourable liking score than books obtained from other sources, and this is perhaps understandable. However, it is also the case that, even if we exclude books owned by the child, books obtained from school sources gain consistently and significantly lower liking scores than books obtained from other sources. This may suggest that the books provided in school and class libraries are often not only outdated and behind the times but also rather ill suited to the needs and interests of the pupils in the age ranges we have been concerned with.

20   Information was also obtained about unfinished books, and these formed a surprisingly high proportion of the whole — about 10%. Books obtained from school sources were significantly more likely to be left unfinished than books obtained from other sources, and this fact tends to reinforce our doubts about the adequacy and suitability of the book provision made in school and class libraries. A further point which was rather striking was the high proportion of re-readings; indeed for the sample as a whole about one book out of five read by each child had been read previously.

21   To supplement the written questionnaires the research team conducted during the school year 1971/72 follow-up interviews with 576 children in 34 different schools spread throughout the country. The distinctive value of these interviews was the way they added flesh to the bare bones of our statistical analysis, but in the nature of things this value resides in the detailed discussion (see Chapter 4) and cannot be reduced to summary form. There were, however, three generalized points which stood out from the impressions we formed. The first was the extent to which the amount, nature and quality of a child's reading is intimately and inextricably bound up with his attainments, interest, personality and total life-situation; each child, we would insist, is a unique person, and can be helped to develop in his reading (as in so many

other matters) only by someone who knows, understands and appreciates this uniqueness. Secondly, we were constantly amazed by the extraordinary diversity in both the amount and quality of the book provision in different schools; we were left in no doubt that, although the home background is undoubtedly of key importance in its influence on a child's reading, an almost equal weight of influence must often attach also to the differing levels of provision made by the school, particularly in regard to such matters as the kind, attractiveness and suitability of the books made available in the school library and the class libraries, the ease of access which children have to them, and the degree to which they are encouraged to make use of them. Thirdly, it was clear to us that a vital factor (sometimes the most important factor of all) was the degree to which individual teachers and teacher-librarians brought to bear upon their pupils' reading an informed and sympathetic concern and interest; in this connection we cannot speak too highly of the enthusiasm, knowledgeability, dedication and tact of a number of the teachers we encountered in these schools, some of whom were achieving wonders in circumstances which were basically unpromising.

22   One of the tasks we had set ourselves was to explore the qualities inherent in the most popular books which lead children to prefer them. Here again the issues raised are so complex (see Chapter 5) that a brief summary cannot help but be bald and unilluminating. We reviewed at some length a number of previous studies, and identified one line of thought which stresses above all the child's quest for instinctual satisfactions in his reading, particularly those related to the emotional conflicts and problems which are uppermost at his particular stage in development. Writers in this tradition have tended to speak in terms of empathy, identification, and disguised or substitute gratification of unconscious wishes; in general their conclusion has been that a major motive leading children to prefer their favourite books is a desire to obtain vicarious imaginative satisfaction of a wish-fulfilment kind, often by means of identification with a hero or heroine not too unlike themselves. There is too much supporting evidence from earlier studies to entitle anyone to brush this line of thinking aside. More recently, on the other hand, some writers have stressed much more the continuity between the reading of fiction and the spectator role which we adopt when we are engaged in a detached evaluative response to events in which we are not actively participating. On this view the reader — whether adult or child — is always aware that what he is reading is 'only a story' and, as an interested onlooker, he sees the fictional happenings through the author's eyes and either takes over or rejects his evaluative judgments on the events described. The implication would seem to be that it is these evaluative judgements which affect us particularly powerfully as we read, and which form the important residue left in our minds from the reading of narrative.

In our own detailed discussion of some of the most popular books in our lists, ranging from *Black Beauty* and *Five on a Treasure Island* to *The Day of the Triffids* and *Jane Eyre,* we formed the impression that these two lines of thought are not only both of them relevant but also indeed mutually support- ing. In all the 'preferred' books we have examined there is at least one character with whom the young reader could be expected to associate himself emotionally, and this sharing of a particular character's experiences normally goes hand in hand with that kind of transposition of the world 'according to an arrange- ment which is more to his liking' which Freud described as characteristic of both the playing child and the poet. It is essential that adults (parents, teachers and librarians alike) should be aware of the importance to the child reader of such emotional satisfactions, and in choosing or recommending books should attach due weight to them, along with such other relevant issues as emotional maturity or linguistic difficulty. On the other hand it is no less important to recognize that these identificatory and wish-fulfilment elements are normally closely intertwined with the evaluative judgements which the reader is invited to take over from the author; the quality of these evaluative responses and their likely impact upon the child reader *at his own stage of development* are issues which we need to keep equally clearly in mind as we attempt to guide the young reader towards experiences which (in the words of the Bullock Report) 'enlarge his understanding of the range of human possibilities'.

One further important point emerges from our detailed discussions. We found ourselves obliged to stress the uniqueness of each individual book, the remarkably varied way in which different fictional elements may be combined within it. In each case generalization can touch only part of what is at stake, and secondhand knowledge derived from book reviews or other people's opinions can never be enough. What we are obliged to insist on is the need for the teacher to know at first hand, and respond sensitively to, both the individual book and the individual child, so that the two may be brought together in the right combination at the right time.

23　　We also examined, in less extensive detail, some of the periodicals which are most widely read by the age group, ranging from *Dandy* and *Beano* through *Bunty* to *Jackie*; and this proved, not unexpectedly, a somewhat depressing exercise. As already mentioned, except for the informational periodicals read by the 14+ boys, and the prose fiction magazines favoured by some of the 14+ girls, these widely read periodicals are now almost exclusively comics in which the stories are told in picture-strips, and in which the amount of verbal content has been dramatically reduced *vis-à-vis* comparable publica- tions from a few decades back. In addition such vocabulary as there is (con- fined now wholly to the balloons issuing from the characters' mouths) is feebly exclamatory and emasculated, and often adds little to the story line as con- veyed by the crudely drawn pictures embellished by cheap and garish colouring. It is indisputable that these uncouth publications offer some emotional satisfactions (however trivial and ephemeral) to their 'readers', and the fact that in the process they contribute virtually nothing to the development of reading ability, and offer nothing in the way of experience save to reinforce conventional stereotyped (and often socially undesirable) attitudes and values, is clearly of no relevance to those publishers whose exclusive concern is with the maximization of profits. Indeed the most deplorable aspect of this part of the 'entertainment industry' is the extent to which many children and young people have come to feel that these adult-produced and commercially motivated comics are essentially their own, a manifestation of their own inner nature rather than a coarse debasement of those parts of it which can be manipulated to the greater profit of a large scale capitalist enterprise. Given such feelings (frequently evidenced in our follow-up interviews), there can be no point in the school setting itself up in overt opposition to the 'culture' of the comics. The most the teacher can do is to take note of the preoccupations this culture testifies to in his pupils' make-up, and then try to find and make available as many books as he can (the more recent in publication date the better) which engage with these preoccupations in a mode which is both more sensitive and more constructive.

24   In moving on now to put forward some positive recommendations based on our research we shall be drawing both upon the findings of our questionnaire survey and upon impressions gained during our follow-up visits to schools. The main burden of our suggestions will be that schools and teachers need to devote more of their energies and resources to the encourage-ment and development of voluntary book reading over the 10—15 age range. The urgency of this need does not arise merely from the likelihood that the average number of books read per head has diminished over the past few decades; most children still read books in their leisure time, and it is natural that they should read fewer books in a cultural climate where strong competing claims upon leisure are made by the audio-visual media (television in particular) and where these media can satisfy some at least of the needs which were formerly met by books alone. What does give reason for concern is the disturbingly high proportion of children (as many as 36% overall) who have either failed to establish or have abandoned the book-reading habit by the age of 14+.

These children suffer in two ways. In the first place their linguistic experience is impoverished to such an extent that in many cases the reading process will never be fully internalized in their own mental make-up. Only extensive reading can produce the really assured and effortless command of the printed word which is necessary for all of us in the modern world (one inter-national authority has contended that children need to have read a million running words before they become fully accomplished in their reading skills, and it is clear that compulsory school reading, even if supplemented by much scanning of contemporary comics, will seldom give enough sheer practice in reading to ensure that even this minimal standard is reached). In the second place, these non-book-readers are unwittingly missing a vital source of enrichment of experience which even a plethora of exposure to the audio-visual media cannot make up for; in saying this we do not denigrate the benefits in stimulus, understanding and emotional satisfaction which can be gained from a medium such as television, we insist only that, in the present state of organization of the television industry in this country, television is unable to do more than cater for the 'big battalions' in ways which are relatively standardized, restricted and trivializing as compared with the variety of opportunity which is opened up to the individual when he becomes free to use the multiple and virtually unlimited diversity of resources available in a library of books.

25   It is true that a considerable number of the non-book-readers are children who are weak in their level of reading attainment, and that most schools devote considerable effort and resourcefulness to improving the reading ability of these backward readers. What our research has uncovered is the existence of a sizeable group in the secondary school whose reading skill would enable them to read interesting books if they chose to do so. The group at risk contains a high proportion of children from manual working class families where books play little part in the life of the home; it also includes a number of children from middle class families, however, and a number who are of high ability in terms of school work — indeed there are more than a few whose attainment in lessons is good enough to conceal from their teachers the deprivation which our own survey has disclosed. Such children are to be found in all types of secondary school, whether grammar, comprehensive or modern; for some reasons not easily explicable there are more of them in mixed schools than in single-sex schools. All schools should be alerted to their responsibility to identify these children and to seek out, provide and recommend the books that will induce them to take up the satisfactions available to them from book reading. One helpful procedure which is widely practised in the primary school but often discontinued in the secondary school is the keeping of book records which are scrutinized from time to time by a teacher. It should be stressed that experience shows that there are very few children, if indeed any, who cannot be 'hooked' on books if the right ones are put in their way.

26   Our study has shown convincingly that the provision of books by the primary school plays an extremely important part in determining what children read, and has suggested that this is also likely to be true in the secondary school, even though at older ages the public library plays an increasing role as a source of books for many pupils. All schools should recognize

the powerful influence they can exercise by making the right books available for leisure-time reading, and while there has undoubtedly been an improvement in provision in recent years many schools need to allocate more of their resources to the purchase of such books and to develop more expertise in their selection.

27   The enormous variety of children's individual choices and preferences lends powerful support to the now widespread practice of catering for their needs by means of an individualized reading scheme rather than by class sets of books. (There is some reason to believe, however, that at some stages in the secondary school and with some groups of pupils the reading together in English lessons of an appropriately chosen book still has a valuable supplementary role to play.) In junior schools such individualized reading schemes almost invariably take the form of a class library; this system has the advantage that the books are continually and readily on hand for all children to make use of, and it does seem to be successful in ensuring that the number of non-readers is kept to a minimum. Secondary schools are more inclined to rely upon the school library, and given certain preconditions – ready access and availability, a varied supply of suitable fiction, an easy borrowing system, regular library periods for browsing and borrowing (and these need to continue, as often they do not, beyond the first or second year), the presence of skilled guidance and supervision, preferably from a knowledgeable librarian or teacher-librarian working in close conjunction with the form's regular English teacher who knows the individual children well – we have good reason to believe that this arrangement can be highly effective.

There are still, however, many schools where the library provision falls far short of this high standard; and we suggest that in these schools English departments need to provide in addition class libraries which are available for borrowing at least during English lessons. We are well aware of the practical difficulties of providing class libraries in a large secondary school where both classes and teachers are on the move from one classroom to another every forty minutes or so; many of these difficulties could be obviated, however, if the school set aside certain rooms as specifically English rooms where class libraries could be housed and where all classes could have at least some of their English lessons. The need for such special accommodation is no less urgent in the case of English than in the case of geography, the sciences or the practical subjects. If they are to do their job effectively class libraries need to be much larger than most of the ones we were able to observe – large enough to provide genuine choice for all pupils, which probably means in practice that there need to be at least three times as many books as there are members of the class. They need also to be varied in scope if they are to cater successfully for the very wide range of reading ability and maturity to be found in most secondary school classes. (Our records show that particularly in a mixed-ability secondary class this range can be quite staggering.) Too many of the class libraries we observed were operating on a shoe string and owed their existence only to the conviction and enthusiasm of an individual teacher. Wherever there is a need for them (i.e. wherever the school library is inadequate or access to it is restricted) the provision of class libraries needs to be given a much higher priority by the school administration.

28   Our discussion so far may seem to suggest that the problem of the non-book-reader is essentially one for the secondary school, and that the primary schools are fulfilling their role with unqualified success. In one sense this is true; there were comparatively very few non-book-readers at 10+, and the ethos of most primary schools did stress book reading as an important activity, even though we would have liked to see more of them encouraging children to take books home to read there as well as at school. Yet we had an uneasy suspicion that in too many cases the seeds of later trouble were observable in the kind and quality of the book provision made at 10+.

In their selection of books for their class libraries many primary schools lay too exclusive an emphasis on the book as a source of information: much money is spent on reference books and on expensive non-fiction, but although fiction of a sort is almost always provided it sometimes seems that little care has been given to its choice and that the teacher's guidance in regard to it is somewhat perfunctory. The reading of fiction and narrative should not be regarded as peripheral to the real business of growth and learning: for most children it is both essential for the establishment of commitment to reading and important as a means of emotional and intellectual development. We think it relevant to recall at this point, moreover, the evidence that children whose reading is confined to non-quality narrative are more likely to discard the reading habit at later ages than those whose book reading has been more wide ranging. We suspected, during our follow-up visits, that our 10+ inter-viewees included a number of children who would later give up book reading in part at least because their experience of it at this stage had never become sufficiently enthralling or rewarding to establish a durable intrinsic motivation towards books. We do not suggest that non-quality narrative should be excluded from junior school classroom libraries (for many children it has its own transi-tional role to play), but we do believe that at present such collections often include many titles that are too vapid, tedious or dated to deserve shelf room. Most primary schools need to update the narrative element in their classroom libraries, and to spend more money on children's fiction of high quality, particularly that which has been written specifically for children of this age during the past quarter of a century.

29   Secondary schools by contrast may be inclined to set their sights rather too high in their choice of narrative titles for class libraries and school

libraries. Pointers to this conclusion are contained in our findings that older children are increasingly disposed to obtain their books from sources other than the school, that books obtained from school sources were consistently awarded lower liking scores than books obtained from other sources, and that quality narrative (often supplied from school sources or upon school recommendation) tended to win lower liking scores than non-quality narrative and to be more often left unfinished. Our interviews left us with the impression that this was often due not to some intrinsic lack of appeal in quality narrative as such (the *right* quality book was often very much enjoyed) but rather to inappropriate recommendation of books that were too difficult or too mature for the child's particular stage of development. We believe that most secondary schools need to include at this level a certain amount of non-quality narrative which will act as an inducement to reluctant readers. Certainly there is a need for more generous interpretation of standards of quality in this area, and a recognition that the relevant evaluation will not be in adult terms but in terms of the current emotional and intellectual maturity of the children concerned. This seems to be particularly important at the stage when children are making the transition from juvenile to adult books: at this point they may often need to regress in terms of quality for a time concurrently with moving forward in terms of the adultness of the themes, characters or settings they read about.

30   Since some boys of secondary school age show a marked readiness to read non-narrative, there is probably a need to include some non-narrative books at a suitable level of difficulty in class libraries, and to reinforce the provision of generalized and popularly written non-narrative (i.e. books which are not specifically harnessed to the didactic purposes of school subjects) in school libraries. The topics which are most likely to pay off include hobbies, sporting activities, animals, science, technology (including all forms of transport) and history. It is difficult to know whether the girls' apparent aversion to non-narrative is to be ascribed in part to the relative sparseness of appropriately written non-narrative books devoted to feminine interests, but where these exist they certainly ought to be sought out, provided and recommended.

Contrariwise, it seems possible that some of the 10% of boys who confine their reading to non-narrative could be induced, by appropriate recommendations, to pursue their interests into the narrative field, and that they would gain something valuable if this could be achieved. (An interest in animals could be channelled in the direction of Gerald Durrell, Jim Corbett and Henry Williamson, for instance; interest in science or technology might lead on to biographies of scientists or inventors, or to some types of sci-fi.) At 14+ many children have begun to form distinct career or occupational interests, and in some cases these could be harnessed towards the reading of either fiction, biography or non-narrative in a way that does not seem to be much in evidence at present.

Since children are such heavy watchers of television it seems reasonable to suggest that this activity also may be used effectively as a cue for reading recommendations. As it happened none of the books at the head of our most widely read lists of individual titles (see Tables 64, 65 and 66) had been serialized on television during the preceding twelve months; but we do know that TV serializations and the reading of extracts from books on such programmes as *Jackanory* often stimulate children to read the books in question (or at any rate to start an attempt to read them), and it would be sensible therefore for teachers to be alert to any such opportunities which present themselves. Nature programmes, science programmes and current affairs programmes might also be used, in appropriate cases, as a jumping-off point for book suggestions and recommendations.

31   The increasing urge to participate in peer-group activities is undoubtedly one of the causes for the drift away from book reading at 12+ and above, but we formed the impression that a further contributory factor, particularly for the more able pupils, may be the somewhat excessively heavy demands which schoolwork makes upon children's leisure time, at any rate for those who are conscientious about it. We suspect that, if schools were to review the overall demands which different subjects make upon their pupils' leisure (particularly in the form of project work which has to be written up at home), they would be surprised at the heavy commitment they are expecting of their pupils. Project work does of course call for reading within books (and too often, alas, results merely in copying unthinkingly from them), but it should not be allowed to crowd out reading as a self-directed activity. It seems unfortunate, also, that examinations in English literature tend to diminish rather than extend voluntary reading, and it is regrettable that their influence in this respect sometimes extends downwards to the fourth and even at times the third year. The O-level GCE exam with its concentration on three set books is especially culpable here; some CSE syllabuses (though not all) are more helpful in their influence on amount of reading. It is to be hoped that, for any common examination which may be established in the future for 16+ pupils, in constructing syllabuses due regard will be paid to the need for fostering extensive as well as intensive reading. More pupils than ever are now working towards external examinations in the secondary school, and they are understandably very much influenced by the underlying ethos of these examinations as the age for them draws near.

32   Our data show a marked association between book ownership and amount of reading, and it seems clear that the possession of books can play an important role in fostering commitment to reading. Unfortunately, however, many children do not have easy access to well stocked bookshops; indeed many parts of the country are singularly ill provided for in this respect. We

recommend that many more schools should organize bookselling schem.
we advise, in particular, the setting up, either regularly or occasionally, of a
bookstall or book exhibition within the school through which children can
buy books (particularly paperbacks) for their own collection. There is no
great difficulty or mystique about this.

A school needs only to find a bookseller willing to supply the books and
then to obtain from the Publishers' Association a Book Agent's licence. The
basic procedure is set out very clearly in an article by Marilyn Davies entitled
'Running a School Book Stall' in the Autumn 1968 issue of *The Use of English*.
(Further relevant articles are 'Enjoying Reading' by Brian Hankins in *The Use
of English*, Summer 1968, 'A paperback display' by E. U. Bramsted in *The Use
of English*, Winter 1969, and 'The school bookshop' by Roger Lewis in *The
Use of English*, Winter 1969). Teachers concerned will also find useful information and advice in *School Bookshop News*, published three times a year
for the School Bookshop Association by Penguin Books. Older pupils can be
involved in the detailed administration of such a venture, and there is a modest
benefit to school funds in the discount normally allowed by the supplier. The
important benefit, however, is the impetus such a scheme gives to the voluntary reading of a wide range of pupils.

33   It is impossible to overstress the influence of the teacher's own
knowledgeability about books. The right book brought forward at the right
time can make all the difference to a child's reading development. Yet the
field is a vast one and to become conversant with its possibilities makes great
demands upon a teacher's leisure time. (Lest this should sound too daunting,
we ought perhaps to remind our readers that most children's books are quite
short and can be read by an adult in a comparatively brief space of time.) Even
since 1971 there has been a useful extension of effort in this connection.
Many local authorities, teachers' centres, colleges of education and institutes
of education have offered courses, organized conferences or set up study
groups at which the relevant experience can be exchanged and made more
widely available. Mention should be made also of the expertise which is on
tap in the school library service of almost all public libraries; help from this
source is invaluable and will always be readily and freely given. Even so, there
is still a need for higher priority to be given in some areas to activities which
develop the individual teacher's ability to act as an effective broker between
the book and the child.

34   Now that a start has been made in establishing a baseline for children's
voluntary reading by means of a national survey, it seems important to us that
monitoring should continue at regular intervals to establish the extent to
which schools are succeeding in this important aspect of their role in society.
We recommend that our own survey should be repeated in, say, 1981, and

thereafter at ten-yearly intervals. A repeat survey would be relatively in-expensive now that the ground has been broken, and the findings would be of great value to all interested parties.

35   It is a commonplace that any research programme is likely to throw up as many new questions as it finds answers to old ones. Our own study has been an exploratory one, drawing upon evidence from a national cross-section of children at three age levels. Through such a survey approach we have been able to draw up an outline of the general terrain and to identify tentatively some of the most important factors at work. The method used does not, however, permit us to draw any firm conclusions about the causes which pro-duce changes in reading patterns from one age to another. What experiences, for instance, have led some children to abandon the reading of books by 14+? What experiences or influences have led other children to move in their read-ing towards more mature or more high quality reading? Does the reading of poor quality books at 10+ form a foundation upon which better reading tastes develop at later ages, or does it lead more typically to a loss of interest in what books have to offer? The answers we have put forward to such important questions as these must of their very nature be tentative and provisional. We suggest that what is needed now is a longitudinal study of a much smaller number of children, in order to follow through their reading over a period of several years and thereby establish the specific determining influences, whether in home, neighbourhood or school, that effect changes in children's reading habits and tastes. The insight and understanding to be gained from such a longitudinal study would be of great practical value to both teachers and children's librarians.

36   In the meantime there is ample scope for individual schools or groups of schools to undertake useful small-scale research into the reading habits and preferences of their own pupils. The Children's Questionnaire reproduced as Appendix II could be used as a starting point, and could be abbreviated or adapted as circumstances make appropriate. Most schools would find it helpful and valuable to compare their own pupils' responses with the national pattern, and they are almost certain to learn some things that they did not know already. Of course when such an inquiry is undertaken in a school setting by teachers the children know, the temptation to give 'expec-ted' answers is more than ever present; but this can largely be overcome by an insistence on anonymity and by explaining frankly the purpose of the questionnaire. We suggest that the role of such investigations should be seen as diagnostic, not for the individual child, but rather for the general book provisions and book selection policy of the school as a whole.

Appendices

I   SAMPLING DETAILS   294

   (a) The sampling frame for primary schools   294
   (b) Distribution of the 197 selected primary schools   295
   (c) The sampling frame for secondary schools   296
   (d) Distribution of the 201 selected secondary schools 298

II   CHILDREN'S QUESTIONNAIRE   299

III   ADMINISTRATION INSTRUCTIONS (Children's questionnaire)   309

IV   ASSESSMENT SHEET   311

V   THE SCHOOL QUESTIONNAIRES   313

   (a) The primary school questionnaire   313
   (b) The secondary school questionnaire   321

VI   AUTHORS OF QUALITY NARRATIVE BOOKS   330

VII   SUPPLEMENTARY PRIMARY SCHOOL QUESTIONNAIRE   334

I Sampling details

APPENDIX I(a) THE SAMPLING FRAME FOR PRIMARY SCHOOLS

Type	Schools/Pupils	School	Region 1	Region 2	Region 4	Region 5	Region 6	Region 7	Region 8	Region 9	Region 10	TOTALS
Junior with infants (boys)	Schools	1							2			3
	Pupils	22							65			87
Junior with infants (girls)	Schools	1		2	3			6	8	4		24
	Pupils	12		69	59			165	287	87		679
Junior with infants (mixed)	Schools	727	458	1 544	996	1 151	786	775	1 728	1 525	1 087	10 777
	Pupils	14 412	10 956	46,711	21 006	33 977	13 128	32 828	46 623	29 449	16 965	266 055
Junior (boys)	Schools	8	8	29	11	5	3	21	12	10	15	122
	Pupils	378	547	1 508	592	264	194	1 339	661	464	681	6 628
Junior (girls)	Schools	9	8	27	8	5	4	17	9	7	16	110
	Pupils	417	501	1 357	531	257	148	1 089	579	360	589	5 828
Junior (mixed)	Schools	295	198	714	380	449	109	665	598	364	390	4 162
	Pupils	20 844	16 856	51 569	30 654	36 071	8 495	55 823	51 948	28 286	22 464	323 010
TOTALS	Schools	1 041	672	2 316	1 398	1 610	902	1 484	2 357	1 910	1 508	15 198
	Pupils	36 085	28 860	101 214	52 842	70 569	21 965	91-244	100 163	58 646	40 699	602 287

(based on DES print-out)

APPENDIX I(b)   DISTRIBUTION OF THE 197 SELECTED PRIMARY SCHOOLS

Type	Region										TOTALS
	1	2	3	4	5	6	7	8	9	10	
Junior with infants (mixed)	5	4	16	7	11	4	11	15	9	6	88
Junior (mixed)	9	6	17	10	12	3	19	18	8	7	109
TOTALS	14	10	33	17	23	7	30	33	17	13	197

APPENDIX I(c)   THE SAMPLING FRAME FOR SECONDARY SCHOOLS

Type	Schools/Pupils	Region 1	2	3	4	5	6	7	8	9	10	TOTALS
Direct grant (boys)	Schools	4	9	24	3	6	6	5	10	13	1	81
	Pupils	697	1 428	4 240	523	1 079	691	858	1 628	1 559	101	12 804
Direct grant (girls)	Schools	6	9	29	5	5	4	16	10	8	3	95
	Pupils	809	1 534	4 564	774	709	478	1 956	1 440	908	314	13 486
Grammar (boys)	Schools	9	23	54	24	39	15	57	53	30	18	322
	Pupils	1 495	3 794	11 322	4 254	6 730	2 080	10 582	9 554	4 780	3 555	58 146
Grammar (girls)	Schools	6	23	57	29	42	14	67	50	27	19	334
	Pupils	1 136	3 901	11 524	4 763	7 577	2 133	11 477	9 809	4 681	3 658	60 659
Grammar (mixed)	Schools	26	10	30	31	33	15	31	31	43	26	276
	Pupils	5 470	1 617	6 527	6 390	5 894	2 623	6 218	6 600	8 046	4 498	53 883
Modern (boys)	Schools	12	18	96	38	52	16	60	73	31	9	405
	Pupils	1 912	3 209	17 925	7 542	9 220	3 511	12 299	16 419	6 329	1 225	79 591
Modern (girls)	Schools	13	21	99	37	51	15	68	73	31	12	420
	Pupils	2 104	3 904	18 164	7 290	9 198	3 206	12 974	15 927	6 136	1 528	80 431

												Total
Modern (mixed)	Schools	96	80	265	155	211	112	116	287	202	104	1 628
	Pupils	17 419	18 118	62 810	30 620	43 787	22 700	26 363	69 710	40 858	19 945	352 330
Comprehesive (boys)	Schools	2	2	14	3	4	2	42	7	4	9	89
	Pupils	703	855	5 080	1 119	1 840	504	14 546	1 720	826	2 519	29 712
Comprehensive (girls)	Schools	4	2	15	2	5	2	41	8	4	8	91
	Pupils	1 180	450	4 662	439	1 583	642	15 272	1 935	935	1 749	28 847
Comprehensive (mixed)	Schools	70	43	99	76	79	6	102	84	91	112	762
	Pupils	22 758	13 507	33 436	24 058	32 313	2 044	37 427	33 147	31 776	35 389	265 855
Other (boys)	Schools	5		13	3	5		27	19	7		79
	Pupils	843		2 147	631	1 101		6 298	3 824	886		15 730
Other (girls)	Schools			8	5	3		24	18	2		60
	Pupils			1 334	1 293	842		5 410	3 773	372		13 024
Other (mixed)	Schools	51	17	12	25	34	2	29	23	4	8	205
	Pupils	12 164	4 180	2 355	7 209	9 532	579	7 242	5 730	740	1 460	51 191
TOTALS	Schools	304	257	815	436	569	209	685	746	497	329	4 847
	Pupils	68 690	56 497	186 090	96 905	131 405	41 191	168 922	181 216	108 832	75 941	1 115 689

(based on DES print-out)

Note: The number for pupils is the combined total of the 10+ and 12+ year groups.

APPENDIX I(d)   DISTRIBUTION OF THE 201 SELECTED SECONDARY SCHOOLS

Type of School	Region 1	2	3	4	5	6	7	8	9	10	TOTALS
Direct grant (boys)	1	–	1	–	–	–	–	–	–	–	2
Direct grant (girls)	–	–	–	1	–	–	1	–	–	–	2
Grammar (boys)	1	1	2	1	1	1	2	2	1	1	13
Grammar (girls)	1	1	2	1	1	1	2	2	1	1	13
Grammar (mixed)	1	1	1	1	1	1	1	1	1	1	10
Modern (boys)	1	1	3	1	2	1	2	3	1	1	16
Modern (girls)	1	1	3	1	2	1	2	2	1	1	15
Modern (mixed)	4	3	10	5	7	4	4	12	6	3	58
Comprehensive (boys)	1	–	1	–	–	–	3	–	–	–	5
Comprehensive (girls)	–	1	1	–	–	–	1	–	1	1	5
Comprehensive (mixed)	5	2	6	4	5	1	6	6	4	6	45
Other (boys)	–	–	2	–	–	1	1	–	–	–	3
Other (girls)	–	–	–	–	1	–	1	–	–	–	2
Other (mixed)	2	1	1	1	2	1	1	1	1	1	12
TOTALS	18	12	33	16	22	11	27	29	17	16	201

II Children's questionnaire

WHAT THIS BOOKLET IS FOR

Many people who take part in your education would like to know what kinds
of book you are interested in reading and what other things you like doing.
We are helping to find this out so that in schools and libraries there will be
more books of the kind that you like and about things that interest you.

WHY YOU HAVE BEEN CHOSEN TO FILL IN THE BOOKLET

Obviously we can't ask everybody who's at school to fill in a booklet; that
would take a very long time and be very expensive. So we got a computer to
take a list of all schools and picked out one school of every sort in each part of
the country. Then we took a list of all the pupils of a certain age in each of
these schools and chose a number of them in a way that was rather like pick-
ing numbers out of a hat. You are one of the pupils who were chosen in this
way and it is very important to us that you should fill in the answers to the
questions as carefully as you can.

HOW YOU FILL IN THE BOOKLET

For some of the questions we shall give you a set of answers and you will just have to choose one that is right for you by putting a tick in the box next to it like this

You will only have to put <u>one</u> tick in <u>one</u> of the boxes.
For other questions, you have to write out the answer. You won't need to write very much and there will be a box to write it in.

Your answers will be completely private. Also do remember that this isn't an examination or a test so don't worry about spelling.

300

1   DO YOU REGULARLY READ ANY MAGAZINES (OR COMICS)?

Put a tick ✓ *in the box by the answer you choose.*

NO
If you answer 'NO'
go on to Question 2.

YES
If you answer 'YES' write a list of
all the magazines (or comics) you
read regularly. Write only one on
each line. If you only read one or
two, put those down.

Read down your list and put a tick ✓ *after the one you most of all look forward to*
reading. Now go on to Question 2.

2   HAVE YOU READ A BOOK (OR BOOKS) IN THE LAST FOUR WEEKS?

Don't count books which a teacher said you must read as part of a lesson or for
homework. Don't count stories which are told mainly in pictures.

NO
If you answer 'NO'
go on to Question 8 on page 4.

YES
If you answer 'YES'
fill in pages 2 and 3.

1

Don't unfold this sheet until you have answered Questions 3, 4 and 5

3   WHICH BOOKS HAVE YOU READ IN THE LAST FOUR WEEKS?

Put down those books you got outside school and those you chose yourself from the class library or the school library.

Don't put down books that a teacher said you must read as part of a lesson or for homework.

Don't put down the names of stories told mainly in pictures.

Now, write down as many of the books that you've read in the last four weeks as you can remember. Put the author's name as well, if you can. It doesn't matter if you've only read one or two books, just put those down.

(We've written two books down to show you how to do it.)

TITLE	AUTHOR	
Journey with a Secret	D. Styles	
The Men and their Boats	B. Ashley	

4   HAVE YOU READ ANY OF THE BOOKS YOU'VE PUT DOWN MORE THAN ONCE? *If you have go back and underline it, like this.*

The Men and their Boats   B. Ashley

5   WERE ANY OF THE BOOKS STORIES WHICH YOU DECIDED NOT TO FINISH? *If they were, go back and put crosses after them, like this.*

Journey with a Secret X   D. Styles

Now unfold the sheet

Don't start this page until you've written your list of books on page 2

| 6 WHERE DID YOU GET THE BOOK FROM? | 7 HOW MUCH DID YOU LIKE THE BOOK? |

Column headings (angled):
- I got it from the class library
- I got it from the school library
- I got it from the Public library
- It belongs to me
- I borrowed it from a friend
- I borrowed it from someone in the family
- I got it somewhere else
- It was one of the best I've ever read
- I liked it very much
- I quite liked it
- I did not like it much
- I did not like it at all

Now, answer two questions about each of the books you've written down.

For every book, choose **one** of the answers to question 6 and **one** of the answers to question 7. Put a tick on the same line as the book under the answer you choose.

(We've put ticks next to our books to show you how to do it.)

After you've filled in the boxes for the books in your list, you can write anything else you'd like to say about any of them in this space.

3

8   DO YOU OWN ANY BOOKS YOURSELF?

NO
*If you answer 'NO'
go on to Question 9.*

YES
*If you answer 'YES' put a tick in
the box by the answer which is
nearest the number of books you
own.*

I own up to 10 books

I own up to 25 books

I own up to 50 books

I own up to 100 books

I own more than 100 books

**9   DO YOU HAVE A FAVOURITE WRITER, ONE WHOSE BOOKS YOU
LIKE READING MORE THAN ANYONE ELSE'S?**

NO
*If you answer 'NO'
go on to Question 10.*

YES
*If you answer 'YES'
write his or her name here.*

10 ABOUT HOW MUCH READING DO YOU THINK YOU DO?
Put a tick in the box by the answer you choose.

A large amount

Quite a lot

About average

Not very much

Only a little

11 DO YOU BELONG TO THE PUBLIC LIBRARY?
Put a tick in the box by the answer you choose.

☐ NO
If you answer 'NO'
go on to Question 12.

☐ YES
If you answer 'YES'
tick the answer which is most nearly
true for you.

☐ I go to borrow books twice a week

☐ I go to borrow books once a week

☐ I go to borrow books once a fortnight

☐ I go to borrow books sometimes

12 DO YOUR PARENTS, OR ANY OTHER ADULTS IN
YOUR HOUSE, READ LIBRARY BOOKS?

☐ NO   ☐ YES   ☐ I DON'T KNOW

13 DO YOU HAVE ANY DAILY OR SUNDAY NEWSPAPERS
IN YOUR HOUSE?

☐ NO
If you answer 'NO'
go on to Question 14.

☐ YES
If you answer 'YES' write down a
list of those you have in your house.
Write only one on each line.

14 DO YOU HAVE A TELEVISION SET AT HOME?

☐ NO   ☐ YES

15 DID YOU WATCH TV LAST NIGHT? (IT DOESN'T MATTER WHETHER IT WAS AT HOME OR SOMEWHERE ELSE.)

☐ NO
*If you answer 'NO'
go on to Question 16.*

☐ YES
*If you answer 'YES'
for how long did you watch?*

☐ Less than 1 hour

☐ More than 1 hour but less than 2 hours

☐ More than 2 hours but less than 3 hours

☐ More than 3 hours but less than 4 hours

☐ More than 4 hours

16 ARE THERE ANY TV PROGRAMMES YOU ALWAYS TRY TO WATCH?

☐ NO
*If you answer 'NO'
go on to Question 17.*

☐ YES
*If you answer 'YES' write down
their names here, one on each line,
just the programmes you always try
to watch.*

17 HOW MUCH DO YOU LIKE SCHOOL?

☐ Very much

☐ Quite a lot

☐ I don't mind it

☐ I rather dislike it

☐ I don't like it at all

17a WHICH OF THE FOLLOWING SENTENCES TELLS HOW
YOU FEEL ABOUT ENGLISH LESSONS?

Put a tick in the box by the answer you choose.

☐ English lessons are my favourite lessons

☐ I enjoy English lessons more than most other lessons

☐ I neither like nor dislike English lessons

☐ I enjoy English lessons less than most other lessons

☐ English lessons are the lessons I most dislike

17b AT WHAT AGE DO YOU EXPECT TO LEAVE SCHOOL?

Put a tick in the box by the answer you choose.

☐ 15

☐ 16

☐ 17

☐ 18

18 DO YOU LIVE WITH YOUR PARENTS?

☐ YES
*If you answer 'YES'
go on to Question 19.*

☐ NO
*If you answer 'NO'
write down whom you live with.*

*Answer Questions 19 and 20 as if they
were about the adults you live with.*

19 DOES YOUR MOTHER GO OUT TO WORK?

☐ NO
*If you answer 'NO'
go on to Question 20.*

☐ YES
*If you answer 'YES'
write down the name of her job.*

Now describe the wort of work she does.

(Note : Questions 17a and 17b were omitted from the 10+ questionnaires.)

7

20 WHAT IS YOUR FATHER'S JOB?

Write down the name of your father's job.

If your father is not working at present, write down the name of his last job.
Now describe the sort of work he does.

21 DO YOU HAVE ANY BROTHERS OR SISTERS?

NO

If you answer 'NO'
go on to Question 22.

YES

If you answer 'YES' how many of them are older than you?
Put the number in the box.

How many of them are younger than you?
Put the number in the box.

22 ARE YOU A BOY OR A GIRL?

Boy

Girl

23 HOW OLD ARE YOU?   *Put your age, in years, in the box.*

24 WHAT IS YOUR DATE OF BIRTH?

Day _____ Month _____ Year _____

III Children's questionnaire administration instructions

1   This questionnaire should be completed on either Tuesday 23rd March, Wednesday 24th March, Thursday 25th March, or Friday 26th March, by the children for whom it is intended. It is important that the children who are filling in the questionnaire should do so as a single group as free as possible from distractions and not in a room with children who are not receiving the questionnaire.

2   Each questionnaire has a code number at the top right-hand corner of the front cover. It is very important that each child should receive the questionnaire which has on it his or her number as indicated on the attached list. An additional copy of the questionnaire is provided for the use of the administrator (please return this to us along with the completed copies).

3   To encourage the children to reply as frankly as possible, we have told them that their answers will be 'completely private'. We should be grateful if the teacher administering the questionnaire could lend strength to this assurance by removing the questionnaires from the envelope in front of the class and replacing them when they have been completed.

4   In general we ask the teacher who administers the questionnaire to show as little interest as possible in the content of children's answers and to confine his or her aid to those difficulties in procedure which the children cannot resolve themselves. Before children start answering please call attention

(a) to the instructions ('How to fill in the booklet') on the inside front cover;

(b) to the phrase 'in the last four weeks' in questions 2 and 3. Children may have difficulty in conceptualizing this period of time, and it would be useful to mention any local circumstance which could help to fix it in their minds. In some schools the questionnaire will be administered

309

approximately four weeks after the half-term break, and reference to this could, in these cases, be helpful.

Apart from these points, the questionnaire will be self-explanatory for most children. However, some of the more backward children may find difficulty in understanding some of the procedures they have to follow. If there is thought to be any likelihood of this please take the children through the introductory paragraphs on the cover and illustrate the instructions about ticking boxes and writing in spaces by reference to page 1.

5   We expect that secondary school children will take between fifteen and thirty-five minutes to complete the questionnaire, and that primary school children will take between twenty-five and forty-five minutes.

6   IF A CHILD IS ABSENT FROM SCHOOL ON THE DAY THE QUESTIONNAIRE IS ADMINISTERED PLEASE WRITE 'ABSENT' ON THE FRONT COVER. If there are any children who are clearly not capable of filling in the questionnaire, it would be of great help to us if the teacher would fill in for the child questions 18 to 24 only, and would write on the front cover of the questionnaire an explanation of why the child is unable to complete it himself, e.g. in terms of 'unable to read', 'backward child', 'recent immigrant' etc.

IV Assessment sheet

Below are listed your pupils who are completing our pupil questionnaire.

For each pupil you are asked to ring the appropriate symbol in each of the 3 columns according to the instructions at the head of the column.

Position in school ability groupings

Please indicate each child's place in your school's general system of ability grouping, streaming, or banding, using one of these categories:

H   High stream (or high set for English).
M   Middle stream (or middle set for English).
L   Low stream (or low set for English).
U   Unstreamed (or unsetted for English).

		H	M	L	U
		H	M	L	U
		H	M	L	U
		H	M	L	U
		H	M	L	U
		H	M	L	U
		H	M	L	U
		H	M	L	U
		H	M	L	U
		H	M	L	U
		H	M	L	U
		H	M	L	U
		H	M	L	U
		H	M	L	U
		H	M	L	U
		H	M	L	U

311

General level of ability and attainment

Please rate each child with reference to *the whole of his or her age group in all schools.* Assume that 20% of all children fall into each of the categories A to E.

A   those capable of passing in four or five subjects at G.C.E. 'O' level.
B   those capable of passing in four or five C.S.E. subjects.
C   those of average ability (some of these being capable of passing one or two C.S.E. subjects; others will not attempt C.S.E. at all).
D   those of below average ability but without serious reading disabilities.
E   backward children — those needing remedial teaching.

Secondary schools will, of course, realise that only a large school with a fully comprehensive intake is likely to have children in all of these categories.

Primary schools are likely to contain some children from each category, and should do their best to apply the categories to their own circumstances.

General attitude

Towards school work

Please assess each child on a three point scale according to his or her attitude towards school work of all kinds.

1   consistent evidence of enthusiasm and perseverance.
2   average or unremarkable show of application.
3   decided absence of response or effort.

A	B	C	D	E	1	2	3
A	B	C	D	E	1	2	3
A	B	C	D	E	1	2	3
A	B	C	D	E	1	2	3
A	B	C	D	E	1	2	3
A	B	C	D	E	1	2	3
A	B	C	D	E	1	2	3
A	B	C	D	E	1	2	3
A	B	C	D	E	1	2	3
A	B	C	D	E	1	2 ·	3
A	B	C	D	E	1	2	3
A	B	C	D	E	1	2	3
A	B	C	D	E	1	2	3
A	B	C	D	E	1	2	3
A	B	C	D	E	1	2	3
A	B	C	D	E	1	2	3

V   School questionnaires

(a) THE PRIMARY SCHOOL QUESTIONNAIRE

University of Sheffield Institute of Education

Schools Council Research Project — **Children's reading habits**

To the Head Teacher

Your school is very kindly helping us with our research programme by arranging for sixteen 10-year-olds to complete our pupil questionnaire. (This pupil questionnaire is currently being administered to a national random sample of 10-year-olds, 12-year-olds, and 14-year-olds). Our programme of research as a whole aims to provide up-to-date factual knowledge on a nationwide scale of what and how much children read voluntarily at different ages, and also to explore their attitudes towards their reading and the relationship between their reading and various environmental factors in school and home. We believe that information of this kind is a prerequisite for sound curriculum planning in reading and literature, and that it will be extremely helpful to teachers in their attempts to guide and evaluate the progress of pupils.

To supplement the information supplied by the pupils, we shall be very grateful if you will complete the attached school questionnaire about library provision and about the part played by literature and reading in the school curriculum. We have tried to keep the questionnaire as short as possible but we think the information we have asked for is essential to enable us to compile a balanced picture of the part played by reading in the pupils' lives. All information which you provide in this questionnaire will of course remain anonymous to anybody outside the research team.

Frank Whitehead
Fred Inglis
Alan Wellings

1   **Which of the following statements best describes the arrangements for your pupils aged 10+?**   (Please tick the appropriate box.)

The timetable for the 10+ pupils is structured according to the usual subject divisions.

The timetable for the 10+ pupils is fully integrated.

The timetable for the 10+ pupils is partly integrated and partly structured according to the usual subject divisions.

2   **Please tick any of these statements which apply to your school's arrangements for the prose reading of pupils aged 10+.**

A collection of miscellaneous non-fiction, novels and short stories is provided in the classroom.

Small sets (say 5–10 copies) of novels, short stories or other prose books are provided at times for use within the class.

Class sets of novels, short stories or other prose books are used at times in the classroom.

The school provides a reading list of titles which pupils are expected to obtain from sources outside the classroom (e.g. the school library, the public library).

3   **About how much time on average each week do the children in your 10+ age group spend listening to the teacher reading stories to them?**

No time at all

Up to 1 hour

Up to 2 hours ☐

Up to 3 hours ☐

More than 3 hours ☐

The time varies too widely for an answer to be possible. ☐

4a Under which of the following circumstances do your 10+ pupils do most of their reading during school time? (Tick the appropriate box.)

During time set aside for individual reading by the whole class. ☐

In a special corner of the classroom while other work is going on at the same time. ☐

As the occasion for reading arises in the course of group or individual work. ☐

b If your 10+ classes are encouraged to keep a record of their individual reading please describe the procedure.

5   **Does your 10+ year group have access to**

School library only?

☐

Class library only?

☐

Both school library and class library

☐

6a   **What is the approximate number of books in the total library bookstock?**
(Include both books owned by the school and those on loan from the
School Library Service. Please ring the appropriate group.)

0–249	1000–1499	3000–3499	5000+
250–499	1500–1999	3500–3999	
500–749	2000–2499	4000–4499	
750–999	2500–2999	4500–4999	

6b   **Please give information which will help us to form a picture of the library
provision in your school.** (e.g. where books are kept – in a specially
designed library, in a central stock, distributed through classrooms etc.)

6c   **Which of the following applies to your school library?** (Please tick the
appropriate box.)

There are arrangements under which the children are allowed
to take books home.

☐

Children are not allowed to borrow books to take home.

☐

7   In your school's teaching of the 10+ age group as a whole, which one of
     the following statements is most nearly true? (Please tick the appropriate
     box.)

The emphasis in reading stories and poems falls upon a few
books which all the class are reading at the same time.

Most classes tend to be reading from a wide selection of books
with little close study.

Most classes tend to be reading from a wide selection of books,
but we reserve a small number for class discussion and reading.

Our practice varies so widely that any generalization is
impossible.

8   Below are some objectives which secondary school teachers of English have
     said should be important in English teaching. Against each one please place
     a tick in the box which shows how important you think it is in the teaching
     of 10+ pupils.

	Very important	Fairly important	Not important
To enable pupils to use language in ways necessary for work after leaving school.			
To help pupils to speak fluently and intelligibly in conversation.			
To foster an awareness of human values inherited from the past.			
To enable pupils to use language as a means of creative expression.			
To encourage an intelligent and critical interest in society.			

	Very important	Fairly important	Not important
To help pupils develop a sense of themselves as individuals.	☐	☐	☐
To teach some knowledge of the uses of language, and its structure.	☐	☐	☐
To enable pupils to examine language critically wherever it is used.	☐	☐	☐
To develop some appreciation of good literature.	☐	☐	☐
To help pupils to organize clear and rational argument.	☐	☐	☐
To encourage the enjoyment of wide reading.	☐	☐	☐
To develop a sensitivity towards other people.	☐	☐	☐

If this list omits some aspect of English which you feel to be very important, please add it here:

9a   Please write your name here:

Mr, Mrs, Miss..

b   Please write down the number of years' teaching experience you have had:
....

c Please write the name and address of your school here:

....

....

....

....

10 Please tick the correct descriptions which apply to your school:

Age range: 5–11   Sex: Mixed
             8–11   Boys only
             8–12   Girls only
             9–13

Status: Maintained   Type of School: Junior with infants
        Voluntary C. of E.   Junior without Infants
        Voluntary R.C.   Middle School
        Voluntary Other

11 Number in school (please ring the appropriate group).

0– 49	250–299	500–549
50– 99	300–349	550–599
100–149	350–399	600–649
150–199	400–449	650–699
200–249	450–499	700+

12 If your school has been affected by reorganization in the last five years, please mention the nature and date of the changes here:

13 Which of the following statements describes your school?

The 10+ year group is streamed by ability. ☐

(If you have ticked this choice, please enter here the number of streams in the year group). ☐

The 10+ year group is taught in mixed ability classes. ☐

The 10+ year group is organized with other years in 'family' or vertical groupings. ☐

14 From which of the following does your school <u>mainly</u> draw its pupils?

A rural area with no town near at hand. ☐

A rural area within easy reach of a town. ☐

A town of between 5–20 000 people. ☐

A town of between 20–50 000 people. ☐

A town of between 50–100 000 people. ☐

A city of between 100–250 000 people. ☐

A large city over 250 000 people. ☐

Please add here and overleaf any comments you wish to make on matters raised in this questionnaire.

APPENDIX V(b) THE SECONDARY SCHOOL QUESTIONNAIRE

University of Sheffield Institute of Education

Schools Council Research Project — Children's reading habits

To the Head of the English Department

As you will know, your school is very kindly helping us with our research programme by arranging for sixteen 12-year-olds and sixteen 14-year-olds to complete our pupil questionnaire. (This pupil questionnaire is currently being administered to a national random sample of 10-year-olds, 12-year-olds and 14-year-olds). Our programme of research as a whole aims to provide up-to-date factual knowledge on a nationwide scale of what and how much children read voluntarily at different ages, and also to explore their attitudes towards their reading and the relationship between their reading and various environmental factors in school and home. We believe that information of this kind is a prerequisite for sound curriculum planning in reading and literature, and that it will be extremely helpful to teachers in their attempts to guide and evaluate the progress of pupils.

To supplement the information supplied by the pupils, we shall be very grateful if you will complete the attached school questionnaire about library provision and about the part played by literature and reading in the English syllabus. We have tried to keep the questionnaire as short as possible, but we think the information we have asked for is essential to enable us to compile a balanced picture of the part played by reading in the pupils' lives. All information which you provide in this questionnaire will of course remain anonymous to anybody outside the research team.

Frank Whitehead
Fred Inglis
Alan Wellings

ENGLISH IN THE SCHOOL

1   Please tick any of these statements which apply to your department's English teaching during the current year (a) with pupils aged 12+ (b) with pupils aged 14+

	12+	14+
Class sets of coursebooks or comprehension books are used.	☐	☐
Class sets of English thematic or topic-based anthologies are used.	☐	☐
Class sets of novels, short stories or other prose books are used.	☐	☐
Small sets (say 5–10 copies) of novels, short stories or other prose books are used within the class.	☐	☐
A class library of miscellaneous titles is provided for pupils to read.	☐	☐
The school provides a reading list of titles which pupils are expected to obtain from sources outside the classroom (e.g. school library, public library).	☐	☐

2   In your department's teaching of the 12+ and 14+ age groups as a whole, which one of the following statements is most nearly true?

	12+	14+
The emphasis in studying litereature falls upon a few books which all the class are reading at the same time.	☐	☐
Most classes tend to be reading from a wide selection of books with little close study.	☐	☐

Most classes tend to be reading from a wide selection of books but we reserve a small number for class discussion and reading.

12+	14+
☐	☐

Our practice varies so widely that any generalization is impossible.

☐	☐

3 **Below are some objectives which teachers of English have said should be important in English teaching. Against each one please place a tick in the box which shows how important you think it is:**

	Very important	Fairly important	Not important
To enable pupils to use language in ways necessary for work after leaving school.	☐	☐	☐
To help pupils to speak fluently and intelligibly in conversation.	☐	☐	☐
To foster an awareness of human values inherited from the past.	☐	☐	☐
To enable pupils to use language as a means of creative expression.	☐	☐	☐
To encourage an intelligent and critical interest in society.	☐	☐	☐
To help pupils develop a sense of themselves as individuals.	☐	☐	☐
To teach some knowledge of the uses of language, and its structure.	☐	☐	☐
To enable pupils to examine language critically wherever it is used.	☐	☐	☐

	Very important	Fairly important	Not important
To develop some appreciation of good literature.	☐	☐	☐
To help pupils to organize clear and rational argument.	☐	☐	☐
To encourage the enjoyment of wide reading.	☐	☐	☐
To develop a sensitivity towards other people.	☐	☐	☐

If this list omits some aspect of English which you feel to be very important, please add it here:

SCHOOL LIBRARY

4   **Which of the following do (a) your 12+ pupils (b) your 14+ pupils have access to?**

	12+	14+
School library only	☐	☐
Class library only	☐	☐
Both school library and class library	☐	☐

5   **Which of the following statements most nearly describes the school library used (a) by your 12+ pupils (b) by your 14+ pupils?**

	12+	14+
The library is in a room designed specially for the purpose.	☐	☐
The library is in a room adapted for the purpose but adequate.	☐	☐
The library is in a room adapated for the purpose but inadequate.	☐	☐
All books are distributed through the school in class libraries and there is no one stock kept for use as a school library.	☐	☐
There is no separate room for a library and the library books are kept in bookcases around the school.	☐	☐

(If none of these statements fits your school please give your own description here).

6   **What is the approximate number of books in the school library?** (Please ring the nearest approximate total).

0– 249	4500–4999	10 000–10 499
250– 499	5000–5499	10 500–10 999
500– 999	5500–5999	11 000–11 499
1000–1499	6000–6499	11 500–11 999
1500–1999	6500–6999	12 000–12 499
2000–2499	7000–7499	12 500–12 999
2500–2999	7500–7999	13 000–13 499
3000–3499	8000–8499	13 500–13 999
3500–3999	8500–8999	14 000–14 499
4000–4499	9000–9499	15 000+
	9500–9999	

7 It would also be most helpful if you add any other information about library use which you feel may be relevant.

8 If your school runs any kind of bookstall or bookselling service, please describe the arrangements for it here.

SCHOOL ADMINISTRATION

9a Please write your name here:
Mr, Mrs, Miss...

b Please write down the number of years' teaching experience you have had:
....

c Please write the name and address of your school here:

....

....

....

....

10 Please tick the descriptions which apply to your school:

Age range:	11–14	Sex:	Mixed
	11–15		Boys only
	11–16		Girls only
	11–18		
	12–16		
	12–18		
	13–16		
	13–18		

Status:	Maintained	Type of School:	Bilateral
	Voluntary C. of E.		Comprehensive
	Voluntary R.C.		Grammar
	Voluntary Other		Secondary Modern
	Direct Grant School		Technical

11 Which of the following statements describes your school?

The school is on a divided site.

The school is on a single campus.

12 Number in school: (Please ring the appropriate group)

0– 49	650– 699	1300–1349	1950–1999
50– 99	700– 749	1350–1399	2000–2049
100–149	750– 799	1400–1499	2050–2099
150–199	800– 849	1450–1499	2100–2149
200–249	850– 899	1500–1549	2150–2199
250–299	900– 949	1550–1599	2200–2249
300–349	950– 999	1600–1649	2250–2299
350–399	1000–1049	1650–1699	2300–2349
400–449	1050–1099	1700–1749	2350–2399
450–499	1100–1149	1750–1799	2400–2449
500–549	1150–1199	1800–1849	2450–2499
550–599	1200–1249	1850–1899	2500+
600–649	1250–1299	1900–1949	

13   Which of the following statements describes your school?

12+

a   The 12+ year group is streamed by ability.

(If you have ticked this choice, please enter here the number of streams in the year group).

The 12+ year group is setted for various subjects, but not for English.

The 12+ year group is setted for various subjects, including English.

English in the 12+ year is taught in mixed ability groups.

14+

b   The 14+ year group is streamed by ability.

(If you have ticked this choice, please enter here the number of streams in the year group).

The 14+ year group is setted for various subjects, but not for English.

The 14+ year group is setted for various subjects, including English.

English in the 14+ year is taught in mixed ability groups.

14   If your school has been affected by reorganization in the last ten years, please mention the nature and date of the changes here:

15 From which of the following does your school <u>mainly</u> draw its pupils?

A rural area with no town near at hand.

A rural area within easy reach of a town.

A town of between 5—20 000 people.

A town of between 20—50 000 people.

A town of between 50—100 000 people.

A city of between 100—250 000 people.

A large city of over 250 000 people.

Please add here and overleaf any comments you wish to make on matters raised by this questionnaire.

VI Authors of quality narrative books

a   AUTHORS OF JUVENILE QUALITY NARRATIVE BOOKS

Joan Aiken: Louisa M. Alcott; Edward Ardizzone: Richard Armstrong; Gillian Avery;

'B.B.'; Enid Bagnold; M. J. Baker; Michael Baldwin; R. M. Ballantyne; Kitty Barne; J. M. Barrie; G. W. Barrington; L. Frank Baum; Nina Bawden; Lilian Beckwith; Hilaire Belloc; Leila Berg; Paul Berna; Michael Bond; Hal Borland; L. M. Boston; C. R. Brink; H. F. Brinsmead; D. K. Broster; Laurent De Brunhoff; Frances Hodgson Burnett; Hester Burton; Sheila Burnford;

W. H. Canaway; Richard Carpenter; Lewis Carroll; S. M. Chauffier; Richard Church; Beverley Cleary; Carlo Collodi; Susan Coolidge;

Roald Dahl; Meindert DeJong; Mary Mapes Dodge; Eleanor Doorly; Arthur Conan Doyle;

Edward Eager; Monica Edwards; T. S. Eliot; Amabel Williams Ellis; Elizabeth Enright;

J. Meade Falkner; Eleanor Farjeon; Sid Fleischman;

Wanda Gag; Paul Gallico; Leon Garfield; Alan Garner; Eve Garnett; Fred Gipson; Elizabeth Goudge; Eleanor Graham; Kenneth Grahame, Frederick Grice; René Guillot;

Leif Hamre; Cynthia Harnett; G. A. Henty; Peter Paul Hilbert; Janet Hitchman; C. Walter Hodges; G. A. Hogarth; Anne Holm; Thomas Hughes;

J. Ingelow;

Will James; Tove Jansson;

Josephine Kamm; Erich Kastner; Clive King; Charles Kingsley; Rudyard Kipling; Phyllis Krasilowsky; H. Kullman;

Selma Lagerlof; C. J. Lambert; Edward Lear; Madeleine L'Engle; C. Day Lewis; C. S. Lewis; Penelope Lively; Marjorie Lloyd; A. Rutgers van der Loeff; Hugh Lofting;

George MacDonald; Allan Campbell McLean; Janet McNeill; Wolf Mankowitz; Frederick Marryat; James Vance Marshall; John Masefield; William Mayne; Spike Milligan; A. A. Milne; Mrs Molesworth; L. M. Montgomery; Honore Morrow; Elizabeth Morse;

Bill Naughton; E. Nesbit; Mary Norton;

Mary O'Hara;

Philippa Pearce; Lucy Fitch Perkins; K. M. Peyton; Beatrix Potter; Alf Prøysen;

Gwynedd Rae; Gerald Raftery; Arthur Ransome; John Ruskin;

Andrew Salkey; Felix Salten; Kate Seredy; Ian Serraillier; E. T. Seton; Dr Seuss; David Severn; Anna Sewell; Margery Sharp; Barbara Sleigh; Dodie Smith; C. D. Snedeker; Ivan Southall; Elizabeth George Speare; Armstrong Sperry Johanna Spyri; R. L. Stevenson; William Stevenson; Mary Stolz; Catherine Storr; Noel Streatfeild; Elizabeth Stucley; Rosemary Sutcliff;

James Thurber; Barbara Euphan Todd; J. R. R. Tolkien; John Rowe Townsend; P. L. Travers; Geoffrey Trease; Henry Treece; Charles Tritten; A. F. Tschiffely; Mark Twain;

Alison Uttley;

Jules Verne; Elfrida Vipont;

Jill Paton Walsh; Jenifer Wayne; Rosemary Weir; Ronald Welch; E. B. White; T. H. White; Oscar Wilde; Laura Ingalls Wilder; Barbara Willard; Ursula Moray Williams; Henry Williamson; P. G. Wodehouse; J. D. Wyss.

b   AUTHORS OF ADULT QUALITY NARRATIVE BOOKS

Brian Aldiss; E. M. Almedingen; Isaac Asimov; Jane Austen;

J. G. Ballard; Lynne Reid Banks; Stan Barstow; Brendan Behan; Arnold Bennett; E. C. Bentley; R. D. Blackmore; Algernon Blackwood; Edward Blishen; Pierre Boulle; Elizabeth Bowen; Ray Bradbury; John Braine; E. R. Braithwaite; Paul Brickhill; Charlotte Brontë; Emily Brontë; Anne Brontë; John Buchan; Pearl S. Buck; John Bunyan; Ivy Compton-Burnett;

Albert Camus; Cervantes; Raymond Chandler; Sid Chaplin; Chaucer; G. K. Chesterton; Sir Francis Chichester; John Christopher; Winston Churchill; Arthur C. Clarke; P. Closterman; Colette; Wilkie Collins; Joseph Conrad; J. Fenimore Cooper; Jim Corbett; Alexander Cordell; Stephen Crane; A. J. Cronin;

R. H. Dana; Daniel Defoe; Charles Dickens; Arthur Conan Doyle; Margaret Drabble; Alexandre Dumas; Nell Dunn; Gerald Durrell;

George Eliot; Antoine de Saint-Exupéry;

Sheridan Le Fanu; Rowena Farr; Thomas Firbank; Gustave Flaubert; C. S. Forester; E. M. Forster; Anne Frank; Christopher Fry; Roy Fuller;

John Galsworthy; Elizabeth Gaskell; Stella Gibbons; Rumer Godden; Goethe; William Golding; Gogol; Robert Graves; F. L. Green; Graham Greene; Walter Greenwood; Arthur Grimble; Giovanni Guareschi;

H. Rider Haggard; Willis Hall; Thomas Hardy; Joseph Heller; Ernest Hemingway; O. Henry; James Leo Herlihy; Thor Heyerdahl; Richard Hillary; James Hilton; Barry Hines; Burt Hirschfeld; David Holbrook; Constance Holme; Homer; Anthony Hope; Geoffrey Household; Fred Hoyle; Richard Hughes; Victor Hugo; Sir John Hunt; Aldous Huxley;

Margaret Irwin;

W. W. Jacobs; Henry James; Jerome K. Jerome; Dennis Johnston;

Nikos Kazantzakis; G. Keller; H. H. Kirst; Arthur Koestler;

D. H. Lawrence; T. E. Lawrence; Harper Lee; Laurie Lee; Ira Levin; Richard Llewellyn; Jack London;

Mary McCarthy; Colin McInnes; Compton Mackenzie; Norman Mailer; W. Somerset Maugham; Daphne du Maurier; Gavin Maxwell; Herman Melville; Henry Miller; Yukio Mishima; Margaret Mitchell; Nancy Mitford Nicholas Monsarrat; Arthur Morrison; Axel Munthe; Robert Musil;

Bill Naughton; P. H. Newby;

Edna O'Brien; George Orwell; John Osborne;

Francis Parkman; Boris Pasternak; Alan Paton; Edgar Allan Poe; Laurens van der Post; H. F. M. Prescott;

Terence Rattigan; Slavomir Rawicz; Margaret Rawlings; 'Miss Read'; Erich Maria Remarque; Mazo de la Roche;

Francoise Sagan; Jeremy Sandford; J. D. Salinger; Jean-Paul Sartre; Siegfried Sassoon; Dorothy L. Sayers; Jack Schaefer; Michael Scott; Sir Walter Scott; Bobby Seale; Shakespeare; Mary Wollstonecraft Shelley; R. C. Sherriff; Nevil Shute; Henryk Sienkiewicz; Alan Sillitoe; Georges Simenon; Joshua Slocum; Betty Smith; C. P. Snow; Alexander Solzhenitsyn; Muriel Spark; Howard Spring; John Steinbeck; J. F. Steiner; R. L. Stevenson; Harriet Beecher Stowe; Lytton Strachey; Jonathan Swift;

Peter Terson; W. M. Thackeray; Dylan Thomas; Russell Thorndike; James Thurber; J. R. R. Tolkien; Tolstoy; Polly Toynbee; Anthony Trollope; Mark Twain;

John Updike; Arthur W. Upfield;

Stephen Vizinczey; Gore Vidal; Virgil;

John Wain; Lew Wallace; Hugh Walpole; Keith Waterhouse; Evelyn Waugh; Denton Welch; H. G. Wells; Franz Werfel; Patrick White; Oscar Wilde; Thornton Wilder; Emlyn Williams; Eric Williams; Tennessee Williams; Henry Williamson; Angus Wilson; Virginia Woolf; Herman Wouk; John Wyndham;

Emile Zola.

VII Supplementary primary school questionnaire

(Sent to 193 schools in January 1972)

AVAILABILITY OF CHILDREN'S BOOKS IN JUNIOR SCHOOLS

Below is a list of 79 books which are sometimes read by children in the top year of the junior school (i.e. by children aged 10–11). Will you please check this list against the books which are currently available in your school for pupils in this year group, and put a tick (√) on the left-hand side of any title which is available for 10–11 year-old children in your school to read *during the Spring Term 1972* either as part of a class library, a school library, or a public library service collection on loan to the school and housed within the school. (Titles which are available in abridgement or adaptation should be ticked in the same way as a complete version).

Alice in Wonderland (L. Carroll)
Around the World in 80 Days (J. Verne)
Bambi (F. Salten)
A Bear Called Paddington (M. Bond)
Black Beauty (A. Sewell)
Black Hearts in Battersea (J. Aiken)
Bobby Brewster (H. E. Todd)
The Borrowers (M. Norton)
The Boy Next Door (B. Cavanna)
The Castle of Adventure (E. Blyton)
Charlotte's Web (E. B. White)
The Children of Green Knowe
   (L. M. Boston)
A Christmas Carol (C. Dickens)
Coral Island (R. M. Ballantyne)
Doctor Doolittle (H. Lofting)
The Eagle of the Ninth (R. Sutcliff)
Earthfasts (W. Mayne)
Emil and the Detectives (E. Kastner)
The Family from One End Street
   (E. Garnett)

Finn Family Moomintroll (T. Jansson)
Five Children and It (E. Nesbit)
Five Go Down to the Sea (E. Blyton)
Five Go Off in a Caravan (E. Blyton)
Five Go Off to Camp (E. Blyton)
Five on a Hike Together (E. Blyton)
Five on a Treasure Island (E. Blyton)
Five Run Away Together (E. Blyton)
Good Wives (L. M. Alcott)
Gulliver's Travels (J. Swift)
Heidi (J. Spyri)
The Hundred and One Dalmatians
   (D. Smith)
The Island of Adventure (E. Blyton)
Jennings and Darbishire (A. Buckeridge)
Jo's Boys (L. M. Alcott)
A Journey to the Centre of the Earth
   (J. Verne)
The Jungle Book (R. Kipling)
Kidnapped (R. L. Stevenson)
The Last of the Mohicans (J. F. Cooper)

Legions of the Eagle (H. Treece)
The Lion, the Witch and the Wardrobe
    (C. S. Lewis)
Little House in the Big Woods (L. I. Wilder)
Little House on the Prairie (L. I. Wilder)
Little Women (L. M. Alcott)
Marianne Dreams (C. Storr)
Mary Poppins (P. L. Travers)
Moominpapa at Sea (T. Jansson)
Moon of Gomrath (A. Garner)
Mrs. Pepperpot (A. Prøysen)
Oliver Twist (C. Dickens)
Paddington Abroad (M. Bond)
Peter Pan (J. M. Barrie)
Pinocchio (C. Collodi)
Prince Caspian (C. S. Lewis)
The Railway Children (E. Nesbit)
Robinson Crusoe (D. Defoe)
The Secret Garden (F. H. Burnett)
The Secret Island (E. Blyton)
The Secret Seven (E. Blyton)
Secret Water (A. Ransome)

Shadow the Sheepdog (E. Blyton)
The Silver Sword (I. Serraillier)
Smith (L. Garfield)
Stig of the Dump (C. King)
Swallows and Amazons (A. Ransome)
The Swiss Family Robinson (J. D. Wyss)
Thimble Summer (E. Enright)
The Three Musketeers (A. Dumas)
Tom Sawyer (M. Twain)
Tom's Midnight Garden (P. Pearce)
Treasure Island (R. L. Stevenson)
Twenty Thousand Leagues Under the Sea
    (J. Verne)
The Viking's Dawn (H. Treece)
The Water Babies (C. Kingsley)
The Weirdstone of Brisingamen (A. Garner)
What Katy Did (S. Coolidge)
The Wheel on the School (M. Dejong)
The Wind in the Willows (K. Grahame)
The Wolves of Willoughby Chase (J. Aiken)
The Woolpack (C. Harnett)

Contents

What is a microhabitat? 4

What lives on plants and flowers? . . . 6

What lives in soil? 12

What lives in a compost heap? 14

What lives in leaf litter and logs? . . . 20

What lives in ponds? 24

What lives in sheds and houses? 26

What is a food chain? 28

Quiz 29

Glossary 30

Find out more 31

Index 32

Some words in this book appear in **bold**, like this. You can find out what they mean by looking in the glossary

What is a microhabitat?

A **habitat** is a place where an animal lives.
Habitats include deserts, rainforests, rivers, oceans
and meadows. A **microhabitat** is a smaller area
where animals live. There are many microhabitats
within a habitat.

Microhabitats

At Home with the Minibeasts

Claire Throp

raintree

a Capstone company — publishers for children

Raintree is an imprint of Capstone Global Library Limited, a company incorporated in England and Wales having its registered office at 264 Banbury Road, Oxford, OX2 7DY – Registered company number: 6695582
www.raintree.co.uk
myorders@raintree.co.uk

Edited by Helen Cox Cannons
Designed by Cynthia Della-Rovere
Original illustrations © Capstone Global Library Limited 2018
Picture research by Tracy Cummins and Heather Mauldin
Production by Tori Abraham
Originated by Capstone Global Library Limited
Printed and bound in India

ISBN 978 1 4747 6629 6
22 21 20 19 18
10 9 8 7 6 5 4 3 2 1

British Library Cataloguing in Publication Data
A full catalogue record for this book is available from the British Library.

Acknowledgements
We would like to thank the following for permission to reproduce photographs: Alamy: Biosphoto/Quentin Martinez, 4, Matthias Lenke, 25, 29 Top Middle, Richard Becker, 11, Robert Pickett, 18, 28 Bottom Left; iStockphoto: athinaenglandphotography, 12, Chris Mansfield, 7, Henrik_L, 17, 29 Top Right, SemenovIgor, 15; Shutterstock: Alena Popova, 16-17 Background, Alex Staroseltsev, 1 Top Right, 31, Allexxandar, 24-25 Background, Astrid Gast, 27, 29 Bottom Right, azure1, 10 Background, Barbro Bergfeldt, 18-19 Background, chanwangrong, 26 Background, Daniel_Kay, 4-5 Background, David Dohnal, 21, Dlabajdesign, 22, Erni, 28 Top Right, Grimplet, 3 Top, Ian Grainger, 8, Ian Rentoul, 28 Top Left, ifong, 12-13 Background, irin-k, Cover Top, Back Cover, 1 Top Left, 1 Bottom, 3 Bottom, 32, Keattikorn, Design Element, kenjii, 6-7 Background, Kiolk, 24, 29 Bottom Middle, Madlen, 14-15 Bottom, Manfred Ruckszio, 26, Marcel Jancovic, 13, Marek R. Swadzba, 20, Maryna Pleshkun, 29 Top Left, Matt Hudson, 16, 29 Bottom Left, mikroman6, 6, NataliTerr, 11 Background, Nutnarin Khetwong, 20-21 Background, PHOTO FUN, 19, SADLERC1, 23, schankz, Cover Bottom, Seksan44, 5, SIMON SHIM, 9, thatmacroguy, 10, windu, 14-15 Background Yulia Kupeli, 8-9 Background, zhekoss, 22-23 Background, 28 Bottom Right

stag beetle

This book looks at habitats you can find in your local area. These include gardens and parks. Microhabitats within these habitats include holes in walls, plants, piles of rotting leaves and spaces under rocks or plant pots. Minibeasts live in these microhabitats. Larger animals often pass by microhabitats looking for something to eat ... like minibeasts!

What lives on plants and flowers?

Plants and flowers are **microhabitats**. They are homes to many minibeasts. Minibeasts can find **shelter** under leaves and food from flowers. Bees and butterflies help to spread **pollen** to make new flowers.

Ladybird

Length: up to 10 millimetres

Eats: aphids, small insects

What eats it: some birds and spiders

How long it lives for: 2–3 years

Aphids and ladybirds

Aphids live and feed on plants. Ladybirds love to eat aphids. The bright colour of ladybirds shows that they are **poisonous** to **predators**. But some birds and spiders can eat the ladybirds.

Aphid

Length: 1–7 millimetres

Eats: plant **sap**

What eats it: ladybirds, some wasps, insect **larvae**

How long it lives for: between 7 and 40 days

Froghoppers

Froghoppers live on plants. They are tiny **insects** that can jump up to 70 centimetres in the air! Their young, called nymphs, are covered in froth. The froth is also known as "cuckoo spit". The nymphs live on plant stems. Froth protects the nymphs from **predators**. The nymphs make the froth themselves. They push air into liquid that comes out of their bottoms.

cuckoo spit

Froghopper

Length: about 6 millimetres

Eats: adults eat plant **sap**; nymphs eat young leaves

What eats it: small birds

How long it lives for: 23 days (adult)

Leaf-cutter bees

Leaf-cutter bees live in holes in plant stems, dead wood or old walls. The females cut discs out of leaves. You may have seen bees carrying bits of leaves in your garden. The bees glue the discs together with saliva. Saliva is a liquid found in their mouths. They use the discs to make "rooms" in which their **larvae** live.

Leaf-cutter bee
Length: 1.3 centimetres
Eats: pollen, nectar
What eats it: some species of wasps feed on their larvae
How long it lives for: 3–4 months (females)

adult cranefly

What lives in soil?

Some minibeasts live in soil.

Leatherjackets

Young cranefly are known as leatherjackets. They live underground and feed on grass roots. Adult cranefly are often known as daddy-long-legs.

Earthworms

Earthworms usually live in the top few centimetres of soil. They help to keep the soil healthy. The hairs on their body allow them to grip the earth and move through the soil. You can find earthworms in your garden or nearby park.

Earthworm

Length: up to 30 centimetres

Eats: rotting roots and leaves, and remains of dead animals

What eats it: birds, shrews, mice, frogs, lizards, beetles, slugs

How long it lives for: 4–8 years

What lives in a compost heap?

A compost heap contains rotting leaves, vegetables and other waste. Many minibeasts live and feed there. They attract **predators** such as hedgehogs and blackbirds. The predators feed on the minibeasts.

Earwigs

Earwigs live in compost heaps as well as under plant pots or rocks. They have wings but rarely fly. Females lay 20–30 eggs. Unlike many **insects**, they look after their young when the eggs hatch.

Earwig

Length: up to 15 millimetres

Eats: plant matter, flowers, small insects, aphids

What eats it: toads, birds, beetles

How long it lives for: 1–3 years

Harvestmen

A harvestman lives in damp places in your garden. It is not a spider. It cannot make webs. Instead, the harvestman uses hooks on the ends of its legs to capture **prey**. If caught itself, it gives off a horrible smelling liquid.

Harvestman
Length: up to 30 millimetres across
Eats: small insects, worms, snails
What eats it: birds, toads, spiders, wasps
How long it lives for: 1 year

Woodlice

Woodlice live in compost heaps or under bark or plant pots in your garden. Pill woodlice are able to curl up in a ball to protect themselves from **predators**. Some woodlice climb trees to find **algae** to eat!

Woodlouse

Length: about 1.4 centimetres

Eats: dead and rotting plants, algae

What eats it: toads, centipedes, spiders

How long it lives for: 2–4 years

Flat-backed millipedes

The flat-backed millipede lives in compost heaps and other dark, damp places in your garden. It has many sections to its body. These are called segments. It has two pairs of legs on each segment. Millipedes can have from 40 to 400 legs!

Flat-backed millipede
Length: 2.4 centimetres
Eats: dead and rotting plants, mildew
What eats it: birds, shrews, badgers
How long it lives for: 2–3 years

The pill millipede looks a lot like the pill woodlouse. The only way to tell them apart is by the number of legs. The pill millipede has only 18 pairs of legs but this is more than the pill woodlouse, which has just 7 pairs.

pill millipede

Buzzing snail hunter

What lives in leaf litter and logs?

Some minibeasts live in piles of rotting leaves called leaf litter. Others live in dead logs. Have a look for them in woods or parks near where you live.

Buzzing snail hunters

The buzzing snail hunter is a beetle. It lives under logs. It buzzes like a wasp if you pick it up. This beetle has a long "snout" that allows it to eat snails.

Common centipede

Length: about 3 centimetres

Eats: small **insects**, earthworms, slugs, spiders

What eats it: birds, toads, shrews, mice

How long it lives for: 5–6 years

Common centipedes

Common centipedes live under rocks, logs and plant pots. Their bodies are made up of parts called segments. Each segment has one pair of legs. They have 15 pairs of legs altogether. They can crawl backwards as well as forwards.

Great grey slug

The great grey slug is also known as the leopard slug. It has spots like a leopard. It lives in leaf litter and in damp places like old logs. You may have seen them feeding on plants in your garden!

Garden snails

Garden snails feed at night. They spend the day in **sheltered** places such as underneath stones or in gaps in trees. If it is too dry, they seal themselves into their shells. They can live like that for months.

Great grey slug
Length: up to 20 centimetres
Eats: plants; other slugs
What eats it: birds, shrews, toads
How long it lives for: up to 3 years

Garden snail

What lives in ponds?

Ponds are home to many different minibeasts. Larger animals such as frogs live there too. Frogs eat minibeasts. If you have a pond in your garden or in your area, try to look for minibeasts in there. Be careful not to fall in!

Pond skaters

Pond skaters are **insects** that live around small ponds or ditches. They can run fast across the water. They use their front legs to snatch up insects that have landed on the water's surface.

Pond skater

Length: 15 millimetres

Eats: small insects

What eats it: frogs, toads, fish, birds

How long it lives for: 1–6 months

24

Whirligig beetles

Whirligig beetles live in ponds and ditches. They spin round on the surface of the water as they look for food. They have one pair of eyes, but each eye is divided into two parts. This is so they can see above and below water at the same time.

Giant house spider

Length of body:
1.4–1.6 centimetres

Leg span: up to 7.5 centimetres

Eats: flies, **insects**, moths

What eats it: cellar spider

How long it lives for:
about 3 years

Peacock butterfly

Wing span: 63–69 millimetres

Eats: nectar; nettles
(caterpillar)

What eats it: birds (caterpillar),
spiders

How long it lives for:
11 months

What lives in sheds and houses?

Some minibeasts live indoors. Spiders live in sheds, garages and houses.

Giant house spiders

A male giant house spider searches for a female in the autumn. They **mate** and then the female eats the male!

Peacock butterflies

In autumn, peacock butterflies drink a lot of **nectar** from flowers such as lavender. This helps them to survive the winter. They live in sheds and garages during those cold months.

What is a food chain?

Food chains show what animals eat.

Foxes eat shrews.

Shrews eat minibeasts such as slugs, snails, beetles, centipedes and millipedes.

The minibeasts eat leaf litter.

Quiz

1. Which minibeast has eyes that are divided in two?

a) earthworm

b) whirligig beetle

c) woodlouse

2. How many pairs of legs does a pill millipede have?

a) 1,000

b) 7

c) 18

3. Which minibeast has hooks on the ends of its legs to help it catch its food?

a) harvestman

b) pond skater

c) peacock butterfly

Glossary

algae plant-like living things with no stems or leaves that grow in damp places

habitat natural place in which a plant or animal lives

insect animal with a hard outer shell, six legs, three body sections and two feelers; most insects have wings

larvae insects at the stage of development between an egg and an adult

mate come together to produce young

microhabitat small part of a larger area, where minibeasts live

nectar sweet liquid found in many flowers

poisonous able to harm or kill with poison

pollen powder made by flowers to help them create new seeds

predator animal that hunts other animals for food

prey animal hunted by another animal for food

sap liquid found inside plants and trees

shelter safe, covered place

Find out more

Books

It's All About … Beastly Bugs (Kingfisher, 2016)

Minibeasts (My First Book of Nature), Victoria Munson (Wayland, 2017)

The Big Book of Bugs, Yuval Zommer (Thames and Hudson, 2016)

Websites

www.buglife.org.uk/activities-for-you/children-and-schools/bug-buddies-activities-young-people

Go to this website and download the Bug Buddies magazines to find out more about minibeasts.

www.dkfindout.com/uk/animals-and-nature/earthworms-and-leeches/earthworms

Learn more about worms on this website.

Index

aphids 6, 7, 15

bees 6
birds 7, 9, 13, 15, 16, 18, 21,
    22, 24, 26
butterflies 6
buzzing snail hunters 20

common centipedes 21
compost heaps 14, 17, 18

earthworms 13, 21
earwigs 14, 15

flat-backed millipedes 18
flowers 6, 15, 27
food chains 28
foxes 28
froghoppers 8, 9
frogs 13, 24

gardens 5, 10, 13, 16, 17, 18,
    22, 24
garden snails 22
giant house spiders 26, 27
great grey slugs 22

harvestmen 16

ladybirds 6, 7
leaf-cutter bees 10
leaf litter 20, 22, 28
leatherjackets 12
leaves 5, 6, 9, 10, 13, 14, 20

minibeasts 5, 6, 12, 14, 20,
    24, 27

parks 5, 13, 20
peacock butterflies 26, 27
pill millipedes 19
plant pots 5, 14, 17, 21
plants 5, 6, 7, 8, 17, 18, 22
pond skaters 24

rocks 5, 14, 21

shrews 28
spiders 6, 7, 16, 21, 26, 27

whirligig beetles 25
woodlice 17, 19

Answers to quiz on page 29
a) harvestman
b) whirligig beetle
c) 18